Joss Whedon and Race

Joss Whedon and Race

Critical Essays

Edited by MARY ELLEN IATROPOULOS
and LOWERY A. WOODALL III

McFarland & Company, Inc., Publishers
Jefferson, North Carolina

LIBRARY OF CONGRESS CATALOGUING-IN-PUBLICATION DATA

Names: Iatropoulos, Mary Ellen, editor. | Woodall, Lowery A., III, editor.
Title: Joss Whedon and race : critical essays /
edited by Mary Ellen Iatropoulos and Lowery A. Woodall III.
Description: Jefferson, North Carolina : McFarland & Company, Inc.,
Publishers, 2017 | Includes bibliographical references and index.
Identifiers: LCCN 2016034275 | ISBN 9780786470105
(softcover : acid free paper) ∞
Subjects: LCSH: Whedon, Joss, 1964—Criticism and interpretation. |
Racism in mass media.
Classification: LCC PN1992.4.W49 J677 2016 | DDC 791.45/6529—dc23
LC record available at https://lccn.loc.gov/2016034275

BRITISH LIBRARY CATALOGUING DATA ARE AVAILABLE

**ISBN (print) 978-0-7864-7010-5
ISBN (ebook) 978-1-4766-2657-4**

Front cover image of J. August Richards as Charles Gunn and David Boreanaz
as Angel in *Angel* (The WB Television Network/Photofest); *background*
downtown Los Angeles at sunset © 2017 Davel5957/iStock

Printed in the United States of America

*McFarland & Company, Inc., Publishers
Box 611, Jefferson, North Carolina 28640
www.mcfarlandpub.com*

Table of Contents

Preface and Acknowledgments

Why a book on race in Whedon? And why now? We thought we'd pinned down an answer when we began this project five years ago, but the world of 2016 in which it will be published is very different from the world of 2011 in which it was conceived. For one thing, back then Joss Whedon was not quite yet the household name that he is today, being praised by comic book fans, cinephiles, critics and mainstream Hollywood folk alike. In 2011, *The Avengers* had not yet assembled to the tune of $1.5 billion at the box office, and the similar box office success of its sequel *Avengers: Age of Ultron* was still years away.[1] The cancellation of *Dollhouse* after only two seasons was still a fresh wound, and *Cabin in the Woods* was still an unanswered question mired in MGM's financial woes. *Much Ado About Nothing* was not yet a glimmer of suggestion in Kai Cole's eye.[2] In the five years and many projects that have unfolded since, Whedon has come into well-earned critical recognition and popular success. The world of Whedon has grown exponentially since we initially undertook this project, and while Whedon scholarship is only just beginning to cover the man's most recent creative engagement (Marvel's *Agents of S.H.I.E.L.D.* TV show, currently in season three)—scholarly and popular interest in the auteur's work has never been higher or more fervent.

The world of critical race studies today also inhabits very different territory than it did during this collection's inception. For one thing, back then, the 2012 election season was still months away, and Barack Obama's re-election (and all the discussions of race in society that it engendered) was still a campaign rather than a certainty.[3] Donald Trump's presidential bid hadn't yet begun its thorough dissemination of ill-received and prejudicial comments on Mexican immigrants and Muslims (among other minority social groups).[4] Arizona had not yet banned ethnic studies classes or as yet enacted a series of controversial immigration laws.[5] Michelle Alexander's seminal work, *The New Jim Crow: Mass Incarceration in the Age of Color-blindness*, had only just begun to make waves with its compelling evidence about how America's mass incarceration system legally disenfranchises millions of citizens each year based mostly on their skin color and what society thinks dark skin signifies, illustrating how "the fact that so many black and brown men are rounded up for drug crimes that go largely ignored when committed by whites is unseen. Our collective colorblindness prevents us from seeing this fact."[6] In other words, even if we have the best intentions, there exist current societal structures constructed around privileging certain groups while disempowering others and the past five years' seeming surge in discourse regarding the institutional-level, large-scale events occurring within institutional frameworks enacting racist practices, are undeniable components of the cultural landscape into which this book is published.[7]

Troublingly, in addition to these institutional, large-scale events, since 2011 we've also seen a sadly steady stream of cases in which the aforementioned race-based practices have heartbreakingly played out on the individual, interpersonal level. Back then, Trayvon Martin was still alive, as were Jordan Davis, Kimani Gray, Jonathan Ferrell, Eric Garner, John Crawford, Tamir Rice, Freddie Gray, Sandra Bland, Ralkina Jones, Michael Brown, Christian Taylor, and LaQuan McDonald.[8] The heated debates surrounding their deaths were not yet a part of the national dialogue, and antiracist activism revolving around the hashtags #BlackLivesMatter, #ICantBreathe, and #SayHerName were not yet being employed to demonstrate to the world the pervasive—yet too often underreported or ignored—life and death consequences wrought by the systemic inequality of America's criminal justice system. As this brief overview of recent critical race studies developments suggests, in the past five years, the topics of how race does or should operate in society have erupted into being a prominent part of national discourse, albeit to exceedingly polarized audiences, as polls perennially suggest that the public's reaction to racially-charged instances falls along starkly divided racial lines.[9] Through the rise of social media and participatory surveillance culture, racism is more visible in our culture than ever, and yet, not everyone can agree on the repercussions of these trends.[10] We asked ourselves whether these developments change what our book means. We agree that it does; we believe that discussing the representation of race in the popular culture texts, images, and narratives we consume and love is even more important now than when we first pitched the idea in 2011, and the subjects comprising this book—race and Whedon—are both more prominent and more powerful than ever before.

Within the thriving environment of the Whedon academic community, a specific interest in exploring race and ethnicity in Whedon's works continues to grow. Many books contain individual essays discussing race and ethnicity, such as: *Seven Seasons of Buffy*, *Investigating Firefly and Serenity*, *The Literary Angel*, and *Joss Whedon's Dollhouse: Confounding Purpose, Confusing Identity* (to name only a few). The issue also perennially appears in presentations at the Slayage Conference on the Whedonverses, as well as many other literary and popular culture association conventions. Despite this demonstrated interest, however, until now, no single volume had devoted itself exclusively to investigating the ways in which race, ethnicity, and nationality operate across the Whedonverses. We felt this was so crucial and fascinating a topic that it deserved more focus and attention than the occasional article or presentation. Our collection seeks to fill this gap while providing both a forum and a resource for investigating race and ethnicity in Whedon's works. What follows is an effort to provide frameworks for discussing, observing, analyzing, explicating, theorizing, and assessing racial, ethnic, and national constructs in all the works which bear Joss Whedon's name (not just those written and/or directed by the man himself, but also those falling under the general Mutant Enemy umbrella, along with their various production teams). Our collection approaches Whedon's works from a variety of disciplines to explore race, ethnicity, heritage, nationhood, nationality, culture, identity, and social hierarchy, privilege and power as they shape, function in and complicate the production realities, characters, narratives, and interpretations of all of Joss Whedon's works.[11] We wanted this to be an enjoyable and informative read for the academic and non-academic Whedon fan alike, and the critical scholarship showcased in these pages provides a template for earnestly and honestly engaging race within Whedon's works and in our greater world outside of them. We've strived to create a tone that's accessible for non-academic Whedon fans while still making an important contribution to the area of Whedon Studies. These conversations have both been going on for far too long, and haven't been going on long for often enough. We offer this book as a way of continuing the conversation.

We wish to clarify some terminology up front. This book will use both "Whedonverse" as a singular noun and "Whedonverses" as a plural noun. We use "Whedonverses" to refer to the creative properties generally associated as belonging, creatively or legally, to Joss Whedon, because these works would not exist without Joss Whedon himself, of course, and his particular brand of creative brilliance makes its mark on anything he touches. Yet there are limits to the auteur approach and to holding Whedon solely responsible for Whedonverse content, due in no small part to the highly collaborative nature of most projects we refer to as "Whedonverses." This is not a discussion about Joss Whedon as an individual, nor about any one writer, director, producer, actor, etc. It's about the works themselves, the power they have over us and the power we have over them. By demonstrating critical race theory as a viewer's tool for social justice, we hope to turn the conversation away from individual blame and back onto the issues of race and representation, onto the larger cultural patterns of oppression in which our beloved characters inadvertently participate, even when they don't mean to, especially when they don't mean to. Because, as we and our contributors demonstrate, in the unintentional we can see the institutional.

We're the first to admit that this book's coverage of the topic is by no means exhaustive. We received enough quality contributions to fill two volumes at least, and we take the fact that our initial CFP received such an enthusiastic response as proof that others agree this conversation deserves more critical attention.[12] While we aimed for a selection of essays that encompass a range of Whedon's works, the majority of the essays here treat *Buffy the Vampire Slayer* and themes that run across Sunnydale and its related 'verse of *Angel*'s L.A., simply because we received so many more abstracts regarding these shows—and no wonder, given that their respective seven- and five-year runs comprise more hours of screen time than all of Whedon's other televisual projects combined.[13] Accordingly, we received comparatively fewer proposals concerning *Firefly/Serenity*, and fewer still about *Dollhouse*, simply, we think, because those shows unfortunately did not receive years of airtime comparable to *Buffy* and *Angel*. For similar reasons, while scholars and fans of Whedon's more recent works may ask why there isn't an essay on *Cabin in the Woods*, *Much Ado About Nothing*, *In Your Eyes*, or either of the *Avengers* films, the answer is simply that we selected our contributors way back in 2011, during a time before any of those works had been released. There are certainly additional dimensions we wish we had time and space to address. We hope that this collection will inspire other scholars to take on the issues of race and ethnicity present in those dimensions of Whedon's work that we couldn't cover. Undoubtedly, there will be even more projects taken on by Mutant Enemy and Whedon himself that we cannot conceive of as yet, ideas for series and films and comic books that are still busy gestating in Whedon's mind. We certainly hope so, and we hope Whedon's new works will encourage even more writers from diverse disciplines to consider his work critically. We can assure those scholars that they are in for an exhilarating and thought-provoking journey. This volume aims to provide a framework for how to approach these forthcoming Whedon properties as critically conscious consumers of his works.

It would be impossible to thank everyone who truly deserves credit for help along the way, but as Captain Mal might do, we'll attempt the impossible here (with thanks to those who have made us mighty!). We'd like to thank our wonderfully astute, insightful, and above all patient contributors: Lynne, Rachel, Joel, Rhonda, Katia, Nelly, Rejena, Brent, Daoine, Mayan, Brandeise, Samira, Candra, Masani, and Hélène. You have helped us make the dream of this book a reality, and we are forever grateful to you for your diligence and understanding throughout what ended up being much longer a process than any of us had thought it would be.

We'd be remiss if we didn't acknowledge the support and collegiality of the Whedon Studies Association. To the founders, current governing board, and wonderful members who work so hard to create such a welcoming, inspiring community of scholars, we thank you for all the work that you do. Particular thanks go to Rhonda V. Wilcox, whose keynote speech at Slayage 2010 prompted the initial thought of a collection on the complexities of race and ethnicity in the Whedonverses to burst into Mary Ellen's brain.

We also owe a great debt to our many mentors throughout this process for providing guidance and encouragement while this book became a reality. Tamy Burnett and AmiJo Comeford, we are forever grateful to you for both opening doors for us and helping us learn the ropes once we'd walked up to the publishing table. Mixed metaphor notwithstanding, we mean it when we say that without you, this book would not have been possible.

Mary Ellen Iatropoulos thanks the scholars who helped her shape her own academic vision and identity. Many thanks to Andrew Higgins, without whose encouragement this book (and the various conference presentations that led to it) wouldn't have been possible. She also thanks the professors who have inspired her over the years: Heather Hewitt, Don Foster, Dean Crawford, Kiese Laymon, Alyson Buckman, Cynthea Masson, Madeleine Muntersbjorn, Lorna Jowett, Stacey Abbott, and Bronwen Calvert. Thanks also to David Satz, who gave immeasurable aid in providing us with transcripts from several live Whedon speaking engagements.

Lowery A. Woodall III thanks the mentors who first opened his eyes to the exciting and challenging world of academic scholarship. Many thanks to Andrew Haley whose constant support and extraordinary insights have been invaluable over the years. Thanks to David Davies who introduced him to historical scholarship and ignited his passion for research. Thank you to Frank Hoffmann, Tony DeMars, Chris Campbell and Gene Wiggins. Most of all, thank you to Regina Cowles who is dearly missed and whose inspiring teachings ring just as true today as they did some 15 years ago.

Both Mary Ellen and Lowery extend their deepest gratitude to everyone at McFarland for their encouragement, support, and again, above all, patience. We would also like to thank Dixie Dunbar, Joan Schmid, and everyone at Ziffren Bittenham LLP, in addition to everyone involved with Time Science Blood Club Limited. Thank you, Mutant Enemy Productions, and all who march under the glorious "Grr! Argh!" flag, and while it may go without saying, we relish the chance to say it, anyway: we cannot thank you enough, Joss Whedon.

Last but most certainly not least, many, many thanks our respective partners, Dan Madsen and Dana Patrick, for supporting us through many long phone calls, weary rounds of late-night editing, and bouts of editorial uncertainty so clouded by exhaustion we couldn't even see the end game. Thank you for supporting us, for making us coffee during conference calls, and for helping us believe in ourselves.

We'd also like to thank you, the reader of this book, as we presume you're reading this because you love Joss Whedon's works, too. As we know now all too well, for the devoted Whedon fan, the conversations contained in and furthered by this book may be very difficult, if not painful. It may help to think of this book's work as an in-depth academic extension of investigation of implicit bias along the lines of "Ur Fave Is Problematic" in that we approach this book's work believing "the fact that your fave is problematic isn't a big deal—the big deal is if you ignore it."[14]

No doubt some will be dismayed by our book's rigorous investigation of the Whedonverses' often-problematic depictions of race and ethnicity that frequently reinforce the very social hierarchies and oppressive institutions they simultaneously challenge. We recognize that, for some, these concepts may be unfamiliar and controversial. No doubt some Whedon fans will think a book devoted to race has been a long time coming, since for many people such issues as problematic televisual representations of race are already on-going conversations. We also recognize that, for some, the arguments voiced in this critical treatise are all too familiar. We're writing for a wide audience.

Either way, the criticisms we raise may be as hard to read and reckon with as they are to analyze and contextualize with a preface. To discuss race in the works of Joss Whedon is inevitably to discuss the problem of race in the works of Joss Whedon, and indeed, the problem of race in our contemporary society, the problem of race rooted deep within ourselves. But our mission here is to question and challenge, not blame or shame. We're delving into a line of inquiry that invariably leads viewers and fans to subject themselves to the same process of interrogation through which we wring Whedon. Our acts of investigation and analysis are not borne of malice, but rather, a passionate enthusiasm and investment in the characters he creates and the stories he tells, complicated, conflicted, and (dare we say it?) occasionally flawed though they may be. And we think this is exactly why his works are so compelling. We recognize in them our own complicated, conflicted, and, yes, occasionally flawed selves.

To paraphrase the great American author James Baldwin, we love Joss Whedon more than any other artist in the world, and exactly for this reason, we insist on the right to criticize his works, lovingly, but perpetually.[15] We hope that the following pages will enlighten, inspire and yes, perhaps occasionally infuriate you. We hope they help you consider issues you may never have considered before. We hope they shed new light onto some of your favorite characters and give you a greater appreciation for Joss Whedon and his amazing, intelligent, inspiring, challenging works. Most of all, we hope that you have as much fun reading, interpreting, and analyzing these essays as we all did editing them.

NOTES

1. *Marvel's The Avengers*, www.boxoffice.com, 2013. The official worldwide box office gross for the film was $1,514,357,910.

2. Joss Whedon's wife, Kai Cole, convinced him to shoot the project in the two-week break he was afforded between the end of filming the *Avengers* and the beginning of post-production for the film. In an interview with *Women and Hollywood* magazine, Cole states that while Joss was "exhausted and more than a little skeptical" she saw this as a wonderful opportunity to "share [one of their Shakespeare at-home reading events] with the world." Kerensa Cadenas, "Interview with Kai Cole—Producer of *Much Ado About Nothing*," *Women and Hollywood*, 2013 (www.blogs.indiewire.com/womenandhollywood).

3. For a more thorough discussion of the ways in which Obama's presidency has been viewed within the scholarly community with regard to concerns of race and ethnicity, please see the following publications: Simone Brown and Ben Carrington, "The Obamas and the New Politics of Race," *Qualitative Sociology*, Vol. 35(2), pp. 113–121, June 2013; Matthew Hughey, "Show Me Your Papers! Obama's Birth and the Whiteness of Belonging," *Qualitative Sociology*, Vol. 35(2), pp. 163–181, June 2012; Bridget Byrne, "Post-Race? Nation, Inheritance and the Contradictory Performativity of Race in Barack Obama's 'A More Perfect Union' Speech," *thirdspace: a journal of feminist theory & culture*, Vol 10(1), pp. 1–18, 2011; Lori Wu Malahy, Mara Sedlins Jason Plaks and Yuichi Shonda, "Black and White, or Shades of Gray? Racial Labeling of Barack Obama Predicts Implicit Race Perception," *Analysis of Social Issues & Public Policy*, Vol. 10(1), pp. 207–222, December 2010; Thomas J. Sugrue, *Not Even Past: Barack Obama and the Burden of Race*, Princeton, NJ: Princeton University Press, April 12, 2010; H. Samy Alim, *Articulate While Black: Barack Obama, Language and Race in the U.S.*, New York: Oxford University Press, October 1, 2012; Michael Tesler and David O. Sears, *Obama's Race: The 2008 Election and the Dream of a Post-Racial America*, Chicago: University of Chicago Press, November 15, 2010; Michael P. Jeffries, *Paint the White House Black: Barack Obama and the Meaning of Race in America*, Palo Alto, CA: Stanford University Press, 2013.

4. Both liberal and conservative news media outlets took Trump to task after his now-infamous derogatory remarks concerning Mexican immigration. See, for example, Michelle Ye Hee Lee, "Donald Trump's False Comments Connecting Mexican Immigrants and Crime." *Washington Post*, July 8, 2015 (https://www.washingtonpost.com/news/fact-checker/wp/2015/07/08/donald-trumps-false-comments-connecting-mexican-immigrants-and-crime/); Dolia Estevez, "Debunking Donald Trump's Five Extreme Statements About Immigrants and Mexico," Forbes.com, September 3, 2015 (http://www.forbes.com/sites/doliaestevez/2015/09/03/debunking-donald-trumps-five-extreme-statements-about-immigrants-and-mexico/); Carolina Moreno, "9 Outrageous Things Donald Trump Has Said About Latinos," *Huffington Post*, August 31, 2015 (http://www.huffingtonpost.com/entry/9-outrageous-things-donald-trump-has-said-about-latinos_us_55e483a1e4b0c818f618904b).

5. For more on the controversy surrounding the immigration laws put in place by the state of Arizona, please see: Daniel J. Tichenor and Alexandra Filindra, "Raising Arizona v. United States: Historical Patterns of American Immigration Federalism," *Lewis & Clark Law Review*, Vol. 16(4), pp. 1215–1247, Winter 2012; Randall Allen, "Arizona's 2010 Immigration Law: Theoretical, Political, and Constitutional Issues," *Journal of Global Intelligence & Policy*, Vol. 3(3), 2010; Emily L. Fisher, Grace Deason, Eugene Borgida and Clifton M. Oyamot, "A Model of Authoritarianism, Social Norms,

and Personal Values: Implications for Arizona Law Enforcement and Immigration Policy," *Analyses of Social Issues & Public Policy,* Vol. 11(1), pp. 285–299, December 2011; Lisa Magana and Erik Lee, Latino *Politics and Arizona's Immigration Law SB 1070* (New York: Springer, 2013).

6. Michelle Alexander, *The New Jim Crow: Mass Incarceration in the Age of Colorblindness* (New York: The New Press, 2012), Kindle Reader e-book.

7. *Ibid.*

8. For further critique of the Trayvon Martin case and how it has altered perceptions of race in America, please see: George Yancy and Janine Jones, *Pursuing Trayvon Martin: Historical Contexts and Contemporary Manifestations of Racial Dynamics,* Lanham, MD: Lexington Books, 2012; Michelle V. Rowley, "'It Could Have Been Me' Really? Early Morning Mediations on Trayvon Martin's Death," *Feminist Studies,* Vol. 38(2), pp. 519–529, 2012; Alex Newman, "The Exploitation of Trayvon Martin's Death," *New American,* Vol. 28(9), pp. 20–26, 2012; Elizabeth Valena Beety, "What the Brain Saw: The Case of Trayvon Martin and the Need for Eye-Witness Identification Reform," *Denver University Law Review,* Vol. 90(2), pp. 331–346, 2012.

9. Recent polls conducted by the Pew Center for Research and ABC/*Washington Post* show that whites and blacks hold very different views on the degree to which race factored into the Zimmerman verdict (http://www.nationaljournal.com/col umns/political-connections/americans-are-once-again-divided-by-race-20130725). For more information on the varied reactions to the Zimmerman decision please see the following: Massimo Calabresi, "The Next Verdict from the Zimmerman Trial," *Time Magazine,* July 14, 2013, www.nation.time.com. Jordan Fabian, "Zimmerman Acquittal: We Don't Live in a Post-Racial America," *ABC News,* July 14, 2013, www.abc-news.go.com. Jonathan Capehart, "Race and the George Zimmerman Trial," *Washington Post,* www.washingtonpost.com.

10. In a 2013 NBC News/*Wall Street Journal* poll, just about half of adults polled said race relations in the U.S. were "good" or "fairly good," a substantial decline from the 70 percent responding that way in similar polls from 2009–2011 (http://firstread. nbcnews.com/_news/2013/07/23/19644475-americas-race-relations-take-hit-after-zimmerman-verdict-nbc-newswsj-poll-finds?lite).

For a more thorough explanation of the persistent problem of racism in modern America, please see: Eduardo Bonilla-Silva, *Racism Without Racists: Color-Blind Racism and the Persistence of Racial Inequality in America,* Boulder, CO: Rowman & Littlefield, 2009; Sabina E. Vaught, *Racism, Public Schooling, and the Entrenchment of White Supremacy: A Critical Race Ethnography,* Albany: State University of New York Press, 2011; Barbara Trepagnier, *Silent Racism: How Well Meaning White People Perpetuate the Racial Divide,* Boulder, CO: Paradigm Publishers, 2010; Tim Wise, *Between Barack and a Hard Place: Racism and White Denial in the Age of Obama,* San Francisco: City Lights Publishers, 2009.

11. Beyond the writers actors and directors that we normally think of as being a part of the television production process, there are a number of other individuals whose work has a noticeable impact on the final product that goes over the airwaves. Although there is not enough space in this volume to identify each of these areas of production, we suggest the following texts as a starting point for better understanding these jobs and how they affect television-programming decision-making. Linda Stradling, *Production Management for TV and Film: The Professional's Guide,* New York: Bloomsbury Methuen Drama, 2010, Herbet Zettl, *Television Production Handbook,* Independence, KY: Cengage Learning, 2011.

12. CFP stands for Call for Papers which is a standard document used in academia asking for submissions of articles for a new book or manuscript collection.

13. There are 144 episodes of *Buffy the Vampire Slayer* and 110 episodes of *Angel*. Averaging 45 minutes for each episode, the shared worlds of *BtVS* and *Angel* comprise 11,430 minutes of screen time. Even if we take a generous approach to defining "televisual projects" for the purposes of calculation, if we allow 45 minutes each for 1 episode of *Glee*, 2 episodes of *The Office*, 3 episode-length acts of *Dr. Horrible,* 14 episodes of *Firefly*, 26 episodes of *Dollhouse*, 67 episodes of *Agents of Shield*, in addition to runtimes for the theatrical versions of *Serenity* (119 minutes), *Cabin in the Woods* (95 minutes), *The Avengers* (143 minutes), *Much Ado About Nothing* (109 minutes), *In Your Eyes* (106 minutes), and *Avengers: Age of Ultron* (141 minutes), all these properties still only add up to a comparatively small 5,798 minutes.

14. Ijeoma Oluo, "Admit It: Your Fave Is Problematic," Medium.com. https://medium.com/matter/admit-it-your-fave-is-problematic-2dfa692f557b#.6dj7p6yj. While the Internet meme existed prior to Oluo's blog post, we find Oluo's critical application of the "Problematic Fave" concept to self-reflective fandom particularly useful.

15. James Baldwin, "Autobiographical Notes," *Notes of a Native Son* (Boston: Beacon Press, 1984), 3–9.

Introduction: The Individual, the Institutional and the Unintentional

Exploring the Whedonverses Through Critical Race Theory

MARY ELLEN IATROPOULOS *and*
LOWERY A. WOODALL III

> The process of breaking a story involves the writers and
> myself, so a lot of different influences, prejudices, and
> ideas get rolled up into it…. I do believe that there is
> plenty to study and there are plenty of things going on in
> it, as there are in me, that I am completely unaware of.[1]
>
> Art isn't your pet … it's your kid. It grows up and
> talks back to you.[2]
> —Joss Whedon

How can an individual be good in a world full of institutional, pervasive, and often-overwhelming evil? It's a question constantly explored in the Whedonverses, albeit carried to different conclusions, as scenarios of struggle with systematized oppression run across shows and stories. Over seven seasons, *Buffy* repeatedly interfaces with many malevolent organizations, from rebelling against the Watchers' Council in Season Two and fighting City Hall in Season Three, to taking on the Initiative in Season Four and mobilizing Potential Slayers to take on the First in Season Seven. *Angel*, of course, presents the metaphor of the evil institution incarnate through Wolfram & Hart, a corporate law firm so powerfully nefarious that the world of *Angel* "doesn't work in spite of evil … it works because of" it, eventually situating Team

Angel against the elite and oppressive Circle of the Black Thorn and the systematized corruption they represent.[3] *Firefly* and *Serenity* offer a world in which our beloved Browncoats endeavor to skirt Alliance authority on the very margins of the 'verse, so that "no matter how long the arm of the Alliance might get, we'll just get ourselves a little further."[4] *Dr. Horrible* shows us a would-be supervillain breaking into the business of established evil, and *Dollhouse* reincarnates *Angel*'s ethical imperative of taking down the system as Echo tackles the Rossum Corporation. The issue's prevalence demonstrates an ongoing concern with the possibilities and limitations of individual action within larger systems. Even when the well-oiled institution's immorality is debatable, characters repeatedly face the narratively significant choice of whether to obey or defy orders from above. In *Cabin in the Woods*, for instance, Dana and Marty decide a world run by systematized sacrifice and a shadowy "Puppeteer" institution isn't worth saving.[5] Even *Marvel's The Avengers* features Nick Fury begrudgingly reporting to a Council who appear glowering down from enormous screens, ordering him to blow up millions of innocent New York citizens, which Fury roundly rejects as a "stupid-ass decision."[6] In a 2013 interview with *Entertainment Weekly*, Whedon himself described this ongoing concern across his works as "something I'm also writing about all the time—the little guy versus the big faceless organization."[7]

While scholars debate the degree to which the Whedonverses reflect a unifying moral ideology,[8] we argue this recurring preoccupation with individual morality and institutional evil substantiates cohesion between his works in that the complex and often contradictory ways in which characters interface with evil institutions are figurative arenas in which Whedon's "narrative ethic" can be observed constructing, as Whedon scholars Richardson and Rabb say, "an indirect argument in which difficult hypothetical cases are imagined and various ways of dealing with them considered."[9] An underlying ethos emerges, conceiving of a moral framework for being good in an evil world that's constructed through interaction with—and, often, rejection or repudiation of—an all-powerful, cruel and uncaring, or downright exploitative system that keeps the world functioning, as Dr. Horrible might say, with the status being "not quo."[10] Moreover, these evil institutions have in common the element of control through surveillance. As these institutions monitor the actions of individuals, their gaze enacts systematic regulation and control to oppress those observed. Who is watching, and why, can determine the world's fate in the battle of good against evil. Of course, this only furthers the real-world parallels, as audiences are also Ones Who Watch, implicating us all as part of the institution.

Now, no one wants to think of themselves as helpless pawns, and as the Whedonverses also show us, individuals do have power to confront and challenge institutions. We are individuals, but we navigate life both within and against much larger governing institutions that impact us all. So how can it be that we think of ourselves as self-determined and in charge of our own lives, but that we also undeniably receive cultural conditioning in symbolic languages much larger than a single person? By applying critical race theory across the Whedonverses, we can use the works we love to better understand how power dynamics between individuals and institutions shape and influence race in the Whedonverses, and how that affects our engagement as viewers and citizens of the world, modifying the question of what it means to try and be good in an evil world for our own book's purposes: how do you appreciate and admire an auteur's works while at once acknowledging and exploring their more problematic aspects? How can we hold in tension our love of the shows with our discomfort recognizing them to also participate in troubling larger social systems? How do we, as individuals, take on the larger institutions, both material and ideological, governing our lives? What happens when we struggle with the system?

At first glance, connections between race, ethnicity, and this recurring existential individual-versus-institution Whedonverse construct may not be readily apparent. Fans and scholars may be prompted to ask, as did many a friend and colleague to whom we've announced the publication of this book, "...*what* race and ethnicity in the Whedonverses?" Indeed, on the surface, the Whedonverses themselves seem to encourage this de-racialized reading. The majority of characters in the Whedonverses are Caucasian and ostensibly of Western cultural descent, race is rarely mentioned by any character, and even situations that do address racial disparities are often only momentarily articulated and tangential to the plot. It may seem, then, that "race" is largely absent from the Whedonverses in terms of cast, character, and content, but to suppose that race doesn't exist in the works of Joss Whedon because he and many of his characters are white is to ignore the very real ways race is constructed in the Whedonverses, albeit at the margins, in largely peripheral characters, through aesthetic strategies normalizing whiteness and marginalizing or exoticizing minorities. For example, take Mr. Trick. "Not exactly a haven for the brothers, strictly the Caucasian persuasion here in the 'Dale,'" he muses (3.3) during his first appearance in *Buffy the Vampire Slayer*, sardonically assessing racism within the *Buffy*verse in the grand tradition of Whedon villains speaking uncomfortable truths.[11] Yet the implications of this line are forgotten nearly the moment it's articulated. The acknowledgment of racism doesn't go far in altering actual racism in Sunnydale, as it is dismissed just as suddenly as it was recognized. But Mr. Trick has clued us in to the fact that it exists, despite its apparent invisibility. Trick's revelation demonstrates that absences matter, and a relative lack of characters of color doesn't mean that race doesn't exist."[12] It just means the effects of race and racism are harder to see and understand, and that what may be presented as "normal" and "neutral" is actually socially constructed, often in harmful ways that are invisible to those with the power to define what "normal" and "neutral" are.

When discussing the construction of normality, pop culture texts provide fascinating sites for observing how institutionalized power dynamics play out. As Jennifer Esposito notes, "representations do not just reflect already determined meanings. Instead, they help contribute to discursive understandings."[13] In other words, representations of race don't just reflect the real world, but also help to shape and construct the world. Studying representations of race in media sheds light onto how systemic inequality manifests itself in seemingly mundane ways. William Ryan asserts that institutionalized oppression perpetuates itself through "systematically motivated, but unintended, distortions of reality" that oppresses and disempower people even as it passes itself off as normal and natural (p. 11).[14] As Srividya Ramasubramanian notes, "through continual habitual exposure to television, media stereotypes become part of the dominant symbolic landscape" which play a crucial role in "forming and maintaining social stereotypes" and racial attitudes.[15]

Put bluntly, popular culture's centralization of whiteness and marginalization of people of color effectively limits the scope of perception of what exists and what is possible—not just on screen, but in the viewer's mind as well. In fact, the very fact that whites are seen as non-raced, as Richard Dyer argues, leads to a social "assumption that white people are just people, which is not far off from saying that whites are people whereas other colors are something else," are Other.[16]

The tendency of Whedonverse properties to present characters of color as Others is well noted. In Pender's words, "*Buffy*'s racial politics are inarguably more conservative than its gender or sexual politics."[17] Matthew Pateman surmises that despite *Buffy*'s disavowal of ontologically fixed categories of identity such as ethnicity, the overwhelming whiteness of the show's cast and the normative exclusionary practices of the characters themselves ultimately result in *Buffy*'s rehearsing and perpetuating cultural practices that lead to the exclusion of groups outside the norm."[18] Despite *Buffy*'s "impressive grappling with all sorts of "difference" and "otherness" ... we will find a lingering preference against the "non-white" or "non–Christian" which subtly undermines the show's message of individual empowerment."[19]

Some critics address this problematic tendency, arguing that in the Whedonverses, vampires, demons and the like inhabit "Other" categories to allegorize interaction with and acceptance of racial Others in viewers' lives.[20] While we agree with this reading, we also note the difficulties of embodying allegorical race relations through mostly white characters with comparatively scarce representation of the people of color to whom such allegories refer. Simply put, to ignore the fact that issues of Otherness are enacted through white bodies means, if nothing else, that the relative absence of actual racial Others becomes normalized. Whedon hasn't received anywhere near the same degree of praise for his representations of race.[21] This is a problem because as Ramasubramanian reminds us, "media portrayals of whiteness as normative and superior are as important as negative stereotypical portrayals of racial/ethnic out-groups as different and inferior in shaping white viewer's racial attitudes."[22]

In other words, there's a connection between foregrounding whiteness and complacently enabling racism to continue; such aesthetic strategies naturalize what is culturally constructed in uncritical terms, and even when they expand to encompass more diverse characters, are not proof-through-absence that there's no race to be found, but rather, illustrate that racism is rooted deeply albeit subtly into the fabric of Whedon's fictional worlds and our own worlds outside of the show. In this way, we can see how Whedon works sometimes (perhaps unintentionally) are rehearsing oppressive/discriminatory practices in one area even as they work to reduce oppression/discrimination in another area.

The Whedonverses, like all televisual representations, reflect the larger systems of social inequality in which they're produced and consumed. To illustrate this point, mentally revisit the aforementioned images of institutions in the Whedonverses, this time considering the role race plays in forming images of power in the Whedonverses. Recognize that the human faces running these institutions are overwhelmingly white. Images matter, and seeing certain images over and over in specific contexts encourages acceptance of an interpretation of those images as self-evident. If we see whiteness as nonraced, we miss that the evil institutions of the Whedonverses present a world in which it's normal for white men to dominate governing forces, possess immense power, command the institutions that inevitably affect our lives. Such imagery of dominant whiteness—critical race theorists would call it evidence of white supremacy, as in the most literal sense we're being shown that it's white people who ascend to the top, whose interests take priority—recurs constantly. The whiteness of the Whedonverses provides a fruitful opportunity to use the works we love to better understand how power dynamics between individuals and institutions shape and influence race in the Whedonverses, as well as to interrogate them: to what degree do Whedon works engage with race and racial stereotypes in order to critique them, to what degree subvert and repudiate them, and to what degree reinforce or reinvest in them—to what degree doing all at once? Since real life puts us in the same position, how does that affect our engagement as viewers and citizens of the world?

Critical Race Theory: Race as Ideological Construction with Material Consequences

Critical race theory, as a school of scholarship, encourages such lines of questioning because it is interested in studying and transforming the relationship between race, racism, and power. It's a crucial endeavor, but also a complicated one, because the factors feeding in are often contradictory and connected to a long, bloody history which few people enjoy revisiting. Michelle Alexander explains, "race makes people uncomfortable ... the striking reluctance of whites, in particular, to talk about or even acknowledge race has led many scholars and advocates to conclude that we would be better off not talking about race at all."[23] This is called the "colorblind" approach, and the flipside of this thinking is that, to mention race is the same thing as being racist. We do sometimes see this in the Whedonverses, as for example in the *Angel* Season Four episode "Calvary," in which the recently de-souled Angelus goads Gunn to jealousy over Fred and Wesley's interest in each other, telling him, "I guess, when you think about it, for the first time in your life you just weren't dark enough."[24] Here, we see the mention of Gunn's race as a function of characterizing Angelus' evilness, and we may be tempted to read the scenes as advocating colorblindness. Yet to dismiss the meanings our brains are trained to take away from recurring visual symbols simply means we're letting them influence us without questioning them. Keeping with the *Angel* example, while it's only evil Angelus who uses racism outright, elsewhere on *Angel*, characters interpret Gunn's skin color as necessitating commentary, as when Gwen (Electrogirl) refers to him as "Denzel,"[25] or necessitating different treatment, as when Fred takes to saying things like "word" and "he lost the mission, bro" to Gunn.[26] Again, those utterances aren't explicitly discriminatory, and yet, they still treat Gunn differently than others based on their perceptions of what his skin color means. Fred doesn't take to uttering Britishisms when dating Wesley, for example. Obviously, people have all sorts of different skin colors, so when one attempts to undertake a "colorblind" approach to the world, one embraces the metaphor of ignoring difference as akin to not participating in race itself—the goal of which is to avoid being racist—but while ignoring racial difference may prevent an individual's blatant racism, in the larger world outside of the individual, the social dynamics using difference as organizational principle continue to operate unabated by the individual's (un)willingness to see it for what it is. Critical race theory teaches us that the more important question is why and how it can be that despite our best intentions as individuals, racism exists and harms people every day, which in turn raises the question, how can an individual can succeed in challenging systemic oppression when the fact of living in that system means inadvertently reinforcing it?

Success depends in part on awareness of key critical race theory concepts. First, race and ethnicity are not one and the same. The textbook definition of "race" is a "notion of a distinct biological type of human being, usually based on skin color or other physical characteristics."[27] Race and racism, however, are not about physical differences themselves, but as author Allan G. Johnson says, what society interprets those differences to mean, and how the world is "organized in ways that encourage people to use difference to include or exclude, reward or punish, credit or discredit, leave alone or harass."[28] By contrast, Delgado and Stefancic define "ethnicity" as a "group characteristic based on national origin, ancestry, language or other characteristic."[29] While modern society often uses the two terms interchangeably, distinctions abound. "Ethnicity" is what a person identifies themselves as, and "race" is a category other people put the person into; one is a claiming of identity, the other an assigning of identity. Again, obviously, physical differences exist between people of all ethnicities, but "race" refers not to these physical differences themselves, but rather, to the practice of participating in the social construction of the meanings assigned to these differences. In comparison to ethnicity, racial categories are, according to Dyer, "not objective, inherent, or fixed, they correspond to no biological or genetic reality; rather, races are categories society invents, manipulates, or retires when convenient."[30] One need only recall America's "One Drop rule" to recognize that one's race is subject to be legislatively altered at a moment's notice.[31] However, to say that race is socially constructed and culturally mediated is not to say that race is made up or make-believe. Rather, as Eduardo Bonilla-Silva points out, such constructs have a "social reality. This means that after race—or class or gender—is created, it produces real effects on the actors racialized as 'black' or 'white.'"[32] Regardless of a person's ethnicity and ancestry, again, when we talk about race, we're not talking about qualities intrinsic to different skin colors, but rather, as Johnson says, what society interprets those differences to mean, and how the world is "organized in ways that encourage people to use difference to include or exclude, reward or punish, credit or discredit, leave alone or harass."[33]

Race and racism are reinforced and perpetuated through privilege and power—or lack thereof—on both individual and institutional levels. Privilege exists when one group has something of value that is denied to others simply because of the groups they're perceived to belong to. Privilege can exist in interpersonal interactions, as for example, when wealthy Manhattan elites at a house party mistook young Illinois senator Barack Obama for a waiter, based simply on his appearance.[34] Yet it also occurs institutionally, in what Peggy McIntosh calls "conferred dominance,"[35] or when one group is given power over another group in structural terms, with organized legal institutions backing them up. This is exemplified by the fact that "studies show that blacks and Latinos who seek loans, apartments, or jobs are much more apt than similarly qualified whites to be rejected, often for spurious or vague reasons."[36] Racism equals prejudice plus power, the ability to take a bias and make it legally sanctioned reality. Through privilege and the lopsided distribution of power that supports it, racism surrounds us everyday, in interpersonal interactions, and through larger cultural narratives and assumptions and the social and legal systems codifying them, albeit in ways not everyone can always see. Race is not the only factor, but race is never *not* a factor. If you don't consider it a factor, it may be because you've never had to. This is how systems of privilege work.

A painful moment in *Angel's* Season Two episode, "The Thin Dead Line" (2.14) illustrates this point. In this episode, police officers (who are actually zombies) are unjustly harassing the homeless youth Anne cares for at her shelter. Gunn and his friends devise a trap to replicate the problem; they'll bring along a video camera, wait for an officer to hassle them, and document the encounter on film. Anne, confused by the plan, asks, "how do you know they will?" to which Gunn replies, matter-of-fact, "'Cause we'll be the ones walking while black."[37] Here, Gunn's certainty and Anne's naiveté demonstrate institutional racism at work. Anne, a white woman, is surprised by Gunn's confidence that the zombie cops will come after him, yet as black men, Gunn and his friends have come to expect such treatment as normal, having been the life-long victims of racial profiling, Anne did not arrange it to be so that she goes unhindered by law enforcement while Gunn and his friends can count on it. It is not her fault, nor is it theirs. And yet, such is the racial reality of the world that they inhabit. If she never heard Gunn describing being racially profiled, she may never recognize that it's happening to other people, just not to her.

Critical race theory also emphasizes the ordinariness and invisibility of institutional racism. As Rinku Sen notes, even though many of us "define racism as individual, overt and intentional ... modern forms of racial discrimination are often unintentional, systemic and hidden."[38] In other words, racism is not about personal antagonism, but rather, about the larger context of a society that rationalizes or minimizes discrimination amidst a legal framework codifying such cultural practices. Racism may proliferate through individual interactions, but these instances are microcosmic enactments of macro-level institutional structures with the power to define status quo. As Delgado and Stefancic relate, "if racism is embedded in our thought processes and social structures ... then the 'ordinary business' of our society—the routines, the practices, and institutions that we rely on to effect the world's work—will keep minorities in subordinate positions."[39]

This issue of the "ordinary business" of institutional racism, the sheer banality of such normalized oppression, is exactly what makes it so hard to successfully challenge. Humans often take the path of least resistance and accept institutions that privilege some while disadvantaging others. Take, for example, the worldview articulated by Cordelia in "Go Fish" (2.20), the episode in *Buffy*'s Season Two: as Willow discusses the unspoken but viscerally felt demand that she raise the grades of a swim-team member, Cordelia responds without any surprise: "the truth is, certain people are entitled to special privileges. They're called winners. That's the way the world works."[40] Xander replies, "what about that nutty 'all men are created equal' thing?" which Cordelia promptly dismisses with "propaganda spouted by the ugly and less deserving."[41] Xander tries again: "I think that was Lincoln!" but again, Cordelia shoots him down: "disgusting mole and stupid hat." Willow intervenes to correct: "actually, it was Jefferson," but Cordelia is undeterred: "he kept slaves, remember?"[42] Here Cordelia connects the episode's narrative to larger systems of institutionally condoned oppression, linking the racist selectiveness of the founding fathers to the "special" treatment received by the swim team at Sunnydale High. She says—and no one successfully contradicts her, she gets the last word here—things that we know to be true yet uncomfortable. In fact, there are many instances where the evil our Scoobies battle manifest as groups of white men exercising unjust advantages and exploiting others: the episode "Reptile Boy" (2.5) where white frat members try to sacrifice innocent women to gain riches from a demon, and then again in "Help" (7.4), where a younger generation of privileged white males attempt the same.[43]

We can observe the flipside of white privilege at work across the Whedonverses as well. In the very first episode of *Angel*, Lindsey McDonald of Wolfram & Hart assures his client, the evil vampire Russell, that he'll get away with murder, that the evil law firm will see to it that Russell won't be associated with the crime, and that instead, witnesses will say they saw a "dark-complected man" exiting the crime scene.[44] While it's a bit of a throwaway line, it also speaks to a much larger cultural understanding: this is the mentality in which people of color are disproportionately imprisoned while white corporate executives go free. According to Joseph Barndt and Charles Ruehle, in America whites are less likely to be arrested than people of color, once arrested, they're less likely to be convicted, and once convicted, are less likely to go to prison.[45] It's easy to link the fictional racism of Wolfram & Hart to actual policies in our everyday world.

We can also find myriad instances where race and racism function in less overt ways. We see characters awkwardly tripping around the idea of race, playing the discomfort for laughs. One such example can be found in the first episode of *Dollhouse*'s Season Two, "Vows," in which Sierra returns from an engagement and, still imprinted, takes one look at Ivy, the technician, and asks if she couldn't have "the other one" administer her treatment (referring to Topher). "I'm not comfortable with Orientals. It's not a racist issue, it's just that your culture's not really the thing, is it?"[46] While Sierra has been programmed at someone's request to exhibit this thinking—a disturbing thought in itself—the tension is compounded by the fact that Ivy, too, is of Asian descent. Sierra's next comment—"although if you were to tie me down and spank me, I could hardly be expected to resist, could I?"—solidifies the humor, but the laughs mask real discriminations Asians face all the time (as contributor Hélène Frohard-Dourlent will discuss in her essay on *Commentary! The Musical* and the song "Nobody's Asian in the Movies"). Further, in an earlier episode, when Sierra infiltrates the NSA, she poses as a worker who happens to be Asian.[47] While Sierra is wearing identical clothes to borrow the woman's identity for the day, the two don't really look alike, yet her ploy is successful, and white man after white man at security checkpoints fail to see Sierra is posing and passing. This reflects an assumption reinforced by systematized racism, namely that all Asian people look alike, a notion so reliably prevalent that Sierra can count on it to execute her mission.

Such systemic bias goes beyond the actions of any one individual, and in fact, make it so that characters we love sometimes reinforce racism on one front even as they simultaneously challenge such oppressions on other fronts. For example, in the *Buffy* Season Two episode "Reptile Boy," we open on Buffy, Xander and Willow watching a film on Buffy's bed.[48] Within seconds, however, the confusion on our beloved Scoobies' faces frames for viewers that this film is foreign and weird. The film's music hearkens to Bollywood cinema, and their mystified attitude imbues this setup with Orientalism and Othering of nonwhite cultures. Buffy and Xander can't even follow the plot. Willow, on the other hand, appears as an emissary of multicultural sensitivity and savvy, as she alone can follow along what's happening in the film. However, Willow is not exempt from participating in the process of centralizing whiteness while marginalizing people of color. Later in the series, as Tara and Willow quarrel in their dorm room in the Season Five episode "Tough Love" (5.19), Willow abruptly leaves in a huff, canceling their plans to attend their college's multicultural fair because "I don't feel real multicultural right now."[49] Multiculturalism, in the sense Willow uses it, is not a vibrant, fleshed out way of regarding the world, but rather, is quartered off to one event, one day a year, connoting the sense that multiculturalism isn't a reality or shared belief system but rather an extracurricular obligation to which one opts in or out. Such rhetoric reveals the cultural constructs embedded in Scooby attitudes, since if one can opt into or out of multiculturalism, "one" must be unmarked as part of any culture, something that further normalizes whiteness. As Johnson says, "whites can choose whether to be conscious of their racial identity or to ignore it" whereas people of color are systematically tagged by racial markers without regard to their consent.[50] In other words, to "not feel real multicultural" is indicative of having the privilege to be able to opt in or out of being seen as ethnic, yet is said in such a way as to obscure the implicit bias at work. Again, despite the best intentions, to ignore race is only to ignore that how such representation is structured around privileging certain groups while disempowering others.

So where do we go from here? As Esposito notes, "popular culture texts … contribute to current discourses on race and racism, which also structure and shape the ways we live."[51] Combining this with the recurring Whedonverses motif of the power of the individual to challenge the institution, we can recognize that we're not helpless pawns in the system at all, but rather, agents for whom the smallest act of rebellion can mean everything. If nothing we do matters, then all that matters is what we do. Whedon shows, films, and characters, much like us as audience members and adoring academics, are capable of acting against oppression on one front even as we may be inadvertently reinforcing that very system in another way. We, just like the Whedonverses we love, sometimes, despite our efforts elsewhere to subvert oppressive dominant paradigms, may also be rehearsing, as Matthew Pateman writes, the very "categories of exclusion that [we] seek to confront elsewhere."[52] The good news, however, is that we've all just taken a step towards doing more challenging and less reinforcing. As Johnson says, "The more you pay attention to privilege and oppression, the more you'll see opportunities to do something about them. You don't have to mount an expedition to find opportunities; they're all over the place, beginning with you."[53] As you will see, our contributors' essays each enact ways of doing something about it. Because one thing is for sure: we can be a part of the evil institution in ways that challenge, confront, and disrupt the institution, or we can merely be a part of the institution. If the Whedonverses teach us anything, it's that despite the system, we, as individuals, still have the power to choose to resist, to build a world more just and equitable, no matter how small the action. Critical race theory shows us how to use the Whedonverses to understand ourselves as caught in a cycle of resisting and reinforcing intersecting oppressions, to understand the aesthetic and cultural mechanics we've been trained to see as neutral that in actuality reinforce the very systems we're trying to oppose. As this dynamic plays out in the Whedonverses, in turn, we may recognize this dynamic playing out in ourselves—helping us, like the characters we love, be better people doing more and fighting harder for a just and equitable world. It's important to explore our participation in exploitative institutions, even if we're not participating consciously, even if our assent is unintentional, in fact, *especially* if it's unintentional. In the unintentional, we can see the institutional.

In keeping with this thought, this book presents 15 essays exploring the vexed relationship between living in, challenging, subverting and reinforcing evil institutions that systematize oppressive race-based practices. We've broken the book into four sections divided along the lines of Whedon's shows themselves. Our book begins with the part of Whedon's career David Lavery refers to as the "Creator" period, with *Buffy the Vampire Slayer*.[54] Our first essay, Lynne Edwards' "'The black chick always gets it first': Black Slayers in Sunnydale," follows this line of thinking to investigate constructions of race at the margins of the narrative. Edwards critically investigates the arcs of the *Buffy*verse's four black Slayers (Rona, Nikki Wood, Kendra, and Sineya, more commonly referred to as the Primitive or the First Slayer) amidst this mostly-white backdrop. Utilizing a foundation of feminist scholarship, Edwards locates each of *Buffy*'s black Slayers within a longstanding cinematic stereotype for Africanized characters. By investigating how Kendra functions as a tragic mulatta figure, how Nikki Wood serves as a Blaxploitation Jezebel figure, how Sineya is represented as a savage, and how Rona functions as a Sapphire figure, Edwards provides a thorough examination of the ironies of Whedon's representations of blackness amidst their respective historical contexts. Edwards traces the various ways in which Whedon's black Slayers are denied power, ultimately citing the show's recurring reliance on racist tropes as grounds for questioning the transgressive nature of Slayerdom as a site of female empowerment.

Buffy has received some praise for its integration of more diverse characters in the form of the Potential Slayers in Season Seven, notably from Jeffrey Middents, who argues that the musical episode "Once More with Feeling" (6.7) provides a turning point for the series.[55] After this episode, Middents suggests, "*Buffy* deals with race by not making it an issue at all, but by slowly adding significant characters of color to the cast without explicit fanfare," which Middents reads as Whedon "subtly readdress[ing]" earlier seasons' lack of diversity through these steps towards inclusiveness.[56] Yet problems of racial representation persist, and our next essay from Rachel McMurray offers a different interpretation, focusing on racial inequalities we can glimpse in the so-called Slayer slang that has been one of the most enduring and recognizable traits of the series. In her essay, "'I have no speech, no name'; The Denial of Female Agency Through Speech in *Buffy the Vampire Slayer*," McMurray argues that speech patterns, accents and linguistic idiosyncrasies displayed by each of the Slayers act as reflections of their agency within the show. McMurray chronicles the ways in which characters of color not subscribing or living up to Buffy Summer's idealized version of Slayerhood encounter challenges to their position and privilege through calculated speech acts. The essay meticulously maps out how the differences in speech exemplified by each of the Slayers complicate potential feminist readings of the program.

Next, Joel Hawkes turns our attention to the Watchers' Council (specifically Rupert Giles and Wesley Wyndham-Pryce) and their role as facilitators of English space and construction of English identities within *Buffy the Vampire Slayer*. In his essay, "'A dodgy English accent': The Rituals of Contested Sacred Space of Englishness in 'Helpless,'" Hawkes identifies the ritual of Cruciamentum (which temporarily strips Buffy of her powers) as a critical moment in the show's developing representation of English cultural identity.[57] Hawkes carefully illustrates the transformative effects of English culture on the competing spaces of America (as embodied by Sunnydale) and the supernatural world (embodied by the Hellmouth). Ultimately, Hawkes argues, the treatment of characters like Giles, Wesley and even Spike become commentaries on the shifting nature of colonialism and ritual within the world of *Buffy*.

Nelly Strehlau also confronts issues of history and representation in her essay "She's White and They Are History: *Buffy the Vampire Slayer*'s Racialization of the Past and Present." Strehlau contends that the show promotes a set of values that glorify the present and future as progressive while denigrating the past as backwards and outmoded. Along these lines, Strehlau finds linkages aligning socially progressive ideology (which, Strehlau argues, the show promotes as favorable) with Caucasian characters, while simultaneously aligning racially Othered characters with the antiquated values of the imagined past (which the show portrays as unfavorable). Exploring *Buffy* through this framework, Strehlau's argument sheds light onto vital questions about the ramifications of this future/present/past dichotomy on the lessons imparted by the show on its viewers.

Rounding out the first section, Rhonda V. Wilcox provides an insightful take on one of *Buffy*'s more explicitly political episodes in her essay "'Let it simmer': Tonal Shifts in 'Pangs.'" Wilcox notes the polarized critical response to the role and representation of the Chumash in the episode's events, citing authors on both sides of the theoretical divide. While some scholars consider this episode a low moment for race relations in the series, Wilcox looks at several early drafts of the episode to establish the nuances that went into forming the often-subtle shifts in tone through dialogue and characterization to complicate the politics of the episode's messages. Noting the ways in which the various ideologies represented by different characters are all eventually undermined through comedic shifts in tone, Wilcox interprets the episode as a problem play that aims to raise, rather than answer, questions of conflicting interests and interpretations regarding racial identity issues on *Buffy*.

As Whedon expanded from working on *Buffy* to working on *Angel* at the same time, so too does our book's second section provide coverage of the two interconnected narrative universes, expanding our academic gaze from

Buffy's Sunnydale to encompass *Angel*'s Los Angeles in our questioning of how racial constructs operate in and inform its narrative world as well. More so than any of Whedon's other properties, these two programs are intimately connected to one another, with characters crossing over and developing arcs that span and affect the worlds of both shows. It seemed insufficient to view them as separate entities, and so the essays in this section of the book focus on how racial and ethnic Otherness have been constructed across *Buffy* and *Angel*. Katia McClain kicks off this section by examining representations of the Roma and Romani identity, a curiously overlooked ethnic group prevalent to the *Buffy/Angel* mythology, considering how important *Angel*'s "Gypsy curse" is to both shows. McClain's essay, "Representations of the Roma in *Buffy* and *Angel*," fills this gap, paying special attention to Jenny Calendar and her character's role as a modern Romani within Sunnydale. McClain also identifies problematic language present in both programs used to articulate the place of the Romani inside Whedon's world. By mapping Whedon's Romani representation amidst the history of "Gypsy" stereotypes and anti–Romani discriminatory tropes that have suffused American cinema, McClain gives readers context and insight into how Whedon's characters advance and stumble in their engagement with the Romani and reconcile the reality of Romani culture with the myths circulating consistently (though incorrectly) through many peoples' perception of this complicated ethnicity.

Angel takes a step towards inclusivity by featuring a black actor in the core group of protagonists, a casting decision which not only brought the immense talent of J. August Richards to Whedon fans the world over but also, with Gunn as a main character with whom viewers are encouraged to identify, occasionally pushed issues of race and racism to the forefront of the show's concerns in ways *Buffy*, without a core protagonist of color, never could. For example, recall the aforementioned moment from Season Two's "The Thin Dead Line" (2.14), in which Gunn and his friends attempt to bait zombie cops into harassing them so he can document it on video, when Wesley asks how Gunn knows the zombie-police will come after him, Gunn responds: "Because we'll be the ones walking while Black."[58] Similar to Mr. Trick's statement, Gunn's words here acknowledge that he, and his racially-coded street family face structural disadvantages due to how society interprets their skin color; similar to Mr. Trick, though, this acknowledgment is brushed aside as the story moves on, throwing Whedon's work right into the debate of whether an ambiguous or even marginalized representation is better than no representation at all. Rejena Saulsberry tackles this question head on in her essay, "An Inevitable Tragedy: The Troubled Life of Charles Gunn as an Allegory for General Strain Theory," as she challenges scholarly readings of Charles Gunn as a stereotype to instead interpret his character as embodying and illustrating the sociological strains placed on young men of color from urban neighborhoods theorized by Emile Durkheim and Robert Agnew. Saulsberry argues for a reading of Gunn's struggle to gain access to privileged institutions as an allegory for Strain Theory that illustrates, dramatizes, and ultimately exposes the unjust societal strains under which young poor men of color are forced to operate. Reading Gunn's character arc in terms of Strain Theory (which posits that deviant behaviors emerge when social pressures prohibit certain groups from legitimately achieving success), Gunn becomes a complex window into the struggles of racial identity in a modern world. Saulsberry contends that strain theory can be used to explain why Gunn attempts to fully acculturate himself into the world of his white colleagues, as well as why, despite his efforts at acculturation, he still maintains an outsider throughout the show. While this representation does present racially problematic elements, she argues that these problems call attention to the strains that structural, systematized racism unfairly places on young urban men of color, and in doing so, offer a more nuanced and complicated representation of a young black man negotiating systemic racism than the color-blind mentality promulgated by other televisual programming would allow.

The next section of our book focuses on the ways in which race and ethnicity operate within *Firefly*, *Serenity*, and *Dollhouse*. We chose to put these two series (*Firefly* and *Serenity* are considered parts of the same series) into the same section for two primary reasons. Since both shows were (in the opinion of the editors, unfairly) cancelled early on, they offer less material to explore and cover. Moreover, they both represent Whedon's forays into science fiction. Whereas his previous work could be seen as exercises in fantasy, these programs grounded their characters in worlds of exciting, promising and more than occasionally terrifying scientific innovation. Despite the shift in genre, however, we see the same tensions and contradictions of the racial representation paradox in these shows that we did in *Buffy* and *Angel*. While *Firefly* represents a relatively diverse ensemble cast, especially when compared to the ostensibly white *Buffy*verse and *Angel*'s arguable tokenization of Gunn as the sole main character of color, *Firefly*'s increased inclusivity doesn't translate into a less problematic representation, as whiteness and white-biased culture constructing themselves as normal and natural still pervade the series. For example, in "Jaynestown" (1.7), as River becomes frightened by Shepherd Book's afro, we see a character elsewhere portrayed as an innocent, helpless victim become terrified of Book's ontology as a black man via his African American hair.[59] While moments before they'd been amicably squabbling over her "revisions" to Book's Bible, once River sees his hair, the marker of racial difference from what counts as normal onboard Serenity upset her, as she runs screaming.[60] Even though the connection is not made explicit by the characters themselves, since River's or Kaylee's (or other white characters) occasionally unruly or bushy hair isn't met with such blatant shock, the fact that Book's hair in its literal natural state is seen as disrupting or challenging the norm reveals how illusory and culturally constructed the dominant, white "normal" paradigm really is, for he must mask his natural state for risk of upsetting things (while this requirement is never placed upon white characters). Along these lines, this moment allows us to see the inequality that arises when race is constructed and operates but remains unspoken or invisible. Further, the normative whiteness we see excluding/marginalizing people of color in both *Buffy* and *Angel* extends into the *Firefly/Serenity*verse as well. In this fictive world, the Chinese superpower has influenced mainstream culture on so large a scale as to ensure that everyone, even the uneducated, speaks both English and perfect Mandarin, and while some critics, notably Susan Mandala, see this codeswitching tendency as having the potential to undermine post-colonial monocultural linguistic oppression, several fans have voiced frustration at the lack of actual Chinese, or even generally Asian, characters enacting this codeswitching.[61] Similarly, several critics question the Reavers as racialized representations, as some interpret them as over-exaggerated stereotypes of Native Americans/American Indians.[62] Again, as with *Buffy* and *Angel*, we see race operating in *Firefly* even if it's not explicitly at the forefront of a given episode's narrative concerns, and again, we see this tension between whether increased diversity of racial representation is better than none at all, and how introducing more characters of color doesn't mean the problematic racial representations have been resolved.

We begin this section with the essay "Race, Space and the (De)Construction of Neocolonial Difference in *Firefly/Serenity*" by Brent M. Smith-Casanueva, which argues that *Firefly* and *Serenity*, unlike some other contemporary space-western worlds, allow a neo-colonial, neoliberal society to emerge, presenting a more nuanced and critical examination than the "essentialized" binaristic discourses of human/alien racial politics that so often stand in place of issues of imperialism and exceptionalism in the universe. Smith-Casanueva contends that Whedon refuses the overly simplistic methodology of direct revolution and an overthrowing of the existing governmental structure. Instead, the show advocates for a more complicated form of resistance in the form of free choice and mobility.

Next, Daoine S. Bachran analyzes the apparent absence of Chicano culture from Whedon productions in "Mexicans in Space? Joss Whedon's *Firefly*, Reavers and the Man They Call Jayne." Bachran locates the world of *Firefly* within a cinematic history of "frontier" space stories used to metaphorically represent U.S.–Mexico border relations. Interpreting Jayne as a vaquero figure, Bachran presents what may be the first close reading of Jayne's character: although displayed as a folk hero, Jayne demonstrates a series of stereotypical tendencies that mark him as less civilized and potentially savage, rendering him a rich but problematic representation of Chicano culture. Bachran also discusses the Reavers as a stand in for the hyperbolic rhetoric typically associated with immigration in the United States, contending that their mythologized nature is reflective of the sentiment used to justify violence and discrimination against Mexicans in the border wars that still engulf the present day United States.

We then have "Zoe Washburne: Navigating the 'Verse as a Military Woman of Color" by Mayan Jarnagin, who identifies Gina Torres' character as one of the most complex and multifaceted portraits of an African American woman in all of science fiction. Jarnagin argues that by situating Zoe as both a competent military commander and a devoted wife, Whedon and his team of writers largely sidestep the common pitfalls of the Strong Black Woman stereotype. Having the ship as a safe haven allows Zoe an outlet for emotional vulnerability that is often not afforded to the SBW stereotype. Further, Zoe's professionalism in her adherence to military codes of conduct (as outlined in comparison to actual U.S. military codes, courtesy of Private First Class Jarnagin's personal experience) render her, in Jarnagin's estimation, a truly nuanced representation.[63]

We see similar instances of race-informed practices with ambiguous implications in *Dollhouse*, as for example when Echo negotiates with Caroline (her former consciousness, who's been dumped into another body by Alpha), over whether she should return to the Dollhouse, persuading herself not to by stating: "I've got 38 brains, and not one of them thinks you can sign a contract to be a slave. Especially now that we have a black president."[64] This statement relies on the audience's acknowledgment and understanding of the history of race and racism in America to carry the meaning that having a black president is a milestone, without articulating the specifics of race and history that makes having a black president a real achievement. And yet, even as it links the brutal history of slavery to an actual black person, the present plot point involving freedom and slavery is being embodied and enacted mostly through white people. Isiah Lavender surmises that *Dollhouse*'s racial politics limit its subversive potential as a progressive television show: despite Echo and Boyd's Active/Handler relationship working as a positive iteration of the historical trope of "a black man 'handling' a white woman" (whereas, historically and stereotypically, black men were lynched for "handling" white women), ultimately, the fact that Boyd is later revealed to be the evil mastermind behind the Rossum Corporation's machinations results in a situation where "the show's primary black character is lynched for his earlier racial transgressions—forcing a white woman into prostitution."[65] As with the world of *Firefly,* the fact that *Dollhouse*'s cast includes more diverse actors of color doesn't necessarily mean the show is exempted from perpetuating problematic racialized practices.

Brandeise Monk-Payton covers this issue by looking at a "post-racial" future as ultimately constructed by the Orwellian Rossum Corporation in her essay "Programming Slavery: Race, Technology and the Quest for Freedom in *Dollhouse.*" Monk-Payton argues that the show takes on a regressive tone by undermining the integrity of its primary African American character Boyd Langton when he is ultimately revealed to be evil. The essay critically examines the role Langton plays as the head of a slave-trade business and how this fits into the larger problematic aesthetic of a post-racial society. It also explores the complications brought about by inserting fantasy elements into the historically racialized narrative of slavery, resulting in a repetition of oppressive power dynamics enabled by forgetting history. The process of historical forgetting through memory wipes is discussed as a site of consternation for the program and its message, as to forget history is to commit to repeating the same mistakes.

Also investigating the show's relationship to history is the next essay, Samira Nadkarni's "'Memory itself guarantees nothing': *Dollhouse,* Witnessing and 'the jews.'" Nadkarni presents evidence linking the events of *Dollhouse* into a metaphorical relationship with the atrocities of the Holocaust. Despite a lack of clearly identified Jewish characters, Nadkarni convincingly connects the Actives of the Dollhouse to victims of concentration camps, exploring specific references to this history (such as Alpha and Echo's conversation regarding their place in society as potential Übermenches) as well as overarching narrative parallels regarding slavery, revolution, and the Jewish Golem myth. Through a comparison of the series to more popular examples of the Golem tradition such as Karel Čapek's play *R.U.R.* (*Rossum's Universal Robots*), Nadkarni is able to establish a specific set of commentaries related to Jewish identity and post–Holocaust guilt within *Dollhouse.*

The final section of essays within the book presents a long view of racial representation across and outside of the Whedonverses, featuring scholars finding overarching themes to Whedon's treatment of race and ethnicity across several shows as well as in meta-narrative commentary upon the larger industry. The first essay in this section, Candra K. Gill's "On Soldiers and Sages: Problematizing the Roles of Black Men in the Whedonverses," takes a multidimensional approach to issues of race and gender within Whedon's televisual properties (in particular, *Buffy, Angel, Firefly* and *Dollhouse*).[66] Gill's essay provides a critical lens for examining peripheral characters in each show who have received comparatively scant scholarly attention up to this point: Mr. Trick, Forrest Gates, Jubal Early and Boyd Langton. Gill lays out a host of tropes to which black men have traditionally been relegated in television as described by Patricia Hill Collins including antagonists, allies, soldiers and sages. By doing so, Gill provides a holistic view of how representations of black men have evolved over the course of Whedon's work in television.

Next, "The Godmothers of Them All: Female-Centered Blaxploitation Films and the Heroines of Joss Whedon" by Masani McGee provides a survey of the relationship between Blaxploitation cinema and the characters of Nikki Wood, Echo, Faith, and Zoe Washburne, deftly tracing the roots of their characterizations to Foxy Brown, Cleopatra Jones, and T.N.T. Jackson. By analyzing aspects of these characters' behavior such as their sexual power and ability to articulate their opinions to other characters within their respective shows, McGee illustrates some complicating factors to the overall narrative of female independence within the Whedonverses, ultimately contending that Whedon's work falls short of the empowering narratives it seeks to emulate in the portrayal of Wood.

In our book's final essay, Hélène Frohard-Dourlent deconstructs the rhetoric of a paratextual accompaniment to Joss Whedon's internet sensation *Dr. Horrible's Sing-Along Blog* in the essay "Someone's Asian in *Dr. Horrible*: Humor, Reflexivity and the Absolution of Whiteness." Although not a part of the web series' three acts, the song "Nobody's Asian in the Movies" appears as part of the *Commentary! The Musical* special feature available on the *Dr. Horrible* DVD, performed and written by Whedon collaborator Marissa Tancharoen.[67] Frohard-Dourlent contends that the song, while on the surface a condemnation of the racially marginalizing practices of Hollywood, also allows a unique space for the writers to admit to some of their own inequities in casting and scripting television programs. Utilizing close reading methodology, Frohard-Dourlent confronts difficult questions raised by the song's content, such as its critique of the role whiteness plays in the film industry, its use of humor as a rhetorical device when dealing with themes of race, and its ultimately ambiguous assessment of how race is understood as a concept in contemporary popular culture.

As Whedon continues working on his televisual creative properties more deeply within the Hollywood institutions, he continues to struggle to interface with the system in his creative decisions. For instance, in the critically acclaimed *Much Ado About Nothing* adaptation, Whedon decided to leave a notoriously racist line from Shakespeare's text in his adaptation, with the intention to have the actors play it as a "Michael Scott" moment functioning to characterize its subject, Claudio, as clueless and ignorant.[68] While such a directorial choice undermines what would have been the line's significance in Shakespeare's time, it nevertheless invokes the cultural framework required for a "Michael Scott" moment to be effective which also takes for granted a world in which uneven and unequal racial representation is still a thing capable of being and needing to be commented upon.[69] Rhonda V. Wilcox reads this line through W.E.B. DuBois' concept of double consciousness, arguing that Whedon's "Ethiope" line offers an opportunity to consider historical double-consciousness, or as she calls it, "cognitive counterpoint," in which the film forces audiences to hold two opposing ideas together at once (the contradiction being are we're both glad Hero's going to marry Claudio after all and that Claudio's the kind of ignoramus who would say such a dreadful thing).[70] While the degree to which this Michael Scott moment is successful remains open for debate, it also demonstrates a continuing concern in Whedon's creative production process; again, at the margins of the narrative, in a momentary utterance that fades as the story moves on, characters perform and practice race and racism, in an ambiguous representation strategy that allows for multiple readings.

The continued regularity of such racially charged moments in the Whedonverses present an opportunity to reflect on what this all signifies in terms of interpreting Whedon's works. Ultimately, inspecting the way institutional oppression plays out in the seemingly neutral actions of characters provides the metaphorical opportunity for us to recognize and examine how institutional discrimination and oppression play out through our own (perhaps unintentional) actions. Oppressive institutions influence us because we're a part of them, there's no escaping that. We are all already part of the problem, but the good news is, as Allan G. Johnson says, we can also be part of the solution as well.[71] The point is that examining race in the works of Joss Whedon gives us an opportunity to investigate and better understand different scenarios of individuals interfacing with the system, to varying degrees of success. Through the Whedonverses, we inhabit the contradiction of attempting to subvert evil institutions while still working from within them, while in some ways perpetuating them even as we fight against them. We understand how characters, and by extension, we as viewers hold the tensions of these contradictions, in the hopes of learning to be more fully human.

NOTES

1. Joss Whedon, quoted in "10 Questions for Joss Whedon." *Time Magazine* video. June 10, 2013.

2. Joss Whedon. Reddit.com AMA. 10 April. 2012.

3. "Reprise," *Angel* 2.15, DVD, written by Tim Minear, directed by James Whitmore Jr. (2001; Twentieth Century Fox Film Corporation, 2007).

4. "Out of Gas," *Firefly* (1.8). Written by Tim Minear, directed by David Solomon (2002; Twentieth Century Fox home Entertainment LLC 2003).

5. *Cabin in the Woods*. DVD. Written by Joss Whedon and Drew Goddard, directed by Drew Goddard (2011; Lionsgate, 2012).

6. *Marvel's The Avengers*, Blu-Ray, written by Joss Whedon (story, screenplay) and Zak Penn (story), directed by Joss Whedon (2012; Marvel Studios, 2012). While critics debate the degree to which characters from Marvel's *The Avengers* can be considered Whedon property, we find it telling that, under Whedon's directorship, even this borrowed universe features a threatening evil institution in line with those featured in his former works.

7. Joss Whedon, interviewed by James Hibberd, *Entertainment Weekly*, No. 1274, August 30th, 2013.

8. While scholars such as Rabb and Richardson find unifying existential threads recurring throughout the Whedonverses, others, such as Lavery and McCown, argue that Whedon fails to theoretically unify all of his creative works. Please see *The Existential Joss Whedon: Evil and Human Freedom in* Buffy the Vampire Slayer, Angel, Firefly, *and* Serenity by J. Michael Richardson and J. Douglas Rabb, and for the opposing viewpoint, see David A. Lavery, "I Wrote My Thesis on You: *Buffy* Studies as an Academic Cult," *Slayage Online Journal*, 13/14 (4.1–2).

9. J. Michael Richardson and Douglas J. Rabb, *The Existential Joss Whedon* (Jefferson, NC: McFarland, 2007), 52.

10. *Dr. Horrible's Sing-Along Blog*. Written by Joss Whedon, Jed Whedon, Zack Whedon, and Maurissa Tancharoen, directed by Joss Whedon (2008; Time Science Blood Club LLC, 2009).

11. "Faith, Hope, and Trick," *Buffy the Vampire Slayer* 3.3, DVD, written by David Greenwalt, directed by James A. Contner (1998; Twentieth Century Fox, 1998). Whedon's works often feature evil characters selectively using the truth to deceive and manipulate others. Spike, for instance, while evil, also utters certain uncomfortable truths others refuse to say. In later seasons, Anya occasionally fills this role, as she relents that "I used to tell the truth all the time when I was evil" ("Sleeper" 7.8). The Master, The Mayor, Angelus, and later in the comics, the snake-goddess Eluwyn also use bits of truth mixed with lies in order to villainously manipulate others.

12. Richard Dyer, *White* (New York: Routledge, 2006), 1–30.

13. Jennifer Esposito, "What Does Race Have to Do with *Ugly Betty*?," 524.

14. William Ryan, *Blaming the Victim*, 2nd ed. (New York: Random House, 1976), 11.

15. Srividya Ramasubramanian, "Pride, Prejudice, and Policy Preferences: Exploring the Relationships Between TV Stereotypes, Racial Attitudes, and Support for Affirmative Action," paper delivered at Annual Meeting of the International Communication Association, 2009, 1–26, retrieved from EBSCO host 21 March 2012. 1–2.

16. Richard Dyer, *White* (New York: Routledge, 2006), 1–30.

17. Pender, 171.

18. Matthew Pateman, *The Aesthetics of Culture in* Buffy the Vampire Slayer (Jefferson, NC: McFarland, 2006), 49.

19. Naomi Alderman and Annette Seidel-Arpaci, "Imaginary Para-Sites of the Soul: Vampires and Representations of 'Blackness' and 'Jewishness' in the *Buffy/Angel*-verse, *Slayage*," *The Online International Journal of Whedon Studies*, 10(3.2).

20. For the definitive reading of this approach, please see Mary Alice Money's essay "The Undemonization of Supporting Characters" in *Fighting the Forces: What's at Stake in* Buffy the Vampire Slayer (Lanham MD: Rowman & Littlefield, 2002), 98–107.

21. This point—that Whedon gives thought and care to representing strong female characters without paying equal attention to representing strong characters of color—is a common refrain many of our contributors will reiterate in their own words. At one point, as it happened, nearly every essay draft we received began with a sentence alluding to this fact!

22. Ramasubramanian, 1–2.

23. Michelle Alexander, *The New Jim Crow: Mass Incarceration in the Age of Colorblindness* (New York: The New Press, 2012), Kindle Reader e-book.

24. "Calvary," *Angel* 4.12, DVD, written by Jeffrey Bell, Steven S. DeKnight, and Mere Smith, directed by Bill Norton (2003; Twentieth Century Fox Home Entertainment LLC, 2007).

25. "Ground State." *Angel* 4.2, DVD, written by Mere Smith, directed by Michael Grossman (2002: Twentieth Century Fox, 2007).

26. "Deep Down," *Angel* 4.1, DVD, written by Steven S. DeKnight, directed by Terrence O'Hara (2003; Twentieth Century Fox, 2007).

27. Richard Delgado and Jean Stefancic, *Critical Race Theory: An Introduction* (New York: NYU Press, 2001), 153.

28. Allan G. Johnson, *Privilege, Power, and Difference* (2nd ed.) (New York: McGraw-Hill, 2006), 16.

29. *Ibid.*, 146.

30. *Ibid.*, 7.

31. Delgado and Stefancic, 153. The Antebellum social and legal principle of the "One-Drop" rule of hypodescent asserted, "any person with discernible black ancestry is black and can never be white," thinking that was used to codify discriminatory housing and voter registration practices (among other policies) in mid–20th Century America.

32. Eduardo Bonilla-Silva, "The Strange Enigma of Race in Contemporary America," *Racism Without Racists: Color-Blind Racism and Racial Inequality in Contemporary America,* 3rd edition (Lanham, MD: Rowman & Littlefield, 2010), 1–24, 9.

33. Allan G. Johnson, *Privilege, Power, and Difference,* 16.

34. In the media buzz surrounding President Obama's recent comments on the Zimmerman verdict and race in America, a 2008 *Wall Street Journal* article recirculated in the blogosphere. It relates the story of the young Obama being casually discriminated against at a gathering of journalists and literary elite. Katherine Rosman, "Before He Was President, Mistaken for a Waiter: A 2003 Encounter with Obama," *Wall Street Journal Online,* 7 Nov 2011 12:34 PM, available here: http://blogs.wsj.com/washwire/2008/11/07/before-he-was-president-mistaken-for-a-waiter-a-2003-obama-meeting/

35. Peggy McIntosh, "White Privilege: Unpacking the Invisible Knapsack," *Understanding Prejudice and Discrimination,* Plous, Scott (Ed.) (New York: McGraw-Hill, 2003), 191–196.

36. Delgado and Stefancic, *Critical Race Theory,* 10.

37. "The Thin Dead Line," *Angel* 2.14, written by Shawn Ryan and Jim Kouf, directed by Scott McGinnis, DVD (2001: Twentieth-Century Fox, 2007).

38. Rinku Sen, "Building a New Racial Justice Movement," Colorlines.com.

39. Richard Delgado and Jean Stefancic, *Critical Race Theory,* 22.

40. "Go Fish," *Buffy the Vampire Slayer* 2.20, written by David Fury and Elin Hampton, directed by David Semel (1998; Twentieth Century Fox, 2006).

41. *Ibid.*

42. *Ibid.*

43. "Reptile Boy," *Buffy the Vampire Slayer* 2.5, written and directed by David Greenwalt (1997; Twentieth Century Fox, 2006); "Help," *Buffy the Vampire Slayer* 7.4, written by Rebecca Rand Kirshner, directed by Rick Rosenthal, DVD (2002; Twentieth Century Fox, 2006).

44. "City of," *Angel* 1.1, written by Joss Whedon and David Greenwalt, directed by Joss Whedon (1999; Twentieth Century Fox, 2007).

45. Joseph Barndt and Charles Ruehle, "Understanding Institutional Racism: Systems That Oppress," in *American's Original Sin: A Study Guide on White Racism,* Eds. Bob Hulteen and Jim Wallis (Washington, D.C.: Sojourners Resource Center, 1992), 12.

46. "Vows," *Dollhouse* 2.1, written and directed by Joss Whedon (2009: Twentieth Century Fox, 2010).

47. "A Spy in the House of Love," *Dollhouse* 2.9, written by Andrew Chambliss, directed by David Solomon (2009; Twentieth Century Fox, 2010).

48. *Buffy*, "Reptile Boy" 2.5.

49. "Tough Love," *Buffy the Vampire Slayer* 5.19, DVD, written by Rebecca Rand Kirshner, directed by David Grossman (2001; Twentieth Century Fox 2006).

50. Allan G. Johnson, *Privilege, Power, and Difference*, 2nd ed. (New York: McGraw-Hill, 2006), 26.

55. Jennifer Esposito, "What Does Race Have to Do with *Ugly Betty*? An Analysis of Privilege and Postracial (?) Representation on a Television Sitcom," *Television New Media*. 10, 2012. 521.

52. Pateman, 61.

53. Johnson, 142.

54. David Lavery, *Joss Whedon: A Creative Portrait* (London: I. B. Tauris, 2013).

55. "Once More with Feeling," *Buffy the Vampire Slayer* 6.7, DVD, written by Joss Whedon, directed by Joss Whedon (2001: Twentieth Century Fox Home Entertainment LLC 2006).

56. Jeffrey Middents, "A Sweet Vamp: Critiquing the Treatment of Race in Buffy and the American Musical Once More (with Feeling)," *Buffy, Ballads, and Bad Guys Who Sing: Music in the Worlds of Joss Whedon,* Ed. Kendra Preston Leonard (Plymouth, UK: Scarecrow Press, 2011), 119–132. 126. Middents notes that, whereas other characters of color on the show (notably Kendra, Mr. Trick, Ampata, Hus, Forrest, Olivia etc.) are killed or simply disappear, in "Once More with Feeling" (6.7), Sweet, the African American-coded singing/dancing villain, does not die, and more importantly, does not lose. While he leaves at the end of the episode, it's of his own volition, and his biting final lines of song illustrate how unsettled the Scoobies remain after his departure, proving the strength of his impact upon them (126).

57. "Helpless," *Buffy the Vampire Slayer* 3.12, DVD, written by David Fury, directed by James A. Contner (1999; Twentieth Century Fox, 2006).

58. "The Thin Dead Line," *Angel* 2.14, DVD, written by David Greenwalt, Shawn Ryan and Jim Kouf, directed by Scott McGinnis (2001; Twentieth Century Fox, 2007).

59. "Jaynestown," *Firefly* 1.7, DVD, written by Ben Edlund, directed by Marita Grabiak (2002; Twentieth Century Fox Film Corporation 2003).

60. *Ibid.*

61. For an account of this argument, please see: Susan Mandala, "Representing the Future: Chinese and Codeswitching in *Firefly*," *Investigating* Firefly *and* Serenity: Science Fiction on the Frontier, Eds. Rhonda V. Wilcox and Tanya R. Cochran (London: I.B. Tauris, 2008). For a fan's perspective on being Asian-American and experiencing the Chinese code-switching without actual Chinese people, see Mike Le's post on racebending.com, "Frustrations of an Asian-American Whedonite," 21.7.2012, http://www.racebending.com/v4/blog/frustrations-asian-american-whedonite/.

62. See Agnes Curry, "'We don't say "Indian"': On the Paradoxical Construction of the Reavers." *Slayage Online Journal of Whedon Studies* 7.1 [25], Winter 2008. See also J. Douglas Rabb and R Michael Richardson, "Reavers and Redskins: Creating the Frontier Savage," *Investigating* Firefly *and* Serenity: *Science Fiction On the Frontier*, Eds. Rhonda V. Wilcox and Tanya R. Cochran (London: I.B. Tauris, 2008), 127–138.

63. Indeed, Whedon seemed to confirm the importance of this aspect of the character when he related the story of the series being picked up by FOX during a Q and A session at the Film Society at Lincoln Center. During the discussion Joss men-

tioned that originally FOX had agreed to pick up *Firefly* on the provision that Zoe and Wash not be married to which he replied: "Then don't pick up the pilot." For the rest of the interview, see Joss Whedon (2013), "An Evening with Joss Whedon," lecture as part of a series at the Film Society at Lincoln Center.

64. "Omega," *Dollhouse* 1.12, DVD, written by Tim Minear, Tracy Bellomo, Andrew Chambliss, Jed Whedon and Maurissa Tancharoen, directed by Tim Minear (2009; Twentieth Century Fox Home Entertainment LLC, 2009).

65. Isiah Lavender III, *Race in American Science Fiction* (Bloomington: Indiana University Press, 2011), 3–4.

66. We note with great excitement that scholarship is beginning to cover *Marvel's Agents of S.H.I.E.L.D.* and look forward to critical applications of these concepts to that show.

67. Jed Whedon and Maurissa Tancharoen, "Nobody's Asian in the Movies," *Commentary! The Musical*, DVD (2008: Mutant Enemy/New Video Group, Inc., 2009).

68. Joss Whedon, "Much Ado About Nothing Screening and Q & A," Brooklyn Academy of Music (BAM), May 31st 2013. Thanks to David Satz for his help in securing transcripts of Whedon's talk that evening.

69. Otherwise, Whedon would have cut or changed the line, as he did in another instance with an anachronistic, racially charged ethnic slur. In Shakespeare's text, Benedick utters the words "If I do not love her, then I am a Jew." Whedon kept the line in but changed the final word to "fool." During the BAM Much Ado screening and Q & A, Whedon explained his thought process with that decision in the following terms: "I don't have Benedick saying, 'If I do not love her, I am a Jew.' I thought, yeah. That's not gonna sell. So I changed it to, 'If I do not love her I am a gay.' No, that doesn't scan, let's go with 'fool'" (Whedon BAM Q&A).

70. Rhonda V. Wilcox, "Much Ado About Whedon," Keynote speech at *Joss In June: A Conference on the Works of Joss Whedon*, 29 June 2013. Thanks to Rhonda for providing us with a copy of her conference paper, the very first academic presentation on Whedon's *Much Ado*.

71. Johnson, 34–5.

PART I

The Caucasian Persuasion Here in the 'Dale

Race and Ethnicity in Buffy the Vampire Slayer

"The black chick always gets it first"
Black Slayers in Sunnydale

LYNNE EDWARDS

I was an avid fan of *Buffy the Vampire Slayer* until November 17, 1997, and then, it happened. The betrayal that black fans dread, yet have come to expect—the moment we are painfully reminded that we are Other. My moment arrived in the cargo hold of an airplane, a tribal drum beat and flute heralding her entrance. She was clearly coded as Other in name, in language, and in her color; she was clearly an outsider to Sunnydale. Her name was Kendra and I knew three things the moment I saw her. She was different. She was dangerous. And she was dead.

As expected, Kendra ultimately died, never to be seen again. I wasn't surprised, given the history of women of color being killed off in television and film, but I was hurt, oddly enough. I thought *Buffy* was going to be different, that she would be transgressive; a powerful role model who took on monsters and race relations head-on. My disappointment, however, was gradually alleviated by the subsequent sisterhood of black Slayers who appeared throughout Buffy's seven-season run. From the First Slayer, Sineya, whose mystical rape in Africa created the Slayer line to Nikki Wood, whose leather coat and ignominious death on a New York City subway contributed to Spike's signature look and "vampire slayer" identity, these women subtly alter the Slayer myth from unquestioned white female privilege to a more difficult feminist narrative about race and shared power.

Race is a social construct that forms a common ground of shared history and culture. As a byproduct of colonialism, slavery, segregation and desegregation, racial discourse in the U.S. is frequently reduced to a black/white binary.[1] In other words, most Americans still typically see racial problems as

37

an issue of black versus white, erasing other non-whites from cultural debates.[2] However, Nell Painter in *The History of White People*, would argue that many whites historically may not have defined themselves as a "race," regardless of their role in the binary.[3]

Blackness functions as a sign and site of cultural struggle and debate about race, but it also serves as a signifier of what Cornell West calls a "system of race conscious people and practices."[4] Not only is the sign of blackness read and constructed against an ever-evolving political context, it is also constructed in relation to whiteness, thereby creating an implicit dichotomy with whiteness.[5] One of the reasons race representations have been explored so much is because of the perceived effects on viewers' perceptions of blacks and even viewers' perceptions of themselves and their racial identities.[6] As Darnell Hunt, in *Channeling Blackness* argues, "Because the black-white binary is so fundamental to our way of thinking in America ... those who attempt to avoid "binary thinking" in their production and/or consumption of representations of Blackness necessarily do so against a cultural milieu that is saturated with the binary."[7] In *Buffy*, the cultural sign of blackness is enacted as a metaphor of liminality, where black characters are the sites of pivotal identity struggles for Buffy and her friends; their presence challenges Buffy's transgressive power. Like white, middle-class Buffy, black Slayers are heroines in Whedon's mythic world. Like Barthes' soldier,[8] however, their racial coding adds a radically different meaning to their characters, evoking black cultural myths from popular media that frame Kendra as a tragic mulatta, Nikki as a Jezebel, Sineya as a savage, and Rona as a Sapphire.

The Centrality of Power in Buffy the Vampire Slayer *Mythology*

Power is a theme explored openly and often in *Buffy*, particularly its abuse by Buffy's friends and their subsequent redemption. Buffy's friendship with Willow and Xander lasts throughout the entire series, and survives a variety of challenges, including Buffy's deaths in "Prophecy Girl" (1.12)[9] and in "The Gift" (5.22),[10] her difficulties in "When She Was Bad" (2.1)[11] as she struggles to come to grips with her death at the hands of the Master, and again throughout all of Season Six as she masks her pain at being yanked out of heaven by her friends. Buffy's friendships also survive the Scoobies' abuse of power. Xander and Willow employ magic to assert control over their lovers' emotions in "Bewitched, Bewildered, and Bothered" (2.16),[12] "Once More with Feeling" (6.7),[13] and "Tabula Rasa" (6.8).[14] Willow and Anya go to murderous lengths in order to cope with grief and to exact revenge in "Two to Go" (6.21)[15] and "Entropy" (6.18).[16] Despite the mayhem and loss of lives they've caused in their abuses of power, these characters are given the opportunity to redeem themselves in the eyes of Buffy and her audience.[17]

The containment of Slayer power by the Watchers' Council is also a recurring theme and the Council's depiction as a neo-colonialist institution provides an ongoing cultural contradiction in Slayer mythology. Located in England, the Council governs Slayer training and education from afar by identifying Potentials and assigning Watchers to them, like colonizing nations identifying fertile new territories rich in natural resources to be managed and reaped by its emissaries. Council members are also the producers and keepers of Slayer knowledge, a consciousness industry that shares only enough information and prophecies to enable the Slayer to perform her duties, while also preventing Potentials from learning about each other and the truth of their shared power.[18]

Ironically, this construction of the Watchers' Council as neo-colonialists whose sole responsibility is to manage the Slayer line masks the contradictions about the realities of racial and gender power inherent in *Buffy* mythology. First, the fact that a transgressive heroine's power in Sunnydale, California, is constrained by a British, predominantly male institution, is clearly problematic. However, the power to control the production of Slayer knowledge disguises the fact that the Council has no power over Slayer reproduction, as it is only the death of *the* Slayer that can activate the next Slayer. We eventually learn that the reproductive death myth was simply another instrument of control utilized by the Council, but it took seven seasons to even raise the question. Second, the representation of the Watchers' Council as British and predominantly white is ironically turned on its head in "Get it Done" (7.15), when Buffy learns that the Shadow Men of Africa were the first Watchers. Coupled with the Slayer's origins in Africa, we are ultimately presented with a narrative about white privilege and power that originates in Africa.[19]

The Watchers' Council is not the only contradictory representation in *Buffy*. Joss Whedon created *Buffy* to be a feminist program, with the blonde girl as hero and not victim.[20] And, to a certain extent, he was successful. Frances Early, in *The Female Just Warrior Reimagined: From Boudicca to Buffy*, argues that Buffy is a "just" warrior who challenges our beliefs about women and aggression.[21] She notes that Buffy "functions as an open image of an empowered transgressive female just warrior" who stands "counterpoised not only against males but also against nonconformist females whose rebellions are located outside the boundary of warriorism as enacted by Buffy."[22]

One critique of *Buffy*'s transgressiveness, however, lies in the reality of the television business. While Buffy does function as the series' warrior hero who does not shy away from violence or valor, she is also a media product constructed to please advertisers and audiences by being beautiful and badass. Toward this end, Buffy fails to push the ideological envelope beyond aggressive female. She is white, middle-class, very attractive, heterosexual, and very feminine. Another contradiction lies in the apparent erasure of race in this feminist text.[23] For the first six seasons, Buffy has no friends of color, nor are there major recurring characters of color, aside from occasional minor players. Arguably, Robin Wood can be seen as a friend and comrade in arms, but not until Season Seven, when Buffy is faced with the seemingly unconquerable First Evil. Although there is no reason why Buffy should have developed friendships with characters of color beyond her core friendship with the Scoobies established in the first season, she does develop other long-term relationships with Anya, Tara, and Spike, so it wouldn't be beyond the realm of possibilities. In contrast, Gunn joins Angel Investigations in Season One ("War Zone" 1.20) and remains by his side until the series end.[24] So where is this cultural progressiveness in *Buffy*? What does the absence of black friends for Buffy signify?

The contested construction of blackness is further complicated, however, when considering gender, where race/ethnicity becomes conflated with gender/sexuality. In *Black Feminist Thought*, Patricia Hill Collins argues that:

> Even when the political and economic conditions that originally generated controlling images disappear, such images prove remarkably tenacious because they not only keep black women oppressed but are key in maintaining interlocking systems of race, class, and gender oppression.... Maintaining images of black women as the Other provides ideological justification for race, gender, and class oppression.[25]

Ideological oppression, particularly in the United States, is an odd exercise in liminalities. The black body is both revered for its supposed sexuality and reviled for its alleged savagery. bell hooks suggests that one reason Otherness is so appealing is because it has become "commodified"—it is the "spice" that livens up white culture.[26] We see this in *Buffy* when Xander falls for Ampata in "Inca Mummy Girl" (2.4)[27] and Lissa ("First Date" 7.14).[28] Giles' relationship with Olivia in Season Four suggests that he is not immune to the charms of the Other, either. *Buffy* mediates these stereotypes by casting Kendra as a tragic mulatta who attempts to share Buffy's Slayer identity, by positioning Nikki as a Blaxploitation Jezebel who was stalked and metaphorically desired by Spike, by constructing Sineya as a savage and demonized rape victim, and by framing Rona as a modern day Sapphire.

Kendra, the Tragic Mulatta

David Bogle charges that media images of black women, like the tragic mulatta, are narrow, stereotypical and unflattering.[29] In the tragic mulatta narrative of the 1930s through 1960s, a biracial woman masks her blackness by trying to pass for white in order to gain access to better opportunities in school, work, and love. Her tragedy lies in her lost potential, her liminal status trapped between black and white communities and denied acceptance by members of both groups. Tragic mulatta characters can be found in novels like Fannie

Hurst's *Imitation of Life* (1933), where black characters attempt to pass as white, and Zora Neale Hurston's *Their Eyes Were Watching God* (1937), in which the mulatta protagonist fights for love and acceptance in and from the black community. We see this in the Whedonverses as well, as *Angel* included a tragic mulatta narrative about a bank employee who is fired after she is discovered to be passing for white ("Are You Now or Have You Ever Been?" 2.2).[30]

Lisa Anderson, in *Mammies No More* argues that, in a society where the distribution of power is rooted in the reading of race, gender, and class, these stereotypes, particularly the tragic mulatta myth, can be seen as a threat to white identity:

> Of all the images of African American women the image of the mulatta, tragic or not, is the most complex one. ... In one sense, the mulatta lies outside the dualism of Western imagination; she is neither white nor black, yet she is both black and white. In the reality of the American (or even Western) racial context, however, she can only be black, even if she passes for white.[31]

As a tragic mulatta, Kendra's narrative presents a threat to Buffy's identity. The story of Kendra is a myth about a failed quest for legitimacy and acceptance. Upon her arrival to Sunnydale, and after the clarification of her identity as the Slayer activated after Buffy's death, Kendra is forced to not only battle vampires but also Buffy, who refuses to acknowledge Kendra as her rightful heir until their final fight. In a scene that signifies their mutual acceptance of each other and, more importantly, Buffy's acceptance of their shared Slayer identity, they share a quip while fighting Spike as he attempts to cure Drusilla through a transfusion of Angel's blood. When Spike asks who Kendra is, Buffy begins to respond in her typical sarcastic fashion, "It's your lucky day, Spike," only for Kendra to join her in the quip, as Kendra calls out "Two Slayers!" followed by Buffy who chimes in "No waiting!" ("What's My Line, Part 2" 2.10).[32]

Within the narrative of "What's My Line? Part 1" (2.9),[33] Kendra's assumption that she will rightfully assume the Slayer identify further adds to her construction as a tragic mulatta. When presented with the opportunity to cede the Slayer identity to Kendra, Buffy opts to fight back, demonstrating a difference in culture between the two, with the show approving of Buffy's method over Kendra's. In terms of the reality of television production, Kendra's significance to the Slayer narrative in *Buffy* is also evidenced by her role in two separate two-episode story arcs (the "What's My Line" arc in 2.9 and 2.10 as well as the "Becoming" arc in 2.21 and 2.22).[34] Interestingly, these arcs' focus on Buffy's acceptance of her Slayer identity and her eventual willingness to fulfill that role at the expense of Angel's life demonstrates Buffy's ascendancy as the Real Slayer while seemingly eliminating the need for any other Slayer, making Kendra the tragic mulatta existing simply to facilitate completing this chapter in Buffy's epic struggle for identity.

As a black Slayer, Kendra also signifies true Otherness; a Slayer seeking to pass for *the* Slayer.[35] Elyce Helford suggests, in "'My Emotions Give Me Power': The Containment of Girls' Anger in *Buffy*," that Kendra provides a foil to Buffy that illustrates "in heightened form the insider/outsider dichotomy based on race and culture that is central to the series."[36] Rhonda Wilcox in "'Who Died and Made Her the Boss?' Patterns of Mortality in *Buffy*" compares Kendra's fate to Faith's, arguing that class difference can be redeemed, but that the "wrong" race can stop a woman from attaining any empowerment.[37] Given her death and lack of resurrection, Kendra obviously has no hope for redemption. In addition to redemption, Slayer credibility also eludes Kendra. Kendra's death, in fact, doesn't even grant Drusilla the same Slayer-slaying credibility that Spike earned.[38] But Kendra's death does grant a metaphoric life, the activation of Faith as the next Slayer. Even this feat only warrants a brief mention when Cordelia figures out that Kendra's death has activated Faith ("Faith, Hope and Trick" 3.3).[39] The only significant impact that Kendra appears to have on the Slayer narrative is activating Faith; otherwise, Kendra embodies that which is deemed "unheroic" in Buffy.[40] Kendra as a tragic mulatta figure also represents a challenge to Buffy's transgressive power. Despite her goal of assuming her role as this generation's Slayer, Kendra lacks the same agency exhibited by Buffy. Kendra's speech style is passive, far more formal and deferential than is Buffy's or the Scoobies'—she is clearly not comfortable interacting with peers.[41] It is not just language that "Others" Kendra, but also her accent; she is exotic whereas Giles is a prim and proper British foreigner.

As our first introduction to additional/alternative Slayers, Kendra signals the potential for the Slayer narrative to continue beyond Buffy's death, that there are others to whom her death would give birth. What her death failed to signal for Buffy, and for viewers, was the need to question the myth of the single Slayer. *Buffy* really is about power. Kendra' activation while this generation's Slayer was still alive technically redefines Slayer power, but her existence at the same time as Buffy should have raised questions about the individual nature of Slayerdom and thereby challenged the Council's hegemonic power. If two activated Slayers can exist at one time, then Slayer power can be shared. Kendra's Slayer identity should have been validated (albeit posthumously) when her death activated Faith. Questions about the solitary nature of Slayer power should have been raised when Faith was activated while Buffy still lived. Kendra's the ultimate liminal Slayer, caught between Buffy and Faith with little agency within or impact on *Buffy*'s narrative. Ironically, the one liminality Kendra is denied is appropriation by The First Evil, who appears as dead friends, family, and loved ones to evoke guilt and fear in the Scoobies and Potentials during Season Seven. Kendra's contribution, like that of all tragic mulattas is that all women can share and gain strength from a common identity, a common destiny. Kendra's existence suggests that the insider/outsider dichotomy is as false as the black/white racial dichotomy.

The mulatta exists in the uncomfortable racial divide. She *is* the divide, the in-between that both sides seek to claim and deny.

Nikki Wood, the Blaxploitation Jezebel

In addition to the tragic mulatta, K. Sue Jewell in *From Mammy to Miss America and Beyond: Cultural Images and the Shaping of U.S. Social Policy* identifies additional stereotypes of the acid-tongued "Sapphire" and the sexually promiscuous "Jezebel."[42] The Jezebel figure embodies the sex act itself; she is promiscuity and blame personified. In films like *Carmen Jones* (1954), the Jezebel is depicted as alluring, sexually arousing, and seductive, thereby reinforcing cultural stereotypes regarding the hypersexuality of black females.[43] This character also re-affirmed the belief that women lack professional or personal agency, focusing their highly sexualized efforts and actions on securing male partners.

Like other Jezebel characters, Nikki Wood lacks any agency beyond her sexualized definition. Nikki's construction as a modern-day Jezebel is accomplished in two ways. Her visual construction is laden with racial and cultural meaning. In "Fool for Love" (5.7), Spike recounts for Buffy how he killed Nikki, and as he talks, their fight replays in flashback form such that we see a sexually explicit battle as Spike narrates.[44] The phallically-named Spike straddles Nikki on a train surrounded by phallic poles as the train plunges into a dark tunnel (Freud much?) and he bites her as she is trapped beneath him. Their battle is accompanied by funky soul music, reminiscent of Blaxploitation-era movie soundtracks. Spike is sexually attracted to Nikki, revealing that he had stalked her and noting that she reminds him of Buffy, that he could have "danced all night" with her as they battled to her death aboard the subway car.[45]

Unlike Jezebel characters of the past, however, Nikki isn't defined solely by her sexual prowess; she is also defined by the consequences of her sexual activity, namely her son, Robin Wood. With Robin, she lives on as an evil version of herself, appropriated by the First Evil to wear away at Buffy's support team by weakening Robin in Season Seven. Nikki Wood, then, is present but without power, both here and not here. Nikki also failed to pass down the Slayer myth. When Nikki died, she left with Robin a collection of shadowcasters that tell the origin myth of the Slayer ("Lies My Parents Told Me" 7.17).[46] In keeping with black Slayers' pivotal roles in Buffy's learning about herself and her Slayer power, and her origins, Nikki's untimely death led to her son, Robin, holding on to and hiding the shadow puppets out of grief and loyalty—until he shares them with Buffy.

Nikki's construction as Other is framed by her location in another place that is distinctly different, almost foreign. While Kendra hails from an unknown, exotic locale (as indicated by her name and accent), Nikki's setting is a well-known, urban center: New York City. The urban site, coupled with the lower-to-working-class setting of public transportation clearly serve to mark this Slayer as Other in comparison to Buffy of middle-class, suburban Sunnydale, California. Nikki's narrative function as an identity challenge for Buffy is a minor one, since the two Slayers don't exist in the same time and place. Like Kendra's story, Nikki's narrative is presented at a time when Buffy is struggling with her identity. Unlike Kendra's tragic mulatta, who directly challenges Buffy's Slayer identity, Nikki visually threatens Buffy's transgressive power by evoking Blaxploitation-era heroines.

Yvonne Sims, in *Women of Blaxploitation: How the Black Action Film Heroine Changed American Popular Culture*, argues that these heroines represent the first non-servile roles for black women, although the genre failed to alter broader stereotypes of black women.[47] In addition to being located in another geographic space, Nikki's narrative is set in the 1970s, an era in American history that is heavily laden with racial and political significance. Visually, Nikki is coded as a Blaxploitation genre heroine with a large Afro, stack-heeled boots, and a long black leather coat that swings aggressively as she fights. Set in the same period as the Civil Rights and Black Power movements, Nikki looks like the transgressive black film heroines *Coffy* (1973) or *Foxy Brown* (1974) and the Blaxploitation era is defined by specific visual significations of blackness, black power, and transgressive black films.[48] Her time and space distance from Buffy prevent obvious comparisons of their agency, as Buffy's strength and independence would seem less unique if Nikki exhibited these same behaviors in the same time and space as Buffy.

Nikki, ultimately, is liminal because we hear about her before we see her, and she's dead before we meet her. Nikki also lacks the Slayer power seen in Buffy's tenure: longevity. The reason we learn Nikki's story is because she died, making her a failed Slayer. She isn't the Slayer whose death contributed to the Slayer line. Rather, her death contributed to Spike's reputation. She, or rather her metaphoric skin, lives on with Spike; forever trapped in leather as her generation's Slayer known not for her victories but for her failure.

Sineya, the Savage Slayer

Bogle argues that the black brute stereotype in Griffith's *The Birth of a Nation* (1915) was a barbaric black out to wreak havoc, his physical violence serving as an outlet for sexual repression. In *The Birth of a Nation*, Bogle argues, the subhuman and feral black brutes, are nameless characters setting out on a rampage full of black rage, brought on by years of abuse.[49] Although these characters were male in Bogle's analysis from a womanist perspective, there are also female characters who embody this untamed rage and abandon.

Sineya, like Nikki Wood, is located in another place and time. Her setting is a sand dune, without dwellings or other structures. She is savage in appearance with wild, unkempt hair and a mud-streaked face. Her fingernails are sharp claws, as are her teeth, and she walks hunched over like an animal. For clothing, Sineya is covered only in a provocatively revealing tattered gauze strip like an unraveling mummy; she is the quintessential "primitive." This primitive image is further enhanced by others not using her name; she is called only "First Slayer."

Unlike Kendra, Sineya is aggressive, full of rage, not tragedy, and is clearly situated in an undeveloped sand dune of another time period. Sineya's transgressiveness lies in her actions, brought about by violations against her body and spirit. Like Bogle's brute, what others see as baseless rage is really a response to repeated abuse. While Kendra embodies emotional constraint and Nikki embodies the sexually mis-appropriated body, Sineya is the exact opposite. Her uncontrolled fury targets those who desecrate her body and spirit.[50] In "Restless" (4.22), Sineya attempts to kill Buffy and her friends in their dreams after they invoked her spirit to help them defeat Adam, symbolically slaying them by taking what they've taken from her in the enjoining spell.[51] In "Get It Done" (7.15), Buffy and the Scoobies learn about Sineya's Slayer origins through shadowcasters. Shadow Men found a girl to fight all demons by chaining her to the Earth and allowing Evil to violate her. She becomes, metaphorically, demonized. In this origin myth, Sineya's savagery doesn't stem from sexual repression but from sexual violation. Despite her position as the mother of all Slayers,[52] Sineya is primarily defined by absence of civility and agency. Sineya's primitive brutality reads as a traditional savage character but with a backstory that contextualizes her violence as the rage of a rape survivor.[53]

The primitive portrayal extends beyond Sineya's appearance and brute force to include her lack of language. In order to communicate with Buffy in "Restless" (4.22), Tara speaks for Sineya in Buffy's dreams, telling Buffy that she has no speech or name, only that she lives in the "action of death," that she is destruction, and that she is alone, The First. In other words, like Spike's narration of Nikki's death, Sineya's story is told in a white character's voice. Unlike Nikki, however, Sineya and Buffy do symbolically inhabit the same space (Buffy's dreams). They fight, but ultimately Buffy wins, besting Sineya not through physical strength but through intellect and language.[54] This defeat, however, is troubling in that it suggests intellectual inferiority on the part of Sineya, a black Slayer.

The liminality of the First Slayer differs from that of Kendra and Nikki. Sineya is trapped between being powerless to stop violations yet empowered by them. While Kendra is trapped between her destiny as this generation's Slayer in Sunnydale and her former life as a potential Slayer in a land unknown, Sineya appears to exist in multiple planes of time, reality and consciousness. But mostly, The First Slayer appears to occupy a liminal space where she is powerless to stop violations that, ironically, affirm her power.

Rona, the Sunnydale Sapphire

In contrast to the tragic mulatta and Jezebel characters, whose historical roots lie in literature and film, there is the Sapphire figure, whose roots lie in radio and television, specifically *Amos and Andy*. Melvin Ely, in *The Adventures of Amos 'n' Andy: A Social History of an American Phenomenon*, describes Sapphire as The Kingfish's strong-willed wife, "...the show's most important female character" who was initially not even referred to by name. Interestingly, when not scolding her lazy husband, Sapphire often spoke "cultivated" English in conversations with other characters.[55] More so than the tragic mulatta and Jezebel stereotypes, the Sapphire character relies upon the presence of a corrupt African American male to justify her continual emasculation and denigration of him.[56]

We see elements of the Sapphire stereotype in Rona, a Potential Slayer introduced in Season Seven. Wearing denim overalls and her hair in shoulder-length dreadlocks, her appearance is the least feminine of all the black Slayers; rather she seems somewhat masculine, or at least androgynous. The greatest significance of Rona's representation as Sapphire is that it implicitly constructs Buffy as the corrupt male figure. Rona's most notable distinction from her sister Slayers, however, is that she is the only black Slayer who acknowledges her race. In a scene during which Buffy uses Spike to test the Potentials' skills, Rona fails to defend herself against Spike and is mock-killed. When Buffy asks Rona why she failed, Rona replies: "the black chick always gets it first?" thereby alerting the audience to the fact that Rona is aware of the stereotype ("Showtime" 7.11).[57] This level of racial awareness is relatively rare in *Buffy*. Aside from Trick's comment about Sunnydale not being a "haven for the brothers" ("Faith, Hope and Trick" 3.3),[58] few other characters in *Buffy* overtly acknowledge race, thereby maintaining the erasure of blackness from the text.

Rona's articulation of this stereotype, however, further contributes to her representation as Sapphire. Rona's frank speech, rather than emasculating a male partner as a traditional Sapphire, instead dis-empowers Buffy and hints, again, at the true, shared nature of the Slayer's power. In fact, as a transgressive warrior, gender is almost rendered irrelevant here. What is relevant in Rona's character, however, is her role in destroying Buffy's "family," verbally tearing it asunder by attacking Buffy's identity as *the* Slayer thereby leaving Buffy no choice except to abdicate leadership. In this final act of verbal transgression, Rona achieves the ultimate challenge to Buffy's power.

As one of the only Slayers of color to exist in the same time period and place as Buffy, Rona is a unique case. First, she is in a time period inhabited by Nikki as the First, and Sineya, whose appearances are tied to their burgeoning narrative development. We learn, for the first time, that Nikki Wood was a mother and Slayer, having already been sexualized in Season Five by Spike. We learn that Sineya is an enraged rape victim, adding new meaning to the term "demonized." This is all relevant to Rona because, unlike these Slayers, Rona has no backstory.

Rona, as a Potential, differs from Kendra's fully-activated Slayerhood. Rona is assertive, looking to be guided and protected by Buffy and Giles, not looking to take her rightful place as this generation's Slayer. Like Kendra and other Potential Slayers in her own time, Rona has travelled to Sunnydale, a place with little black presence, as shown by Amanda, the Potential who already lives in Sunnydale, being a young white woman. Rona and the dead black Slayers raise a troubling question about Kendra's lack of impact on Buffy. In the Seventh Season, the First appears as characters whose deaths have emotional, guilt impact on their targets. Joyce appears to Buffy and Dawn, Tara indirectly appears to Willow, Nikki Wood appears to Robin, and the Mayor appears to Faith. Kendra, as the first Potential and ascending Slayer that Buffy meets, who dies on Buffy's watch, apparently died a meaningless death, lacking the power to evoke any guilt or insecurities on Buffy's part. Rona initiates Buffy's ousting from the Summers' home in "Empty Places" (7.19) and celebrates with a sarcastic *Wizard of Oz* reference: "Ding dong, the witch is dead."[59] This challenge to Buffy's identity brings Faith into the role of "the" Slayer, which ironically sets up the visual reversal that takes place in the climactic battle in "Chosen" (7.22).[60] She brings the black/white shared Slayer identity full circle in the apocalyptic final episode; as Buffy lays severely injured by one of the Turok-han, she tosses the Scythe to Faith who uses it to kill several of them before tossing the scythe to Rona, who then kills several more before tossing the Scythe back to a now-standing Buffy, signifying that, finally, they are all equal Slayers working together.

Consequences of Power Denied

Black Slayers inhabit a space between victim and villain, a line where they are punished for assuming the position of the Slayer and villainized for even attempting to take it. They are not fully integrated or connected with other characters and their lack of relationships hearkens back to stereotypical portrayals of servitude and ineptitude. They are liminality personified. *Buffy*, too, is a contested site of social construction. In *Buffy the Vampire Slayer*, as in the real world, assimilation passes for acceptance, tokenism looks like tolerance, and mere presence equals power. Blackness remains a contested construct and there is no easy solution to this struggle as we all continue to search for a way to live together. hooks argues that "integration within a racist system is ineffective because it merely gives the appearance of tolerance or progress where none (or little), in fact, exists."[61]

The greatest irony in the Slayer narrative, of course, is the Season Seven revelation that true Slayer power is shared, that all Potential Slayers can be activated at once rather than the one Slayer per generation lie maintained by the Watchers. What makes this irony a bitter one, however, is the evidence of this great truth provided by Kendra's tragedy. Her activation along with Buffy in Sunnydale clearly demonstrated the possibility of this shared power. And when the truth is revealed by the Guardians, there is no expression of remorse or regret for not realizing or suspecting this truth with Kendra's arrival, but rather outrage at the Council's duplicity. In a narrative that is presented as ideologically transgressive because of the physical and emotional strength of its heroine, the opportunity for another form of transgression was lost, a more socio-political transgression that doesn't just *share* power across different races but acknowledges and celebrates these shared differences.

NOTES

1. Herman Gray, *Watching Race: Television and the Struggle for "Blackness"* (Minneapolis: University of Minnesota Press, 1995), 42.

2. Lisa Anderson, *Mammies No More: The Changing Image of Black Women on Stage and Screen* (Lanham, MD: Rowman & Littlefield, 1997), 49.

3. Nell Irvin Painter, *The History of White People* (New York: W.W. Norton & Company, 2010), 8, 383.

4. Cornell West, *Race Matters* (New York: Vintage Books, 1994), 39.

5. Gray, *Watching Race*, 42.

6. Gail E. Coover, "Television and Social identity: Race Representation as White Accommodation," *Journal of Broadcasting & Electronic Media*, Summer 2001 v. 45 no. 3, p. 427.

7. Darnell M. Hunt, "Making Sense of Blackness on Television," in *Channeling Blackness: Studies on Television and Race in America*, ed. Darnell M. Hunt (Oxford: Oxford University Press, 2005), 4.

8. Roland Barthes, "Myth Today," in *A Barthes Reader*, ed. Sonia Sontag (New York: Hill and Wang, 1982), 101–102.

9. "Prophecy Girl," *Buffy the Vampire Slayer* 1.12, DVD, written by Joss Whedon, directed by Joss Whedon (2001: Twentieth Century Fox 2001).

10. "The Gift," *Buffy the Vampire Slayer* 5.22, DVD, written by Joss Whedon, directed by Joss Whedon (2003: Twentieth Century Fox 2003).

11. "When She Was Bad," *Buffy the Vampire Slayer* 2.1, DVD, written by Joss Whedon, directed by Joss Whedon (2002: Twentieth Century Fox 2002).

12. "Bewitched, Bothered and Bewildered," *Buffy the Vampire Slayer* 2.16, DVD, written by Marti Noxon, directed by James A. Contner (2002: Twentieth Century Fox 2002).

13. "Once More with Feeling," *Buffy the Vampire Slayer* 6.7, DVD, written by Joss Whedon, directed by Joss Whedon (2004: Twentieth Century Fox 2004).

14. "Tabula Rasa," *Buffy the Vampire Slayer* 6.8, DVD, written by Rebecca Rand Kirshner, directed by David Grossman (2004: Twentieth Century Fox 2004).

15. "Two to Go," *Buffy the Vampire Slayer* 6.21, DVD, written by Doug Petrie, directed by Bill Norton (2004: Twentieth Century Fox 2004).

16. "Entropy," *Buffy the Vampire Slayer* 6.18, DVD, written by Drew Z. Greenberg, directed by James A. Contner (2004: Twentieth Century Fox 2004).

17. Several other Scoobies and one-offs have also behaved reprehensibly—even

murderously—yet were allowed to redeem themselves. For example, Spike attempted to rape Buffy and kills while under the control of The First, Angel killed Jenny Calendar, Oz killed Veruca, and Xander attempted to rape Buffy while under a spell.

18. It is likely, however, that the Women in White, or the Guardians, may have kept the scythe secret from the Watchers. This seems a reasonable extension of the extremely clandestine nature of their work throughout the majority of the series.

19. "Get It Done," *Buffy the Vampire Slayer* 7.15, DVD, written by Douglas Petrie, directed by Douglas Petrie (2004: Twentieth Century Fox 2004).

20. Lorraine Ali, Jeff Giles and Marc Peyser, "Newsmakers," *Newsweek.* 14 Jan, 2002. LexisNexis.

21. Frances Early, *The Female Just Warrior Reimagined: From Boudicca to Buffy*, in *Athena's Daughters: Televisions New Women Warriors*, eds. Frances Early and Kathleen Kennedy (Syracuse, NY: Syracuse University Press, 2003), 55–65.

22. Early, *The Female Just Warrior*, 57–60.

23. bell hooks, *Feminism Is for Everybody: Passionate Politics* (Cambridge, MA: South End Press, 2000), 59.

24. "War Zone," *Angel* 1.20, DVD, written by Garry Campbell, directed by David Straiton (1999, 2000: Twentieth Century Fox 1999, 2000).

25. Patricia Hill Collins, *Black Feminist Thought: Knowledge, Consciousness and the Politics of Empowerment* (New York: Routledge, 1991), 68.

26. hooks, *Feminism*, 22.

27. "Inca Mummy Girl," *Buffy the Vampire Slayer* 2.4, DVD, written by Matt Kiene & Joe Reinkemeyer, directed by Ellen S. Pressman (2002: Twentieth Century Fox 2002).

28. "First Date," *Buffy the Vampire Slayer* 7.14, DVD, written by Jane Espenson, directed by David Grossman (2004: Twentieth Century Fox 2004).

29. Donald Bogle, *Toms, Coons, Mulattoes, Mammies and Bucks: An Interpretive History of Blacks in American Films*, 3rd ed. (New York: Continuum Publishing Company, 1996), 9.

30. "Are You Now or Have You Ever Been," *Angel* 2.2, DVD, written by Tim Minear, directed by David Semel (2000, 2001: Twentieth Century Fox 2000, 2001).

31. Anderson, *Mammies No More*, 48.

32. "What's My Line? Part 2," *Buffy the Vampire Slayer* 2.10, DVD, written by Marti Noxon, directed by David Semel (2002: Twentieth Century Fox 2002).

33. "What's My Line? Part 1," *Buffy the Vampire Slayer* 2.9, DVD, written by Howard Gordon and Marti Noxon, directed by David Solomon (2002: Twentieth Century Fox 2002).

34. "Becoming, Part 1," *Buffy the Vampire Slayer*, written and directed by Joss Whedon (1998: Twentieth Century Fox Film Corporation, 2006). "Becoming, Part 2," *Buffy the Vampire Slayer*, written and directed by Joss Whedon (1998: Twentieth Century Fox Film Corporation, 2006).

35. Lynne Edwards, "Slaying in Black an White: Kendra as Tragic Mulatta in *Buffy*," in *Fighting the Forces: What's at Stake in Buffy the Vampire Slayer*, Eds. Rhonda Wilcox and David Lavery (Lanham, MD: Rowman & Littlefield, 2002), 85–97.

36. Elyce Rae Helford, "'My emotions give me power': The Containment of Girls' Anger in *Buffy*," in *Fighting the Forces: What's at Stake in Buffy the Vampire Slayer*, Eds. Rhonda Wilcox and David Lavery (Lanham, MD: Rowman & Littlefield, 2002), 27.

37. Rhonda Wilcox, "'Who died and made her the boss?': Patterns of Mortality in *Buffy*," in *Fighting the Forces: What's at Stake in Buffy the Vampire Slayer*, Eds. Rhonda Wilcox and David Lavery (Lanham, MD: Rowman & Littlefield, 2002), 21.

38. Editors' note: while Drusilla's slaying of Kendra doesn't garner her the same praise/acknowledgement from multiple characters that Spike receives for having killed the Chinese Slayer and Nikki Wood, she does receive this nod of approval from Spike: "Dru bagged a Slayer? She didn't tell me! Good for her!" (Becoming, Part 2, 2.22).

39. "Faith, Hope, & Trick," *Buffy the Vampire Slayer* 3.3, DVD, written by David Greenwalt, directed by James Contner (2002: Twentieth Century Fox 2002).

40. Elyce Rae Helford, "'My emotions give me power': The Containment of Girls' Anger in *Buffy*," in *Fighting the Forces: What's at Stake in Buffy the Vampire Slayer*, Eds. Rhonda Wilcox and David Lavery (Lanham, MD: Rowman & Littlefield, 2002), 30.

41. Karen Eileen Overbey and Lahney Preston-Matto, "Staking in Tongues: Speech Act as Weapon in Buffy," in *Fighting the Forces: What's at Stake in Buffy the Vampire Slayer*, Eds. Rhonda Wilcox and David Lavery (Lanham, MD: Rowman & Littlefield, 2002), 82.

42. K. Sue Jewell, *From Mammy to Miss America and Beyond: Cultural Images and the Shaping of U.S. Social Policy* (New York: Routledge, 1993), 46.

43. Jewell, *From Mammy to Miss America*, 46.

44. "Fool for Love," *Buffy the Vampire Slayer* 5.7, DVD, written by Douglas Petrie, directed by Nick Marck (2003: Twentieth Century Fox 2003).

45. *Ibid.*

46. "Lies My Parents Told Me," *Buffy the Vampire Slayer* 7.17, DVD, written by David Fury and Drew Goddard, directed by David Fury (2004: Twentieth Century Fox 2004).

47. Yvonne Sims, in *Women of Blaxploitation: How the Black Action Film Heroine Changed American Popular Culture* (Jefferson, NC: McFarland, 2006), 8.

48. Ed Guerrero, *Framing Blackness: The African American Image in Film* (Philadelphia, PA: Temple University Press, 1993), 69.

49. Bogle, *Toms, Coons, Mulattoes, Mammies and Bucks,*13.

50. J. P. Williams, "Choosing Your Own Mother: Mother-Daughter Conflicts in *Buffy*," in *Fighting the Forces: What's at Stake in Buffy the Vampire Slayer*, eds. Rhonda Wilcox and David Lavery (Lanham, MD: Rowman & Littlefield, 2002), 63.

51. "Restless," *Buffy the Vampire Slayer* 4.22, DVD, written by Joss Whedon, directed by Joss Whedon (2003: Twentieth Century Fox 2003).

52. Willow refers to Buffy as the daughter of Sineya when she invoked the enjoining spell in "Restless" (4.22).

53. "Get It Done," *Buffy the Vampire Slayer* 7.15, DVD, written by Douglas Petrie, directed by Douglas Petrie (2004: Twentieth Century Fox 2004).

54. J. P. Williams, "Choosing Your Own Mother," 62.

55. Melvin Patrick Ely, *The Adventures of Amos 'n' Andy: A Social History of an American Phenomenon* (New York: The Free Press, 1991), 28.

56. Jewell, *From Mammy to Miss America*, 45.

57. "Showtime," *Buffy the Vampire Slayer* 7.11, DVD, written by David Fury, directed by Michael Grossman (2004: Twentieth Century Fox 2004).

58. "Faith, Hope, & Trick," *Buffy the Vampire Slayer* 3.3, DVD, written by David Greenwalt, directed by James Contner (2002: Twentieth Century Fox 2002).

59. "Empty Places," *Buffy the Vampire Slayer* 7.19, DVD, written by Drew Z. Greenberg, directed by James A. Contner (2004: Twentieth Century Fox 2004).

60. "Chosen," *Buffy the Vampire Slayer* 7.22, DVD, written by Joss Whedon, directed by Joss Whedon (2004: Twentieth Century Fox 2004).

61. hooks, *Feminism*, 10.

"I have no speech, no name"

The Denial of Female Agency
Through Speech in
Buffy the Vampire Slayer

RACHEL MCMURRAY

On the surface, Joss Whedon's series *Buffy the Vampire Slayer* depicts a seemingly positive female role model in the form of the title character and several powerful women as secondary characters. As with most texts on the subject of representation, however, the reality of *Buffy*'s positive embodiment of feminist ideals is problematic. The issue is further complicated when delving into the mythology of the Slayer—one girl in all the world, a chosen one. In Season Seven, it is revealed that the First Slayer was a young African girl imbued with the essence of a pure demon by a group called the Shadow Men ("Get It Done" 7.15).[1] This demonic energy is where the Slayer gets her strength, speed, agility, quickened healing powers, and heightened senses. Yet these impressive powers come at a troubling price, notably the First Slayer's lack of speech. Since the Slayer line is matrilineal, a new Slayer is called only when the old Slayer dies, suggesting a traditional paradigm wherein power is not meant to be shared. All of this information complicates the idea of the Slayer and what her power actually means for a feminist reading of the show. A great deal of discussion has already taken place about whether *Buffy* succeeds at presenting positive feminist ideals, some specifically dealing with third-wave feminism.[2] Third-wave feminism is a term that can only be loosely defined, because there are many different variants within any theoretical and ideological movement. In relation to *Buffy*, I would like to focus on some specific ideas that third-wave feminism began to explore as a response to, and criticism of, second-wave feminism.[3] These ideas include the need to value different cultural, economic, social, and sexual experiences equally in public discourse; a continuing fight against misogynistic violence; the tension between individual and group empowerment; and paradox and contradiction, specifically in the "willingness to use beauty, sex, and power strategically."[4] While the series as a whole (and Season Seven in particular) does attempt to incorporate some of these key concepts of third-wave feminism, the narrative ultimately fails as a third-wave feminist text—and in fact, reinforces second-wave feminism—because the series finale still privileges the white, American, middle-class experience over all others. Further, this privilege is most clearly enacted through speech and the denial of speech to characters of different cultural, economic, and social experiences—especially Slayers and Potential Slayers. By looking at agency through speech throughout the series, the denial of third-wave feminist ideals is revealed.[5]

Many scholars have attempted to answer the question "Is *Buffy* feminist?" with varying degrees of success.[6] The show's writers and producers have said in multiple forums (interviews, DVD commentaries, press junkets, etc) that *Buffy* is a feminist show.[7] Some scholars adamantly deny feminist readings, while others gloss over the complications and limitations of the show, reading *Buffy* as what Charlotte Brunsdon calls an "Ur-feminist text."[8] These strategies tend to reduce the show to an either/or position; either the show is decidedly feminist, or it is not. I have taken my reading from St. Louis and Riggs, who suggest that while the show does strive to embody "liberal, emancipatory, discursive feminism," ultimately "a reading of this effort reveals gaps, inconsistencies, and contradictions within both the show's version of feminist empowerment, and within the larger world's feminisms also."[9]

A few scholars have looked at the depiction of race and Otherness in the show,[10] and some critics have investigated roles played by speech acts,[11] but no one has looked at the ways that these two concepts are intertwined as a means of creating/denying female power. By looking at female speech acts in the show, especially those of women of color and women from cultural or economic backgrounds different from Buffy herself,[12] we can investigate some of the clearest contradictions to *Buffy*'s proclaimed feminist agenda.

Analyzing Buffy Summers's Speech

There are three main types of speech acts: locutionary, illocutionary, and perlocutionary.[13] Locutionary speech acts occur when sounds and phonemes are organized into a recognizable shape, i.e., actual words and sentences (not just babbling). Illocutionary speech acts are locutionary acts that also make some sort of change in the world. One example would be "I thee wed" because "it makes a statement, thus declaring that the world is in such-and-such a state, and it performs an action, pronouncing a couple to be married."[14] Perlocutionary acts are illocutionary acts that also have an effect on a listener or reader's behavior. To follow the wedding example, "You may kiss the bride" is a perlocutionary act because it "is an utterance made by someone in authority to effect a change in the behavior of others."[15] Perlocutionary acts have the most tangible consequences on *Buffy* because of Buffy's position of power over those to whom she speaks. Her perlocutionary acts often take precedence over everyone else's, especially over other women who do not share her experience as a white, middle-class American. While Karen Eileen Overbey and Lahney Preston-Matto have examined the use of speech in *Buffy* in their essay "Staking in Tongues: Speech Act as Weapon in *Buffy*,"[16] no scholars have looked at the connection between speech and the denial of other women's agency. If anything, Overbey and Preston Matto's essay, which delves furthest into the ways that speech acts are used as weapons in the show, emphasizes the white privilege that is taking place, because it states, without critical attention to the racial dynamics at work, "Buffy *is* the speech act. She is the utterance that communicates meaning.... Other Slayers have never confronted such a powerful foe or managed such harmonic power; they are solitary and silent."[17] I argue that the reason these other Slayers are solitary and silent is because Buffy herself often is the one who denies them speech.

Speech and its associated agency have long been understood as important to both postcolonial and feminist discourses.[18] In her watershed article, "Can the Subaltern Speak?" Gayatri Chakravorty Spivak describes the subaltern as a person denied subjecthood because of his or her social status, and makes this connection to feminist theory: "If, in the context of colonial production, the subaltern has no history and cannot speak, the subaltern as female is even more deeply in shadow."[19] Though Spivak's use of the term subaltern is specifically referring to those who are placed outside the hegemonic discourse on the South Asian subcontinent, I am using the more general meaning of marginalized peoples who are deprived of agency specifically because of their social status or class. Marta Caminero-Santangelo quotes noted French feminist scholar Christine Makward when describing the trend in feminist theory of embracing madness and non-reason in women's tests, yielding the result that "women are resigning themselves to silence and to nonspeech. The speech of the other will then swallow them up, will speak for them, and instead of them."[20] Buffy becomes the force that speaks *for* and *instead* of other women throughout the series, and especially when she encounters her two fellow Slayers, Kendra and Faith.

Buffy and Other(ed) Slayers

The few other modern-day Slayers we see besides Buffy are all women of color or of different socioeconomic classes than her. While this seems to indicate diversity of experience and an equal opportunity chance to become a Slayer, these women do not subscribe to the normative pattern established by Buffy, and thus are punished with either death or incarceration. Throughout the course of the series, we see four other Slayers besides Buffy: Kendra, who is killed; Faith, who turns herself in to serve prison time for murder; Nikki Wood in the 1970s whom Spike kills; and an unnamed (!) Chinese Slayer during the Boxer Rebellion who also falls victim to Spike.[21]

Lynne Edwards reads Kendra, the first Slayer introduced besides Buffy, as a tragic mulatta who is killed as a result of her attempts to assimilate into Buffy's circle of friends.[22] Kendra, played by the African American woman Bianca Lawson, was called to be the Slayer after Buffy (temporarily) died ("Prophecy Girl" 1.12).[23] Kendra speaks with a heavy yet unidentified accent that vaguely sounds like Jamaican patois. Her legitimacy is called into question immediately upon her introduction to Buffy and the rest of the group in the two-part episode "What's My Line."[24] When Buffy and Kendra first meet, Buffy refers to herself as "the *real* Slayer" (2.9; emphasis mine).[25] Later, Buffy and Willow discuss Kendra's training as a Slayer and the fact that Kendra and Giles have a natural rapport. Willow reassures Buffy that she will always be Giles's favorite because "you're *his* Slayer. The *real* Slayer" (2.10; emphasis mine).[26] These perlocutionary acts are potent because they isolate Buffy and privilege her individual power over group empowerment. As the episodes unfold, Kendra attempts to be a part of Buffy's social group and to include herself in the category of Slayer, but Buffy continually shuts her down.

Buffy's interactions with Kendra are condescending and sarcastic throughout this two-part episode. At various times she speaks to Kendra like a dog ("Down girl!"), mocks Kendra's heavy Caribbean accent ("I tink we might make him"), and uses racist language in order to explain the distinct Anglo teen SoCal vocabulary she uses.[27] When Kendra doesn't understand the phrase "you promise not to go all wiggy until we can go to my Watcher and figure this out," Buffy defines "wiggy" by saying, "You know. No kick-o, no fight-o?"[28] It is only when Kendra begins to perform her slaying duties more like Buffy that she begins to be accepted. In an attempt to get Kendra to show more emotion—a strategy that Buffy uses when she fights, and thus identifies as the 'proper' way for a *real* Slayer to behave—Buffy deliberately provokes Kendra, telling her that she would have eventually defeated her because "power alone isn't enough. A good fighter needs to know how to improvise, to go with the flow."[29] This comment incites Kendra's anger, which causes Buffy to praise her assimilation into normative Slayer behavior. This is a powerful perlocutionary act because of Buffy's successful attempt to make Kendra angry. Once again, Buffy denies Kendra the status of a true Slayer, this time by implying she is not a full-fledged Slayer. Though Buffy's perlocutionary acts have power over Kendra's behavior, Kendra's do not have the same effect on Buffy. When Buffy threatens a snitch for information, Kendra demands, "Just hit him, Buffy!" which causes Buffy to address the snitch—not Kendra—and say, "She likes to hit."[30] Buffy's actions and emotions are not affected by Kendra's utterance, and in fact, Buffy does not even reply to Kendra after this perlocutionary act. All of these speech-related slights accrete into an overarching dynamic that validates Buffy's privilege at the expense of Kendra.

Despite the constructs of white privilege working against her, Kendra continues to attempt to assimilate. Though she has her reservations about a Slayer saving a vampire's life, she and Buffy fight side-by-side in the final battle of "What's My Line Part 2" (2.10) to save Angel. Kendra willingly compromises to meet Buffy's agenda, and even borrows one of Buffy's shirts for her journey back home, showing (in accordance with the tragic mulatta myth) that, "Kendra becomes dissatisfied with her life when introduced to Buffy's world; however, Kendra is not readily accepted" by Buffy and the Scooby Gang until *after* Kendra changes her slaying style, her perspective on vampires, and her clothes.[31] It is at this point that Buffy finally proffers an olive branch, saying thank you for Kendra's help in saving Angel and acknowledging that she, Buffy, is not the only Slayer anymore.

Kendra's final appearance on the show occurs in the first part of the two-part Season Two finale ("Becoming Part 1" 2.21), in which she comes back to Sunnydale a seemingly assimilated part of the group. There are cues in Buffy's speech that indicate that Kendra is still an outsider, however. When Kendra first appears, she sneaks up on Buffy and when Buffy is startled, she says "You know, polite people call before they jump out of the bushes and attack you,"[32] a sentiment that highlights the differences between her own expectations of "politeness" and that of other females, foreshadowing her exchange with the First Slayer in "Restless."[33] After Buffy regains her bearings, she asks "Which begs the question, and don't think I'm not glad to see you, but, why are you here?"[34] When Kendra starts to answer, Buffy interrupts her, imitating her accent: "Oh, wait. No, let me guess. Your Watcher informed you dat a very dark power is about to rise in Sunnydale."[35] Though the meaning of her speech seems to indicate that she is glad to see Kendra and that Kendra has been fully accepted, Buffy still interrupts her and does not allow her to speak for herself, going so far as to take the words right out of her mouth by imitating Kendra's accent. However, Kendra shows more emotion and warmth in this episode, an attempt at assimilation which Buffy immediately takes advantage of when she convinces Kendra to help her kill Angelus. As Lynne Edwards astutely points out, Kendra's assimilation is ultimately the cause of her death; the newly accepted Kendra participates in Buffy's flawed plan to challenge Angelus, and in keeping with her status as a tragic mulatta, assimilation equals death for blacks.[36] Though Kendra is a more accepted part of the group during this second visit to Sunnydale, her assimilation is not enough to earn the right to speak, but it is enough to get her killed. Because Kendra is the first non-white recurring character on the show, and because she is killed after only two appearances, it is clear that "*Buffy* (often embraced by the popular press for providing liberating images of girls and women) nevertheless conveys debilitating images of and ideas about people of color."[37]

The show also depicts differences of class in a problematic light. Faith Lehane, the Slayer called after Kendra, is a white American like Buffy. She has dark hair, pale white skin, and a penchant for dark, tight clothing. She comes from the wrong side of the tracks in Boston and is the opposite of Buffy, and the creators describe her story arc as a view of what the "road not taken" would look like for the Slayer.[38] She has no family or friends, and is often considered the "working class Slayer."[39] She and Buffy clash from the start, although the rest of Buffy's group is much quicker to "go out on a limb and say there's a new Slayer in town" (3.3) than they or Buffy were upon meeting Kendra, seemingly because she is white and she is American—much closer to the representation of a Slayer than they're used to.[40] Faith becomes an antagonist for Buffy, and even though Faith is a formidable foe, her own speech still positions Buffy as the center of the narrative universe. Faith describes her position as marginalized Other, even when given leadership in the penultimate episode of Season Seven: "My whole life I've been a loner…. No ties, no buddies, no relationships…. Me, by myself, all the time. I'm looking at you, everything you have and, I don't know? Jealous. Then there I am, everybody's looking to me, trusting me to lead them and I've never felt so alone in my entire life."[41] The show's attempts to widen the gap between Buffy and Faith here are undercut when, describing the loneliness of being a Slayer, Faith quips, "thank God we're hot chicks with superpowers" and Buffy replies, "takes the edge off."[42] Though she does occupy a marginalized position, Faith is still a white American female like Buffy, and this allows her some access to the privileged space within the show and the use of the same humor and wit Buffy uses in her perlocutionary acts. This is why a straightforward feminist reading of the characters is incredibly complicated. The characters' speech and actions are paradoxical, especially when it comes to using traditional notions of beauty, sex and power. Such complexity of representation is typical of third-wave feminism, but the relationship between Buffy and Faith undermines this complexity because a hierarchy in status still exists between them, with Buffy on top, revealing a simplistic binary at the core.

Faith represents the only real threat to Buffy's legitimacy as a Slayer, but Faith's jealousy of Buffy's top ranking leads her to abandon the Slayer role. Faith even recognizes Buffy's perlocutionary power and attempts to undermine it in "Enemies" (3.17).[43] When Buffy cries, "Faith, listen to me!" Faith asks, "Why? So you can impart some special Buffy wisdom … say it, you think you're better than me!"[44] Faith is calling Buffy out on her privilege, and Buffy affirms her superiority, stating, "I am. Always have been."[45] When Faith backhands her in an attempt to shut her up, Buffy smirks, "You had to tie me up to beat me. There's a word for people like you, Faith. Loser."[46] Up until this point, Faith's rage has been controlled and contained, but Buffy's words do have power over her, and Faith has to resort to physical, rather than verbal, violence to do any harm to Buffy. Faith has an advantage though that Kendra doesn't because Faith does spar verbally with her enemies, including Buffy. However, Faith's displays of power (as this exchange demonstrates) remain rooted in the physical, while Buffy clings to her position at the top of the narrative's hierarchy of power by exerting her dominance over others both physically *and* verbally.

Faith does eventually become Buffy's ally, like Kendra, but as with Kendra, Buffy is the catalyst for the transformative effect on Faith. Kendra assimilates. She adopts Buffy's slaying style, her clothes, and her social norms. Upon her return to Sunnydale, Buffy and her group accept Kendra much more openly. In "This Year's Girl" and "Who Are You?" (4.15 and 4.16), through the use of a spell, Faith and Buffy end up wearing each other's bodies.[47] Faith wears Buffy's skin and lives life as Buffy, surrounded by family and friends. Even though Faith speaks, it is Buffy's voice, Buffy's body. Faith (in Buffy's body) mouths the phrase "Because it's wrong" as an outright mockery of Buffy's position as the "good Slayer"—first it's sanctimonious, then teasing and seductive.[48] Finally, however, when Faith-as-Buffy actually attempts to prevent some vampires from killing innocents, we see that being treated like Buffy has the desired rehabilitative effect on Faith and she again utters the phrase "Because it's wrong," this time genuinely.[49] The act begins as locutionary, becomes illocutionary, and then finally becomes perlocutionary. Living as Buffy allows Faith to experience the luxuries of Buffy's class that Faith has not had access to: stable, healthy relationships with family and friends; easy access to a college education and people who value higher education; a loving and supportive boyfriend who respects her and does not objectify her. These benefits of Buffy's class combine with the privilege the show grants Faith as a white American to provide Faith-as-Buffy the perlocutionary power that Buffy always wields so effortlessly.

Once the bodies are switched back, Faith is radically changed; she begins the path to atonement for her crimes and eventually turns herself in for murder. If "Buffy *is* the speech act," as Overbey and Preston-Matto point out, her body and its racial, socioeconomic, cultural, and gendered signifiers are part of that speech act, and those signifiers are shown to be preferable to the signifiers that Kendra and Faith exhibit.[50] As a result of her Buffy-aided transformation, Faith chooses to spend the next three years in prison until the

First Evil becomes active, and then she heads back to Sunnydale to fight the good fight. Faith's character proves that "nurture" is much more important than "nature" when it comes to Slayers. Though they come from the same raw materials, Buffy and Faith are wildly different, and the stereotypical normative experience of Buffy is clearly the ideal.

The other two Slayers that we see during the series do not fare any better than Kendra and Faith. They are also women of color. In the Season Five episode "Fool for Love" (5.7), we see Nikki Wood, an African American Slayer in 1977, and the Chinese Slayer during the Boxer Rebellion of 1900.[51] Both are killed by Spike, and he recounts these experiences to Buffy. These fights are both intriguing because neither Slayer speaks at any point during the fight. Once Spike has fought, taken a hold of, and bitten the Chinese Slayer, she speaks to him in Chinese, saying, "Tell my mother I'm sorry...." Spike replies, "I'm sorry, love. I don't speak Chinese" and throws her lifeless body to the ground.[52] Later in the same episode, Spike fights Nikki Wood, and she never says a word. As he fights Nikki in flashback, he addresses Buffy in the present, and when his speech is done Buffy says coldly "Get out of my sight. Now."[53] Buffy has the power here, in shutting off Spike's speech, refusing his kiss, and walking away. Buffy is the Slayer still standing; she and Spike have fought countless times, and she has never lost, in no small part because of her ability to defend and disarm through speech. Neither the Chinese Slayer nor Nikki has that luxury. Buffy is a fierce and powerful warrior, just as these other Slayers are, but Buffy's speech acts are the mechanisms that reveal the show's problematic message about Buffy's superiority over other Slayers as a white, middle-class American Slayer.

There is one more Slayer in the series who is denied the power of speech. The First Slayer appears in the series as a silent, feral, half-wild African woman, focused only on hunting and killing. Caminero-Santangelo connects madness and silence to ideas about race and ethnicity in American literature, asserting, "the African American or Latina madwoman ... suggest[s] the dangers of complicity with an oppressive dominant culture."[54] This oppression is suggested in the First Slayer's naming (or lack thereof). The First Slayer is referred to as Sineya once during the three episodes in which she appears, but the circumstances are obscure. During a spell, Willow asks that "we may inhabit the vessel, the hand, daughter of Sineya, first of the ones," which has caused speculation that Sineya may be the name of the First Slayer.[55] However, in scripts and promotional materials she is called the Primitive.[56] She first appears in "Restless" (4.22) in response to Buffy, Giles, Xander and Willow joining their essences together to form an *uber*-Buffy in order to defeat Adam. The Primitive hunts each member of the group in their dreams and tries to kill them for calling on the source of her power. She is seen in flashes and glimpses during the first three acts, and is only fully seen in the fourth act, which is Buffy's dream. The Primitive has dark skin, unkempt dreadlocks, and white paint on her face, with black paint around her eyes and mouth. Before the group realizes what is trying to kill them, in Giles's dream Willow describes her as "like some primal, some animal force" and Giles sings that "The spell we cast with Buffy must have released some primal evil … a warrior beast."[57] Once Giles realizes it is the First Slayer, he tries to reason with her when she attacks him, saying "I can defeat you with my intellect. I can cripple you with my thoughts."[58] Thus, before she is even fully seen, the group has characterized the Primitive as just that—primal, animalistic, evil, and a beast who is easily defeated by higher cognitive processes. Because speech is one of these higher cognitive processes that the Primitive seemingly does not have access to, Giles's illocutionary act is intended to disarm and defeat her, which foreshadows Buffy's later defeat of the Primitive through perlocutionary acts.

Buffy's confrontation with the First Slayer in her dream is the most illuminating encounter with this woman. Tara, who is another white, middle-class, American female, appears in Buffy's dream as a translator for the First Slayer, saying "Someone has to speak for her."[59] Buffy charges, "Let her speak for herself. That's what's done in polite circles," highlighting the class differences between herself and the Primitive.[60] Buffy has been raised in those aforementioned polite circles and demands that those she fights follow these same rules. Later, when Buffy's questions to the First Slayer are ambiguously answered through Tara, Buffy gets frustrated and commands "Make her speak."[61] The First Slayer replies through Tara, "I have no speech. No name. I live in the action of death, the blood cry, the penetrating wound."[62] Buffy reveals her own position of privilege when she assumes that a fellow privileged female, Tara, has the power to make the First Slayer speak through a perlocutionary act.

When the Primitive actually does speak for herself, once, she reiterates the differences between her experience and Buffy's, saying "No friends! Just the kill. We … are … alone."[63] This shows that the Primitive is *able* to speak, but her speech does not seem to matter. It is only after the Primitive speaks that Buffy is able to defeat her. They have a physical fight in the dream that ends with Buffy re-materializing back in her living room and the First Slayer jumping out and stabbing Buffy repeatedly, to no effect. Buffy's ultimate conquest of the First Slayer occurs when Buffy says, "It's over, okay? I'm going to ignore you, and you're going to go away. You're really gonna have to get over the whole primal power thing. You're *not* the source of me" and then actually wakes up.[64] Though the First Slayer does eventually speak for herself, Buffy's denial of that speech—both the locutionary act itself and the illocutionary meaning of the words—is what allows her to triumph.

The last appearance of the Primitive occurs in "Get It Done" (7.15). Buffy is transported through a portal to Africa to meet the Shadow Men, who explain that they are the ones who created the First Slayer. Though they are speaking an unidentified African language that sounds like Swahili, Buffy can understand them perfectly and they can understand her. Given the difficulties that other Slayers and Potentials (for example, Kendra, the Chinese Slayer in 1900, and Chao Ahn the Potential) have with language barriers, the ease with which Buffy understands the Shadow Men, and they her, highlights how the show privileges Buffy above all others. The Shadow Men tell her, "We are at the beginning. The source of your strength. The well of the Slayer's power. This is why we have brought you here."[65] Confused, Buffy responds, "I thought I brought me here. Listen, you guys. I'm already the Slayer, bursting with power. Really don't need any more."[66] The Shadow Men are put off, claiming, "The First Slayer did not talk so much."[67] Buffy's disrespect and petulance towards the Shadow Men displays a sense of entitlement that underscores how often Buffy unequivocally gets her way. This exchange serves to reinforce Buffy's previous treatment of the First Slayer, because the Shadow Men also deny and diminish the Primitive's ability to speak. As her origin story in "Get It Done" shows, the First Slayer's lack of speech seems to very clearly "suggest the dangers of complicity with an oppressive dominant culture."[68] By pointing out the marked difference between Buffy's speech and the First Slayer's, the Shadow Men are, in turn, emphasizing Buffy's agency through language.

Buffy is then knocked out, chained to the ground, and commanded to accept the Shadow Men's offer of power by allowing the spirit of a demon to "become one with" her and make her "less human," just as the First Slayer did so long ago.[69] Buffy is resistant and screams as the demon spirit attempts to enter her body, and her screams render it impossible for the spirit to enter her. In this case, it is her speech—her screams of protest, a perlocutionary act—that save her from being violated. Buffy then rips her chains out of the ground, fights the Shadow Men, and breaks the magical staff they were holding, which makes the demon disappear.[70] As the Shadow Men point out, this rebellion—the option to say "no" to their offer of power—is more than the First Slayer ever enjoyed. The Primitive is the subaltern; she is not allowed to speak or enact choice or free will, and this enforced silence results in the Primitive being symbolically raped and forced to incorporate the demonic power the Shadow Men offered into herself. By saying no to the Shadow Men, Buffy denies the legacy of misogynistic violence that they represent, which is a decidedly feminist action. However, Buffy also denies and rejects the experience of the First Slayer when she rejects the Shadow Men's offer. The privilege carried by Buffy's social status endows her with an agency simply unavailable to the Primitive, and so while she succeeds in rebelling against the Shadow Men where the Primitive could not, Buffy's success also invalidates the experience of the First Slayer. Buffy has the luxury of saying no to darkness, and her privileged agency allows her to find a successful way to engage her enemies.

Buffy and the Potentials

Buffy's race, class, and experience are still privileged in the final season of the show, even as more women join the recurring cast of characters. Potentials from all over the world begin arriving at Buffy's door in Season Seven, to help fight the First Evil, or "the First," literally the source for all evil in the world. Agents of the First are killing all of the Potential Slayers around the world in order to wipe out the Slayer line. Four attacks take place in other countries before any violence is done on American soil. No American Potentials are killed until *after* these attacks on foreign soil have taken place, and neither of the white American Slayers are threatened by the First until later in the season. In "Bring on the Night" (7.10), Giles tells Buffy of the First's plan, "to erase all the slayers in training and their Watchers along with their methods" and Buffy finishes, "And then Faith, and then me."[71] It's not "and then Faith and me"—there is a clear hierarchy at play. The show is placing white Americans over all others and placing Buffy at the very top, because she is of a higher class than Faith. As before, this reinforces Buffy as the center of the narrative universe and reaffirms her position as the only *real* Slayer.

As the Potentials train and band together to form an army against the First, more and more girls become involved in planning and strategizing, adding more and more voices to the mix of perspectives and ideas about how to defeat the evil they're up against. Though Season Seven emphasizes repeatedly that the Potentials are coming to Sunnydale from all over the world, the only specific places of origin mentioned for the Potentials who come to train with Buffy are the USA, the UK, and China. Of the approximately thirty Potentials, five are women of color: Kennedy, the wealthy, stubborn Latina girl who eventually becomes Willow's girlfriend[72]; Chao Ahn, who is from Shanghai and speaks no English; Rona, who is African American and very outspoken and resistant to Buffy's leadership; Chloe, a reluctant and scared Latina Potential who kills herself after being tormented by the First; and Caridad, who is Dominican and speaks only twice. Rona, Chloe, and Caridad are all marginalized in their own ways through speech. Rona consistently complains about Buffy's leadership to the Potentials and, eventually, to Buffy's face in "Empty Places"(7.19).[73] However, when Buffy is deposed as leader and Rona flexes her newfound power through speech by saying "ding dong the witch is dead," Dawn (neither a Slayer, nor a Potential, but a white, middle-class American) says "shut your mouth," and Rona does.[74] Additionally, all of Rona's speech acts challenging Buffy's power are essentially discredited when the group suffers heavy casualties without Buffy as leader. Chloe is provoked into permanent silence by the First when she commits suicide, and Caridad barely speaks at all. While all these women of color are being presented to the audience as representatives of diversity, their voices are shut down, ignored, unheard, or mute.

Kennedy and Chao Ahn are the most representative examples of the ways in which Potentials' speech acts are portrayed in the show. Kennedy's representation is complicated because of her positions of privilege/marginalization, and Chao Ahn's representation is arguably the most damaging to a third-wave feminist reading of the show because of her continued attempts to communicate with the others and their inability (or unwillingness) to understand what she says. On the surface the show's attempt to depict a globalization of Slayer power is somewhat successful, but in the words of Pender, "its use of formulaic markers of cultural difference to distinguish the international Slayers"[75] is problematic at best. Buffy chafes against these ambiguous racial politics because "living crammed into a house full, or a world full, of very different people can be an uncomfortable business, and Buffy shows us how not to do it ... we see her failing to really get to know the Potentials— even to learn their names."[76] As more and more Potentials arrive in Sunnydale, Buffy begins to make more and more speeches, a fact that is pointed out, and occasionally poked fun at in multiple episodes in Season Seven like "Storyteller" (7.16) and "Touched" (7.20).[77] Herein lies the problem with the show's attempts at a positive message of communal female empowerment: the series, up until this point, has positioned Buffy at the center of a group that supports her and often acts as a valuable resource, but in spite of having a much larger group of invested and capable fighters around her, Buffy's leadership becomes authoritarian and autocratic over the course of Season Seven, continually re-establishing and reinforcing a hierarchy in which Buffy emerges on top.

Kennedy provides a perfect example of how this complicated hierarchy functions. The actress who plays Kennedy, Iyari Limon, is clearly Latina, yet Kennedy is never identified as such. However, Kennedy is one of the only women on the show who interrupts, talks over, or stymies Buffy, and later, Faith, with her speech. In "Bring on the Night" (7.10) Kennedy reveals that she comes from a wealthy family when she speaks of her house with multiple wings and her summer home in the Hamptons.[78] Kennedy has a higher status than other Potentials because of her American identity, but in particular because of her wealth, giving her the privilege to be able to counter Buffy in her speech. Kennedy is also a lesbian involved in a romantic relationship with Willow. This is one of the many ways the series presents a complicated third-wave feminist reading; though Kennedy's agency through speech seems to be a positive marker for the representation of non-heterosexual females, her status as a Potential and as a secret Latina still put her in a lower hierarchical position than Buffy, the *real* Slayer. Kennedy is one of the most vocal opponents of Buffy's in "Empty Places" (7.19), which leads to Buffy's excommunication as leader. Kennedy then challenges Faith's new position as leader in "Touched" (7.20). When she suggests a plan, Faith cuts her off with "Let's not get ahead of ourselves…. So we know we've got a lot of enemies. We'll start there."[79] Kennedy interrupts again, saying, "Faith, I'm sorry—" and Faith presses, "I got this, okay?"[80] None of the other Potentials attempt to disarm Faith's leadership like Kennedy, and her socioeconomic standing seems to be the source of Kennedy's sense of entitlement to disrupt the hierarchy—yet, she is still ultimately silenced here. Kennedy is one of the few Potentials to consistently stand up to the Slayers, and her privileged position of wealth and class indicate that the hierarchical structure is still in play when it comes to who is challenged in speech and who isn't. Kennedy's intersection of privileged identities (wealthy, American) and marginalized identities (Latina, lesbian, Potential) demonstrates again that Season Seven's attempts at a third-wave feminist representation of female power are still being undermined by traditional markers of privilege.

Chao Ahn's character is also complicated, because her position as a Potential is particularly ambiguous in regard to the positive depiction of cultural diversity and shared global power espoused in Season Seven. Many viewers saw Chao Ahn, who is from Shanghai and speaks no English, as being played just for laughs, a characterization that is demeaning, given her inability to be understood by those around her—she is, essentially, muted.[81] Rhonda Wilcox, however, asserts that Chao Ahn is not being played for laughs, but that the language barrier between her and Giles actually calls into question *his* attitudes and choices, not hers, and that "the cultural presumption of some globalizers, well-intentioned though they may be, is gently mocked."[82] In "First Date" (7.13), Giles takes Chao Ahn to the mall , and when the group asks how he and Chao Ahn got along, he says, "As I suspected, ice cream is a universal language."[83] Chao Ahn (in subtitles) says, "Like many from Asia, I am lactose intolerant. I'm very uncomfortable."[84] Giles then (mis)translates for her, saying, "She's grateful to be in a land of plenty."[85] Chao Ahn's presence as one of the few Potentials of color both supports and complicates the ways in which the show tries to create a sense of global community and female power. If the goal is third-wave feminist consciousness-raising, as advocated for by Rory Dicker and Alison Piepmeier, the "gentle mocking" approach to interpreting Giles's cultural presumption doesn't go far enough in taking that feminist perspective out into the world as a motivation for activism, since such thinking obscures how Giles' actions deny Chao Ahn's agency through speech.[86] This is particularly troubling given Giles's position as an authority figure whose actions and wisdom Buffy and her friends so often look to for guidance. In portraying Giles's encounters with Chao Ahn, while none of the other Potentials or Scoobies have much interaction with her, the show portrays a complicit acceptance of his impressions as law when it comes to best understanding foreign visitors, if they bother to understand them at all.

As the army of Potentials gets closer to war with the First, Buffy's increasing use of speeches while resisting outside suggestion prompts the Potentials to begin to mount against her. In "Get It Done" (7.15), Buffy lashes out in frustration at the group, in particular Xander, who reminds her that she is their leader, to which she responds, snapping "Well from now on, I'm your leader as in 'do what I say.'"[87] This exchange is a turning point in the season, because of the very clear perlocutionary act being performed by Buffy here. Not only is she telling the group to do what she says, but also, her leadership methods are clearly being enacted here through her speech. Dubbed the "'Everyone Sucks But Me' speech" by Anya, this scene causes characters to complain about Buffy's position as leader, indicating that Season Seven's goal of showcasing a more diverse collection of female experiences and perspectives is finally being enacted.[88]

"Empty Places" (7.19) offers the most explicit example of multiple perspectives actually being put into action, as the group stages a coup and kicks Buffy out of her house. This scene is pivotal because of its clear reversal of Buffy's usual demonstration of power through speech. When Buffy claims, "you need someone to lead you," Anya challenges her, saying, "and it's automatically you. You really do think you're better than we are."[89] When Buffy attempts to deny this, Anya interrupts her *twice*, claiming that Buffy "came into the world with certain advantages…. They were just handed to you. So that doesn't make you better than us. It makes you luckier than us."[90] For the first time, Buffy is rattled by another woman's ability to use speech to gain power over her, and demands that the group "fall in line" because she is "still in charge here," but Rona asks her why and points out that Faith is also a Slayer.[91] Buffy continues to repeat the rhetoric that she used against Kendra, that she is the *real* Slayer, and thus her perspective is the clear and proper path to follow. Her willingness to "talk strategy" is still singularly focused, because "this is the plan."[92] As usual, others may "talk strategy" but Buffy will not listen. Notice also that Anya, who is neither a Slayer nor a Potential, (but another white, middle-class American) is able to interrupt Buffy twice and turn the tide against her. Now that the Slayer power hierarchy has finally been challenged, Rona is able to use speech to gain her own power and call into question Buffy's claim to legitimacy, thus undermining Buffy's perlocutionary act ("you have to fall in line!") and turning it into an illocutionary act.[93] As a result of this challenge and the transformation of Buffy's speech acts, "Empty Places" (7.19) is the clearest example of globalization and privileging of outside, non-white, non–American, non-middle class perspectives this season, because the group finally challenges Buffy's actions, rather than letting her continue her autocratic regime.

Unfortunately, all of this work is undone in "Chosen" (7.22), the Season Seven, and series, finale. Buffy returns to the fold after Faith makes a bad call as leader, costing several Potentials their lives in "End of Days" (7.21).[94] She also returns with a new weapon, a scythe built by female Guardians who've kept watch over the Slayer line for centuries.[95] The leader of the Guardians gives Buffy the scythe, once more re-establishing her as the center of the narrative. And when Buffy uses the scythe to rescue Faith and the Potentials from a deadly trap, her white, middle class American privilege is rewarded once again. In "Chosen" (7.22), as Buffy and the rest of the group face the final battle against the First, Willow is able to channel the power of the scythe and ensure that every Potential Slayer all over the world becomes an *actual* Slayer immediately.[96] The army of Potentials becomes an army of Slayers to fight the minions of the First. As Arwen Spicer points out in her excellent resistant reading of "Chosen," Buffy's plan to fight the First Evil is characterized as "brilliant" when it is actually "tactically absurd."[97] Because Buffy regains her status at the top of the Slayer hierarchy when she is given the scythe, her plan is unquestioned; thus the group's decision to follow her "is only made possible by the final episode's rejection of an open exchange of perspectives. Ultimately, Season Seven sabotages its own claims to a feminist deconstruction of patriarchal authority by refusing the feminist multivocality it supposedly supports."[98]

As in "Empty Places" (7.19), Buffy's plan in "Chosen" (7.22) is not up for discussion. When she first introduces it, the Potentials are not in the room; later, she presents the plan to the Potentials as a choice, asking if they want the power that she and Faith have. We hear this speech in voice-over as Buffy's plan goes into action onscreen: "From now on, every girl in the world who *might* be a Slayer, *will* be a Slayer.… Make your choice. Are you ready to be strong?"[99] This speech is disturbing both because of its implications of singular, dictatorial leadership again—this time without being questioned by the Potentials—and also because of its rhetorical similarities to the proposal the Shadow Men gave to Buffy. Asking these girls to accept a mystical force into themselves in order to be powerful enough to defeat the First is precisely what Buffy fought against in "Get It Done" (7.15). Buffy unilaterally decides that the only way to defeat the First is to accept the Shadow Men's model of power by taking on the role of oppressor and forcing girls to accept this power into their bodies. In spite of the choice she offers to the Potentials, if one of the girls decided to say no and walk away from the fight, she would still have this power forced into her body when the spell was cast. We see this in the montage of girls onscreen during Buffy's speech—girls who were offered no choice about whether they wanted this power.[100] This "make your choice" speech is arguably the most powerful perlocutionary act that Buffy utters in the series, because the choice these Potentials all over the world make can only be "yes"—it can only be the choice Buffy has made. Her plan is proposed, accepted, and enacted simultaneously onscreen, creating a globally connected female community forged in the power of Slayerdom. Though the end of "Chosen" seems positive, the fundamental feminist paradox is a lack of dialogic decision-making, which essentially silences the very people who are supposed to be communally empowered. Buffy's plan, though tactically absurd, is the one that is enacted, and her authority is never questioned or attacked upon her return as the head of the mission to kill the First because she was handed the scythe and what it represents (much like her status as the *real* Slayer) because of her position of privilege.

It's not surprising that a show called *Buffy the Vampire Slayer* would take great pains to ensure that its title character was strong, well-spoken, and powerful in order to avoid cartoonish or hollow characterization. What is surprising is the way in which this power is denied to other females along lines of race and class, given the show's feminist agenda. In some ways, the complications that I have pointed out here in depictions of race, class, and power are an accurate representation of the struggles that feminists the world over struggle with today. As Pender points out, "the fact that [*Buffy's*] success in critiquing its own cultural privilege is equivocal should be read less as a straightforward sign of failure than as a reflection of the redoubtable contradictions that characterize third wave feminism itself."[101] However, the *Buffy* story lives on. The Season Eight and Season Nine series of comic books and motion comics have been released. The global power sharing that is created in "Chosen" (7.22) now has an outlet to be explored further, and unless other females—specifically other Slayers—are allowed to create the powerful perlocutionary acts that Buffy uses so frequently, Whedon and his creative team, will continue to deny "the show's intended message of a disseminated, multivocal, and critical female empowerment."[102] As Buffy is introduced to a new generation of young females (and males), I sincerely hope that the writers will be able to embrace more of the third-wave feminist issues that Season Seven engages in by distributing the power of speech acts to other females and going beyond the white, middle-class, American privilege that Buffy herself has enforced for so long.

NOTES

1. "Get It Done," *Buffy the Vampire Slayer* 7.15, DVD, written and directed by Douglas Petrie (2003: Twentieth Century Fox, 2004).

2. See Rhonda Wilcox, "Show Me Your World: Exiting the Text and the Globalization of *Buffy*," in *Why Buffy Matters: The Art of Buffy the Vampire Slayer* (London: I.B. Tauris, 2005), 90–107; Renee St. Louis and Miriam Riggs, "'And yet': The Limits

of *Buffy* Feminism," *Slayage: The Journal of the Whedon Studies Association* 8.1 (2010), http://slayageonline.com/Numbers/slayage29.htm; and Patricia Pender, "'Kicking ass is comfort food': *Buffy* as Third Wave Feminist Icon," in *Third Wave Feminism: A Critical Exploration,* eds. Stacy Gillis, Gillian Howie, and Rebecca Munford (New York: Palgrave-McMillan, 2004), 164–74.

3. Some of these ideas were borrowed from Pender, "'Kicking ass is comfort food,'" 164–74.

4. Rory Cooke Dicker and Alison Piepmeier, "Introduction," in *Catching a Wave: Reclaiming Feminism for the 21st Century* (Boston: Northeastern University Press, 2003), 3–28.

5. Second-wave feminism primarily focuses on gender equality, and is sometimes referred to as the Women's Liberation Movement. Hallmarks of second-wave feminism include support for the Equal Rights Amendment, passage of the Equal Pay Act of 1963, and *Roe vs. Wade.* While all of these were landmarks in the fight for gender equality, in the 1980s it became clear that the movement did not represent all women's views or experiences, and third-wave feminism arose out of the desire to encourage equality for women of all races, sexual orientations, and social classes. For further discussions of second-wave feminist ideals, see Jane F. Gerhard, *Desiring Revolution: Second-Wave Feminism and the Rewriting of American Sexual Thought, 1920 to 1982* (New York: Columbia University Press, 2001); Robin Morgan, *Sisterhood Is Powerful: An Anthology of Writings from the Women's Liberation Movement* (New York: Vintage Books, 1970). For further discussion of third-wave feminist ideals, see Gloria Anzaldua, *Borderlands/La Frontera: The New Mestiza* (San Fransisco: Aunt Lute Books, 1987); Audre Lorde, "Age, Race, Class, and Sex: Women Redefining Difference," in *Literary Theory: An Anthology,* ed. Julie Rivkin and Michael Ryan (Malden: Blackwell, 2004), 854–60.

6. For discussions of *Buffy* as a non-feminist show, see Sherryl Vint, "'Killing us softly'? A Feminist Search for the 'Real' Buffy," *Slayage: The Journal of the Whedon Studies Association* 2.1 (2002), http://slayageonline.com/essays/slayage5/vint.htm; Zoe-Jane Playdon, "'The Outsiders' Society': Religious Imagery in *Buffy the Vampire Slayer,*" *Slayage: The Journal of the Whedon Studies Association* 2.1 (2002), http://slayageonline.com/essays/slayage5/playdon.htm; and Wilcox, "Show Me Your World," 90–107.

7. "Season 3 Overview," Joss Whedon et al., *Buffy the Vampire Slayer the Complete Third Season DVD Special Features* (Twentieth Century Fox, 2001).

8. This means that a critic identifies problematic issues in terms of feminist concerns in a text with a central female character or that addresses a female audience. Once these issues are identified and explored, the author shows the ways in which the text is actually successful at portraying a female living in a patriarchal world. Charlotte Brunsdon, "The Feminist in the Kitchen: Martha, Martha and Nigella," in *Feminism in Popular Culture,* ed. Joanne Hollows and Rachel Moseley (New York: Berg, 2006), 41–56.

9. St. Louis and Riggs, "'And yet': The Limits of *Buffy* Feminism," 3.

10. See Kent A. Ono, "To Be a Vampire on Buffy the Vampire Slayer: Race and ('Other') Socially Marginalizing Positions on Horror TV," in *Fantasy Girls: Gender in the New Universe of Science Fiction and Fantasy Television,* ed. Elyce Rae Helford (Lanham, MD: Rowman & Littlefield, 2000), 163–86.

11. See Alice Jenkins and Susan Stuart, "Extending Your Mind: Non-Standard Perlocutionary Acts in 'Hush,'" *Slayage: The Journal of the Whedon Studies Association* 3.1 (2003), http://slayageonline.com/Numbers/slayage9.htm; Cynthea Masson, "'Is

that just a comforting way of not answering the question?' Willow, Questions, and Affective Response in *Buffy the Vampire Slayer*," *Slayage: The Journal of the Whedon Studies Association* 5.4 (2006), http://slayageonline.com/essays/slayage20/Masson. htm.

12. One of the few ways that *Buffy* does recognize and validate a traditionally non-normative perspective, thus succeeding at the attempts of third-wave feminism to address non-heterosexual experiences, is through its thorough and nuanced depiction of lesbian characters (Willow, Tara, and Kennedy). For further reading about queer perspectives on *Buffy*, see Cynthea Masson and Marni Stanley, "Queer Eye of That Vampire Guy: Spike and the Aesthetics of Camp," *Slayage: The Journal of the Whedon Studies Association* 6.2 (2006), http://slayageonline.com/PDF/Masson_Stanley.pdf; Malin Isaksson, "Buffy/Faith Adult Femslash: Queer Porn with a Plot," *Slayage: The Journal of the Whedon Studies Association* 7.4 (2009), http://slayageonline.com/PDF/Isaksson.pdf.

13. I am greatly indebted to Jenkins and Stuart's article, "Extending Your Mind: Non-Standard Perlocutionary Acts in 'Hush'" for its excellent synopsis of speech acts and the ways that they can be applied to a specific episode of *Buffy*. I have extrapolated their applications to analyze the episodes discussed in this essay. It is also worth noting here that locutionary, illocutionary, and prelocutionary speech acts as literary terms can be traced back to author J. L. Austin and his book *How to Do Things with Words*, published in 1975.

14. Jenkins and Stuart, 3.

15. *Ibid.*

16. See Karen Eileen Overbey and Lahney Preston-Matto, "Staking in Tongues: Speech Act as Weapon in *Buffy*," in *Fighting the Forces: What's at Stake in Buffy the Vampire Slayer*, ed. Rhonda Wilcox and David Lavery (Lanham, MD: Rowman & Littlefield, 2002), 73–84.

17. Overbey and Preston-Matto, 83.

18. For examples of postcolonial literary criticism see: Edward Said, *Orientalism* (London: Vintage, 1978). Gayatri Spivak, *In Other Worlds: Essays in Cultural Politics* (London: Routledge, 1987). Homi K. Bhabha, *The Location of Culture* (London: Routledge, 1994).

19. Gayatri Cakravorty Spivak, "Can the Subaltern Speak?" in *Marxism and the Interpretation of Culture*, ed. Cary Nelson and Lawrence Grossberg (Urbana: University of Illinois Press, 1988), 83.

20. Christine Makward, "To Be or Not to Be … a Feminist Speaker," in *The Future of Difference*, eds. Alice Jardine and Hester Eisenstein (Boston: C.K. Hall, 1980), 100, emphasis in original.

21. Editors' note: while the Chinese Slayer doesn't have a name in the world of the show, her name is revealed to be Xin Rong in the *Spike and Dru: All's Fair* comic. That a figure so pivotal to the episode would only receive a name in an apocryphal text serves to reinforce McMurray's point. Please see: *Spike and Dru: All's Fair*, written by Christopher Golden, art by Eric Powell, Drew Geraci, Keith Barnett and Guy Major (Milwaukie, OR: Dark Horse Comics, 7 December 2000).

22. Lynne Edwards, "Slaying in Black and White: Kendra as Tragic Mulatta in *Buffy*," in *Fighting the Forces: What's at Stake in Buffy the Vampire Slayer*, ed. Rhonda Wilcox and David Lavery (Lanham, MD: Rowman & Littlefield, 2002), 85–97.

23. "Prophecy Girl," *Buffy the Vampire Slayer*, 1.12, DVD, written and directed by Joss Whedon (1997: Twentieth Century Fox, 2002).

24. "What's My Line Part 1," *Buffy the Vampire Slayer* 2.9, DVD, written by Howard Gordon and Marti Noxon, directed by David Solomon (1997: Twentieth Century Fox, 2002).

25. *Ibid.*

26. "What's My Line Part 2," *Buffy the Vampire Slayer* 2.10, DVD, written by Marti Noxon, directed by David Semel (1997: Twentieth Century Fox, 2002).

27. "Becoming Part 1," *Buffy the Vampire Slayer*, 2.21, written and directed by Joss Whedon (1998: Twentieth Century Fox, 2002).

28. "What's My Line Part 2," *Buffy the Vampire Slayer,* 2.10.

29. *Ibid.*

30. *Ibid.*

31. Edwards, 92.

32. "Becoming Part 1," *Buffy the Vampire Slayer*, 2.21.

33. "Restless," *Buffy the Vampire Slayer* 4.22, DVD, written and directed by Joss Whedon (2000: Twentieth Century Fox, 2003).

34. "Becoming Part 1," *Buffy the Vampire Slayer*, 2.21.

35. *Ibid.*

36. Edwards, 94.

37. Ono, 163.

38. Whedon et al., "Season 3 Overview."

39. *Ibid.*

40. "Faith, Hope & Trick," *Buffy the Vampire Slayer* 3.3, DVD, written by David Greenwalt, directed by James A. Contner (1998: Twentieth Century Fox, 2003).

41. "End of Days," *Buffy the Vampire Slayer* 7.21, written by Jane Espenson and Doug Petrie, directed by Marita Grabiak (2003: Twentieth Century Fox, 2004).

42. *Ibid.*

43. "Enemies," *Buffy the Vampire Slayer* 3.17, DVD, written by Doug Petrie, directed by David Grossman (1999: Twentieth Century Fox, 2003).

44. *Ibid.*

45. *Ibid.*

46. *Ibid.*

47. "This Year's Girl," *Buffy the Vampire Slayer* 4.15, DVD, written by Douglas Petrie, directed by Michael Gershman (1999: Twentieth Century Fox, 2006); "Who Are You?" *Buffy the Vampire Slayer* 4.16, DVD, written and directed by Joss Whedon (2000: Twentieth Century Fox, 2003).

48. *Ibid.*

49. *Ibid.*

50. Overbey and Matto, 83.

51. "Fool for Love," *Buffy the Vampire Slayer* 5.7, DVD, written by Douglas Petrie, directed by Nick Marck (2000: Twentieth Century Fox, 2003).

52. *Ibid.*

53. *Ibid.*

54. Marta Caminero-Santangelo, *The Madwoman Can't Speak, Or, Why Insanity Is Not Subversive* (Ithaca: Cornell University Press, 1998), 11.

55. "Primeval," *Buffy the Vampire Slayer*, 4.21, DVD, written by David Fury, directed by James A. Contner (2000: Twentieth Century Fox, 2003).

56. Though she is never referred to as the Primitive on screen, this is her name in the script and in the credits of the episodes she appears in ("Restless" 4.22, "Intervention" 5.18, and "Get It Done" 7.15). See "Restless—Complete Script," Buffyworld.com, http://www.buffyworld.com/buffy/scripts/078_scri.html. The inherent racism of an

African woman with this name, her wild hair and tribal makeup, and her inability to speak is less than subtle.

57. "Restless," *Buffy the Vampire Slayer*, 4.22.

58. *Ibid.*

59. *Ibid.*

60. *Ibid.*

61. *Ibid.*

62. *Ibid.*

63. "Restless," *Buffy the Vampire Slayer*, 4.22.

64. *Ibid.*

65. "Get It Done," *Buffy the Vampire Slayer*, 7.15.

66. *Ibid.*

67. *Ibid.*

68. Caminero-Santangelo, 11.

69. "Get It Done," *Buffy the Vampire Slayer*, 7.15.

70. Editors' note: interestingly, Buffy's screams also enact this same power to defend herself and defeat her enemies through her voice alone in "Hush" (4.10). Notably, though she is not exempt from losing the power of speech through the Gentleman's spell, it is the recovery of her speech, and hers alone, that ultimately brings about their end.

71. "Bring on the Night," *Buffy the Vampire Slayer* 7.10, DVD, written by Marti Noxon and Douglas Petrie, directed by David Grossman (2002: Twentieth Century Fox, 2004).

72. While Kennedy is never explicitly identified as Latina, her character is played by Iyari Limon, a Latina actress, leading fans and critics to interpret the character as Latina.

73. "Empty Places," *Buffy the Vampire Slayer*, 7.19, DVD, written by Drew Z. Greenberg, directed by James A. Contner (2003: Twentieth Century Fox, 2004).

74. *Ibid.*

75. Pender, 9.

76. Wilcox, 102.

77. See "Storyteller," *Buffy the Vampire Slayer* 7.16, DVD, written by Jane Espenson, directed by Marita Grabiak (2003: Twentieth Century Fox, 2004); "Touched," *Buffy the Vampire Slayer* 7.20, written by Rebecca Rand Kirshner, directed by David Solomon (2003: Twentieth Century Fox, 2004).

78. "Bring on the Night, "*Buffy the Vampire Slayer*, 7.10.

79. "Touched," *Buffy the Vampire Slayer*, 7.20.

80. *Ibid.*

81. The popular discussion forum Whedonesque.com features many comments from viewers who gather to discuss all of the works of Joss Whedon, and include discussions and commentary on the treatment of race and class in *Buffy*. For Chao Ahn's treatment as comic relief see rufustfyrfly, May 18, 2008 (21:41 CET), comment on Simon Fraser, "Dead Bro Walking: Characters of Color in Joss Whedon's *Buffy*verse," *Whedonesque* (blog), May 18, 2008, http://whedonesque.com/comments/16368; the ninja report, May 19, 2008 (00:41 CET), comment on Simon Fraser, "Dead Bro Walking: Characters of Color in Joss Whedon's *Buffy*verse," *Whedonesque* (blog), May 18, 2008, http://whedonesque.com/comments/16368.

82. Wilcox, 96.

83. "First Date," *Buffy the Vampire Slayer*, 7.14, DVD, written by Jane Espenson, directed by David Grossman (2003: Twentieth Century Fox, 2004).

84. *Ibid.*

85. *Ibid.*

86. Rory Cooke Dicker and Alison Piepmeier. 2003. Introduction. *Catching a Wave: Reclaiming Feminism for the 21st Century*, eds. Rory Cooke Dicker and Alison Piepmeir (Boston: Northeastern University Press, 2003), 3–28.

87. "Get It Done," *Buffy the Vampire Slayer*, 7.15.

88. *Ibid.*

89. "Empty Places." *Buffy the Vampire Slayer*, 7.19.

90. *Ibid.*

91. *Ibid.*

92. *Ibid.*

93. *Ibid.*

94. "End of Days," *Buffy the Vampire Slayer*, 7.22, DVD.

95. "Chosen," *Buffy the Vampire Slayer* 7.22, DVD, written by Joss Whedon, directed by Joss Whedon (2003: Twentieth Century Fox, 2004).

96. *Ibid.*

97. Arwen Spicer, ""It's bloody brilliant!' The Undermining of Metanarrative Feminism in the Season Seven Arc Narrative of Buffy," *Slayage: The Journal of the Whedon Studies Association* 4.3 (2004), http://slayageonline.com/essays/slayage15/Spicer.htm.

98. *Ibid.*

99. "Chosen," *Buffy the Vampire Slayer*, 7.22.

100. *Ibid.*

101. Pender, 11.

102. Spicer, 18.

A Dodgy English Accent

*The Rituals of a Contested Space
of Englishness in "Helpless"*

JOEL HAWKES

In the *Buffy the Vampire Slayer* episode "Helpless" (3.12), Buffy Summers nears her eighteenth birthday.[1] A series of injections are surreptitiously administered to the Slayer by her Watcher, Rupert Giles, at the request of the Watchers' Council, in preparation for a coming-of-age rite of passage. The injections temporarily rob Buffy of her superhuman strength, readying her for the commencement of the rite called the "Cruciamentum," during which she is locked in a dilapidated boarding house (a kind of tomb) with a psychotic vampire (3.12). Trapped, she must prove herself without her powers, a rite of passage each Slayer must undergo, and a turning point in *Buffy* through which we can more carefully examine the role that ritual and ethnicity play in the show.[2]

Rites of Passage In-Between
Three Different Spaces

The episode illustrates the narrative functionality of a rite of passage as first outlined in detail by the anthropologist Arnold van Gennep in his seminal work *Rites de Passage*. In van Gennep's study, rituals among so-called "semicivilized peoples" are seen to accompany rites of passage found within all societies, such as puberty, marriage and death.[3] The use of the word "semicivilized" both problematizes and illuminates our understanding of ritual, and its relation to *Buffy*. The word suggests a discourse of cultural origins, the earlier stages of humankind's development, but it also places van Gennep's text within a European colonialist narrative. "Semicivilized" rituals are frequently illustrated with examples from less-developed nations of the period and the past. This definition is an act of colonialism, reflected in the practices of, for example, the British Empire, with its introduction, indeed enforcement, abroad of its more "civilized" ceremonies.

Similar to European "civilization" in van Gennep's work, a comparable English presence in *Buffy* is both problematic and illuminating. It is a very English Watchers' Council that plans and controls the rite of passage in "Helpless" (3.12). They are a group that have always trained, guided and governed the Slayer in her fight against evil, but who, up until this episode, have remained an obscure force.[4] What we might call an "English space"— a space of history, authority, ritual, knowledge and tradition—lies just behind the events of "Helpless" and behind many other occurrences in the television show. An older, even sacred, English space is found behind (physically, culturally and temporally) what I will call the two other spaces (worlds) of *Buffy*: America (the everyday small town Sunnydale) and its seeming antithesis in the Otherworldly (the space of magic, demons, and their evilest paragons in the Hellmouth). The role of English space in *Buffy* is not unlike that of historical English colonialism, at times enforcing its own "civilizing" mission on American space, an intersecting relationship whose meanings are explored in *Buffy* with the aid of the third Otherworldly space.

Englishness, I argue, assists, and instigates, various rites of passage in *Buffy*, and helps the development of the other two spaces, while also driving the story and characters forward on their various quests. This ritualized English space is not a benign space though; it is not an inert space of old books, English accents and polite tea drinking (some of its rituals)—though at first it appears to be just this. Neither is it the same as England itself. English space (like its American and Otherworldly counterparts) is a cultural and mythic space rather than a mappable location, a distilling and imagining of what those locations hold and represent. And as transformative spaces, these three are locations of violence and conflict.

We witness something of this vexed and violent ritual in "Helpless" (3.12).[5] House and episode are similarly ritually-structured locations that offer a clearly defined framework within which we might read the ritual significance of *Buffy*. The episode is also a *transition* point, as we will later see, in the role Englishness plays in the show. Conforming to the three stages of this threshold rite, the action of the "Helpless" episode/house can be divided into three parts: "*separation, transition,* and *incorporation.*"[6] In fact, van Gennep identifies such a transforming ritual with a "*territorial passage,* such as the entrance into a [...] house."[7] Victor Turner illustrates the tripartite ceremony by giving the example of an individual entering a temple (a sacred space), where he/she is divided from the rest of society; a ritual act assists spiritual progress or social development, whereupon the individual re-enters society at an elevated level.[8] The rite can be read as a symbolic death and rebirth of the initiate. This is the type of rite Buffy must complete to prove herself as Slayer in the abandoned boarding house, as she symbolically dies and is reborn,[9] and makes the *transition* into adulthood, and to an advanced (and, importantly, recognized—by the Council) position as Slayer.[10]

A reading of *Buffy* as ritual space is strengthened when we consider *Anthropology of Religion*, in which Bobby Alexander gives a broad definition of ritual as a performance that "effects a transition from the everyday life to an alternative context within which the everyday is transformed."[11] Described as a "transition," we become aware of a ritual's liminality (its in-betweenness) and transformative power more generally. *Buffy's* world of demons and magic has a transformative effect on the everyday world of Sunnydale, and we can observe a plethora of rituals (performed by demons, witches, Watchers, vampires, and Slayer) that help achieve this transition in the show.

A ritual is a very physical performance: "communication in ritual" is primarily "through the bodies of the actors."[12] This is illustrated by numerous rites enacted in *Buffy*, of which fighting and slaying might be counted, through their embodiment (their making physical) of the sacred duty of the Slayer.[13] Buffy's coming-of-age rite is itself a very physical test, and one that traditionally conforms to strict rules and regulations, as it scripts preparation, entry into the house, and the completion of the task. But the rite goes beyond the physical world. The performance of a religious ritual might, for example, strive to link the practitioner from the seen world to the unseen, the profane to the sacred, humankind (or, in *Buffy*, monsterkind) to the gods (or demons). In a sense, it is a rite of passage from one space (realm) to another metaphysical one.

The *transition* part of a rite of passage (as Turner notes) not only aids the social/spiritual progression of the individual but also helps designate the location of the rite as a sacred liminal space—a "cultural realm that is defined as 'out of time.'"[14] Mircea Eliade sees this space as "reversible," in the sense that it is a "*primordial mythical time made present*," and the ritual a "re-actualization of a sacred event that took place in a mythical past, 'in the beginning.'"[15] Past and other(worldly) times and places are constantly re-actualized in *Buffy* through numerous rituals performed by a variety of different characters, who utilize sacred texts, sacrifices, and spells to achieve transformation.[16] The re-actualization of English space, in particular, is a powerful force in *Buffy*, and plays an important role in the numerous rites of passage that we might read as key constructs of the *Buffy*verse.

Developing High School and England in BtVS *Seasons One to Three*

Englishness is first introduced through Buffy's Watcher, Giles, who is already present at Sunnydale High School when Buffy arrives. Giles's first task is to set Buffy back on the Slayer path which she is intent to escape so that she might lead a "normal" American high school life.[17] Giles is narratalogically positioned as an origin, as he is quite literally there before Buffy, and (re)initiates Buffy's own rite of passage as Slayer. He also represents an English cultural origin—a source (and a point of re-actualization) of wisdom, knowledge and traditional guidance to the Slayer. The school library becomes a microcosm of the Watchers' world, a manifestation of old and distant English space. Giles and his occult books offer insight into the demon world that "everyday" small town America cannot, and the library becomes a sanctuary (a sacred space) that allows Buffy and her friends, Willow Rosenberg and Xander Harris, to negotiate—from a position of relative safety—not only the Otherworldly but "everyday" America as well.

In these early episodes there is an almost elementary understanding of what constitutes these three intersecting spaces. What is English, what is American, and what is Otherworldly (specifically, evil) are very simply sketched; they repeatedly conform to stereotype and cliché, as in "I Robot... . You Jane" (1.8), which sees Moloch as Otherworldly space, Buffy and Willow (and Jenny Calendar) as American, and Giles as English.[18] The Otherworldly provides a space in which the relationship between the other two spaces can be explored, helping transfigure the seeming clichés—represented in "I Robot.... You Jane" (1.8) in the cultural bickering between Giles and Jenny—and enabling the two cultural spaces to follow their own rites of passage in development, alongside the first three seasons' more ostensible concerns with teenage rites of passage.

These teenage ceremonies are chiefly explored through the experiences of high school.[19] Directing our attention to this particular reading, Giles tells Buffy of her SATs, "It isn't meant to be easy, you know, it's a rite of passage," to which Buffy replies "Is it too late to join a tribe where they pierce something or cut something off?"[20] Such teenage experiences are threshold rites towards adulthood. The teenage angst, the fighting of monsters, and the show's quirky humor never mask but actually accentuate the importance of each rite of passage, allying teenage events with the fighting of various demonic threats, while never taking itself too seriously. Joss Whedon explains that during high school years one "blow[s] everything out of proportion, and the tiniest thing can set you off."[21] The intensities of one world/space illustrate the horrors of the other, though it is not always clear which way this spatial synonym works.

The first three seasons culminate in the rite of high school graduation ("Graduation, Part One and Two" 3.21 and 3.22), where transformation into adulthood is paralleled with the "ascension" of Sunnydale's Mayor into demonic snake form. The two spaces mirror and contrast each other, complementing and encroaching. In the end it is the united graduating students who defeat the Mayor and his minions. As the school lies in ruins after the Mayor's defeat, Oz observes, "we survived.... Not the battle. High school."[22] Another rite of passage has been completed. We are left to ponder which is the greater battle, but given how closely related the spheres have become, rituals occur within both American and Otherwordly spaces.

While it is Giles' job to oversee Buffy's fight with evil, he also assists in Buffy's, Willow's and Xander's American high school battles. He advises them on relationships, helps Buffy prepare for the SATs, and comforts them when they are upset (often as regards relationship issues).[23] He is a fatherly figure, and is at first introduced as a slightly bumbling, well spoken, occasionally pretentious tweed-clad librarian version of this (Buffy says "his diapers were tweed").[24] He is edged towards English cliché through some very English idiosyncrasies but also through the perceptions of his students who project their stereotypes onto him. Englishness is here a paternal space intersecting with a child-like one, while Giles's superior Otherworldly knowledge reinforces a position that is at times reminiscent of a kindly yet condescending colonialism. This simple cultural/historical structuring of the relationship complements the cliché of American high school experience, and Giles's own readings of cultural stereotypes onto it.

The same use of stereotype informs Buffy herself, who is a slightly vain and ditzy, short, blonde cheerleader, but only at first sight. While Whedon quickly explodes the Buffy stereotype, he seems determined to explore it more fully in Giles. Giles is set apart from America and the Otherworldly, fighting the latter, while unsure, and lightly mocking, of the former. A cultural contrast of England and America is established, managed through the humor of cultural stereotyping. Giles' old man/Old World technophobia and reliance on tradition help illustrate this position early on. Gesturing to the only computer in the school's library, Giles asks Buffy and friends (The "Scoobies") if they can "wrest some information from that dread machine."[25] An askew look from the group elicits an addendum from Giles: "That was a bit, um, British, wasn't it." "Welcome to the New World," replies Buffy.[26] This half-joking definition of the Englishman is continued in "I Robot.... You Jane," when Giles again rages against the computer as an alternative depository of information to books.[27] It is the Old World looking down on the New, supposing it holds (in its more "civilized" ways) the history and knowledge the other lacks. But at the same time, it is the New World mocking the Old by putting such words in its mouth. This episode is the first time that Giles' English traits are significantly insulted, so maintaining his "set-apart" qualities, but through mockery rather than respect, thereby questioning the authority of the English space he embodies.

In contrast to Giles, the new computer teacher Jenny appears to represent modern America, though again in clichéd form—loving football and monster truck rallies. Jenny's New-World sensibilities label Giles a snob, and reject his claims that knowledge should be held in books, arguing that there, it is only accessible to the rich, old, white men who have traditionally governed and shaped society.[28] A criticism of privilege is leveled at Giles, and at the Englishness he represents, by a female figure who is both Giles' equal and opposite as an American high school teacher with her own "band" of students who meet in the computer lab rather than the library. If we are in any doubt of this other group's allegiance to the New World, a later scene in the same episode cements the cultural connection with its not-so-subtle inclusion of an American flag hanging in Jenny's classroom.[29]

A metaphorical relationship of nations, of trust and mistrust, begins between Giles and Jenny. On a date to watch high school football, Giles mocks the un-masculine nature of the sport, questioning the need to put on heavy protective clothing just to play rugby ("Some Assembly Required" 2.2).[30] Continuing the cultural sparring, Jenny insists that Giles "read[s] something that was published after 1066," suggesting[31]—before the later questioning of England in "Helpless"—that English origins and knowledge might be outdated.[32] Jenny's greeting to Giles of "Morning England" further reinforces his cultural significance.[33] Buffy, too, mocks Giles, his sense of duty, and its English roots: "I know this one: slaying entails certain sacrifices, blah blah biddy blah. I'm so stuffy get me a scone."[34] In these relationships we see a reflection of America past, growing, struggling for independence against an older England that was once its antecedent. It is a moment of struggle in-between, a threshold point as outlined by van Gennep.

The half-joking, friendly yet adversarial relationships of Giles, Jenny, Buffy, and friends are caught in a process of *transition*, in-between the two worlds of America and England. This liminal position is accentuated in Buffy, whose American life is dramatically affected by a sacred birthright that in part originates from England. But despite the unsettling position of being in-between, the intersecting stereotypes of England and America contrast the threat of the Otherworldly, so providing a safe, "knowable" space to defend, and retreat into. Both worlds are offered like a memorized liturgical order, learnt through repetition, and given solid and comforting form in their dogmatic appearance. The re-actualization of England, in particular, offers reassurance, even though it is, at times, mocked—a technique that softens and makes more palatable its authoritative position, allowing a sympathetic narrative of British colonialism in an American show. Origins (social, religious, historical, and cultural) have always helped to give structure and meaning to society, and they reassure us in an ever-changing world. Giles' mastery of these origins helps Buffy defeat their shared foes. Yet, even as Whedon creates these cultural certainties, he begins to question them, threatening their destruction by locating within them the darkness of the Otherworldly.

The Growing Darkness of England: English Culture in Seasons Two and Three

As the relationship between Giles and Jenny evolves, the jokes and the couple's battles begin to reveal a greater complexity to the seeming cliché of their polarized cultural positions. Jenny is a Neo-Pagan, and her seemingly American naiveté is partly dismissed ("cultured") with some knowledge of the Otherworldly—a learning traditionally aligned with English Watchers. The revelation of Giles's past brings greater discord, so testing the pleasant English cliché. The transformation of the viewer's perception begins with the arrival of the trickster figure, Ethan Rayne, an old university friend of Giles, who, with the help of the god Janus, transforms people into the costumes they have brought from his store.[35] The double face of Janus seems at first to reflect two faces, one of Giles, the other of Ethan (order vs. chaos). But with Ethan's exposure of Giles' past, we realize that Buffy's Watcher is a form of Janus himself, with a dark history, when he, too, played with majicks and rebelled against order. We are shown just how the past man informs the present when the aggression of a younger Giles is manifested in a ruthless beating of Ethan for information.[36] This violence between the two destabilizes our envisioning of English culture, which is beginning to reveal its other face. There are those from within (Ethan, and later Watcher turned bad, Gwendolyn Post) who rebel against a sacred English tradition of a "civilizing"/controlling mission over the forces of the Otherworldly, to seek instead personal gain or chaos. With Ethan and Gwendolyn's betrayal of the Watcher's cause, the violence of enforcement, emergent at first through Giles, casts doubts on the integrity of the Watcher's stated mission. What is more troubling is the greater brutality revealed in the Watchers' Council, which increasingly resembles the repressive aspects of a British colonial past.

Giles' own questionable beginnings are not discovered by the Scoobies until Ethan's return in "The Dark Age" (2.8), when the raising of the demon by Ethan, Giles and friends in their university days is exposed.[37] Giles explains to Buffy that he never wanted her to see this part of him—a side we have already glimpsed more fully in his violence against Ethan.[38] This exposes another face of Giles and the Watcher profession he represents; it is a smashing of the loveable tweed-wearing cliché that, at this stage, the viewer and

Buffy can readily accept. Like Buffy, the viewer can forgive Giles, being able to identify with the Watcher, whose past failings humanize him, and even align aspects of English and American culture. Here, Giles' early misdeeds are not so different from those committed by Sunnydale's high school students even as they continue on to Sunnydale University. The other darker implications of his chosen profession are not as yet recognized. The Watcher's youthful rebelling is itself a rite of passage undertaken by many adolescents— a kind of "dropping out" from society, protesting its rules and elders. The Otherworldly again functions as a metaphor for the events of American and English society, with drink, drugs, and parties replaced by indiscreet magic. The Otherworld provides a space for Ripper's rite of passage.

At the same time, Giles' mythic and timeless qualities as representative of England and Englishness must be reconsidered, as they become more closely connected to the Otherworldly. This is a troubling position because such alignment questions the purity of Giles's mission, but at the same time allows further development and realization for all involved. The moment is another threshold point that enables a maturing of Giles. We glimpse a darker side of the Watcher and Englishness, but begin to understand that while the "origins" of both are not as comforting and reassuring as we supposed they were, an English space cannot just be made of tea and tweed if it is to effectively battle the Otherworldly threat. The moment is also a threshold point for Jenny who, rather than being fully traumatized by her own possession by the demon Eyghon, is perhaps more affected (a moment of self-realization) by a consideration of her own as yet unrevealed duplicitous position.

A switch occurs here, and roles reverse in another Janus-like move when soon after Jenny's "righteous" outrage at Giles' "betrayal," Giles feels similarly betrayed when Jenny's double role as a spy is revealed.[39] Jenny has not only repeated Giles' subversion of the purity they both supposedly represent, she has also shown Old World origins by means of her "gypsy" connection to Europe, so she assumes aspects of both the darkness and wisdom that is associated with Giles' Englishness.[40] Jenny is now linked to something of America's European cultural origins—the persecution once fled from in Europe (from which the Roma suffered), but also the oppression that grew in America under colonial rule. She is not entirely honest, and nor is she an American unencumbered by European influence, so she inhabits a liminal point that again destabilizes English, American and Otherworldly boundaries.

The Otherworldly space offers an in-between location in which we can examine and negotiate the truths and lies of cultural stereotypes embodied in Jenny and Giles, while never destroying the humor of these clichés that ensures our continued acceptance of characters who are flawed and even dangerous. Humor allows our continued enjoyment of Ethan's destructive influence, but is denied to the "humorless" Gwendolyn, whose "cold" Englishness seems a stereotype too far. Like Ethan she not only threatens American space through use of the Otherworldly, she has also betrayed her own English origins. While humor saves Ethan from his dishonesty and betrayals, these same flaws almost redeem Giles from too much humor, allowing an evolution of character into a more effective Watcher, who can in turn better effect transformation in those under his care. This gradual "darkening" of Giles foreshadows the greater manifestation of Englishness as duality of profane and sacred, fully manifesting in "Helpless" (3.12) where the Watchers' Council enables the ritual becoming of the Slayer despite her conceptions of Englishness.[41]

Inside the House: The Turning Point of Englishness in Season Three

"Helpless" (3.12) is an essential rite of passage for Buffy, and a liminal point for Englishness in the show. The ritual not only transforms Buffy, it also transfigures the space in which the ritual is performed, connecting time and space in the house to something beyond the seen. The rite is a physical practice (a fight), and the space a practiced space—practiced physically by movement within it, and culturally by the cultural significance the English/Watcher ceremony assigns to it. The "Cruciamentum" is firstly a re-actualization of previous Slayer tests: all those who have survived to their eighteenth birthday have entered a similar ceremonial arena, though this is a forced lineage, in a sense a ritual rape of the unknowing Slayer.[42] Secondly, the rite is a smaller manifestation of the greater search for sacred origins, the mystical "in the beginning" that often haunts culture and religion—for example, Christianity with its concerns of God, creation, and the fall from paradise—as it does *Buffy*, most notably in later concerns with the First Slayer,[43] and the First Evil.[44] Thirdly, another kind of time and space "origin" manifests and haunts *Buffy*: Englishness. The force and power of this English space is fully manifested in the ceremony that Senior Watcher (and leading member of the Council), Quentin Travers, explains is "a time-honored rite of passage."[45] The rite is a symbolic journey of death and rebirth, but here threatens real death, aiming a rebirth of a physically and mentally stronger Slayer, with closer ties to supporting Watchers and Council.

While the rite is technically a success, with Buffy assuming greater strength and maturity through the experience, her re-*incorporation* into her Watcher-governed world fails. Her newly acquired strength and knowledge force her to challenge the Council's authority. With Giles' forced betrayal of Buffy, and the risk posed by the test, the rite's place in the modern world is questioned. The rite of passage is completed but not in the expected way.

Tradition is broken. Giles is the first to rebel, scorning the event as an "archaic exercise in cruelty," countermanding orders not to reveal the hidden test to an unwitting Buffy.[46] This brings about Giles's second betrayal, namely, of the English space he represents. Picking up the show's colonialist discourse, we can compare Giles's shifting in-between English and American spaces with the questioning of British rule in America by once-loyal members of the colonial government, who might have once been complicit in its "exercise(s) in cruelty."[47] The ceremony in "Helpless" has become a different kind of rite of passage, beginning a transition away from English rule. Giles remains mentor to Buffy but is freed from the official English position he had held. He is even accused of becoming "a bit American" by rogue Watcher Gwendolyn Post.[48] But while Gwendolyn's betrayal ultimately reveals the more ruthless side of an English space, Giles' betrayal shows a consideration of values that bring him closer to Buffy and to an American space. Travers even fires Giles, accusing him of being too much like a father figure to Buffy, rather than the Watcher he should be.[49]

Replacement Watcher, Wesley Wyndham-Pryce, reinstates the earlier clichéd Englishness found in Giles, but in a more exaggerated form.[50] His clueless, bumbling Englishness undermines his English authority (as do his inappropriate feelings for Cordelia Chase) rather than legitimize it as it did for Giles, while knowledge of the ruthlessness that lies behind this comic representation is now understood. The Council is transformed into a harsh, uncaring space, while Giles, distanced from old England and his former Watcher ties, retains our sympathy, becoming less and less the English stereotype, as seen for example when he refuses to have a cup of tea in a time of crisis, eliciting Xander's reply: "Okay, but you're destroying a perfectly good cultural stereotype here," in "Graduation Part Two" (3.22).[51] A final movement away from Englishness, reflecting, even lightly parodying, America's own historical rejection of English rule on July 4, 1776, is completed in Season Three's "Graduation" episodes. The Council's refusal to help the poisoned Angel finally causes Buffy to abjure them. Wesley tells Buffy that you "can't turn your back on the Council," to which she replies, "They're in England, I don't think they can tell which way my back is facing," demonstrating an outright rejection of the English authoritative space they represent.[52] When Wesley accuses Buffy of "mutiny," the reference to English origins and American independence is unambiguous.[53]

England ceases to be a relevant cultural and mythic space in the same way, thereby altering the fundamental role it continues to play in later seasons.[54] Buffy graduates from the Council and England just as she and her fellow students do from high school, but America's cultural antecedent lingers still. Giles remains at Buffy's side, while the rites of graduation in Sunnydale High see the students parade to their seats accompanied by British composer

Edward Elgar's "Pomp and Circumstance." In 1902, A. C. Benson wrote words to Elgar's composition at the suggestion of King Edward VII to create the hugely British nationalistic song, "Land of Hope and Glory," at a time in Europe when it was thought a sense of national unity needed to be reinforced.[55] We are reminded of America's English origins, and the part England played in bringing forth a new nation, just as Englishness has played its role in Buffy's own *transition. Incorporation* for a nation, and for Buffy, are both outside an English space, but still affected by it. Elgar is something very English taken and reused to produce new purpose and meaning, becoming part of an American high school rite of passage.

Spike, the Last English Hero: Origins and Endings

The Council returns in Season Five in an attempt to exert authority over the Slayer through testing once again ("Checkpoint" 5.12), echoing the earlier forced rite of passage in "Helpless."[56] Though Buffy refuses to participate in their second game, she agrees to work with the Council, claiming that they need her more than she needs them.[57] But this is only a half-truth; she is still beholden to the Council for its knowledge and history, which helps Buffy identify and destroy the hell god Glory.[58]

At the same time, the brutalities of the Council that have ostensibly been rejected by Buffy still remain a presence through Giles. Indeed, it is only because of the darker part of the Watcher that Buffy is able to defeat Glory in the finale of Season Five. Giles claims: "I've sworn to protect this sorry world, and sometimes that means saying and doing what other people can't," a commitment he demonstrates in killing Ben, the innocent vessel holding the hell god Glory.[59] Buffy could not do it ("she's a hero") so someone must do it for her.[60] Buffy's own sacrifice, moments later, to save Dawn and the world, seems contrasted with the murder by Giles, yet both acts remain sanctioned ritual events in the context of the greater rite Glory is performing, which seeks to bring about the end of the world.[61] René Girard might label both deaths "sacrificial violence": sanctioned brutality to "protect the community from its own violence."[62] Giles's bloodletting stops Glory's greater evil, and quells the need for greater violence. Ben and Buffy, caught at the intersections of American, Otherworldly, and for Buffy, English, spaces, make ideal scapegoats, dying on behalf of the American space whose own violence against itself is often transformed into the metaphor of Otherworldly figures. To save the world from Glory, both acts of sacrifice in "The Gift" (5.22) are necessary: Buffy cannot complete her own death if Giles has not brought about the other. An English space is still relevant.

Buffy never fully rejects the Council, but with the destruction of its headquarters in London, the presence of an English space is dramatically reduced, allowing Buffy and an American space to develop more independently.[63] That the Council is ultimately unable to defend itself demonstrates its archaic and irrelevant position, an empire in full decline. The Old World's time has passed; it is an American space now that must stand against the Otherworldly in the final season.

With another betrayal of Buffy by Giles in the final season (colluding with Principal Wood to kill Spike), English space is again diminished, forcing the Slayer to realize she has nothing more to learn from her Watcher.[64] Yet, Englishness is still not fully rejected, only transformed. One English Space replaces another, with Spike having grown more like the earlier embodiment of Englishness in Giles. We might even read Giles' collusion with Wood to kill Spike not only as a misguided attempt (sacrifice) to protect the group, but as an attempt for self-preservation (of identity), as Giles's role of support to the Slayer is usurped. Buffy's decision to remove Spike's chip is an acceptance of his new position, and an evolution in Buffy; whereas assistance once came from a father figure, Giles, it now comes from a protagonist who is both hero and lover, revealing Buffy's maturation and coming of age.[65]

Spike's own journey, or rite of passage, begins in a state of stilted immortality but ends in liberation through death. As a vampire, Spike has been sired, another mystical blood rite, this one initiating a vampire through a passage of death and rebirth. The threat from this creature is then not death but eternal life: a "perversion of Christ's resurrection."[66] The First Evil, the Mayor, and Glory all promise a similar form of immortality to those who will obey them. But while evil offers life to its adherents, it frustrates and interrupts the renewal found within the cycles of rites of passage experienced by good characters. In Season Seven, Buffy is offered a variant form of immortality in a re-actualization of the creation of the First Slayer that, like a vampire's siring, would imbue her with extra power. Her decision to reject this power is again a rewriting of the expectations of another rite of passage for Buffy, thereby creating a new rite affirming her rejection of the Council, of Giles, and of the English, patriarchal cultural space they represent.

In later episodes, we glimpse Spike's origins as a vampire, sired by Drusilla,[67] and see that this is not a true origin, but merely an event in his development, another *transition*.[68] Wilson suggests that Spike sees his "siring as salvation,"[69] and in a sense it is, in that it allows Spike to follow a path towards self perfection. David George suggests that, perhaps more important than religion's obsession with origins (e.g., God, Eden), is the search for perfection (e.g., heaven, redemption).[70] It is a spiritual quest, and the initiation of this type of journey might be read in the stages of the rite of passage, "*separation, transition*, and *incorporation*."[71] One can read the rite of passage as an act of pilgrimage—a journey from one point to another—to a place marked as sacred, itself an image of "perfection."[72] That which is sought in the self can be read as being embodied in place. It is another form of spiritual quest, and one that necessarily involves an arduous route, the suffering experienced during the pilgrimage being essential in definition of the journey and the sacred site. This suffering offers "grace" and redemption, in other words, rebirth.[73] Though many of *Buffy*'s characters follow such a quest, Spike provides the most comprehensive experience of this spiritual rite of passage.

Spike cannot reject his immortality, since he's already sought the ability to be more than a mere vampire, which he does in the final moments of Season Six with his acquisition of a soul.[74] However, as Angel demonstrates, a regained soul does not complete or begin the journey. Spike's rite of passage of redemption begins much earlier, assisted by an increasing Englishness and its associated comedy. In Spike, we see a re-actualization of English space that both aids his development and those around him. In early seasons of *Buffy* Spike remains an undeveloped character, though his English credentials begin to be established with the use of memorable Englishisms like "Nancy-boy" in "School Hard" (2.3). Whedon had originally planned to kill Spike off after a few episodes in the second season, but changed his mind, and the character was allowed to develop.[75] A more pronounced Englishness allows for this in the later part of Season Two, often achieved through a humor of English sayings and colloquialisms, with phrases like "Goodbye Piccadilly, farewell Leister bloody square," as a response to Angelus's desire for apocalypse.[76] English slang aids the manifestation of Englishness in the vampire and so humanizes the creature.[77] Words like "shag" ("Lovers Walk" 3.8)[78] increase in usage by Season Four where in "The Harsh Light of Day" (4.3) we are given an assortment: "mate," "sod off" and "bint," while Buffy refers to him as the "English guy."[79] Elsewhere, Willow calls him the "undead English patient" ("Something Blue" 4.9).[80] As with Giles, comedy plays an important role in the development of the English character, cultivating sympathy, while showing that Englishness must again come in comedy form to find a place in the *Buffy*verse, a position highlighted in the choice of James Masters, an American, to play this part. Spike inhabits the intersection of, and unites, English, American and Otherworldly spaces.

At the same time there is a gradual shift to bring Spike closer to Giles, and what he represents. In the surreal dream sequence of "Restless" (4.22) we see Spike and Giles dressed in matching tweed suits, swinging on playground swings, where Giles declares Spike is like a son to him.[81] In "Tabula Rasa" (6.8), Spike again cycles through comical English slang as he realizes his cultural origins ("bloody hell, sodding, blimey, shagging, knickers, bollocks"), while wearing the same tweed suit from "Restless."[82] Suit, English accent and slang lead Giles and Spike (now "Randy Giles") to the erroneous conclusion that they must, in fact, be father and son. In reality, they are quite different. Giles as a character evolves as he moves from English stereotype into a darker self, while Spike softens and assimilates as his Englishness helps make him something more than just a villain and vampire.

Where Giles has assisted Buffy, sometimes doing what she *will not* do, Spike does what she *cannot*, wearing the amulet brought to Sunnydale by Angel, Spike ultimately defeats the First Evil. He is destroyed along with the Hellmouth and Sunnydale. A freedom is achieved from the conflicting and violent trinity of England, America and Otherworldly spaces, but only in the finality of death. In a literal death, Spike is reborn—an *incorporation* back into the world as a hero, and with his humanity regained he becomes more than human (though of course, his story continues in Season Five of *Angel*). Buffy's own freedom mimics Spike's sacrifice, but hers is once more a symbolic death, with the loss of her home, her enemy, and the individual nature of her Slayer powers, she completes a rite of passage that means she no longer has to be alone. She is for the first time fully incorporated back into a community.

In these last moments, Englishness is also redeemed through its manifestation in Spike's heroics. An English space has challenged, and threatened the various characters in the show, but in its Janus-faced role, it has assisted numerous transformative rites of passage, in its manifestations as Council, Giles and Spike. It has helped the becoming, or final *incorporation*, in the last moments of Season Seven, of Slayer and Spike. At the same time, Englishness has itself undergone a rite of passage, reinvented from a colonial narrative embodied in the Council, made acceptable through comedy and Giles, but only redeemed in a final act of self-sacrifice, where the Old World dies, in Spike, to allow the New World to continue. This last rite destroying Sunnydale and the Hellmouth unites the complementary and antagonistic creative and destructive rituals of English, American and Otherworldly spaces, offering freedom in a final symbolic death and transcendence.

NOTES

1. "Helpless" *Buffy the Vampire Slayer* 3.12 DVD, written by David Fury, directed by James A Contner (1998: Twentieth Century Fox, 2005).

2. *Ibid.*

3. Arnold van Gennep, *The Rites of Passage*, trans. Monika B. Vizedon and Gabriel L. Caffee (London: Routledge & Kegan Paul, 1960), 3.

4. "Helpless," *Buffy the Vampire Slayer* 3.12, DVD, written by David Fury, directed by James A. Contner (2001: Twentieth Century Fox, 2001).

5. *Ibid.*

6. Victor Turner, *From Ritual to Theatre: The Human Seriousness of Play* (New York: PAJ Publications, 1982), 24.

7. Van Gennep, *The Rites of Passage*, 192.

8. Turner, *From Ritual to Theatre*, 24.

9. By going inside the house Buffy is entering a tomb-like space, in a symbolic death, while her re-emergence is her coming back to life (it might be seen as a quest into the underworld). Her loss of powers, her battle, and her later reacquisition of her power as the drugs wear off also map a symbolic death, and a struggle to reclaim her power in the underworld, matched with her right to live and continue as the Slayer in the eyes of the Council upon completion of the task. If Buffy died in the house, her power, mission and life would be forfeit.

10. A number of essays on *Buffy* address the influence of a similar tripartite structured quest concerning the figure of the hero on the show, with reference to Joseph Campbell's discussion of the journey of the archetypal hero in *The Hero with a Thousand Faces*. Here, the hero's journey is also a rite of passage. Campbell writes, "A hero ventures forth from the world of common day into a region of supernatural wonder: fabulous forces are there encountered and a decisive victory is won: the hero comes back from this mysterious adventure with the power to bestow boons on his fellow man" (Joseph Campbell, *The Hero with a Thousand Faces* [Princeton: Princeton University Press, 1968], 30). On this subject and *Buffy* see Lynne Edwards, "Slaying in Black and White: Kendra as Tragic Mulatta in *Buffy*," in *Fighting the Forces: What's at Stake in "Buffy the Vampire Slayer?,"* ed. Rhonda V. Wilcox and David Lavery (Lanham, MD: Rowman & Littlefield, 2002), 85–97, and the chapter "Pain as Bright as Steel: Mythic Striving and Light as Pain," in Rhonda V. Wilcox, *Why Buffy Matters: The Art of Buffy the Vampire Slayer* (New York: I. B Tauris, 2005), 30–45.

11. Bobby Alexander, "Ritual and Current Studies of Ritual: Overview," in *Anthropology of Religion: A Handbook*, ed. Stephen D. Glazier (Westport, CT: Greenwood Press, 1997), 139.

12. David Torevell, *Losing the Sacred: Ritual, Modernity and Liturgical Reform* (Edinburgh: T & T Clark, 2000), 32.

13. Slaying is Buffy's birthright (or birth*rite*), a sacred duty that is closely governed, scripted and prepared for. Slaying is the physical practice of Slayer and Watcher culture. Klaus-Peter Köpping, Bernard Leistle and Michael Rudolph write that ritual is a way of making culture real; it transfers it to the physical world (Klaus-Peter Köpping, Bernard Leistle and Michael Rudolph, introduction to *Ritual and Identity: Performative Practices as Effective Transformations of Social Reality*, ed. Klaus-Peter Köpping, Bernard Leistle and Michael Rudolph [Berlin: Lit Verlag, 2006], 21). Buffy and Giles achieve a similar transformation through their actions, researching, preparing, and in battle, giving form to Council and Slayer ideology, history and tradition.

14. Turner, *From Ritual to Theatre,* 24.

15. Mircea Eliade, *The Sacred and the Profane: The Nature of Religion*, trans. Willard R. Trask (London: Harcourt Brace, 1987), 68–69.

16. A list of examples of ritually re-actualized past and Otherworldly spaces used to achieve transformation in *Buffy* would fill multiple pages. Various spells conjured by the likes of Giles, Anya, Amy, and Willow achieve this, tapping into older, and Otherworldly, forces. The ritual summoning the First Slayer to help Buffy defeat Adam is a powerful example ("Primeval" 4.21). Sacrifices (usually of the blood variety) re-actualize older rites and events to find benefit from the Otherworldly (e.g., "Reptile Boy" 2.5). Other rituals also help manifest the Otherworldly to achieve transformation in an individual, as adherents of the First Evil attempt to do when they try to call back Angelus in "Amends" (3.10).

17. "Welcome to the Hellmouth," *Buffy the Vampire Slayer* 1.1, DVD, written by Joss Whedon, directed by Charles Martin Smith (2001: Twentieth Century Fox, 2001).

18. "I Robot … You Jane," *Buffy the Vampire Slayer* 1.8, DVD, written by Ashley

Gable and Thomas A. Swyden, directed by Stephen Posey (2001: Twentieth Century Fox, 2001).

19. The school prom (referred to by Buffy as an "end of high school rite of passage thingy" in "The Prom" 3.20); first sexual experiences ("Surprise" 2.13 and "Innocence" 2.14); career day ("What's My Line, Part One and Two" 2.9 and 2.10); dating (in almost every episode); and the SATs ("Band Candy" 3.6) all come under scrutiny as rites of passage.

20. "Band Candy," *Buffy the Vampire Slayer* 3.6, DVD, written by Jane Espenson, directed by Michael Lange (2001: Twentieth Century Fox, 2001).

21. Joss Whedon, quoted in Candace Havens, *Joss Whedon: The Genius Behind Buffy* (Dallas: Banbella Books, 2003), 33. That high school is hell is an established metaphor in Buffy. In particular see Tracy Little, "High School Is Hell: Metaphor Made Literal in *Buffy the Vampire Slayer*," in *Buffy the Vampire Slayer and Philosophy: Fear and Trembling in Sunnydale*, ed. James South (Chicago: Open Court, 2003).

22. "Graduation Day Part 2," *Buffy the Vampire Slayer* 3.22, DVD, written by Joss Whedon, directed by Joss Whedon (2001: Twentieth Century Fox, 2001).

23. Giles's role as parent/advisor/teacher/Watcher during the seven seasons of *Buffy* goes beyond high school advice. It allows the Otherworldly guidance of Willow, assisting her transformation into a witch. His later support for Anya, which includes giving her work at the magic shop, aids a rite of passage, which moves the individual in the other direction, from Otherworldly space into American (or human) space, transforming Anya, and restoring her humanity.

24. "The Dark Age," *Buffy the Vampire Slayer* 2.8, DVD, written by Dean Batali and Rob Des Hotel, directed by Bruce Seth Green (2001: Twentieth Century Fox, 2001).

25. "The Harvest," *Buffy the Vampire Slayer* 1.2, DVD, written by Joss Whedon, directed by John T. Kretchmer (2001: Twentieth Century Fox, 2001).

26. *Ibid.*

27. "I Robot ... You Jane," *Buffy the Vampire Slayer* 1.8, DVD, written by Ashley Gable and Thomas A. Swyden, directed by Stephen Posey (2001: Twentieth Century Fox, 2001).

28. *Ibid.*

29. *Ibid.*

30. "Some Assembly Required," *Buffy the Vampire Slayer* 2.2, DVD, written by Ty King, directed by Bruce Seth Green (1997: Twentieth Century Fox, 2001).

31. "School Hard," *Buffy the Vampire Slayer* 2.3, DVD, written by David Greenwalt, directed by John T. Kretchmer (2001: Twentieth Century Fox, 2001).

32. Interestingly, 1066, the year of the Battle of Hastings, is itself a threshold event for England. The Norman conquest of England, with its defeat of its Anglo-Saxon rulers in this battle, was a *transition* for the nation that utterly transformed England's society and culture. The implication is that Giles is yet to change.

33. "The Dark Age," *Buffy the Vampire Slayer* 2.8, DVD, written by Bean Batali and Rob Des Hotel, directed by Bruce Seth Green (2001: Twentieth Century Fox, 2001).

34. "Inca Mummy Girl," *Buffy the Vampire Slayer* 2.4, DVD, written by Matt Kiene and Joe Reinkemeyer, directed by Ellen S. Pressman (2001: Twentieth Century Fox 2001).

35. "Halloween," *Buffy the Vampire Slayer* 2.6, DVD, written by Carl Ellsworth, directed by Bruce Seth Green (2001: Twentieth Century Fox 2001).

36. *Ibid.*

37. "The Dark Age," *Buffy the Vampire Slayer* 2.8, DVD, written by Dean Batali

and Rob Des Hotel, directed by Bruce Seth Green (2001: Twentieth Century Fox, 2001).

38. "Halloween," *Buffy the Vampire Slayer* 2.6, DVD, written by Carl Ellsworth, directed by Bruce Seth Green (2001: Twentieth Century Fox, 2001).

39. "Innocence," *Buffy the Vampire Slayer* 2.14, DVD, written by Joss Whedon, directed by Joss Whedon (2001: Twentieth Century Fox, 2001).

40. Editors' note: As will be discussed in a later essay in this collection, the term "gypsy" is seen as a derogatory slur for the Roma. However, given that characters in the show repeatedly use the term, including Jenny herself, its inclusion here is warranted. Please see Katia McClain's essay in this collection for a thorough explanation of the slur's history and its usage on *Buffy* and *Angel*.

41. "Helpless," *Buffy the Vampire Slayer* 3.12. DVD, written by David Fury, directed by James A. Contner (2001: Twentieth Century Fox, 2001).

42. *Buffy the Vampire Slayer*, "Helpless," 3.12.

43. The First Slayer, named Sineya is endowed with her power by three shamans (The "Shadow Men"), who chain her to the floor, and force her power and position upon her, in a kind of mystical rape. The forced rites of the "Cruciamentum" can be read as a reflection of this early rite first creating the Slayer, revealing the forced nature of the Slayer's position, and the male-centered brutality that first creates, and later governs it. The "Cruciamentum" is then another re-actualization, but of a more sinister kind.

44. The *Buffy*verse reverses traditional Christian storytelling by presenting a new origin myth, where the world began as hell, where demons ruled. Humankind did not fall; they ascended, throwing off the rule of hell to allow the earth to develop. However, similar to Christian mythology, demons continue to walk the earth in the *Buffy*verse, working towards the demise of earth and humankind.

45. Reference to this traditional test is also made in *Angel*, where Wesley Wyndham-Pryce (Watcher in *Buffy*, later working for Angel, in *Angel*) is regressed by magic to his teenage self being trained as a Watcher. This younger Wesley tells of rumors of a rite, a "secret gauntlet that only the most cunning can survive," where you are locked in a house with a vampire and must survive. He adds, "It's been done in the past with Slayers" ("Spin the Bottle" 4.6, *Angel: Special Collectors Set* [CA: Twentieth Century Fox, 1999–2004], DVD release 2006). All further references to *Angel* refer to the *Special Collectors Set* and appear in parenthesis in the text.

46. "Helpless *Buffy the Vampire Slayer* 3.12, DVD, written by David Fury, directed by James A. Contner (2001: Twentieth Century Fox, 2001).

47. *Ibid.*

48. "Revelations," *Buffy the Vampire Slayer* 3.7, DVD, written by Doug Petrie, directed by James A. Contner (2001: Twentieth Century Fox, 2001).

49. *Buffy the Vampire Slayer*, "Helpless," 3.12.

50. Like Giles, Wesley also goes through a transformation from English stereotype to a darker and more complex character. His journey/rite of passage is taken in *Angel*, where he is allowed to evolve from foolish, pompous comic relief into a melancholy warrior. In *Angel* he too, like Giles, represents England. For example, Charles Gunn identifies him with his cultural origin, naming him "English," ("Blood Money" 2.12), just as Jenny had called Giles "England" in *Buffy*.

51. "Graduation Day Part 2," *Buffy the Vampire Slayer* 3.22, DVD, written by Joss Whedon, directed by Joss Whedon (2001: Twentieth Century Fox, 2001).

52. "Graduation Day Part 1," *Buffy the Vampire Slayer* 3.21, DVD, written by Joss Whedon, directed by Joss Whedon (2001: Twentieth Century Fox, 2001).

53. *Ibid.*

54. In later seasons, England and Englishness continue as an origin, a source of knowledge, but their position to govern is removed. Offering a sanctified space in Season Seven for Willow's recovery, we are presented with green and pleasant lands, tinged with mysticism—not England, but an English space that is looked for today on the tourist trail, a country's persona reinvented after the collapse of empire into a place of history and heritage.

55. Editors' note: more information on Elgar can be found at http://www.elgar.org/3pomp-a.htm.

56. "Checkpoint," *Buffy the Vampire Slayer* 5.12, DVD, written by Doug Petrie and Jane Espenson, directed by Nick Marck (2001: Twentieth Century Fox, 2001).

57. "Checkpoint," *Buffy the Vampire Slayer* 5.12.

58. *Ibid.*

59. "The Gift," *Buffy the Vampire Slayer* 5.22, DVD, written by Joss Whedon, directed by Joss Whedon (2001: Twentieth Century Fox, 2001).

60. *Ibid.*

61. *Ibid.*

62. René Girard, *Violence and the Sacred*, trans. Patrick Gregory (Baltimore: Johns Hopkins University Press, 1979), 40.

63. Moments before the Council's destruction, Travers stands in the chambers speaking of the fight against the First, claiming "We are still masters of our fate, and still captains of our souls" ("Never Leave Me" 7.9). Travers' words are in reference to the poem "Invictus" (1875) by English poet William Ernest Henley (1849–1903). "Invictus" is Latin for "unconquerable." The work is a poem of Empire, but has come to stand for ideas of freedom over the years. Travers' use of it moments before the Council's demise is nicely ironic, but also suitable as a battle cry, and again reminds us of old England, and the British Empire, upon which it was said the sun would never set.

64. "Lies My Parents Told Me," *Buffy the Vampire Slayer* 7.17, DVD, written by David Fury and Drew Goddard, directed by David Fury (2001: Twentieth Century Fox, 2001).

65. "The Killer in Me," *Buffy the Vampire Slayer* 7.13, DVD, written by Drew Greenberg, directed by David Solomon (2001: Twentieth Century Fox, 2001).

66. Melanie Wilson, "She Believes in Me: Angel, Spike, and Redemption," in *Buffy Meets the Academy* (Jefferson, NC: McFarland, 2009), 137.

67. *Buffy* and *Angel* revel in the use of origin flashbacks, showing us Old World Europe and the siring of many of the vampire characters there. We see Angel's siring by Darla, and Angel's siring of Drusilla. It is a way for the show to tell numerous backstories, setting the scene for modern events, but also continues the show's repeated concerns with origins and how characters and events develop from them.

68. With Whedon's exploration of other characters' origins, we begin to realize that many of the villains of the show are not originally evil. The Mayor was once human, and loved his wife; Angelus was once a man, as was Adam. The name "Adam" alludes to questions of origin (as does the power of the First Slayer called upon to defeat him in "Primeval" (4.21), and a fall from paradise—a descent from perfection. It is perfection Adam seeks to re-attain, misguidedly—as many of the villains do—in a super-nature and immortality. Spike's own search (though initially one centered around immortality) reveals his vampire nature to be a moment of *transition*—an in-between point of becoming, as it is for Angel—another rite of passage to be negotiated, leading to point where he replaces Giles.

69. Wilson, "She Believes in Me," in *Buffy Meets the Academy*, ed. Durand (Jefferson, NC: McFarland, 2009), 145.

70. David George, "On Origins: Behind the Rituals," *Performance Research: A Journal of Performing Arts*, 3, 3 (1998), 12.

71. Turner, 24.

72. Alan Morinis, introduction to *Sacred Journeys: The Anthropology of Pilgrimage*, ed. Alan Morinis (Westport, CT: Greenwood Press, 1992), 2.

73. John Eade and Michael J. Sallnow, introduction to *Contesting the Sacred: The Anthropology of Christian Pilgrimage*, ed. John Eade and Michael J. Sallnow (Urbana: University of Illinois Press, 2000), 17, 21.

74. "Grave," *Buffy the Vampire Slayer* 6.22, DVD, written by David Fury, directed by James A. Contner (2001: Twentieth Century Fox, 2001).

75. Nikki Stafford, *Bite Me! An Unofficial Guide to the World of Buffy the Vampire Slayer* (Toronto: ECW Press, 2002), 75. It is interesting to note that when reading for the part of Spike, James Masters first read the role with an American Southern accent, not English (Stafford, *Bite Me!*, 75).

76. "Becoming Part 2," *Buffy the Vampire Slayer* 2.22, DVD, written by Joss Whedon, directed by Joss Whedon (2001: Twentieth Century Fox, 2001).

77. Spike's accent also plays a part in the development of his character. In flashback scenes that show the still-human Spike (William) we hear his posh English accent ("Fool for Love" 5.7); later, as a vampire, Spike deliberately turns this to a more "common" and rough cockney (5.7), seemingly to reflect his new depraved nature. Giles' reversion to his younger self, Ripper ("Band Candy" 3.6), makes for an interesting comparison, as we hear Giles' darker self with an affected cockney accent. Spike's accent becomes a sign of his evolution (for Giles it is a sign of regression) alongside his vampiric transformation, though it is mocked by Angel, and later by Cordelia who refers to Spike, in *Angel*, as the "little cockney" ("In the Dark" 1.3), so again coloring an English space as a comedic space, allowing it to mediate and lighten the tone of the darker side of transformation (that cockney also seems to designate) when American, English and Otherworldly spaces intersect.

78. "Lovers Walk," *Buffy the Vampire Slayer* 3.8, DVD, written by Dan Vebber, directed by David Semel (2001: Twentieth Century Fox, 2001).

79. "The Harsh Light of Day," *Buffy the Vampire Slayer* 4.3 DVD, written by Jane Espenson, directed by James A. Contner (2001: Twentieth Century Fox, 2001).

80. "Something Blue," *Buffy the Vampire Slayer* 4.9, DVD, written by Tracey Forbes, directed by Nick Marck (2001: Twentieth Century Fox, 2001).

81. "Restless," *Buffy the Vampire Slayer* 4.22, DVD, written by Joss Whedon, directed by Joss Whedon (2001: Twentieth Century Fox, 2001).

82. "Tabla Rasa," *Buffy the Vampire Slayer* 6.8, DVD, written by Rebecca Rand Krshner, directed by David Grossman (2001: Twentieth Century Fox, 2001).

She's White and They Are History

Buffy the Vampire Slayer's *Racialization of the Past and Present*

NELLY STREHLAU

The past, the present and the future collide forcefully in the mythology and in the aesthetic of *Buffy the Vampire Slayer*. After the show began airing in March 1997, its protagonist soon became an icon of a new femininity, which can variously be described as third-wave feminist, Californian, commercial and, above all, modern.[1] While a character like Buffy Summers may not have been possible without earlier portrayals of action heroines such as *Alien*'s Ripley or *The Terminator*'s Sarah Connor,[2] at the same time, her youthful modernity taps into the 1990s zeitgeist romanticizing portrayals of commodified femininity that so popularized *Sex and the City* in following years.[3] Combining fashion consciousness with athleticism, self-confidence with disregard for any notion of "destiny" and girliness with a hip vernacular, *Buffy* was clearly meant to appeal to the relatively young audiences of The WB by being believably current. Concurrently, the contemporariness of Buffy's world is far from uniform, inhabited as it is by ancient powers and mythical creatures which (and sometimes whom) Buffy fights with the help of magic spells spoken in Latin (though definitely not by *her*) and weaponry ranging from the iconic pointy stick to a rocket launcher. In fact, as Susan Owen describes it in her 1999 essay, "[m]ost of the series' humor derives from the (sometimes contrived) irony of postmodern teens dealing with premodern monsters."[4] However, even as the show allowed Buffy to be powerful and feminine at the same time, it was notably "problematic [in its] politics of racial representation."[5] One facet of this at times less-than-perfect track record lies, as this essay aims to show, in the association drawn between characters of color and the past.

This essay contends that *Buffy*'s racial politics are significantly connected with the show's portrayal of the past and the future, as whiteness comes to signify the present and the future, whereas the past can be seen as associated with non-white ethnicities. In order to illustrate this point, the initial part of this essay discusses the politics of the imagined past on the show and how *Buffy* constructs the past as a source of danger connoting female powerlessness, as well as proposes that Buffy and her friends are, by contrast, associated with modernity as a milieu in which women can be powerful and successful. By comparing this with the portrayal of Slayers played by actresses of color, as well as discussing the appearances of those antagonists of the week who are non-white and anachronistic at the same time, I illustrate my hypothesis about the racialization of the past and the present. I follow this with an overview of European characters to conclude by reflecting on the significance of the patterns of racialization traceable in Buffy.

Negotiating Modernity: Buffy and the Gang

Modernity can most broadly be used to understand the historical period after the Middle Ages, or, as the sociologist Anthony Giddens puts it, to signify "modern society or industrial civilization."[6] As such, modernity is associated with a dynamic, post-traditional society, dominated by market forces, and with the rising importance of individualism, as opposed to religion. Furthermore, when it comes to interpersonal relationships, Giddens associates modernity with friendships and sexually-based ties, as opposed to the kinship ties occupying a central role in pre-modern societies.[7]

Within the narrative of *Buffy the Vampire Slayer* a similar opposition between modernity and pre-modernity can be traced. Buffy's identity as an exceptionally successful Slayer is linked to the contrast between her archaic occupation and up-to-date personality, a conflict that also translates into the generation gap between her and her humorously old-fashioned father figure, Giles. The duties and expectations arising from Slayerdom are far from compatible with the modern world for a number of reasons, ranging from the toll they impose on Buffy's schoolwork and social life, to the difficulty she experiences when attempting to explain them to the scientifically-minded Initiative, and to the preferably silent obedience the Watchers' Council requires from the Slayer. Pre-modernity and the past signify tradition, religion and hierarchy, which in turn can be connected to patriarchal oppression.[8] Modernity, in turn, connotes adaptability and modification, rationalization (demanding explanations rather than believing in established rules), as well as friendship and individualism. Within the show, markers of modernity, or simply contemporariness, can also be seen in clothing styles and language use.[9]

Perhaps the most prevalent indications of Buffy's contemporariness as a heroine for the late 1990s and early 2000s come from her fashion sense. As Leigh Clemons describes in her essay dedicated to the semiotics of fashion in *Buffy*, the clothing choices of the costume designers for the series aimed "to keep a clear focus on the show's contemporary feel."[10] This is particularly true of the protagonist's attire in the early seasons, where the short skirts and fitted tops serve to emphasize both her youth and trendiness. Buffy, as a hip young woman, embraces trends and change, as her varied hairstyles and fashionable make-up attest. In fact, her awareness of trends sets her apart from the monsters she fights and often proves useful on patrol, as in the first episode of the series ("Welcome to the Hellmouth," 1.1), when Buffy identifies a vampire in the crowd not due to some special Slayer sense, as Giles would expect, but because of his clothing.[11] As Clemons notes, this is a fairly regular occurrence on the show, with vampires typically choosing distinct clothing styles, most of which are characterized as far from modern.[12] Furthermore, in her analysis, Clemons suggests that what distinguishes Buffy's fashion sense is the "adaptability" of her attires: Buffy typically wears clothing that is both comfortable and trendy.[13]

Another marker of Buffy's contemporariness can be seen in the speech patterns she shares with her friends. Their language constitutes a conspicuous slang, peppered as it is with phrases and pop-cultural references, some of which the Slayer and Scoobies presumably coin.[14] Rather than cling to traditional forms and functions, Buffy chooses to modify speech and clothing to make them more useful to her as resources, signaling her very modern approach to change and fluidity. Buffy's ingenuity in the face of supernatural danger strongly shows her adaptability; when tradition would have Buffy resort to the stake (or at least to a sword), her adaptability enables her to make innovative use of weapons, from her unusual use of holy water in "Helpless" (3.12), to the modern technology of the rocket launcher in "Innocence" (2.14).[15] The latter situation, in particular, shows Buffy's ability to deal with a crisis caused by an ancient problem, as summed up in the irreverent approach to tradition contained in her final words to the Judge: "That was then. This is now."[16] Finally, Buffy is willing to destroy the established order if she perceives it to be oppressive. In her speech in "Chosen" (7.22), when she states, "I say we change the rule,"[17] she continues remaking the Slayer system she has always rebelled against, from enjoying friends and family whereas most Slayers don't, to surviving prophecies proclaiming her demise, as in Season One's "Prophecy Girl" (1.12).[18]

The characterization of Buffy's closest friends often emphasizes their contemporariness. Even though Willow Rosenberg is initially shown dressed in old-fashioned, childish clothing, serving to illustrate her shyness and lack of social skills, she is at the same time a nerd whose impressive computer skills almost overshadow her bookishness. Frequently her proficiency with technology gives an advantage to her and her friends, reinforcing the privileged position occupied by modernity within the narrative. Xander, in turn, represents modern rather than traditional masculinity, being in touch with his emotions and upwardly mobile in terms of his social class.[19] Furthermore, it is his contemporary pop-cultural interest in comic books and science-fiction which serves him as a source of textual references, situating him as relatable to the presumably similarly "fannish" audience. Thus, Buffy's core group of friends is doubtlessly predominantly associated with the present, and grounds Buffy's own association with it. Such a connection is essential for Buffy not only in that it makes her recognizable to the viewers as their contemporary, but also as it proves to be a valuable resource. While in "What's My Line Part 2" (2.12) she claims that "her emotions" (which are therein associated with her friends) constitute the source of her power, nevertheless, the same claim can be made for her up-to-date identity, to which her friendships contribute.[20] This can be seen for instance in "Restless" (4.22), where Buffy's dream quest to find and protect her friends is at odds with the Slayer ethos, embodied by Sineya—and it is Buffy who prevails in the arising conflict.[21]

This young and modern Slayer, however, performs a distinctly old-fashioned job, entangled in a variety of traditions frequently proving to be counter-productive rather than helpful to her. The juxtaposition of late Twentieth and early Twenty-First Century life and the function of the Slayer is brought to the forefront in a number of episodes.[22] Furthermore, in this binary opposition modernity comes to be associated with emancipation and female empowerment, whereas history and tradition appear to be largely construed as a source of danger as well as being the time/tool of patriarchal oppression. The Season Three episode "Helpless" (3.12) may represent one of the clearest examples of this trend.[23] The narrative shows Giles facing the dilemma of either betraying Buffy's trust, or refusing to participate in the long-established rite of passage, which supposedly constitutes an important part of the Slayer lore. Giles, at least initially, lets himself be persuaded that the cruel ritual of Cruciamentum will eventually prove beneficial to Buffy. His decision to participate, while eventually reversed when he runs to Buffy's aid despite orders not to do so, nevertheless can be seen as contributing to him being characterized as attached to tradition and the past. The heroine herself, however, has less trust in what she, presumably alongside the viewers, perceives as a dated and oppressive institution. Buffy's subsequent announcement in "Graduation Day Part 1" (3.21) that she will no longer operate under the supervision of the Watchers' Council is mirrored by her estrangement from her own father. The rejection of convention translates into embracing feminine independence through the choice of friends over familial ties.[24] A similar situation of Buffy's refusing to allow the past to shape her destiny and define her identity occurs in "Restless" (4.22) when the protagonist faces the wrath of her Slayer ancestress. The First Slayer, Sineya, attempts to impress on Buffy the impossibility of sharing her burden with anyone, by naming Buffy a "killer" and trying to deprive her of her friends. To this Buffy responds with a monologue about the passage of time and the changes it has brought to the Slayer's life, exclaiming that "[she doesn't] sleep on a bed of bones" and that the First Slayer is "not the source of [her]."[25] This, once again, frames the juxtaposition between Buffy and previous Slayers in terms of progress, where Buffy's independence is explicitly linked with her rejection of tradition and presented as an advantageous characteristic.

While Buffy's modern mentality allows her to survive dangers previous Slayers did not manage to withstand, the past returns as a source of danger and as a time of female powerlessness on a number of occasions. This tendency to portray the past as a source of women's disempowerment can be illustrated for instance by the events of the Season Two episode "Halloween" (2.6), when Buffy attempts to make herself more attractive to Angel by donning historical attire, and a spell causes her to revert to the persona she is pretending to be.[26] Wearing an "18th century gown" of a European aristocrat, not only does Buffy become unable to defend herself from Spike, but she also presumes that others will protect her.[27] Buffy's semi-nostalgic restaging of the past through costume may have been intended as light-hearted fun. Nevertheless, it results in her temporary incapacitation, lending credence to the conclusion that the past oppresses women in the narrative, and that it is unwise, or even censurable, to forget that.

Furthermore, even when the connection to women's oppression is absent, when the past returns in *Buffy's* Sunnydale, it is usually associated with danger, as an analysis of the series' villains may attest. Although in Seasons Four and Six Buffy faces down technological enemies clearly associated with progress-gone-awry, all other "Big Bads" possess a clear connection to the past. The Master is an exceptionally old vampire, Angelus constitutes Angel's historical identity, Mayor Wilkins has ruled Sunnydale from its inception, Glorificus, despite her rather modern attire, is a primordial "hellgod" with faux-Middle Ages acolytes, and the First Evil boasts of being even older than the ancient Slayer line. Furthermore, one can notice that within the politics of the show, a character's acceptance of progress and change is frequently associated with redemption. Admittedly, a few contrary examples can be listed here, most notably associated with the Season Four and Six Big Bads, but also with Glory, who is ambiguously associated with the present through characterization, as she delights in both modern conveniences and the past through other narrative signals, such as the rituals she engages in, the aforementioned worshippers, and her mythological origins.[28] Nevertheless, such a pattern can, for instance, be detected when it comes to Anya, who is discussed in more detail later in the essay. Finally, in the case of Angel, not only is his current persona presented more positively than the soulless Angelus, whose association with the past is emphasized in the Latinate name alone, but also than that of Angel's past human identity, Liam.

Is the Future Whiter Than the Past?

If an analysis of modernity in *Buffy* reveals that the show constructs the past as dangerous and disempowering for women (in contrast to the present's association with progress and women's emancipation), then viewing this construct through the lens of ethnicity reveals a more problematic relation between the past and the present. *Buffy* can be seen to racialize this binary opposition, as the following discussion demonstrates, both through presenting a number of villains of color whose primary association is with the past, and by conflating historical gender inequality with non-whiteness.

The racialization of the opposition between the past and the future is far from a new concept, and in fact has long been present in anthropological discourse as well as in speculative fiction. Following now outdated nineteenth-century scientific beliefs concerning evolution, the field of anthropology often conceptualizes the difference between the presumably white scientists and the dehumanized objects of their inquiry in terms of an "anachronism, an incongruous co-habitation of the same moment by people ... from different times."[29] This racist rhetoric presenting people of color as belonging to earlier stages of human development is to an extent mirrored by neo-colonialist discourse of progress and human rights. As Chandra Talpade Mohanty surmises, the distinction made within some feminist scholarship between the theoretical constructions of Western and non–Western femininity operates on the basis of an implicit, simplistic opposition between an "average Third World woman [leading a life] based on her feminine gender (read: sexually constrained ... ignorant, poor, uneducated, tradition bound ... victimized, etc.)" and a "self-representation of Western women as educated, as modern, [and possessing] the freedom to make their own decisions."[30] In the model of thinking Mohanty criticizes, African, Asian and particularly Muslim cultures are depicted as oppressive towards women and thus "reactionary" in comparison to Western cultures, which are supposedly supportive of "liberated" femininities, thereby using the axes of gender to deem "Third World" ethnicities inferior. As Carolyn Pedwell demonstrates by critiquing feminist scholarship which equates "Muslim veiling and so-called Western fashion and beauty practices," such an analogy requires separation of axes of oppression and prioritizes gender-based ones, inadvertently erasing ethnicity as a factor to be considered.[31] While the aim of these texts is presumably to underline the continuity of gender oppression across cultures, they also reenact a problematic colonial dynamic valuing Western over non–Western cultures. Such a hierarchy of oppression, so defined, can likewise be seen in *Buffy the Vampire Slayer*, where gender oppression is explicitly problematized, as the narrative shows all the Slayers suffering from the same gender oppression, even as it narratively associates non-whiteness with the past and disempowerment, resulting in problematic portrayals of ethnicity on the show.

Firstly, the characters who are played by persons of color seem to be frequently associated with the past in its dangerous and oppressive aspect. Admittedly, such a correlation is far from universally consistent throughout the show, since characters such as Mr. Trick in Season Three or Robin Wood (to an extent, given the significance of his parentage) in the final season are portrayed as predominantly modern. The former, in fact, appears to be a vampire particularly well-adapted to the contemporary world, even going so far as to use the phrase "modern vampire" in self-reference.[32] The latter, in turn, is at first chiefly characterized by his relative youth for someone occupying the position of school principal. Wood's association with the present is accentuated by his appearance, including an ear piercing, as well as by his romantic associations (first, briefly, with Buffy, and subsequently with Faith). Nevertheless, even his character has marked ties that figure him as a signifier of the past when it comes to the history of Slayerdom, as he is unable to come to terms with the tragic death of his mother, a Slayer killed by Spike. Instead of moving on, in "Lies My Parents Told Me" (7.17) Wood unsuccessfully attempts to avenge his mother, almost resulting in his exclusion from the group led by Buffy.[33] Therefore, even though Spike is the older of the two characters, and the one aesthetically aligned with the past, characterization suggests that Robin Wood is the one facing greater difficulty in adapting to the changing situation and living in the present.

Nevertheless, other, more marginal characters likewise contribute to the link between the oppressive past and characters of color in a more direct manner. In the Thanksgiving episode "Pangs" (4.8), the colonial past returns to haunt the present in the form of Hus, a Chumash ghost awakened when construction work uncovers the ruins of an old mission building.[34] While the writing may suggest an effort to be culturally sensitive, as the characters themselves appear largely conflicted about the ethics of fighting the vengeful ghost, the result is an egregiously stereotypical portrayal of a Native American warrior, signifying not only the past, but a colonial past in the form imagined by the white majority, at that.[35] This encounter is particularly telling when it comes to the narrative depiction of Native Americans as belonging to the American past rather than present, considering the scarcity of indigenous characters on the show.

In fact, the only other episode of the show to feature a storyline related to indigenous characters takes place in Season Two. The main villain of the episode, while sympathetic to an extent, is nevertheless Othered on a variety of narrative levels (even should her gender be removed from the equation). Ampata, from whom the episode derives its title, is an "Inca Mummy Girl" (2.4), and her non-white, "immigrant" ethnicity is strictly bound up in her relegation to the past.[36] As a "monster of the week" in television idiom, Ampata occupies a similar position to that of Hus due to the fact that she is primarily dangerous by reason of being temporally displaced. She does not belong in the present, and the violence she perpetrates and affects is committed as she attempts to survive in an alien world. Unlike Hus, whose only aim was seemingly to enact revenge on the modern world, Ampata makes some attempts to fit into Sunnydale society, which prove to be unsuccessful, as she can only survive by harming others. Also unlike Hus, Ampata has a second function in the storyline; namely, she acts as a foil for Buffy in her sacrificial capacity. Like the Slayers, the Incan princess was supposedly sacrificed for the good of her people, and thus her appearance associates the past not only with a source of danger but also with women's lack of power. Through analogy, this character of color showcases the outdated nature of Buffy's occupation, even as she allows the current Slayer to seem more modern on the individual level. While Ampata only attempts to blend in among the contemporary teens by using borrowed clothes and make-up, Buffy is empowered and emancipated in her femininity. Ultimately, despite her redemption, the character of Ampata returns to the past from which she emerged, leaving Sunnydale all but unchanged, much like the unambiguously villainous Kakistos or The Master.

A number of other characters played by women of color serve as warnings or foils for Buffy within the narrative of the history of the Slayer line. In fact, it is only in the Season Seven finale that white Slayers other than Buffy and Faith are introduced into the narrative of the television series. Before that, the show features two initially nameless Slayers killed by Spike, namely, Nikki Wood and Xin Rong. Both of them are non-white, as is the First Slayer, Sineya. Furthermore, both of them are given very little narrative space, achieving relevance to the plot primarily because of their deaths. In a mythological/narratological sense, they constitute Buffy's ancestresses, passing on to her their inheritance of Slayer power and self-sacrifice, which is inextricably bound with this legacy. Buffy, whose ethnicity can in fact be seen as prominently emphasized through her appearance and relative privilege, not only succeeds them, but also succeeds where they did not, due to learning from their mistakes.[37] While they were both killed by Spike, Buffy retains an advantage over him, as well as survives a number of powerful foes.

Admittedly, this sequence of power, originating from African men and passed from the Asian and black Slayers to the more successful white one is by no means as simple as the racist images of ethnic "evolution," wherein the development of humans has typically been traced from hairy, dark-skinned figures to modern European ones. In fact, Buffy herself is followed in the Slayer line by Kendra, whose ethnicity or nationality is never explicitly discussed, but who is doubtlessly as non–American as she is non-white.[38] However, while Kendra is the Slayer called after Buffy's first death, and thus her successor, she can be seen as a return to the kind of Slayer that existed before Buffy, and that Buffy has worked to modify and modernize: alienated from her family and friendless, dedicated solely to her calling, obedient, and dependent on her Watcher. Remarkably, Kendra herself, in turn, is followed by Faith, who is both white and decidedly more current in her portrayal.

What constitutes a particularly troubling aspect of Kendra's characterization in the series is how close she comes to a number of racist stereotypes. She has been analyzed as a "tragic Mulatta" figure, or a "fiery.... Islander"; however, in this analysis particular attention is to be paid to her being constituted as Buffy's *disempowered* and *outdated* foil.[39] Kendra embodies a number of the aforementioned characteristics listed by Mohanty regarding the construct of an "average Third World woman" as envisioned by the feminist theory Mohanty criticizes.[40] Owning only the one shirt she is wearing, unable to speak to boys, somewhat disoriented in the American surroundings and unquestioningly obedient to her Watcher, Kendra is supposed to be the perfect Slayer, following the rulebook Buffy has never seen but that Kendra has all but memorized. This characterization of Kendra serves to highlight Buffy's individualistic and nonconformist nature, however, it does so by making the darker-skinned Slayer an Other. While both Buffy and Kendra are presented as oppressed by the same structure of domination, namely, the patriarchal Watchers' Council, it is Kendra who internalizes the oppression and Buffy who attempts to "liberate" her. Thus, it is the American Slayer who offers Kendra aid and advice, trying to teach her how to be more independent as it could prove to be essential in her Slayer duties. As Buffy explains to Kendra, emotions and the support system of her friends and her boyfriend, Angel, are sources of strength to her rather than disadvantages, whereas following the Watchers' orders unquestioningly can put their lives in danger.[41] This independence is clearly articulated as related to Buffy's modernity: Kendra's outlook, in comparison, seems outdated and tradition-bound. The importance of modern disobedience is clearly emphasized by the narrative. While Kendra directly suggests that Buffy's unwillingness to follow orders may have been the reason for her death in Season One, it is precisely obedience that ultimately results in Kendra's death at Drusilla's hands. Unlike Buffy, who has managed to withstand vampire hypnotic abilities in "Prophecy Girl" (1.12), Kendra is unable to resist Drusilla's will and ultimately succumbs to the vampire's magic, becoming defenseless and thus sharing the fate of all (non-white) Slayers before her (2.21).[42]

The last Slayer played by an actress of color to be discussed here is the very first one, referred to variously as "Sineya" and "the First of the Ones" in the episode "Primeval" (4.21) and, disturbingly, as "the Primitive" in the *Angel* episode "Damage" (5.11).[43] Created by the group of black shamans in a ritual strongly evocative of both demonic possession and rape, the First Slayer's very humanity seems to be questioned, as the power she has gained is related to the demonic element she now carries.[44] Furthermore, she is predominantly wordless; in "Restless" (4.22), she needs a medium in order to communicate with Buffy, since she can hardly speak, and when she finally does, her speech consists of awkward, short and simple utterances, unlike that of Buffy, who is, in fact, able to use speech as her weapon, for instance to distract her opponents or to threaten them.[45] The contrast between Sineya's negatively-perceived traditionality and Buffy's progressive modernity can also be seen through their repective guardians, the shamans and the Watchers' Council—and Giles.[46] While the former two embody the history of patriarchal oppression, Giles, with Buffy's help, seems to evolve towards modernity, especially in Seasons Four and Five, following his expulsion from the Watchers' Council.

Finally, it bears reflection that the First Slayer functions as an ambiguous figure not only in regard to her humanity, but also due to her internalization of the structure of domination. Sineya poses direct danger to Buffy and her friends in "Restless" (4.22) when she threatens them with death due to what she perceives as an inappropriate relationship between a Slayer and "civilians"; tradition-bound, she cannot abide the Slayer having friends and a life of her own.[47] What is more, the advice she gives Buffy in "Intervention" (5.18), is for Buffy to be self-destructive. Although the protagonist's choice to save her sister's life by sacrificing her own may be noble, the death wish Buffy denied having in "Fool for Love" (5.7) ultimately appears to constitute a sanctioned part of being a Slayer, embraced by the First Slayer and now by Buffy, resulting in her (second) death.[48] It is precisely when Buffy ultimately rejects the remnants of the past, represented by the shamans and Watchers' Council, by revolutionizing the very institution of Slayerdom that being a Slayer becomes a communal experience rather than an individual burden.[49]

Accordingly, it is not only the characters of color who encounter oppression within the structures of patriarchal domination. Within the show's narrative, the problematized violence as associated with the dangerous past is also perpetrated against Native Americans, women of color, and Slayers in particular; furthermore, in the last case, the continuity and similarity of oppression appears to be emphasized.[50] However, among those groups, it is white Slayers who are shown in the privileged position of successfully tackling the oppression they experience and of affecting a change due to their progressive / modern attitudes and methods. While white Slayers in general, and Buffy in particular, come to be associated with revolution and empowerment, Slayers of color as well as villains of color remain oppressed and disempowered by the past they cannot escape.

However, it is only when those examples are viewed alongside the portrayal of other characters associated with the past or with difficulty adjusting to modernity, namely the main vampire characters and the two Watchers, Rupert Giles and Wesley Wyndam-Pryce, that we can fully see the manner in which the narrative conducts a racialization of the past.

From the "Old World" Toward Contemporariness

Being from Europe (and especially being English) also seems to be connected with being "stuck in the past" or at least with having one's roots in it. The two major vampire characters, Angel and Spike, are both connected with the past not only due to their nature as traditional Gothic literary monsters, but also quite literally, as the former was born in the Eighteenth, and the latter in the Nineteenth Century. Similarly, Darla and Drusilla are connoted as belonging to a bygone era not only directly, but also through their clothing styles, which can be age-inappropriate (for instance Darla's school uniform) or which resemble period clothing (such as Drusilla's gowns). Furthermore, while Buffy's modernity was emphasized by her use of modern, witty language, Drusilla's poetic, semi-incoherent speech can be perceived as dated. Nevertheless, these vampire characters survive for a long time on *Buffy the Vampire Slayer*, and both Spike and Darla go on to appear in *Angel*, perhaps due to their ability to pass for contemporary characters. Angel in particular, since he is the most positively portrayed, appears capable of blending into the culture of the 1990s and 2000s, due to his neutral clothing and an American accent. Furthermore, although Darla's backstory as a prostitute dying from a venereal disease might point to the aforementioned oppressiveness of the past as it concerns females, and while Drusilla suffers because of the historical prejudice against her supernatural ability, in the course of the series they both appear mostly capable of standing up to the patriarchal sources of oppression, unlike the female characters of color.[51] Despite the fact that Darla is at times forced to do The Master's bidding, she is portrayed as an independent character with her own mind and opinions. Drusilla, despite being portrayed as mentally unstable, can also survive on her own and is in fact the one vampire Buffy never manages to defeat. The relative independence and empowerment of Darla and Drusilla's past-ness, when compared to the disempowered and outdated characterization of the characters of color, shows us that white female characters in the series appear to find it easier to adjust to modernity and are less oppressed by their connection with the past, reinforcing the racialization of history.

The Watchers constitute another group whose depiction connects them to the past. However, their relationship with it is not completely stable. While the institution of the Watchers' Council is doubtlessly associated with tradition and oppression, the same is not necessarily true for Giles and Wesley as individual characters. As immigrants from "the Old World," they have their customs mocked, as their mannerisms and overly formal clothing situate them as belonging to older generations not fully adjusted to the 1990s and 2000s reality of American life. Already in "The Harvest" (1.2) Giles is shown expressing his distrust of computers, referring to one as a "dread machine," only to have Buffy welcome him "to the New World."[52] Nevertheless, both their character arcs involve gradual modernization in terms of clothing, speech and association with oppressive patriarchal organizations.

In Wesley such a transformation commences on *Buffy* to continue on *Angel*, where it often proves to be a difficult if not traumatic process. However, it is clearly already begun when he aids Buffy in the finale of Season Three. Giles, in turn, initially becomes disassociated from the Watchers' Council in the aftermath of the Cruciamentum in "Helpless" (3.12).[53] His supposed Americanization, referenced by Gwendolyn Post in "Revelations" (3.7), coincides with his clothing and behavior becoming more up-to-date, and culminates with him renouncing the patriarchal institution and recognizing the value of Buffy's more modern approach to Slayerdom.[54]

Also portrayed as related to the past is Jenny Calendar, Giles's first romantic interest. Although she is initially contrasted with Giles through her association with modernity (due to her computer skills and attitude), the past is likewise present in her characterization (predominantly through witchcraft). Nevertheless, when the narrative strengthens her association with the latter, it does so at the same time as her identity as a Romani woman is revealed with the appearance of her uncle, Enyos. The legacy of her ethnicity connects her to the past (as she is obliged to carry out a revenge promised to Angelus by her ancestors), as well as disempowers her; although it is the source of her magic, it also limits her use of it, enforcing her obedience to family, and more particularly, to its male representative, the aforementioned uncle.[55]

Anya, the last European character to be discussed here, has an association with the past and the present that can be considered one of the most multifaceted. When she first appears on the show in Season Three, it is as the demon Anyanka, under the guise of Anya, a high school student. Anya is coded as current to the point of being able to convince Cordelia, a supposedly astute judge of style, that she possesses a relevant fashion sense. In

"The Wish" (3.9), Anya's ability to pass for a modern teenager, wearing inconspicuous clothing and speaking without a foreign or dated accent, seems rather indisputable.[56] However, in the very same episode her identity as an ancient vengeance demon is revealed. As Anyanka, the character's primary association is clearly with the past, as established through flashbacks and through her involvement with an oppressive patriarchal institution, since, being a vengeance demon, she works for D'Hoffryn, whose "employees" are all women, and who exerts absolute power over them.[57] Nonetheless, despite her much-emphasized idiosyncrasies, such as her comically literal speech pattern, Anya is associated with the present through her adaptability and ability to change: for instance, while flashbacks show her to be an enthusiast for Bolsheviks, her current values are strictly capitalist. This ability may be seen to contribute to her ultimately being able to break away from patriarchal institutions and oppression. Following "Selfless" (7.5), she is neither a vengeance demon, nor does she base her identity on her relationship with Xander, as was the case earlier in the series.[58]

Racializing the Present/Past Binary, Whitewashing the Future

More could doubtless be said for instance about Willow, or the female Guardians introduced towards the end of the show, who constitute a unique positive force related to the Slayers and associated with the past. Nevertheless, the manner in which *Buffy* associates the past with characters of color and the present with those who read as white reveals that nationalities other than American and races other than white frequently, if not almost exclusively, connote a connection with tradition and history, which are marked by female powerlessness and gendered oppression, and exist as sources of predominantly supernatural danger. By pinpointing the multiple ways in which the show illustrates characters' connections with modernity/tradition/history, as well as the connotations carried by the past in the narrative, we can see arising a disturbing tendency that connects being modern, white, and American with being better equipped to survive, even as it connects Slayers and characters of color to a past aligned with gendered oppression.[59] Furthermore, while Buffy herself doubtlessly experiences and recognizes institutionalized sexism in the very form of the institution of the Watchers' Council and even the Slayer occupation itself, her recognition thereof is connected with her appropriating a messianic role in relation to other Slayers, who are predominantly women of color. Unlike them, she is presented as capable of subverting power structures, largely due to her modern and, therefore, independent personality. It can be concluded that it is the Othering of women of color as oppressed and unable to successfully negotiate their positions in the power structures (an Othering which is contingent on the prioritizing of gender over other systems of domination) that allows Buffy to assume the role of the ultimate subversive figure.

NOTES

1. For a detailed discussion of the application of the term "third-wave feminist" to *Buffy*, please see Patricia Pender, "'Kicking ass is comfort food': Buffy as Third Wave Feminist Icon," in *Third Wave Feminism: A Critical Exploration*, eds. Stacy Gillis, Gillian Howie and Rebecca Munford (New York: Palgrave Macmillan, 2004).

2. Gallardo Ximena C. and Jason Smith, *Alien Woman. The Making of Lt. Ellen Ripley* (New York: Continuum, 2004), 4. For examples of the analysis of the *Alien* franchise protagonist, Ripley, as a feminist icon, consult Gallardo and Jason Smith's *Alien Woman* or Elizabeth Hills' article "From 'Figurative Males' to Action Heroines: Further Thoughts on Active Women in the Cinema" *Screen* 40.1 (1999): 38–50. For examples of analysis of Sarah Connor from *Terminator* as a feminist icon, see Yvonne Tasker, *Spectacular Bodies. Gender, Genre and the Action Cinema* (London: Routledge, 1993).

3. For an analysis of the discourse surrounding *Sex and the City*, see for instance Angela McRobbie, "Young Women and Consumer Culture: An Intervention," *Cultural Studies* 22 (2008): 531–550, where she discusses the notion of "commodity feminism."

4. Susan A Owen, "*Buffy the Vampire Slayer*: Vampires, Postmodernity, And Postfeminism," *Journal of Popular Film and televIsion* 27.2 (1999): 24–25.

5. Patricia Pender, "'Kicking ass is comfort food,'" 164.

6. Anthony Giddens and Christopher Pierson, *Conversations with Anthony Giddens. Making Sense of Modernity* (Cambrige: Polity Press, 1998), 94.

7. Anthony Giddens, *The Consequences of Modernity* (Cambridge: Polity Press, 1990), 102 (Table 1).

8. Gidden in *The Consequences of Modernity*, 102, lists religion and tradition as particularly important for pre-modernity. Interestingly, he also makes an argument concerning reflexivity and self-reflexivity in modernity, which could likely be applied quite well to discussing *Buffy the Vampire Slayer* and its modern and postmodern features, however, it would likely require a separate essay to do so.

9. Contemporary and modern are used interchangeably in the essay. A distinction could be made between the two, as well as between modernity and postmodernity, however, its importance is negligible for the purpose of this argument. Arguably, adaptability and modification, which I go on to associate with modernity, could be more readily linked with postmodern culture.

10. Leigh Clemons, "Real Vampires Don't Wear Shorts: The Aesthetics of Fashion in Buffy the Vampire Slayer," *Slayage: The Journal of the Whedon Studies Association* 22 (2006), http://slayageonline.com/essays/slayage22/Clemons.htm, paragraph 9.

11. "Welcome to the Hellmouth," *Buffy the Vampire Slayer* 1.1, DVD, written by Joss Whedon, directed by Charles Martin Smith (1997: Twentieth Century Fox, 2008).

12. Clemons, "Real Vampires," paragraph 10.

13. Clemons, "Real Vampires," paragraph 14.

14. Michael Adams "Beyond Slayer Slang: Pragmatics, Discourse, and Style in *Buffy the Vampire Slayer*," *Slayage: The Journal of the Whedon Studies Association* 20 (2006), http://slayageonline.com/PDF/Adams.pdf.

15. "Helpless," *Buffy the Vampire Slayer* 3.12, DVD, written by David Fury, directed by James Contner (1999: Twentieth Century Fox, 2008); "Innocence," *Buffy the Vampire Slayer* 2.14, DVD, written by Joss Whedon, directed by Joss Whedon (1998, Twentieth Century Fox, 2008).

16. *Buffy*, "Innocence," 2.14.

17. "Chosen," *Buffy the Vampire Slayer* 7.22, DVD, written by Joss Whedon, directed by Joss Whedon (2003: Twentieth Century Fox, 2008).

18. "Prophecy Girl," *Buffy the Vampire Slayer* 1.12, DVD, written by Joss Whedon, directed by Joss Whedon (1997: Twentieth Century Fox, 2008).

19. For a detailed analysis of Xander Harris's plotline as an example of a story about achieving maturity, see Lorna Jowett, *Sex and the Slayer: A Gender Studies Primer for the Buffy Fan* (Middleton, CT: Wesleyan University Press, 2005), 134–144.

20. "What's My Line Part 2," *Buffy the Vampire Slayer* 2.10, DVD, written by Marti Noxon, directed by David Semel (1997: Twentieth Century Fox, 2008).

21. "Restless," *Buffy the Vampire Slayer* 4.22, DVD, written by Joss Whedon, directed by Joss Whedon (2000: Twentieth Century Fox, 2008).

22. Compare, e.g., "Bad Eggs," *Buffy the Vampire Slayer* 2.12, DVD, written by Marti Noxon, directed by David Greenwalt (1998: Twentieth Century Fox, 2008), where Buffy's family trip to the mall is interrupted by Slayer duties, or "The Freshman," *Buffy the Vampire Slayer* 4.1, DVD, written by Joss Whedon, directed by Joss Whedon (1999: Twentieth Century Fox, 2008), where Buffy must reconcile being a Slayer with going to college.

23. *Buffy*, "Helpless," 3.12.

24. "Graduation Day Part 1," *Buffy the Vampire Slayer* 3.21, DVD, written and directed by Joss Whedon (1999: Twentieth Century Fox, 2008).

25. *Buffy*, "Restless," 4.22.

26. "Halloween," *Buffy the Vampire Slayer* 2.6, DVD, written by Carl Ellsworth, directed by Bruce Seth Green (1997 Mutant Enemy/Kuzui Enterprises Incorporated in association with 20th Century Fox, 2008).

27. Clemons, "Real Vampires," paragraph 23.

28. Another essay could perhaps be written addressing the association between religion and time within the *Buffy* narrative, considering the large number of religious rituals that take on negative associations on the show, including Glory as well as Caleb or even the Master. A more detailed discussion on religion in *Buffy* can be found in *Faith and Choice in the Works of Joss Whedon*, edited by K. Dale Koontz (Jefferson, NC: McFarland, 2008).

29. John Rieder, *Colonialism and the Emergence of Science Fiction* (Middleton, CT: Wesleyan University Press, 2008), 5.

30. Chandra Talpade Mohanty, *Feminism without Borders: Decolonizing Theory, Practicing Solidarity* (Durham: Duke University Press, 2004), 22.

31. Carolyn Pedwell "The Limits of Cross-Cultural Analogy: Muslim Veiling and 'Western' Fashion and Beauty Practices" in *New Femininities: Postfeminism, Neoliberalism and Subjectivity*, eds. Rosalind Gill and Christina Scharff (Houndmills, Basingstoke, Hampshire: Palgrave Macmillan, 2011), 188; 192; 197.

32. "Faith, Hope and Trick," *Buffy the Vampire Slayer* 3.3, DVD, written by David Greenwalt, directed by James Contner (1998: Twentieth Century Fox, 2008).

33. "Lies My Parents Told Me," *Buffy the Vampire Slayer* 7.17, DVD, written by David Fury and Drew Goddard, directed by David Fury (2003: Twentieth Century Fox, 2008).

34. "Pangs," *Buffy the Vampire Slayer* 4.8, DVD, written by Jane Espenson, directed by James Contner (1999: Twentieth Century Fox, 2008).

35. For a more detailed discussion of the "Pangs" episode, see for instance Sally Emmons-Featherston, "Is That Stereotype Dead? Working with and Against 'Western' Stereotypes in Buffy," in *The Truth of Buffy: Essays on Fiction Illuminating Reality*, ed. Emily Dial-Driver, 55–66.

36. "Inca Mummy Girl," *Buffy the Vampire Slayer* 2.4, DVD, written by Matt Kiene and Joe Reinkemeyer, directed by Ellen Pressman (1997: Twentieth Century Fox, 2008). To call Ampata's presence in the United States "immigration" may be somewhat paradoxical, as the episode reinforces Ampata's foreignness by having her be mistaken for an "exchange student."

37. Irene Karras, "The Third Wave's Final Girl: Buffy the Vampire Slayer," *thirdspace: a journal of feminist theory & culture* 1.2 (2002), http://www.thirdspace.ca/index.php/journal/article/view/karras/50.

38. Consult, e.g., Monique Scott, *Rethinking Evolution in the Museum. Envisioning African Origins* (New York: Routledge, 2007), particularly chapter 3 "Revisiting Victorian Progress" for a discussion of the "march of progress" imagery and for suggestions for further reading.

39. Lynne Edwards, "Slaying in Black and White: Kendra as Tragic Mulatta in *Buffy*," in *Fighting the Forces: What's at Stake in "Buffy the Vampire Slayer*," eds. Rhonda V. Wilcox and David Lavery (Lanham, MD: Rowman & Littlefield, 2002), 85–97; Elyce Rae Helford, "'My emotions give me power': The Containment of Girls' Anger in *Buffy*," in *Fighting the Forces*, eds. Wilcox and Lavery, 28.

40. To reiterate, according to Chandra Talpade Mohanty, the "average Third World woman" is portrayed as "sexually constrained ... ignorant, poor, uneducated, tradition bound ... [and] victimized," *Feminism without Borders*, 22.

41. "What's My Line Part 2," *Buffy the Vampire Slayer* 2.10, DVD, written by Marti Noxon, directed by David Semel (1997: Twentieth Century Fox, 2008).

42. "Prophecy Girl," *Buffy the Vampire Slayer* 1.12; "Becoming part 1," *Buffy the Vampire Slayer* 2.21, DVD, written and directed by Joss Whedon (1998: Twentieth Fox, 2008).

43. "Primeval," *Buffy the Vampire Slayer* 4.21, DVD, written by David Fury, directed by James A. Contner (2000: Twentieth Century Fox, 2008); "Damage," *Angel* 5.11, DVD, written by Steven S. DeKnight and Drew Goddard, directed by Jefferson Kibbee (2004: Twentieth Century Fox 2007).

44. Rhonda V. Wilcox, *Why Buffy Matters: The Art of Buffy the Vampire Slayer* (London: I. B. Tauris, 2005), 104.

45. "Restless," *Buffy the Vampire Slayer* 4.22.

46. Other episodes which feature Sineya include also "Intervention," *Buffy the Vampire Slayer* 5.18, DVD, written by Jane Espenson, directed by Michael Gershman (2001 Mutant Enemy/Kuzui Enterprises Incorporated in association with 20th Century Fox, 2008) and "Get It Done," *Buffy the Vampire Slayer* 7.15, DVD, written and directed by Douglas Petrie (2003: Twentieth Century Fox, 2008).

47. *Buffy*, "Restless," 4.22.

48. *Buffy*, "Intervention," 5.18; "Fool for Love," *Buffy the Vampire Slayer* 5.7, DVD, written by Douglas Petrie, directed by Nick Marck (2000 Mutant Enemy/Kuzui Enterprises Incorporated in association with 20th Century Fox, 2008); "The Gift" *Buffy the Vampire Slayer* 5.22, DVD, written and directed by Joss Whedon (2001: Twentieth Century Fox, 2008).

49. *Buffy*, "Chosen," 7.22.

50. Compare for instance *Buffy* "Get It Done" 7.15, where Buffy undergoes a trial similar to the demonic rape of Sineya—with a vastly different outcome, due to her independence and ability to stand up for herself.

51. This subject deserves a more detailed analysis; however, it bears noting that while self-sufficiency of both Darla and Drusilla appears to be somewhat disputable in the light of their (co-)dependent relationships with Angel and Spike, their contemporariness and arguable liberation is emphasized by sexual agency and the ultimatums posed by them when their vampire partners fail to meet their expectations by acquiring a conscience and falling in love with the Slayer, respectively.

52. "The Harvest," Buffy the Vampire Slayer 1.2, DVD, written by Joss Whedon, directed by Charles Martin Smith (1997: Twentieth Fox, 2008).

53. *Buffy,* "Helpless," 3.12.

54. "Revelations," *Buffy the Vampire Slayer* 3.7, DVD, written by Douglas Petrie, directed by James A. Contner (1998: Twentieth Century Fox, 2008). Admittedly, Giles may be perceived to retain a connection to the past which is reaffirmed by his return to the United Kingdom, and which for him constitutes a source of power rather than disempowerment, as his use of magic in Season Six attests. Nevertheless, following his first expulsion from the Watchers' Council, he is shown to be capable of modifying and modernizing the past, which showcases his adaptability and reinforces a tie with the present.

55. In fact, Enyos explicitly contrasts their Romani clan with "modern man" on the subject of vengeance in "Innocence" (2.14).

56. "The Wish," *Buffy the Vampire Slayer* 3.9, DVD, written by Marti Noxon, directed by David Greenwalt (1998: Twentieth Century Fox, 2008).

57. "Selfless" *Buffy the Vampire Slayer* 7.5, DVD, written by Drew Goddard, directed by David Solomon (2002: Twentieth Century Fox, 2008);

58. *Buffy,* "Selfless," 7.5. Indubitably, Anya dies whether or not she achieves narrative empowerment. However, it seems clear that her narrative arc culminates with her having achieved a degree of self-liberation and re-affirmation of her ability to function in modern times.

59. All other Slayers—including Faith—serve as foils for the protagonist. Nevertheless, it is only Buffy and Faith who, due to their longevity within the show, have their own storylines, with elements separate from their occupation as the Chosen Ones, whereas the non-white Slayers remain defined by their function and, by extension, the oppression they seem to accept.

"Let it simmer"
Tonal Shifts in "Pangs"[1]

Rhonda V. Wilcox

BUFFY: Will, you know how bad I feel about this. It's eating me up—[to Anya:] (a quarter cup of brandy and let it simmer)—but even though it's hard, we have to end this. Yes, he's been wronged. And I personally would be willing to apologize—

SPIKE: Oh, someone put a stake in me.[2]

In his *Buffy Goes Dark* essay "Understanding the Espensode," David Kociemba argues that "what defines a series like *Buffy the Vampire Slayer* is not just the big moments in narrative arcs.... A series is also defined by how it gets to the end of those narrative arcs: by its dialogue, its voices, and its tone."[3] Paying attention to the nuances of a show is an important way to illuminate it and, one hopes, avoid the mistake of bending the evidence to fit a theory. As Douglas Pye says in *Movies and Tone*, "The centrality of tone to our experience of films is indisputable—and, presumably, to our experience of television."[4] In this essay, I want to talk about Jane Espenson's Season Four episode "Pangs" (4.8), and more specifically what we might call the problem of "Pangs." It is unquestionably one of the most controversial episodes of *Buffy*. It is also one of *Buffy* creator Joss Whedon's declared favorites.[5] As Espenson says, "The core of it was something Joss had wanted to do for a long time, which is have a dead Indian at Thanksgiving—a very poetic illustration, I think, that we do kind of live in this country by virtue of some very ugly conquest. And the next thing you know we had a very non-threatening bear and some funny syphilis."[6] The risky complexity of tone is clear in her comment. I want to look at "Pangs" briefly in terms of the big narrative picture for the series, but also to focus on some of the significant specifics of tone. I

108

accept the premise that each viewer will have his or her own experience of the show, and his or her own interpretation; I can't unring the *Buffy* bell you hear in your own mind. Certainly I do not expect in one brief essay to solve the problem of "Pangs" (4.8). However, I will try to make a case that the episode is progressive in its social stance and that this progressive stance is created in part by the episode's effectively nuanced tonal shifts. In fact, I would argue that "Pangs" is an exemplary case of the use of tone in television.

To begin with, let me say that I think the episode has two major jobs to do: one, the presentation of the Indigenous/Native American subject, and two, a shift in the through-story in terms of Buffy's relationship to Angel and her relationship to Spike (not to mention Spike's relationship to the Scoobies as a whole). The first job is by far the one that has received the most critical attention (in all senses of that phrase). The second job is usually commented on more casually. I think, however, that the two of them can be seen as working well together to make the meaning of the episode. As I examine each of them, I will also draw on Jane Espenson's draft versions of the episode, to enhance understanding of the final version by comparing some of the choices available to the writers.[7] It is also worth noting that Espenson reports that Whedon did "extensive rewrites" and that "much of Acts Three and Four are pure Joss, not me."[8,9]

Dominic Alessio, in 2001, sounded the first major note in the debate on "Pangs" (4.8) with his condemnation of the episode as essentially colonialist.[10] In 2003, Gregory Stevenson, in his book *Televised Morality*, acknowledged the controversial nature of "Pangs," emphasizing the importance of seeing the ethical meaning of a series through its long-term narrative, and he argues for "Pangs," saying that while both the colonizers and the indigenous people used violence, Buffy, in his declared Christian view, represents moving on to forgiveness, because of the fact that she and the Scoobies take in both the ex-demon Anya and the vampire Spike—and vampires and demons can represent oppressed, demonized peoples.[11] J. Michael Richardson and J. Douglas Rabb acknowledge Stevenson and further emphasize the fact that *Buffy*, as a television series, will have done a great deal to bring to light the atrocities inflicted on Native Americans by the colonizers—much more than the books that Willow unearths, and that Giles seems to think sufficient to have spread the truth.[12] As viewers may recall, Willow represents concern for the Native Americans; Spike represents an imperialist view; and Giles represents a pragmatic view, while Xander is the representative for syphilis and Buffy is the representative for pie.[13] In contrast to Richardson and Rabb, Jes Battis calls the episode "infamous,"[14] and declares it "a highly misguided and patronizing attempt to discuss cultural relativism within *Buffy*," saying that the "didactic, as well as subversive, value of laughing at what is clearly a tokenized aboriginal history within the all-white-all-the-time universe of Sunnydale is virtually nil."[15] Sally Emmons-Featherston offers more or less the same perspective, also reiterating, with more specific data, Alessio's important point that while the episode presents the Chumash as "exterminated," there are in fact "approximately 3,500 Chumash living across the United States, some still in California."[16] In another of the major analyses, Matthew Pateman notes "Buffy's reluctance to accept Willow's version" of history, and adds that "the show's subtle endorsement of that reluctance persists throughout, despite some excellent writing by Jane Espenson, whose capacity for dialogue-as-debate is very impressive."[17] And while he thinks that the show itself sympathizes with the view that treatment of the indigenous has been "shameful," Pateman argues nonetheless that "the resolution of the episode … is much closer to Philip Sheridan, the infamous nineteenth-century army general, whose comment that 'the only good Indian is a dead Indian' is disturbingly mirrored."[18] Nikki Stafford, on the other hand, states that "Pangs" "lay[s] out both sides of the Thanksgiving debate without ever taking sides."[19] As for Whedon himself, he says that "Pangs" is "to me, among the most radical and potentially offensive and necessary messages we ever played. American History has fictionalized itself, and in an attempt to deconstruct it, we find ourselves repeating it."[20]

I would remind you that the sides of this historical-social debate are not the only source of complexity in "Pangs" (4.8); there is also the personal element. Of course, most *Buffy* episodes contain both social symbolism and personal story: "Pangs" is more overtly on the social issue than most *Buffy* plots, which normally incorporate social symbolism—but we should not underestimate the personal here, especially if we remind ourselves that the personal is political. The unusually discursive presentation of the social issue may be a tribute to the issue's intractability. It may also turn the form on its head, and use the social as symbol of the personal instead of vice versa. For some viewers, both symbolisms will operate simultaneously.

In any case, the complexity of the subject matter is reflected in the complexity of the episode's tone. Every *Buffy* episode is complex in tone, that is part of its art; however, probably none is more complex or displays more instances of tonal shift than does Espenson's "Pangs." There are many different categories of tonal shift. There can be a shift in tone within one character's single speech (as in this essay's epigraph); there can be, for one character, a shift in tone from one speech to another; there can be a shift from one to another character's tone in juxtaposed scenes; and naturally, there can be a shift from one character to another in the same scene. These are categories of tonal shift as expressed through wording of the dialogue and actors' voices, facial expression, and body language, but of course the episode's tone is conveyed not only through conversational discourse but in many other ways as well, such as music and visuals—the non-diegetic and diegetic music and sounds, the mise-en-scène, visual tropes, costumes, and camera work, etc. Other than diegetic music (which is not applicable here), "Pangs" illustrates all of these.

First let us consider a case of clear-cut shift in tone from one character to another within a scene. This shift occurs when the social debate begins to be overtly presented in the scene immediately after the credits. In preface, however, let me note that the teaser, before the credits, touches on both of the two jobs I've mentioned for the episode: Buffy confronts a vampire who asks "Why don't you go back where you came from?" and implicitly connects her with the colonizers and the vampire with Native Americans[21]; and she pauses after dusting him, subconsciously aware that she is being watched by Angel, whom we see hiding as he observes her. Angel and the Indigenous are the two major subjects of the show. More specifically, the two major subjects are Buffy's *attitude* towards the Indigenous and Angel.

But to return to the post-credits scene, the beginning of Act I. The young women of the Scoobies—Buffy, Willow, and the still-peripheral Anya—are watching the University of California–Sunnydale Cultural Partnership Center's groundbreaking, in which Xander participates as a construction worker. The tone of the discourse shifts from speaker to speaker. Dean Guerrero and the Center's curator, Professor Gerhardt, use typically cliché-ridden ceremonial language, the dean referring to his colleague's "dream" and the professor, in explaining the move to a bigger building, saying, "it was like seeing one's child grow up and move on to better things," her use of the third person singular possessive "one's" emphasizing the formality of her language.[22] There is wonderful realism in the difference of tone in the quiet chatter of the audience while the ceremonial discourse proceeds publicly: the thousand-year-old ex-demon Anya, in her usual unadorned directness, tells Buffy, Willow, and viewers, that she is imagining having sex with the hard-hatted Xander, while Buffy and Willow comment on Xander's pre-construction-worker jobs; they focus on their private lives even while observing the ceremony. When Professor Gerhardt praises the "melting pot" (with smiling disregard of any questions about this term), the episode undercuts her formal tone and the official line even further by having a car alarm horn sound repeatedly in the distance as she speaks.[23] Thus the official point of view that failed to acknowledge the damages colonization inflicted on the Chumash and other tribes— that pompously expressed view is already being subtly undercut by its reception on-screen even before Willow more directly challenges it with "What a load of horse hooey!"[24] For the quiet, intellectual Willow, this is particularly abrupt language, expressing anger much more directly than she usually allows herself to do. The newly collegiate Buffy replies with a much more moderate tone, using language more characteristic of Willow: "We have a counterpoint?" she asks. Later in the episode, as she tries to persuade Willow to have Thanksgiving dinner in spite of her reservations, Buffy uses academic language again, citing her psychology professor Maggie Walsh, and referring to "sense memory" to justify what she admits is a desire to return to childhood, to being eight years old, in response to seeing so much change in her life (going to college, losing Angel).[25]

But for now, while the official speaker drones on, Willow's much more informal tone and self-deprecation—acknowledging that she "sounds a little overwrought"—carries much more emotional impact as she reminds us of the "destruction of the indigenous peoples."[26] As for Anya, as Pateman points out, she performs an anthropological function by defining the holiday. It is, she says, "a ritual sacrifice, with pie."[27] This bald description is not only humorous but accurate; her objective tone might make us laugh, but it might also make us look at ourselves from a slightly different, thousand-year-long perspective. In fact, she seems in this moment a more useful anthropologist than the speechifying Professor Gerhardt, perhaps in part because Anya's analytic gaze is directed at the behavior of the majority. The scene's tonal shift from character to character opens the debate in a very real way, making the differences more than didactic.

In spite of my dismay at Professor Gerhardt's linguistic style, I would not wish her dead, though she soon ends up that way. Of course her death is more likely attributable to her position as traditional authority figure than to her discourse; in fact, the characters assert as much. In earlier drafts, Professor Gerhardt even more emphatically represented traditional authority, because she was a he: Espenson created both the dean and professor as males.[28] The male Catholic priest Father Gabriel, representing the religious establishment, also ends up dead—as does Hus, the vengeance spirit of the Chumash, who was in draft versions identified by the characters as a shaman, a priest of an indigenous tradition.[29]

Hus is not only connected to the professor and the priest in his demise; he is also connected to the professor linguistically (the priest never speaks). While the emotional tone of the two characters is quite opposite—the curator complacent, while the vengeance spirit is outraged—nonetheless they are both, one might say, linguistically dead. Sally Emmons-Featherston describes Hus's language as "clipped, simple English."[30] In his first encounter with Buffy, she finds Hus with the dead body of Father Gabriel, cutting off the priest's ear. "You can't stop me," he says, "I am vengeance. I am my people's cry. They call for Hus, for the avenging spirit to carve out justice." "They tell you to start an ear collection?" Buffy replies.[31] Now this reply at first seems to be an example of Buffy's signature wit, and its lively contrast to the pompous language of the Chumash spirit shows to her advantage. Her tone is not only acerbically humorous but also steeped in moral righteousness. But her wit is born of ignorance. Not much later in the episode she learns that the ear-cutting began with the *settlers'* mutilation of the Chumash, as a form of proof of death. Thus Buffy's seeming linguistic dominance is undone; the complacency of her confrontation with Hus was based on mistaken assumptions.

In the earlier drafts of the episode, Espenson also gave Hus a much more human voice and, in fact, a name. She had *his* character present the case about the atrocities in his own words—still impassioned, but in much less stilted language. Huluyanawchet and Buffy have an actual conversation, and among other things he says

> our people were slaughtered! Imprisoned in your Missions [sic], forced into labor. Cut down by the thousands by your diseases. Our lands taken. Our women raped. Our children starved. The men driven to theft. And when we fought back, we tried to take back what was ours ... we ended up like the priest here. Like this seller of lies.[32]

The contrast between the original Hus and Buffy is much less in terms of language and tone; Hus's—or Huluyanawchet's—language and tone are farther from the empty ceremonial statements of the academics, and closer to the voice of our hero. In the broadcast version, the information about atrocities is presented mainly by Willow rather than Hus. This transfer of presentation results in at least two effects. First, Hus seems to be less of a person and more of a symbol—as the story specifies, a spirit rather than a living being; and second, we hear about these atrocities and are likely to think about them through the point of view of one of the Scoobies, someone with whom we as audience members presumably already have an emotional connection. Clearly there are both advantages and disadvantages to this transfer. As Whedon has said, he did not write *Buffy the Lesbian Separatist*—because he wanted to effect change indirectly, not so much through confrontation.[33] Having Willow speak seems in line with this plan. In her essay "'We Don't Say Indian,'" Agnes Curry has voiced her shock at the angry reactions of some who have been denied the comfort of their prejudices.[34] On the other hand, denying Hus his voice—or limiting him to a voice that speaks in a pompous tone—helps explain why critics like Battis call the episode "patronizing."[35] Nonetheless, eventually within the episode, the voice of Hus is shown to have justification and Buffy's flippant mockery of it is very clearly shown to be mistaken, while the similarly pompous academic voices of Gerhardt and Guerrero are never unmocked, so to speak.

The positioning of Hus and the tone of his presentation are also affected by his placement within a visual trope in the episode, a set of variations on thresholds. In "Pangs" (4.8), there are two sets of three instances, the first set relating to windows and the second set relating to doors. As has been noted, the teaser seems to connect vampires with Native Americans—or, more specifically, Buffy's (and some audience members') attitudes to Native Americans, as does the series of window images. Angel, who left Buffy at the end of Season Three, has secretly returned to town because of a prediction that Buffy is in great danger. He is repeatedly shown standing alone outside, looking wistfully in through a window at Buffy. In the first draft he tells Giles, "being a spectator just outside her life is the most painful thing I can imagine."[36] But in the final version his statement is phrased so as to allow for more general application: "To be on the outside looking in at what I can't … yeah, I'd forgotten how bad it feels."[37]

The episode then immediately cuts to the second of the three instances, and perhaps I should say three characters, of the window trope: the vampire Spike. The dynamically vicious Spike is shown reduced to starvation (having been "chipped," rendered harmless, by the secret U.S. military group the Initiative), staring through a dirty window at a vampire version of a Thanksgiving feast, a group of vampires with an older one patting a younger one on the back to offer him a turn at their nice big turkey, a human stretched out on a table. While the tone of this passage could be (and in part is) played for humor, the dinner shot is followed by a close-up of a pathetic expression on actor James Marsters' face accompanied by drippingly sympathetic music. The scene clearly represents the outsider looking in, as identified moments before by Angel in the preceding scene. It is one of many parallels of Spike to Angel, foreshadowing Spike's later role in Buffy's life. But for now it is more obviously a parallel granting sympathy, though in Spike's case, with a touch of gruesome humor. As Espenson describes it in the first draft, the vamp dinner is "a heartwarming domestic scene," and Spike is "a picture of misery and longing."[38]

The third instance of the window trope in "Pangs" (4.8) involves Hus himself, in the incarnation of a coyote. In the first draft, Buffy opens Giles's front door to see a coyote flash by. When Willow suggests it is Hus and Buffy starts to follow it, Spike immediately appears in the doorway.[39] The equation of Hus and Spike is thus quite direct. It is still present, however, in the final version, as Angel, Spike, and Hus form a trio of outsiders, looking in the window. In fact, Hus's part of the window trope amounts to a voiceless conversation. The coyote, unseen by Buffy, Willow, or Giles in the broadcast version, looks in at them through the window while they debate their reaction to Hus. The coyote only stops listening and turns away at the moment when Giles says, "No, I think perhaps we won't help the angry spirit with his rape and pillage and murder."[40] Giles, Buffy, and Willow are voicing the debate, but as Curry says in another context, the visual has "enormous epistemological privilege," and here we share the point of view of the coyote looking in through the window.[41] Giles, Buffy, and Willow are unaware of the coyote's perspective, but we are aware—a fact that I think shifts the tone of the episode, along with Hus's placement in parallel with Angel and Spike—characters who are problematic but in the end worthy of emotional investment.

To return, however, from the visual to the voice: Willow, Buffy, and Giles are not the only characters to voice elements of the debate. As many critics have noted, Spike vividly does so as well. As a British character born in the nineteenth century, he not surprisingly expresses an imperialist colonialist view with emphatic zest: "You won. All right? You came in and you killed them and you took their land. That's what conquering nations do. It's what Caesar did, and he's not going around saying, 'I came, I conquered, I felt really bad about it.' The history of the world isn't people making friends. You had better weapons, and you massacred them."[42] And the other two males in the room agree with him. Spike speaks with the kind of certainty of tone Buffy used in her "ear collection" line. The character of Spike has been given some of the most memorable speeches in the Whedonverses, and this one, while harsh, is unquestionably eloquent. The lucid, verbally controlled, supercilious tone is an absolute contrast to another brief line of Spike's, later in the episode. More than once I have seen an email signature incorporating this quote: "A bear! You made a bear!"[43] Hus has earlier taken the shape of a flight of birds, then a coyote, and in the climactic battle, he becomes a giant grizzly in Giles's living room. Later in the episode, Giles talks about losing control in violence, and Spike comments "that's the fun."[44] Part of the fun of this moment of bear-confrontation is Spike's lack of control linguistically. Here, we do not have condescending eloquence, but instead brief, blurted childlike words and simple syntax. "Undo it! Undo it!" he shouts, and our vampire imperialist no longer seems so smooth.[45] The contrast in the tone of his "Caesar" speech and his bear blurt undermine the political position he has voiced, and his visual correlation with the outsider makes his role in the episode even more complex. Spike reminds us that things are never simple in a Whedon series.

Spike is also part of a second visual trope in "Pangs" (4.8). In addition to the Angel-Spike-Coyote Hus window pattern, there is also a three-part doorway pattern. Buffy has told Giles that, while her mother is away, he must host the Thanksgiving festivities because he is the "patriarch"—a term not used in the earliest drafts, but which emphasizes Giles's alignment with traditional forces—even while serving to let Buffy humorously underscore her recognition of the patterns of the ritual, *and* "stick [Giles] with the clean-up."[46] A magical three times in a row, Buffy the cook and Giles the patriarch open the door upon people who come to participate in the ritual. First comes Willow, who brings a large stack of books topped by a much smaller stack of boxes of frozen peas—in fact, information is her main contribution to the occasion. Next comes Xander (assisted by Anya), dreadfully infected by the mystical venereal disease from the old mission: "You look like death!" says Giles. "You didn't bring rolls?" says Buffy.[47] Last comes Spike, who pathetically says, "Help me" to Buffy, who reaches for a stake. "You haven't murdered anybody lately? Let's be best pals!" Her dismissal of him is just as glib as was her earlier rejection of Hus, though with more justification. But Spike is allowed in when he offers, like Willow, to provide information—though for completely selfish reasons. "I came to you in friendship," he says, and—off Buffy's quizzical glare—"Well, all right, seething hatred."[48] Even the slap on the head she gives him seems strangely casual and intimate—not the tone of body language one would use with a mortal enemy. Spike is being domesticated, and the trio of threshold-crossings brings the point home. Hus, who shared Spike's position in the window trope as outsider looking in, is never invited in through the threshold of the door; instead he breaks in and then is killed. He is never domesticated, and he remains an outsider.

The significant tonal shift from one speech by a character to another by the same character, then, is memorably exemplified by Spike when we move from the debate to the fight scene. But an even more memorable shift comes in the middle of a single speech by a single character. At the height of the debate on how to deal with Hus, Buffy talks with Willow while simultaneously giving Anya cooking directions. When Willow says Hus is just "one lonely guy" (not the only one in this episode)—that he is an "oppressed warrior guy who's just trying to—" and when she pauses, Buffy fills in with "Kill a lot of people?" "I didn't say he was right," concedes Willow; and Buffy launches into her speech: "Will, you know how bad I feel about this. It's eating me up—[to Anya:] (a quarter cup of brandy and let it simmer)—but even though it's hard, we have to end this. Yes, he's been wronged. And I personally would be willing to apologize—" "Oh, someone put a stake in me," Spike injects.[49] This passage is perhaps richest in implication of any in the episode; it is exceptionally illuminating in it use of tonal shift. Pateman also singles it out, saying, "[Buffy's] pragmatic and unconcerned response to the situation is very funnily presented ... the rhetoric of historical concern is wonderfully juxtaposed with the reality of immediate need."[50]

In most ways I agree with Pateman's assessment of the passage, but I quibble with his description of Buffy as "unconcerned," and I would also like to further examine the implications of the passage. Here we have a clear case of a shift in tone within a single speech, and it is the passage which led me to write on this subject. Buffy's remarks in earlier scenes suggest she is genuinely troubled by her confrontation with Hus; she is not just attempting to pacify Willow. To Giles, she has said, "I like my evil like I like my men—evil. You know, straight up, black hat, tied to the train tracks, soon my electro ray will destroy Metropolis bad. Not all mixed up with guilt and the destruction of an indigenous culture."[51] And as Richardson and Rabb point out, this speech emphasizes a visual of costuming that many have noted: Buffy herself is wearing a black cowboy hat in the debate scene during the groundbreaking ceremony.[52] Her confusion about what is wrong suggests that her concern is genuine. But it is ludicrously undercut when she stops to give cooking instructions—right after having said that the Chumash problem is "eating her up," no less.[53] Yes, she does have food on her mind. As Angel says much earlier in the episode (and as most viewers likely notice), she seems "intense about this Thanksgiving thing," and Giles responds that he thinks she is "lonely"— using the same term Willow has applied to Hus.[54] What I am saying here builds on what others have said before, but with a different focus. We are not just talking about pangs of hunger, but pangs of guilt. I think Buffy is truly concerned about the plight of the Chumash and the right way to react to Hus. At the same time, she is desperate for the comforting ritual of the holiday dinner. Consider the brief scene in "The Body" when she either fantasizes or recalls a holiday dinner with all of the Scoobies and her mother, and she and Joyce cut and drop the pie—one could write a whole essay on pie.[55] And as Kociemba reports, Espenson loves writing about food.[56] With Buffy's "quarter cup of brandy" interruption, there is the intrusion of the personal into the political. I would not say that the effect is to make a mockery of concern for the Chumash; instead, it makes a mockery of the speaker, fond of her though many of us may be. The tonal shift suggests not a debasement of the significance of the issue, but a weakness in Buffy—a very human weakness in a person many of us identify with—a weakness in someone who asserts conscientious consideration for the social issue, but who at this moment is more involved in getting dinner than righting wrongs. How many of us can claim to be much different? We may express liberal sympathies (and if you are reading an essay on the Whedonverses, there is a fairly good chance that you express liberal sympathies), but how easy is it to go no farther than words? I believe that kind of weakness, more than anything else, is what is mocked in this passage. When I laugh at that speech, I laugh at myself. And I'm not really happy about it.

At the same time, I think the ritual of the shared dinner is important, and is valorized by the episode. We have to take time to be human, and the ritualized sharing of food is eminently human. It is yet another case of the great Buffy divide—the "Vampire Slayer" versus the Buffy. She is strong because she is both—human and hero. So while I laugh at the tonal shift of this speech, while I feel excruciating embarrassment for her failure to recognize the conjunction of the two different tones, I am nonetheless touched by her human weakness. And in fact, as many have noted, throughout the episode there are similar passages in which Buffy retreats from the pain of a seemingly insoluble ethical question (how to respond to Hus) and the pain of her lonely life by immersing herself in batter. Or cranberries. This is simply the passage in which the tonal shift is most marked.

And so we return to the personal, ever a part of the political. Many of the nuances of tonal shift suggest that the Scoobies' response to the Chumash situation is problematic (which suggests that the episode's response is less so). The tonal shift involved in the second major subject of the episode, the Angel / Buffy relationship (or, if you prefer, the Angel / Buffy / Spike relationship) is indirectly connected to the social subject in the broadcast version, and more directly connected in earlier drafts. Angel disappears when Hus disappears—though in many other ways they are far from equivalent. Recall that in worrying about the justice in Hus's motivation (the "I like my evil" speech), Buffy compares Hus to her "men."[57] But after all, Angel is Buffy's undead beloved, and Hus is the vengeance spirit of the dead Chumash.[58] Hus is largely presented as an enemy or a problem, not someone with whom Buffy enters into a real relationship—though Xander inadvertently reminds us of the parallel between the vengeance spirit Hus and Xander's vengeance demon girlfriend Anya—who also points out that automatically slaying either of them without thought is wrong. But as for Buffy's boyfriend, or former boyfriend, for her he seems mainly to be a part of the personal life that Buffy so desperately wants and finds so hard to maintain. Yet he has returned to Sunnydale only to secretly help in part of her Slayer life—the attack by Hus and the dead fighters he calls up.[59] Nonetheless, the tone of Angel's presentation focuses mainly on personal emotion. And the tone gradually shifts from the beginning of the episode to the end. "Pangs" (4.8) was broadcast immediately before "Something Blue," (4.9) the hilarious episode in which Willow unwittingly bespells Spike and Buffy to plan a wedding.[60] In terms of the big narrative picture, the serious tone of the Buffy / Angel relationship moves in "Pangs" to a middle ground of humor for both the Buffy / Angel and the Buffy / Spike relationship; then the Buffy / Spike relationship gradually, over years, moves to a more serious tone.

As for the tonal shift from the serious to the humorous for Buffy and Angel in "Pangs," the episode begins with Angel in the dark—where we so often find him—watching Buffy without her knowledge—as he so often does.[61] He is hidden in the foliage nearby as Buffy fights the vampire who tells her to go back where she came from, and poignant music plays the scene out. The significance of their relationship is reemphasized by the fact that Buffy seems to somehow recognize that she is being watched—as she does repeatedly during the episode when he watches her. Her awareness lessens the suggestion of weakness on her part and heightens the suggestion of connection. Not only the knowledge of their past, but also Angel's face in the dark, the music, and Buffy's reaction contribute to the seriousness of the tone.

As the episode proceeds, the tone varies. In Angel's discussion with Giles, he voices his sadness at the separation from Buffy and, as already noted, the window trope adds to that effect. But along with the repeated visual imagery, we have a running joke about Angel: "You're evil again!" Willow accuses, as he grabs her in the Espresso Pump.[62] His repeated denials put salt in the emotional recipe of the episode. By the time he leaves, the sad music goes with him. And then there is the very last shot.

The last *scene* of "Pangs" has the Scoobies plus Anya and Spike sitting around the Thanksgiving dinner table in Giles's home. In Espenson's earlier version, the dinner has failed, and Spike is eating raw turkey, while the rest of them go hungry.[63] Also in an earlier draft, Espenson has Riley and the other Initiative soldiers note that the "Hostile" (i.e., vampire) needs a pint of blood a week,[64] and in a different scene she has Buffy say that she will get blood from the butcher tomorrow.[65] In the broadcast version, though the pilgrim centerpiece has an arrow through it, the group except for the still-hungry Spike has thoroughly enjoyed their dinner after all. Buffy has throughout the episode referred to this dinner as a way to hold on to the past—her eight-year-old self—and the private scene between Angel and Giles reminds us that she is missing her more recent past as well. Alessio notes that she has also wished to hold on to a more innocent, or perhaps naïve, view of our national past as well.[66] It also seems to be a desire for order and control, and sitting in the disorder of Giles's apartment after the fight, there is still some order as the six of them, including the rope-tied Spike, sit around the table. Repeatedly through the episode, characters have complained that everything seems to be changing. The dinner was Buffy's valiant attempt to hold on to the past. And in the end, Willow, having condemned herself for joining in the violence, now focuses on the comfort: "At least we all worked together; it was like old times." Then comes Xander's addition: "Yeah, especially with Angel being here and everything."[67]

That last shot of the episode that I mentioned occurs at this point. The point of view is Buffy's, and with a Frasier lens we share her sight of all five of the others—Spike with a quiet, knowing smirk (and his face is the largest), Anya looking at Spike, Giles looking down, and Willow and Xander looking guilty. This is the image included for the episode in Nancy Holder's *Watcher's Guide*.[68] The painful humor of the situation is clear, as the image cuts to the credits and we hear Xander's voice say "Oops."[69] So the solemn poignancy of the opening scene's Buffy / Angel tone has shifted to a grimace or a wince. The effect is to leave Buffy seeming vulnerable and very human. The last note of the episode, if I may use a musical metaphor, does not emphasize heroism but personal limitation—a rather likeable impression, in my view.

And it may help console us for her limitations in resolving the social issue as well. In earlier drafts of the episode, Espenson has Buffy frantically hunting for the mate to the little pilgrim man centerpiece; there was also a little pilgrim woman—something from her past, her home: "It's not here—Mom's centerpiece. This little pilgrim couple. I only have Michael. Lisa Marie is missing." "You're joking, right?" says Willow. And Buffy replies, "I named them when I was twelve. I had high hopes for those kids."[70] Many viewers had high hopes for Buffy and Angel, too, but they were just as doomed as Michael Jackson and Lisa Marie Presley. Clearly the separated couple of the centerpieces suggests the separated couple of Buffy and Angel, whose changed relationship is one of the two major subjects of the episode. But Michael and Lisa Marie the pilgrim couple also connect to the idea of the second subject, the colonists versus the Chumash, and remind us of the naiveté of that part of Buffy's world view—and for some of us, by extension, our own. As I hope I've shown in my earlier comments, I believe the broadcast episode also establishes these parallels, but Michael and Lisa Marie may sing out a little more clearly.

"Under-explain," says Jane Espenson in her essay in Stacey Abbott's *Cult TV Book*.[71] This episode certainly qualifies in that regard. "Pangs" is a problem play, not a solution play. The problem of the U.S. past with Native Americans is certainly not sorted out in this 48-minute television show. And the lessened humanity in the depiction of the Chumash Hus does not help, nor does his demise; as Pateman reminds us, citing Frank Kermode by way of David Lavery: endings have heavy weight.[72] But the narrative of "Pangs" (4.8) is more troubling if we do not attend to these touches of tone—conveyed in dialogue, music, and visual patterns. And the *very* ending of the episode, and its tone, remind us of the weakness of our hero. Thus the show as a whole may remind us *why* the problem is not solved. Throughout the episode Buffy is barely, if at all, conscious of the outsiders looking at her through the window. She is caught up in her very human desire for comfort and sustenance, both emotional and physical. She is holding on to a past that was never there. In the last shot she and we are very conscious of those looks that tell us how much we have not known. And if we have paid enough attention to the subtle tonal shifts of "Pangs," it is possible we will come up with a recipe for action outside the episode—if we just let it simmer.

NOTES

1. This essay was first published in *Slayage* 9.1 [33], Spring 2011, and is reprinted here with permission from journal editor and author. An earlier version of this essay was presented as a keynote speech at the fourth biennial *Slayage Conference on the Whedonverses*, Flagler College, St. Augustine, FL, June 3–6, 2010.

2. "Pangs," *Buffy the Vampire Slayer* 4.8, DVD, written by Jane Espenson, directed by Michael Lange (1999: Twentieth Century Fox 2001).

3. David Kochiemba, "Understanding the Espensode," *Buffy Goes Dark: Essays on the Final Two Seasons of Buffy the Vampire Slayer on Television*, ed. Lynne Y. Edwards, Elizabeth L. Rambo, and James B. South (Jefferson, NC: McFarland), 2009. 24.

4. Douglas Pye, "Movies and Tone," *Movies and Tone; Reading Rohmer; Voices in Film*, Ed. John Gibbs and Douglas Pye. Close-Up Series 02 (London: Wallflower Press, 2007), 8.

5. Joss Whedon, "Joss Whedon's Selection of His Favorite *Buffy* Episodes," The Chosen Collection DVD Boxed Set Episode Guide (Beverly Hills: Twentieth Century Fox Home Entertainment, 2005), p. 3.

6. Jane Espenson, "Writing the Vampire Slayer," *Reading the Vampire Slayer: The New, Updated Unofficial Guide to Buffy and Angel,* Ed. Roz Kaveney (London: Tauris Parke, 2004), pp. 111–112.

7. My thanks to Jane Espenson for giving me permission to consult the drafts and to Matthew Pateman for providing me with pdf copies. I was also given the caveat that, among the various drafts, some were mislabeled and/or had missing material, and that there were problems in some cases with material translated ineffectively from one computer program to another. However, as far as I can observe, these problems do not apply to the "Pangs" drafts.

8. Jane Espenson, "Writing the Vampire Slayer," *Reading the Vampire Slayer: The New, Updated Unofficial Guide to Buffy and Angel,* Ed. Roz Kaveney (London: Tauris Parke, 2004), p. 112.

9. My thanks to Doug Rabb and Mike Richardson for reminding me (at SCW4) of Espenson's comments on this matter.

10. Dominic Alessio, "'Things are different now?' A Post-Colonial Analysis of Buffy the Vampire Slayer," *European Legacy,* 6.6 (2001): 731–40.

11. Gregory Stevenson, *Televised Morality: The Case of Buffy the Vampire Slayer* (Dallas: Hamilton Books, 2003).

12. J. Michael Richardson and J. Douglas Rabb, *The Existential Joss Whedon: Evil and Human Freedom in Buffy the Vampire Slayer, Angel, Firefly, and Serenity,* (Jefferson, NC: McFarland, 2007).

13. In "Pangs," Buffy fixates on the Thanksgiving food, and the pie in particular. See Kociemba 34–35 on Espenson's frequent focus on food and its significance; and see further discussion later in this essay. Xander, while working construction, gets a case of mystical syphilis from the old mission where the Chumash were imprisoned and given various illnesses.

14. Jes Battis, *Blood Relations: Chosen Families in Buffy the Vampire Slayer and Angel* (Jefferson, NC: McFarland, 2005), p. 93.

15. *Ibid.,* p. 94.

16. Sally Emmons-Featherston, "Is That Stereotype Dead? Working with and Against 'Western' Stereotypes in Buffy," *The Truth of Buffy: Essays on Fiction Illuminating Reality,* Ed. Emily Dial-Driver et al. (Jefferson, NC: McFarland, 2008), p. 63.

17. Matthew Pateman, *The Aesthetics of Culture in Buffy the Vampire Slayer* (Jefferson, NC: McFarland, 2006), p. 79.

18. *Ibid.,* p. 83.

19. Nikki Stafford, *Bite Me!: An Unofficial Guide to the World of Buffy the Vampire Slayer. Rev. and Updated to Season 6* (Toronto: ECW Press, 2002), p. 269.

20. Joss Whedon, "Joss Whedon's Selection of His Favorite *Buffy* Episodes," The Chosen Collection DVD Boxed Set Episode Guide (Beverly Hills: Twentieth Century Fox Home Entertainment, 2005), p. 3.

21. My thanks to the blind reviewer who commented on the possible implicit insult in the symbolic equivalence of vampires and Native Americans. I hope my revisions have made clearer that (in my view) the symbolism is associated with the problem in Buffy's (and others') attitude, which this episode explores. There is also a history of Whedon scholarship discussing the symbolic equivalence of vampires and various outsider groups. For two of the many divergent views on this subject, see Kent Ono, "To Be a Vampire on Buffy the Vampire Slayer: Race and ('Other') Socially

Marginalizing Positions on Horror TV," *Fantasy Girls: Gender and the New Universe of Science Fiction and Fantasy Television*. Ed. Elyce Helford (Lanham, MD: Rowman & Littlefield, 2000), 163–86, and Mary Alice Money's "The Undemonization of Supporting Characters in Buffy," *Fighting the Forces: What's at Stake in Buffy the Vampire Slayer*. Ed. Rhonda V. Wilcox and David Lavery (Lanham, MD: Rowman & Littlefield, 2002), 98–107. See also Stevenson, as referenced above.

22. "Pangs," Buffy the Vampire Slayer, 4.8, DVD, written by Jane Espenson, directed by Michael Lange (2001: Twentieth Century Fox 2001).

23. The professor's rather surprising apparent ignorance of postcolonial theory allows her to provide viewers an implicit postcolonial lesson.

24. *Ibid.*

25. *Ibid.*

26. "Pangs," *Buffy the Vampire Slayer*, 4.8.

27. Matthew Pateman, *The Aesthetics of Culture in Buffy the Vampire Slayer* (Jefferson, NC: McFarland, 2006), p. 79.

28. Jane Espenson, "'Pangs': Outline." N.d. PDF emailed to Matthew Pateman and forwarded to the author. 4 July 2008. Pp. 3–3.

29. Jane Espenson, "'Pangs': Writer's First Draft." 4 Oct. 1999. PDF emailed to Matthew Pateman and forwarded to the author. 4 July 2008. p. 27; "'Pangs': Writer's Second Draft." 6 Oct. 1999. PDF emailed to Matthew Pateman and forwarded to the author. 4 July 2008, p. 26.

30. Sally Emmons-Featherston, "Is That Stereotype Dead? Working with and Against 'Western' Stereotypes in Buffy," *The Truth of Buffy: Essays on Fiction Illuminating Reality*, Ed. Emily Dial-Driver et al. (Jefferson, NC: McFarland, 2008), p. 59.

31. "Pangs," Buffy the Vampire Slayer, 4.8, DVD, written by Jane Espenson, directed by Michael Lange (2001: Twentieth Century Fox 2001).

32. Jane Espenson, "'Pangs': Writer's First Draft." 4 Oct. 1999. PDF emailed to Matthew Pateman and forwarded to the author. 4 July 2008. Pp. 24–25.

33. Emily Nussbaum, "Must-See Metaphysics," *New York Times*, 9 Sept. 2002, *Joss Whedon: Conversations*. Ed. David Lavery and Cynthia Burkhead (Jackson: University Press of Mississippi, 2011), p. 65.

34. Agnes B. Curry, "'We don't say "Indian"': On the Paradoxical Construction of the Reavers," *Slayage: The Online International Journal of Buffy Studies*, 7.1 (Winter 2008). Special Issue on *Firefly* and *Serenity*. Ed. Rhonda V. Wilcox and Tanya R. Cochran (Web. 20April 2010), note 5.

35. Jes Battis, *Blood Relations: Chosen Families in Buffy the Vampire Slayer and Angel* (Jefferson, NC: McFarland, 2005), p. 94.

36. Jane Espenson, "'Pangs': Writer's First Draft." 4 Oct. 1999. PDF emailed to Matthew Pateman and forwarded to the author. 4 July 2008. p. 18.

37. "Pangs," *Buffy the Vampire Slayer*, 4.8, DVD, written by Jane Espenson, directed by Michael Lange (2001: Twentieth Century Fox 2001).

38. Jane Espenson, " Pangs': Writer's First Draft." 4 Oct. 1999. PDF emailed to Matthew Pateman and forwarded to the author. 4 July 2008. p. 18.

39. *Ibid.*, p. 34.

40. *Ibid.*

41. Agnes B. Curry, "'We don't say "Indian"': On the Paradoxical Construction of the Reavers," *Slayage: The Online International Journal of Buffy Studies*, 7.1 (Winter 2008). Special Issue on *Firefly* and *Serenity*. Ed. Rhonda V. Wilcox and Tanya R. Cochran (Web. 20 April 2010), par. 19.

42. *Buffy the Vampire Slayer*, "Pangs," 4.8.

43. *Ibid.*

44. *Ibid.*

45. *Ibid.*

46. *Ibid.*

47. *Ibid.*

48. *Ibid.*

49. *Ibid.*

50. Matthew Pateman, *The Aesthetics of Culture in Buffy the Vampire Slayer* (Jefferson, NC: McFarland, 2006), p. 80.

51. "Pangs," *Buffy the Vampire Slayer*, 4.8, DVD, written by Jane Espenson, directed by Michael Lange (2001: Twentieth Century Fox 2001).

52. J. Michael Richardson and J. Douglas Rabb, *The Existential Joss Whedon: Evil and Human Freedom in Buffy the Vampire Slayer, Angel, Firefly, and Serenity*, (Jefferson, NC: McFarland, 2007). p. 163.

53. "Pangs," *Buffy the Vampire Slayer*, 4.8, DVD, written by Jane Espenson, directed by Michael Lange (2001: Twentieth Century Fox 2001).

54. *Ibid.*

55. "The Body," *Buffy the Vampire Slayer*, 5.16, DVD, written by Joss Whedon, directed by Joss Whedon (2001: Twentieth Century Fox 2001).

56. David Kochiemba, "Understanding the Espensode," *Buffy Goes Dark: Essays on the Final Two Seasons of Buffy the Vampire Slayer on Television*, Ed. Lynne Y. Edwards, Elizabeth L. Rambo, and James B. South (Jefferson, NC: McFarland), 2009. pp. 34–35.

57. *Buffy the Vampire Slayer*, "Pangs," 4.8.

58. As Emmons-Featherston notes, in the real world the Chumash are by no means all dead.

59. Like Willow in the episode, Alessio points out that the Chumash have been historically peaceful (735).

60. "Something Blue," *Buffy the Vampire Slayer*, 4.9, DVD, written by Tracey Forbes, directed by Nick Marck (2001: Twentieth Century Fox 2001).

61. For a discussion of this pattern in their relationship, see my essay "The Darkness of 'Passion': Visuals and Voiceovers, Sound and Shadow" in *PopMatters* and in *Joss Whedon: The Complete Companion*, ed. Mary Alice Money (London: Titan Books, 2012), 102–112.

62. "Pangs," Buffy the Vampire Slayer, 4.8, DVD, written by Jane Espenson, directed by Michael Lange (2001: Twentieth Century Fox 2001).

63. Jane Espenson, "'Pangs': Outline." N.d. PDF emailed to Matthew Pateman and forwarded to the author. 4 July 2008. P. 11; Jane Espenson, "'Pangs': Writer's First Draft." 4 Oct. 1999. PDF emailed to Matthew Pateman and forwarded to the author. 4 July 2008. Pp. 35–37; Jane Espenson, "'Pangs': Writer's Second Draft." 6 Oct. 1999. PDF emailed to Matthew Pateman and forwarded to the author. 4 July 2008, pp. 35–37.

64. *Ibid.*, Outline p. 9.

65. *Ibid.*, First Draft p. 42; *Ibid.* Second Draft p. 41.

66. Dominic Alessio, "'Things are different now?' A Post-Colonial Analysis of Buffy the Vampire Slayer," *European Legacy*, 6.6 (2001): p. 736.

67. "Pangs," *Buffy the Vampire Slayer*, 4.8, DVD, written by Jane Espenson, directed by Michael Lange (2001: Twentieth Century Fox 2001).

68. Nancy Holder, *Buffy the Vampire Slayer: The Watcher's Guide. Vol. 2* (New York: Pocket Books, 2000, p. 214.

69. "Pangs," Buffy the Vampire Slayer, 4.8.

70. Jane Espenson, "'Pangs': Writer's First Draft." 4 Oct. 1999. PDF emailed to Matthew Pateman and forwarded to the author. 4 July 2008. p. 33. "'Pangs': Writer's Second Draft." 6 Oct. 1999. PDF emailed to Matthew Pateman and forwarded to the author. 4 July 2008, p. 33.

71. Jane Espenson, "Playing Hard to 'Get': How to Write Cult TV," *The Cult TV Book*. Ed. Stacey Abbott (London: I.B. Tauris, 2010), p. 46.

72. Matthew Pateman, *The Aesthetics of Culture in Buffy the Vampire Slayer* (Jefferson, NC: McFarland, 2006), p. 79.

PART II

From *Buffy* to *Angel*

Racial Representation Across Sunnydale and L.A.

Representations of the Roma
in *Buffy* and *Angel*

KATIA McCLAIN

Starting with *Buffy the Vampire Slayer*, the "genre defying/genre bending" Joss Whedon has been praised for creating "cutting edge, subversive television."[1] Whedon's works create worlds where the "categories of good and evil are explicitly and repeatedly dismantled."[2] His programs ask viewers "to interrogate their beliefs and systems of thought while terrifying them, delighting them or breaking their hearts."[3] Despite this characteristic of Whedon's work and its focus on the deconstruction of cultural myths and cinematic conventions, scholars have shown that it is, at times, also "complicit in dominant culture and ideologies."[4]

One area where Whedon's shows have not been able to resist "the internalized forces of the dominant culture" is in their representation of race and ethnicity.[5] Scholars have analyzed Whedon's representation of characters of color and non-majority ethnicities and found them problematic.[6] Their analyses suggest that, in representing race and ethnicity, Whedon's series sometimes reinforce "the very categories of exclusion" that he "seeks to confront elsewhere."[7] Interestingly, the portrayal of the Roma, an ethnicity central to the mythology of the *Buffy/Angel*verse (in which a Romani punishment turns the vampire Angelus into Angel, by giving him a soul), has failed to attract much discussion, even from Whedonverse scholars focusing on race and ethnicity.[8] This essay will examine the treatment of the Roma in *Buffy* and *Angel* to determine whether their representation goes beyond "the age-old stereotypes from the pre-romantic era," found in their earlier literary and cinematic appearances.[9]

Origins

The Roma are a people who originated in northern India, entered Europe at the end of the thirteenth century, and who speak (or are descended from ancestors who spoke) the Romani language.[10] Perceived as having darker complexions than most Europeans, speaking an unfamiliar language and with no local origin, the Roma were seen as an excludable "Other" from almost the first moment that they entered Europe.[11] Their rich and complex culture was ignored as they were treated as pariahs, subjected to restrictive laws in many countries, forced into centuries of slavery in what is now Romania and nearly exterminated by the Nazis during the Holocaust. Many Roma immigrated to the Americas (mainly Argentina and the United States) after the abolishment of slavery in the mid nineteenth century.[12] The prejudice against them found in Europe continued in the United States, where laws specifically targeting the Roma were on the books, in some cases into the 1980s.[13]

The term "Gypsy," historically applied to the Roma by English speakers is both inaccurate (since it is derived from their imagined origin in Egypt) and problematic (because it has accrued a pejorative resonance from the long history of marginalization, persecution and racism to which the Roma have been subjected).[14] The encoding of the inaccurate and racist stereotypes that echo in the name is shown in this definition from the 1828 edition of Noah Webster's *American Dictionary of the English Language*[15]:

> GIP'SEY, n. The Gipseys are a race of vagabonds which infest Europe, Africa and Asia, strolling about and subsisting mostly by theft, robbery and fortune-telling. The name is supposed to be corrupted from Egyptian, as they were thought to have come from Egypt. But their language indicates that they originated in Hindoostan.

It is not surprising, then that many Roma in the United States, ordinary people, scholars and activists alike, are deeply offended by the use of the term, "Gypsy" (hereafter "the inaccurate/problematic term"), because of its long history of disparaging usage.[16] Community members and scholars have worked since the first World Romani Congress in 1971 to encourage media and governmental agencies to replace the inaccurate/problematic term with a word from the Romani language.[17] The term "Roma" was proposed at the World Congress, since it means Romani people in many dialects of the Romani language. It has become the standard term for many in the Romani diaspora, international agencies and Romani Studies scholars. However, although many Romani communities refer to themselves as Roma, some Romani groups had developed local names (Sinti in Germany, Romanichal in the UK, Machwaya in Serbia, Manouche in France, etc.) and are less comfortable with Roma as a general term.[18] A second term, "Romanies," derived from the adjective Romani, used by all groups, has been suggested as way of overcoming the problem, and may replace Roma at some point.[19] In this essay, I will use Roma, since it is the term still most commonly used in both Romani scholarship and activism. The inaccurate/problematic term will only be used in quotations from Whedonverse texts and from other authors.

Representational Tropes

The representations of the Roma, growing out of their historical marginalization and exclusion, were codified in nineteenth century European literature.[20] They fall into two categories. A set of pejorative images associate the Roma with darkness, dirtiness, the occult and supernatural (especially fortune-telling and curses), theft (including the stealing of children), con-artistry (scams), seduction, hot-bloodedness, and vengeance.[21] Because real Roma had often been excluded from towns and cities and forced to live on the margins of developed areas, a second type of pseudo-positive representation was developed. Literary Roma were thought to inhabit an imagined, attractive, pastoral space of wagons and campfires where one could go to escape the drudgery or ordinariness of the urban industrialized world.[22] Representations in this category associate the Roma with carefree, wandering nomadism and colorful music and dance.[23] The imagined Roma look alike, women wearing long skirts, with both men and women wearing scarves and gold earrings.

The representations of the Roma in early American cinema follow this model. D.W. Griffith's first silent short, in 1908, *The Adventures of Dollie*, includes the tropes of child stealing and vengeance by Romani characters.[24] The bulletins provided by the film company, often used verbatim in newspapers, provide synopses of the plot that reinforce the stereotypes.[25] The Roma in *Dollie* are described as "a band of those peripatetic Nomads of the Zingani type, whose ostensible occupation is selling baskets and reed ware, but [whose] real motive is pillage."[26] They are "swarthy" with "black" hearts.[27] A portion of the film takes place in a cinematic Romani camp, complete with campfires and wagons. Griffith's *An Awful Moment*, also from 1908, creates Romani characters that engage in criminality and vengeance.[28] He uses his 1910 film, *What the Daisy Said*, to associate Roma with fortune telling and seduction.[29] Griffith sets two 1911 films featuring stereotypical Romani characters, outside of the United States, in Andalusia and Corsica. *The Spanish Gypsy* features singing, dancing, vengeance and a "hotblooded" character that "loves with extreme ardor" and "can hate just as intensely."[30] *A Romany Tragedy* features vengeance.[31]

Two other early silent films based on nineteenth century literary pieces also helped solidify the representational tropes of the Roma in American popular culture.[32] Cecil B. DeMille's *Carmen* (1915) combines the trope of the seductive, hyper-sexualized Romani woman with that of general Romani criminality.[33] *The Hunchback of Notre-Dame* (1923) has its Romani characters either stealing children or singing and dancing.[34] Unusually, Esmeralda, the main Romani character, is kind and good. This potential challenge to the trope is undercut when it turns out that she is not Romani at all, but has been stolen by the Roma as a baby.[35]

One of the key films codifying imagined Romani culture in the horror film genre is Universal Picture's 1941 film *The Wolf Man*.[36] The Roma are associated with wandering nomadism (they drive colorful wagons and come to town once a year) and the occult (they provide fortune-telling services, and believe in charms and spells and that people can turn into wolves). Their behavior is colorful (violin playing and dancing). They are dressed in colorful pre-modern outfits: swirling skirts, scarves and dangling gold earrings. Most importantly for the reinforcing of cinematic/televisual stereotypes, the film is associated, in the popular imagination, with the trope of vengeance and curses. Modern American viewers often misinterpret the transformation of the human character into a werewolf as an "ancient Gypsy curse," but this is inaccurate, as in the film, the Romani character suffers from the "curse" of being a werewolf.[37]

The tropes remain remarkably stable in American televisual and cinematic culture up to and after *Buffy* and *Angel*. Romani characters carry out their vengeance with curses (Stephen King's 1996 film *Thinner* and Sam Raimi's 2009 *Drag me to Hell*).[38] Disney's 1996 animated remake of *The Hunchback of Notre-Dame* eliminates the child-stealing trope, but Esmeralda still wears a low cut blouse, swirling skirts and a gold earring and goes barefoot throughout the film, even as she dances for money in the streets of Paris.[39] The images of the Roma remain "one of [the] few mysterious, unspoken currencies of cinema, concentrated around identifiable stereotypes."[40]

Language, Names and the Roma in "Angel"(1.7) and "Surprise" (2.13)[41]

The use of names to add texture and meaning to the narrative of the Whedonverse is well known.[42] Sometimes the names are used for humor, as when Buffy attempts to tell Giles the name of the demon Kakistos in Season Three, guessing that his name might be "kissing toast" or "taquitos."[43] At other times, as when an amnesiac Buffy, not knowing that she's the Slayer, still names herself after another powerful woman warrior, Joan of Arc, "Whedon and his company of writers use names very consciously to advance meaning."[44] How do the names chosen by Whedon and his creative team frame the representation of the Roma in the *Buffy/Angel*verse?

In "Angel" (1.7), a crucial episode in the first season of *Buffy,* as Buffy and Angel battle each other at the Bronze, Buffy and the viewers find out about Angel's past as the evil Angelus, replete with a life of killing "with a song in [his] heart."[45] The critical importance of the Roma to the *Buffy/Angel*-verse is also revealed when Angel explains why he changed.[46] Angel explains that he, "fed on a girl about your age … beautiful … dumb as a post … but a favorite among her clan."[47] Buffy doesn't understand what he means, asking, "clan?"[48] To explain, Angel says, "Romani."[49] Buffy's face shows no understanding, and he continues, "Gypsies. The elders conjured the perfect punishment for me. They restored my soul."[50]

What does the use of names in this episode reveal about the representation of the Roma? Unusually for a work of popular culture, *Buffy* first references the Roma with an appropriate word from their language (the feminine adjective "Romani"), rather than the problematic/inaccurate term discussed above. All Roma accept the adjective and "will readily admit to being a Romani person, to speaking the Romani language, and maintaining Romani culture."[51] This appears to be exactly the way Angel uses the word in "Angel" (1.7), as an adjectival modifier for the word clan.[52] By using a name that originates with the Roma, Whedon and his creative team take a step towards avoiding the age-old stereotypes associated with the problematic/inaccurate term. This positive step is at least complicated by Angel's reference to the young Romani woman he killed as "dumb as a post."[53] While not one of the more ugly stereotypes (dirtiness, thievery), it is certainly not a positive or neutral representation.

Unfortunately, Buffy's blank reaction to Angel parallels that of mainstream American society, most of whom have never heard the word Romani. Angel's response to her lack of comprehension is to explain the term by using the popular inaccurate/problematic term. The discussion between Buffy and Angel in "Angel" (1.7) reflects the difficulty in talking about the Romani people in English without introducing names that encode problematic representations.[54] Angel, the older, experienced person of European origin, uses an accurate term—Romani. However, to communicate with Buffy, who, "lives very much in the now," he resorts to the inaccurate/problematic term.[55] Although the focus of this tense scene (where Angel needs to convince Buffy not to kill him) would most likely not allow Angel to enlighten Buffy (and the viewers) about the problem with the pejorative resonance of the inaccurate/problematic name, it might have been possible to include it elsewhere. Giles, Buffy's Watcher, who does the "heavy lifting for the show with all that exposition," could have easily been given one of his many explanatory monologues to address the issue.[56]

The second place where the representation of the Roma via names may be examined is in the second season episode "Surprise" (2.13).[57] In a heated discussion between Jenny Calendar, newly revealed to be a Romani person, and her uncle Enyos, the tension between terms continues, albeit with a different set of names.[58] Jenny and her uncle discuss whether the punishment of Angel is still in effect. When her uncle reminds her of her "responsibility to [her] people," she reassures him that "the curse still holds."[59] He reminds her that Angel murdered the "the most beloved daughter of [her] tribe."[60] As Jenny tries to defend her actions, he angrily replies, "What? You thought that you are Jenny Calendar now? You are still Janna of the Kalderash people! A gypsy."[61]

Here, the usage of names parallels that found in the scene between Buffy and Angel. A character initially refers to a group of Roma with an actual Romani name, followed by the inaccurate/problematic term. Here the name is Kalderash, designating several groups of Roma who migrated out of present-day Romania (then Wallachia) in the 1860s, when they were liberated after some 500 years of slavery.[62] Many people from Kalderash groups eventually settled in the United States. Again, it seems someone on Whedon's creative team did enough research to find a real name, designating a real group of Romani people with a distinct culture and history. In this scene as in the earlier scene with Buffy and Angel, the Romani name is immediately followed by the inaccurate/problematic term. While it may have been used to define "Kalderash" for viewers who are unfamiliar with the name, it has the unfortunate effect of reducing the Roma to the cinematic stereotypes encoded in the inaccurate/problematic term. The use of the inaccurate/problematic term is even more disturbing, as it is used by Roma talking about Romani identity. It has the result of having Uncle Enyos remind Jenny not that she is Kalderash, with a rich, complex history, but that she is the cinematic stereotype encoded by the inaccurate/problematic term. Since one of Whedon's stated goals was to create "a fantasy that was emotionally, completely realistic," this conversation could have been an opportunity to have Romani characters, who must deal with stereotypes invoked by the inaccurate/problematic term on a day-to-day basis, introduce the problem to the viewers.[63] It is disappointing that a show that was said to have, "a real commitment to, and respect for, the intelligence of its viewers," chose to leave the viewer with the inaccurate/problematic term, thereby reinforcing, rather than subverting Western cinematic stereotypes.[64]

What does the nomenclature in "Angel" (1.7) and "Surprise" (2.13) tell us about the representation of Roma in the Whedonverse?[65] First, both episodes initiate the representation with appropriate names for the Roma from their own language—Romani and Kalderash—something atypical of film and television. However, if this is an attempt to subvert the dominant representational patterns, it is undercut when the appropriate names are immediately followed by the inaccurate/problematic term. Whether the inaccurate/problematic term is used only because the mainstream audience would be unfamiliar with the appropriate terms or whether the two types of names are used to highlight the representational issue in nomenclature, neither episode takes the opportunity to interrogate the inaccurate/problematic term and show that it is not representationally equivalent to the Romani names. This is especially striking in the scene in "Surprise" (2.13), in which the discussion is precisely about Romani identity.[66] As a result, the viewer is left with only the inaccurate/problematic term, which upholds the cinematic/tele-visual stereotypes.

Discriminatory Language and the Question of Intentionality in Buffy *and* Angel

Although Romani characters—Jenny Calendar, Uncle Enyos and their ancestors who originally punished Angel—appear or are referenced in several more episodes of *Buffy* and *Angel*, names referring to Romani ethnicity are rare. On the few occasions when they are used, only the inaccurate/problematic term appears. Whedon and his creative team have abandoned their practice of at least introducing names like Romani or Kalderash as in the early episodes of "Angel" (1.07) and "Surprise" (2.13).[67] Instead of "constantly and pervasively draw[ing] on its own history," as typically found in the Whedonverses, the terms for the Roma in *Buffy* and *Angel* draw upon the cinematic norm.[68] This undercuts one of the striking aspects of Whedon's shows, one that has contributed to its characterization as "Quality TV," and that is memory.[69] The texts of the Whedonverse are so rich, because "characters remember, and we remember with them."[70] Here, as in the larger mainstream culture, the empowerment of the Roma through accurate naming, attempted in the early episodes, has been forgotten.

Even though all the examples use the inaccurate/problematic term, they differ along a continuum of intentionality towards the representational tropes. In the first examples, there is no evidence of any extra-linguistic pejorative attitude toward the Roma in the use of the name, although the use of the inaccurate/problematic term still brings with it the basic cinematic stereotypes.

The Season One episode of *Angel* "Five by Five" (1.18) features references to the Roma that are of relatively low intentionality.[71] In the episode flashback, scenes showing Angel's punishment by the Roma in 1898 Romania frame scenes set in the present examining similar issues of evil, punishment, and redemption concerning Angel and Faith. The first flashback scene details what Angel described about his backstory in "Angel" (1.7).[72] We see Darla giving Angelus the Romani girl as a surprise birthday gift and his sexualized feeding off the girl, causing her death. Angelus responds to the gift, by noting: "She's a Gypsy."[73] Although the name invokes the inherent cinematic stereotypes, there is no evidence that Angelus is intentionally going beyond that to push any particular representational tropes. Darla's response, "I looked everywhere," while not connected to naming, exoticizes the girl, implying that the marginalized Roma are a rare treat for vampires.[74]

The second flashback, taking place after Angelus has been punished, is similar. Darla is suddenly repulsed by him and asks what has happened. He replies, saying: "That Gypsy girl you brought me, her people found out. They did something to me," referring to the restoration of his soul.[75] Later in the interaction, Darla says, "the spell. They gave you a soul. A filthy soul!"[76] Again Angel's use of the name is of low intentionality, although the term itself is problematic. As in the first flashback, Darla's language, while not directly naming the Roma, is deliberately pejorative and evokes two negative cinematic stereotypes—connection to the supernatural and dirtiness.

The inaccurate/problematic term is also used in the part of the show set in the present. Wesley and Cordelia are talking in the office while Angel interrogates a minor character. Wesley expresses his faith in Angel's ability to convince the minor character to do the right thing and testify, while Cordelia argues that people like this character don't change. When Wesley reminds her that she could be describing Angel (who did change), Cordelia says, "Oh, please, he was cursed by gypsies. What's Angel going to do, drag a bunch of them in here to shove a soul down this guy's throat?"[77] Again the inaccurate/problematic term is not used in an intentionally pejorative way by the character. But like the second flashback scene, it invokes the cinematic trope associating the Roma with the supernatural. Although the scenes in "Five by Five" (1.18) adhere closely to the cinematic stereotypes, in naming and in evoking representational tropes, the naming practice itself shows relatively little pejorative intent.

Other references to the Roma are more troubling. In two episodes in *Buffy* and one episode in *Angel*, the inaccurate/problematic term for the Roma is used in an intentionally pejorative way. The first instance occurs during the Season Two episode of *Buffy*, "Passion" (2.17), an episode noted for, among other things, the first loss of a major character in the Whedonverses.[78] Angelus is taunting Jenny Calendar and playing with the Orb of Thesaluh. He wonders whether she knows why he hates the orb. When she doesn't reply, he smiles and smashes the orb, saying, "They're so damn fragile. Must be that shoddy Gypsy craftsmanship, huh?"[79] After a harrowing chase through the halls of the deserted school, Angelus kills her. The one non–Romani character who has used the term "Romani," deliberately uses the inaccurate/problematic term. Furthermore, he uses it intentionally to invoke the pejorative representational trope of the Roma as con-artists. He wields the term to disempower Jenny Calendar herself as well as the Roma as a group, and ultimately kills the last remaining representative of the Roma in this universe. Angelus's unchallenged use of the inaccurate/problematic term reinforces Western cinematic stereotypes about the Roma.

The second instance occurs in the Season Five opening episode, "Buffy vs. Dracula" (5.1).[80] Riley interrogates Spike, wondering whether Spike knows anything about Dracula, who has recently arrived in Sunnydale.[81] At Riley's suggestion that Dracula is "not just a regular vampire" but might have "special powers," Spike, scoffs, "Nothing but showy Gypsy stuff," again utilizing the inaccurate/problematic term.[82] Spike's outburst invokes the same cinematic stereotype, con-artistry, that Angelus used in "Passion" (2.17).[83] In seeking to put down Dracula, Spike actually disempowers the Roma, reducing them to the cinematic stereotype. His use of the offensive word and its accompanying trope go unchallenged within the show.

What are we to make of the offensive utterances from "Passion" (2.17) and "Buffy vs. Dracula" (5.17)?[84] It is difficult to argue that they are being used to encourage "an audience critique of the … characters' xenophobia and racism."[85] First, there is no evidence within the Whedonverses that either Angel or Spike are coded as overtly racist. Second, the scenes are not cinematographically arranged to bring the utterances to the audience's attention. That is exactly the point—offensive references to the Roma are so normalized by cinematic practice that they can go by unnoticed and unchallenged. In "Passion" (2.17) and "Buffy vs. Dracula" (5.17) the outbursts by Angel and Spike are rooted in unplanned emotion, vicious anger on the part of Angel or jealousy on the part of Spike, but their use of the inaccurate/problematic term is intentional.[86] The utterances are completely based on representation, as their accusations against the Roma—shoddy workmanship and showy powers—are factually untrue within the series. Romani power and workmanship are "precisely what Miss Calendar and her clan used to re-ensoul Angel."[87] More significantly, the utterances characterizing the Roma are used not to direct anger or jealousy at a person who happens to belong to a larger group. Instead it is the entire group that is denigrated, a classic example of offensive, racist usage. The representation of the Roma in these utterances, of a people that sell shoddy goods while distracting their victim with a showy display, is one of the strongest of the Western cinematic tropes. Although, there are con-artists among the Roma, just as there are among any other race or ethnicity, the problem lies in attaching the stereotype, "to an identifiable ethnic group, as an embedded and defining characteristic—a supposedly inherent trait."[88] By allowing the utterances to go unchallenged Whedon allows the cinematic stereotype of Roma as con-artists to be reinforced.

This cinematic representation is, perhaps unknowingly, also reinforced by another term used at least once in *Buffy*. At the end of the Season Two episode, "Inca Mummy Girl" (2.4), Buffy and Xander are discussing the fate of Ampata, a 500-year-old Peruvian girl, victim of a ritual sacrifice, who is in Sunnydale masquerading as an exchange student.[89] When she tried to take their lives, they were forced to let her die. When Xander talks about his bad taste in women, Buffy says that Ampata wasn't evil at first, and mentions that she had cared about Xander. When Xander quips that the "whole sucking the life out of people thing" would have been a problem, Buffy responds, "She was gypped. She was just a girl, and she had her life taken away from her."[90] Here Buffy uses a term that clearly means being cheated and which is etymologically derived from the inaccurate/problematic term for the Roma.[91] Ironically she uses it in expressing sympathy for a character of color, marginalized in white Sunnydale. It is possible, however, that Whedon and his team were unaware of the connection.[92] Using the term in a work of popular culture like *Buffy*, however unknowingly, reinforces the Western cinematic stereotype of con-artistry as an inherent quality of the Roma.[93]

The last example of language use that needs to be examined occurs in *Angel's* Season Five, in the episode "The Girl in Question" (5.20).[94] In this episode Angel and Spike meet the Italian CEO of Wolfram and Hart, Ilona Costa Bianchi, dressed in a low-cut sundress that barely contains her cleavage. Speaking exuberantly, performing as a cinematic Italian, she responds to Angel's assertion of his identity as Angel, "Ah yes, of course. The gypsies they gave you your soul. The gypsies are filthy people!"[95] She then bends over and spits loudly towards the floor and continues, "And we shall speak of them no more."[96] In her next scene, Ms. Bianchi, now eating chocolates and smoking a cigarette in an overly long holder, explains that the Immortal "doesn't use spells. He considers them dirty. Dirty tricks for dirty people. Like gypsies."[97] Again she turns to the side and spits. She then repeats, "We will speak of them no more."[98] Bianchi's utterance, "dirty tricks," invokes the same cinematic stereotype as those used by Angel, Spike and Buffy, that of con-artistry.[99] The character, however, adds an even more pejorative cinematic trope, dirtiness.[100] "Bringing dirt and disease ... is one of the most common and yet least challenged myth[s]" about the Roma.[101] In fact, the Roma have a very strict belief system regarding cleanliness.[102]

Unlike the example in "Inca Mummy Girl" (2.4), in which Buffy may not be aware of the meaning of the term she uses, the use of the inaccurate/problematic term in "The Girl in Question" (5.20) is presented in an intentional and overtly racist way.[103] In contrast to the scenes with language use by Angel and Spike in "Passion" (2.17) and "Buffy vs. Dracula" (5.01), Bianchi's utterances are cinematographically foregrounded, framed with repetition and actions (spitting) designed to highlight the offensive language use.[104] Thus the final example of naming practice in the *Buffy/Angelv*erse is different from the earlier ones. On the surface, the utterances evoke the cinematic stereotypes of con-artistry and dirtiness. However, by having the lines spoken by an evil character in an exaggerated, ridiculous fashion, the scenes draw attention to the racism in the utterances in a way the earlier examples did not. This at least allows for a reading of the text that subverts the pejorative cinematic representations of Romani characters, rather than reinforcing them.

Vengeance Not Justice: Distortions of Romani Images

The *Buffy/Angel*verse representation of Romani culture is inextricably tied to the punishment received by Angel. The details of the punishment are well known: Angelus killed a young Kalderash girl in 1898, her family devised an unusual punishment for him, and Angelus was inflicted with a soul causing him to suffer painful remorse.[105] Unbeknownst to Angel, as revealed in "Surprise" (2.13), an ancillary clause specified that if he experienced one moment of true happiness, his soul would leave him and he would revert to Angelus.[106] Further details are revealed in "Innocence" (2.14), and "Becoming, Part 1" (2.21).[107] What picture of Romani culture do we get from this cluster of episodes?

In the *Buffy/Angel*verse the Roma, especially older Romani women, are closely tied to magic and the occult. A flashback in "Becoming, Part 1" (2.21) illustrates this.[108] The locale is given in a title as "Rumanian Woods, 1898."[109] An older woman is reciting a spell that will punish Angelus. She is outdoors, under a canopy, a crystal ball in front of her, surrounded by candles. This upholds the cinematic stereotype, in which the Roma "have consistently been associated with the supernatural," especially fortune-telling.[110] In most cases, the spirituality imagined for the Roma is not based on their own complex belief system, but on an image that non–Roma project onto them.[111] The intersection of spirituality and occupation is varied in Roma society. In some communities, "comparatively few Gypsy women practice fortune-telling," while in others, "fortune-telling is a widespread means of income."[112] Of course, when not excluded from the educational system or the job market by the dominant society, Roma are not limited to any particular profession. Not surprisingly, the positive type of spirituality attributed to women like Willow and Tara in the *Buffy/Angel*verse is not found in the representation of spirituality of the woman who punished Angelus, since she is not a nuanced character, but a stereotyped representation.

In the Whedonverses, the Roma are not only associated with magic, but with using that magic to punish. Angelus's punishment was originally described with just that word: punishment. By the end of Season Two, his punishment has morphed into a "gypsy curse."[113] Whedon gives his take on the issue in the commentary to "Innocence" (2.14): "Some say the Gypsy curse—a hokey concept. But, Danish curse just doesn't sound as good. You know how I love the classics."[114]

The Roma, a group with "no legal means of redressing wrongs against it" throughout much of their history, may have sometimes used fear to keep "outsiders at arm's length," but were more likely to be victimized by the majority population.[115] Whedon's own description of the curse as a classic suggests that its origins are to be found not in actual Romani culture, but in cinematic representations. Popular culture has a definite notion as to where the "classic" curse can be found. That notion is illustrated in the quote in the introduction, as well as this one: "The granddaddy of all Gypsy curse movies is, of course, Universal's _The Wolf Man_ (1941.)"[116] It appears that the show that loves to mock the conventions of its genre(s), has instead embraced a venerable cinematic trope. If this is the classic that Whedon is referencing, as discussed above, he is actually mistaken, as the Roma do not punish or curse anyone in the film. Instead both Lon Chaney and the Romani character (Bela Lugosi), who bites him, are actually portrayed as unfortunates, who suffer "through no fault of [their] own."[117] The linking of the Roma with the cinematic stereotype of the curse continues to thrive. _Drag Me To Hell_, referenced in the introduction, is one of the more recent examples.[118]

Finally, in the Whedonverse we learn that the Roma are not driven to seek justice, but to seek vengeance. As Uncle Enyos, declares, "To the modern man vengeance is a verb, an idea.... Not with us. Vengeance is a living thing. It passes through generations."[119] This attribute excludes Whedon's Roma from the modern world. Whedon admits that this idea was something he created, not something he based on actual Romani culture. He describes the process in the commentary to "Innocence" (2.14), in which he says, "I remember walking along the Santa Monica Pier desperately trying to figure out how I was going to do this scene and, uh, then coming up with this and realizing with that one phrase, 'Vengeance is a living thing,' we could just sort of make everybody accept what had gone before, make it make some kind of sense."[120] In this, as with the "curse" motif, Whedon adheres tightly to the cinematic stereotype of the Roma. The very earliest representations of the Roma in American cinema, such as those of D.W. Griffith, use the vengeance trope. Examining the representation of the Roma in the _Buffy/Angel_verse reveals that, in both naming practices and cultural representation, Whedon reinforces, rather than subverts, stereotypes of the Roma. While Whedon has the creative license to give his fictional Roma any characteristics he wishes, these particular representations demonstrate that, by using stereotyped depictions of marginalized characters like the Roma, Whedon has not advanced their representation beyond "the age-old stereotypes from the pre-romantic era," typically found in their literary and cinematic appearances.[121]

Notes

1. Jes Battis, *Chosen Families in* Buffy the Vampire Slayer *and* Angel (Jefferson, NC: McFarland, 2005), 47. I will refer to the television shows created by Joss Whedon as his work. As Roz Kaveney, *Reading the Vampire Slayer: An Unofficial Critical Companion to* Buffy *and* Angel (London: I.B. Tauris, 2001), 3; Candace Havens, *Joss Whedon: The Genius Behind Buffy* (Dallas: BenBella, 2003), 50–51; Rhonda Wilcox, *Why Buffy Matters* (London: I.B. Tauris, 2005), 5–8; and Stacey Abbot, *Angel*, Detroit: Wayne State University Press, 2009), 25–26; all discuss, Whedon's shows may also be understood as a collaborative effort, as he pulled together a collective of writers, producers and other creative individuals to work with him. However, it seems clear that, especially in the early years of *Buffy* the controlling vision for the show came from Whedon. Jane Espenson, for example, says in Roz Kaveney, "Writing the Vampire Slayer: Interviews with Jane Espenson and Steven S. DeKnight," *Reading the Vampire Slayer: The New, Updated Unofficial Guide to* Buffy *and* Angel, ed. Roz Kaveny (London: I.B. Tauris, 2004), 101, "it is so Joss's show" or in Jane Espenson "Introduction," Michael Adams, *Slayer Slang: A* Buffy the Vampire Slayer *Lexicon* (Oxford: Oxford University Press, 2003), ix, "Joss is *Buffy*'s father, the creator and show-runner, the king of us."

2. Cynthea Masson, "'Evil's spreading, sir—and it's not just over there!': Nazism in *Buffy* and *Angel*," in *Monsters in the Mirror: Representations of Nazism in Post-War Popular Culture*, ed. Sara Buttsworth and Maartje Abbenhuis (Oxford: Praeger, 2010), 177. Many other works focus on this topic, including Gregory Stevenson, *Televised Morality: The Case of* Buffy the Vampire Slayer (Dallas: Hamilton, 2003), J. Michael Richardson and J. Douglas Rabb, *The Existential Joss Whedon: Evil and Human Freedom in* Buffy the Vampire Slayer, Angel, Firefly *and* Serenity (Jefferson, NC: McFarland, 2007) and K. Dale Koontz, *Faith and Choice in the Works of Joss Whedon* (Jefferson, NC: McFarland, 2008).

3. Matthew Pateman, *The Aesthetics of Culture in* Buffy the Vampire Slayer (Jefferson, NC: McFarland, 2006), 12.

4. Lorna Jowett, *Sex and the Slayer: A Gender Studies Primer for the* Buffy *Fan* (Middletown, CT: Wesleyan University Press, 2005), 2.

5. Naomi Alderman and Annette Seidel-Arpaci, "Imaginary Para-Sites of the Soul: Vampires and Representations of 'Blackness' and 'Jewishness' in the Buffy/Angelverse," *Slayage: The Online International Journal of Buffy Studies*, 3, no. 2 (November 2003).

6. For works that specifically focus on race and/or ethnicity in *Buffy* and *Angel*, see Kent A. Ono, "To Be a Vampire on *Buffy the Vampire Slayer*: Race and ('Other') Socially Marginalizing Positions on Horror TV," in *Fantasy Girls: Gender and the New Universe of Science Fiction and Fantasy Television*, ed. Elyce Rae Helford (Lanham, MD: Rowman & Littlefield, 2000), 163–186; Lynne Y. Edwards, "Slaying in Black and White: Kendra as Tragic Mulatto in *Buffy the Vampire Slayer*," in *Fighting the Forces: What's at Stake in* Buffy the Vampire Slayer, ed. Rhonda V. Wilcox and David Lavery (Lanham, MD: Rowman & Littlefield, 2002), 85–97; Elyce Rae Helford, "'My emotions give me power': The Containment of Girls' Anger in *Buffy*," in *Fighting the Forces: What's at Stake in* Buffy the Vampire Slayer, ed. Rhonda V. Wilcox and David Lavery (Lanham, MD: Rowman & Littlefield, 2002), 18–34; Mary Alice Money, "The Undemonization of Supporting Characters in *Buffy*," in *Fighting the Forces: What's at Stake in* Buffy the Vampire Slayer, ed. Rhonda V. Wilcox and David Lavery (Lanham, MD: Rowman & Littlefield, 2002), 98–107; Naomi Alderman and Annette Seidel-Arpaci,

"Imaginary Para-Sites of the Soul: Vampires and Representations of 'Blackness' and 'Jewishness' in the Buffy/Angelverse," *Slayage: The Online International Journal of Buffy Studies*, 3, no. 2 (November 2003); Vivian Chin, "Buffy? She's Like Me, She's Not Like Me—She's Rad," in *Athena's Daughters: Television's New Women Warriors*, ed. Frances Early and Kathleen Kennedy (Syracuse: Syracuse University Press, 2003), 92–102; Matthew Pateman, "'You say tomato': Englishness in *Buffy the Vampire Slayer*," *Cercles: Revue Pluridisciplinaire du Monde Anglophone* 8 (2003), 103–113, http://www.cercles.com; Donna L. Potts, "Convents, Claddagh rings, and Even The Book of Kells: Representing the Irish in *Buffy the Vampire Slayer*," *Studies in Media & Information Literacy Education* 3, no. 2 (May 2003), 1–9; Candra K. Gill, "Cuz the Black Chick Always Gets It First: Dynamics of Race in *Buffy the Vampire Slayer*," in *Girls Who Bite Back: Witches, Mutants, Slayers and Freaks*, ed. Emily Pohl-Weary (Toronto: Sumach Press, 2004), 39–55; Matthew Pateman, *The Aesthetics of Culture in* Buffy the Vampire Slayer (Jefferson, NC: McFarland, 2006); Cynthia Fuchs, "'Did anyone ever explain to you what 'secret identity" means?' Race and Displacement in *Buffy* and *Dark Angel*," in *Undead TV: Essays on* Buffy the Vampire Slayer, ed. Elana Levine and Lisa Parks (Durham: Duke University Press, 2007), 96–115; Victoria Pettersen Lantz, "Numero Cinco, Border Narratives, and Mexican Cultural Performance in *Angel*," in *The Literary* Angel: *Essays on Influences and Traditions Reflected in the Joss Whedon Series*, ed. AmiJo Comeford and Tamy Burnett (Jefferson, NC: McFarland, 2010), 98–111; and Jeffery R. Middents, "A Sweet Vamp: Critiquing the Treatment of Race in *Buffy* and the American Musical Once More (with Feeling)," in Buffy, *Ballads, and Bad Guys Who Sing: Music in the Worlds of Joss Whedon*, ed. Kendra Preston Leonard (Lanham, MD: Scarecrow Press, 2011), 119–132. Also published in *Slayage: The Online International Journal of Buffy Studies*, 5, no. 1 (June 2005). Also presented at the *Slayage Conference on* Buffy the Vampire Slayer (Nashville, Tennessee, May 28–30, 2004); Ewan Kirkland, "The Caucasian Persuasion of *Buffy the Vampire Slayer*," *Slayage: The Online International Journal of Buffy Studies*, 5, no. 1 (June 2005).

For works that focus on race and/or ethnicity in Whedon's later works see Agnes B. Curry, "'We don't say "Indian"': On the Paradoxical Construction of the Reavers," *Slayage: The Online International Journal of Buffy Studies*, 7, no. 1 (Winter 2008); and Eric Hung, "The Meaning of 'World Music' in *Firefly*," in Buffy, *Ballads, and Bad Guys Who Sing: Music in the Worlds of Joss Whedon*, ed. Kendra Preston Leonard (Lanham, MD: Scarecrow Press, 2011), 255–273.

7. Matthew Pateman, *The Aesthetics of Culture in* Buffy the Vampire Slayer, 61.

8. Jeffrey Middents notes the lack of scholarly attention, writing: "no one has addressed the complicated racial dynamics surrounding the Romani character Jenny Calendar (Robia La Morte)." Middents, Jeffery R. "A Sweet Vamp: Critiquing the Treatment of Race in *Buffy* and the American Musical Once More (with Feeling)." In Buffy, *Ballads, and Bad Guys Who Sing: Music in the Worlds of Joss Whedon*. ed. Kendra Preston Leonard (Lanham, MD: Scarecrow Press, 2011), 129. First published in *Slayage: The Online International Journal of Buffy Studies*, 17 (2005). Also presented at the *Slayage* Conference on Buffy the Vampire Slayer, Nashville, May 2004.

Kent Ono mentions the topic very briefly, writing: "[a]t a school setting after that, Xander laments having horrible taste in women, and Buffy says that Ampata was "gypped," using a derogatory term referring to gypsies, even though Ms. Calendar, herself, is a gypsy." Ono, Kent A. "To Be a Vampire on Buffy the Vampire Slayer: Race and ('Other') Socially Marginalizing Positions on Horror TV," in *Fantasy Girls: Gender and the New Universe of Science Fiction and Fantasy Television*, ed. Elyce Rae Helford (Lanham, MD: Rowman & Littlefield, 2000), 176. [Not that it mitigates the use of a discriminatory term, but at the time that the episode aired that Ono is referring to, neither the characters nor the viewers knew that Jenny Calendar was a Romani person.]

Brief discussions of the Roma can also be found in K. Dale Koontz, *Faith and Choice in the Works of Joss Whedon* (Jefferson, NC: McFarland, 2008), 35 and Nikki Stafford, *Bite Me! An Unofficial Guide to the World of* Buffy the Vampire Slayer: *The Chosen Edition* (Toronto: ECW Press, 2007), 167–168. Pateman (*The Aesthetics of Culture in* Buffy the Vampire Slayer, 50–51) offers a brief discussion of the Romani character, Jenny Calendar, within his wide-ranging analysis of ethnicity in *Buffy*.

A brief, but interesting discussion of the Roma in *Buffy*, especially Jenny Calendar, can be found in Nikolina Ivantcheva Dobreva, "The Curse of the Traveling Dancer: Romani Representation from the 19th Century European Literature to Hollywood Film and Beyond," (Ph.D. thesis, University of Massachusetts Amherst, 2009).

9. Dina Iordanova, "Mimicry and Plagiarism: Reconciling Actual and Metaphoric Gypsies," *Third Text*, 22, No. 3 (May, 2008), 306.

10. The ethnonym Roma, a plural form (singular: Rom; original meaning: a married Romani male) is widely used in Romani Studies and Romani human rights activism as an umbrella term for all the Romani people. For discussion, see Ilona Klímova-Alexander, *The Romani Voice in World Politics: The United Nations and Non-State Actors* (Hants, England: Ashgate, 2005), 13–15. Ian Hancock, noted American Romani scholar prefers Romanies. See Ian Hancock, *We are the Romani people* (Hertfordshire: University of Hertfordshire Press, 2002), xviii–xxi.

11. For a discussion of the history of the Roma, with a focus on marginalization and persecution, see Ian Hancock, *The Pariah Syndrome: An Account of Gypsy Slavery and Persecution* (Ann Arbor, MI: Karoma Publishers, 1987); Angus Fraser, *The Gypsies* (Cambridge: Blackwell, 1992); Donald Kenrick and Grattan Puxon, *Gypsies under the Swastika* (Hatfield, England: University of Herfordshire Press, 1995); Hancock, *We are the Romani People*; Susan Tegel, "Leni Riefenstahl's 'Gypsy Question,'" *Historical Journal of Film, Radio and Television*, 23:1 (2003), 3 10; Nicholas Saul and Susan Tebbutt, ed. *The Role of the Romanies* (Liverpool: Liverpool University Press, 2004); Valentina Glajar and Domnica Radulescu, ed. *"Gypsies" in European Literature and Culture* (New York: Palgrave, 2008); Eve Rosenhaft, "Blacks and Gypsies in Nazi Germany: the Limits of the 'Racial State,'" *History Workshop Journal*, Issue 72 (Autumn 2011), 161–170.

12. Hancock, *Pariah Syndrome*, 37.

13. *Ibid.* 105–114.

14. According to Kenrick, "the French word *gitan* and Spanish *gitano* also come from this etymology. The German word *Ziguener* and Slav *tsigan* or *cigan* have a different source. They come from the Greek word athinganos, meaning 'heathen.'" Donald Kenrick, *Historical Dictionary of the Gypsies (Romanies)* Second Edition (Lanham, MD: Scarecrow Press, 2007), xxxvii.

15. Noah Webster, *An American Dictionary of the English Language* (New York: Converse, 1828), http://machaut.uchicago.edu/websters. The 1828 and 1913 editions have been digitized by the ARTFL project at the University of Chicago at: http://machaut.uchicago.edu/websters. The entry in the 1913 edition (http://machaut.uchicago.edu/websters) retains some of the racist language: "One of a vagabond race, whose tribes, coming originally from India, entered Europe in 14th or 15th century, and are now scattered over Turkey, Russia, Hungary, Spain, England, etc., living by theft, fortune telling, horse jockeying, tinkering. Etc. Cf. Bohemian, Romany."

The 1966 *Webster's Third New International Dictionary of the English Language*

Unabridged (Springfield, MA: G & C Merriam Company, 1966) still retains the stereotypes (and even adds some new ones), but has removed the overtly racist language: "One of a dark Caucasoid people coming originally from India and entering Europe in the 14th or 15th century that are now found chiefly in Turkey, Russia, Hungary, Spain, England and the U.S. Still maintain somewhat their itinerant life and tribal organization, and are noted as fortune-tellers, horse traders, metalworkers and musicians."

16. For scholarly work, see references in Endnote 11. For voices from the Romani community, see, for example, Kay Randall, "What's in a Name? Professor Takes on roles of Romani Activist and Spokesperson to Improve Plight of his Ethnic Group." *University of Texas at Austin* (2003), Interview with Ian Hancock, http://www.utexas. edu/features/archive/2003/romani.html; "Breaking 'Gypsy' Stereotypes," *Voice of Roma*, http://www.voiceofroma.com/culture/gyp_vs_rom.shtml; Paul Dean, "Gypsies Are Banding Together to Fight Age-Old Stereotypes," *Los Angeles Times* (October 5, 1986), http://articles.latimes.com/1986-10-05/news/vw-4311_1_gadjo. While the information given by the Roma interviewed focused on combating racism, the reporter seems to be unable to get away from using stereotypes. Finally, it should be noted that not all Romani communities in the U.S. feel that the inaccurate/problematic term should be eliminated. Some feel that it should be reclaimed by the community and re-shaped in a positive way.

17. The slowness of the progress can be seen in the effort to reform terminology in the Library of Congress Subject Headings. The discriminatory language was first noted by Sanford Berman in the early 1970s, in his study of racism and sexism in the Library of Congress terminology, where he found "Rogues and vagabonds" listed as the cross reference for the subject "Gipsies." See Sanford Berman, *Prejudices and Antipathies: A Tract on the LC Subject Heads Concerning People* (Metuchen, NJ: The Scarecrow Press, 1971), 72–75. The Library of Congress only made the change to "Romanies" as the Subject Heading in 2001. See Robert M. Hiatt, ed. "Revised LS Subject Headings," *Cataloging Service Bulletin*, No. 93 (Summer 2001), 50–56 and http://groups.yahoo.com/group/AvenAmentza/message/92, where an LC official writes to Ian Hancock detailing the reasons for finally making the change.

A parallel struggle over naming practices also took place, as Romani activists tried to persuade media organizations to at least capitalize the initial letter of the inaccurate/problematic term, if they were going to use it, to show that the Romani people are an ethnicity, not a "lifestyle." Hancock (*We Are the Romani People*, 67) reports that an editor of a Texan newspaper wrote in 1975 that "[a] lower-case g will continue to be used, for the simple reason that gypsies are a contrived people and not a legitimate ethnic group." There was some success in this battle. For example, the style policy at the *New York Times* was finally changed in 1992. See Toby F. Sonneman, "Dark Mysterious Wanderers: The Migrating Metaphor of the Gypsy," *Journal of Popular Culture* 32, no. 4 (Spring 1999), 119 and Hancock, *We Are the Romani People*, 64–69.

18. The tension between local and general terms is noted on the European Commission website, which states that the "use of the term Roma is in no way intended to downplay the great diversity within the many Romani groups." http://ec.europa. eu/justice/discrimination/roma/index_en.htm.

19. Hancock, *We Are the Romani People*, xix.

20. Some of the key works in the codification process were Alexander Pushkin's 1824 poem *Tsygany* (*The Gypsies*), Victor Hugo's 1831 novel *Notre-Dame de Paris*, Prosper Mérimée's 1845 novella *Carmen* (popularized in Georges Bizet's opera of the

same name in 1875). British novels with stereotyped Romani characters include Jane Austen's *Emma* (1815), Charlotte Bronte's *Jane Eyre* (1847), and Emily Brontë's *Wuthering Heights* (1847), among others. For further discussion see Katie Trumpener, "The Time of the Gypsies: A 'People without History' in the Narratives of the West," in *Identities*, Kwame Anthony Appiah and Henry Louis Gate, Jr., ed. (Chicago: University of Chicago Press, 1995), 338–379; Sonneman, "Dark Mysterious Wanderers"; Anat Zanger, "Desire Ltd: Romanies, Women, and Other Smugglers in Carmen," *Framework* 44, no. 2 (Fall 2003), 81–93 and Glajar and Radulescu, *"Gypsies" in European Literature and Culture.*

Similar representations of Roma can be found in both British and American children's literature, starting in the nineteenth century and continuing throughout the twentieth century. For discussion see Ian Hancock, "The Origin and Function of the Gypsy Image in Children's Literature," *The Lion and the Unicorn*, 11, no. 1 (June 1987), 47–59; Nancy Tillman Romalov "Lady and the Tramps: The Cultural Work of Gypsies in Nancy Drew and Her Foremothers," *The Lion and the Unicorn*, 18, no. 1 (June 1994), 25–36; Jodie Matthews, "Back Where They Belong: Gypsies, Kidnapping and Assimilation in Victorian Children's Literature," *Romani Studies*, 20, no. 2 (December 2010), 137–159.

21. Colin Clark "'Severity has often enraged but never subdued a gipsy': The History and Making of European Romani Stereotypes," in Nicholas Saul and Susan Tebbutt, ed. *The Role of the Romanies: Images and Counter-Images of 'Gypsies'/Romanies in European Cultures* (Liverpool: Liverpool University Press, 2004), 226–246. Ronald Lee "Roma in Europe: 'Gypsy Myth' and Romani Reality—New Evidence for Romani History," in Valentina Glajar and Domnica Radulescu, ed.*"Gypsies" in European Literature and Culture* (New York: Palgrave, 2008), 1–28.

22. Hancock, *We Are the Romani People*, 65; Lee "Roma in Europe," 10.

23. *Ibid.*

24. *The Adventures of Dollie*, directed by D.W. Griffith (1908; American Mutoscope and Biograph).

25. Stanley Kauffman, *American Film Criticism: From the Beginnings to Citizen Cane* (New York: Livright, 1972), 7–8.

26. Eileen Bowser, *Biograph Bulletins* 1908–1912 (New York: Octagon Books, 1973), 1. Griffith, well known for his racist images of African Americans in later work, produced a series of films that featured immigrants as exotic and dangerous. See Scott Simon, *The Films of D. W. Griffith* (Cambridge: Cambridge University Press, 1993), 48–50.

27. Bowser, *Biograph Bulletins*, 1.

28. *An Awful Moment*, directed by D.W. Griffith (1908; American Mutoscope and Biograph).

29. *What the Daisy Said*, directed by D.W. Griffith (1910; American Mutoscope and Biograph).

30. *The Spanish Gypsy*, directed by D.W. Griffith (1911; American Mutoscope and Biograph). Quote from *Bowser Bulletins*, 286.

31. *A Romany Tragedy*, directed by D.W. Griffith (1911; American Mutoscope and Biograph).

32. For an exploration of Romani images in early American films, see Dobreva, "The Curse of the Traveling Dancer," 73–97.

33. *Carmen*, VHS, directed by Cecil B. DeMille (1915; Kino International, 1997). A potential counterexample can be found in Charlie Chaplin's parody of *Carmen*, in which he plays with the stereotypes of the genre. *A Burlesque on Carmen*, directed

by Charlie Chaplin in *Chaplin's Essanay Comedies*, Vol. 03 (1915, Image Entertainment, 1999).

34. *The Hunchback of Notre Dame*, DVD, directed by Wallace Worsley (1923; Image Entertainment, 2007).

35. For further discussion of the representation of female Romani characters, see Zanger, "Desire Ltd."; Ian Hancock, "The 'Gypsy' Stereotype and the Sexualization of Romani Women," *"Gypsies" in European Literature and Culture*, ed. Valentina Glajar and Domnica Radulescu (New York: Palgrave MacMillan 2008), 181–191; and Dobreva, "The Curse of the Traveling Dancer."

36. *The Wolf Man*, DVD, directed by George Waggner (1941; Universal Studio, 1999).

37. According to one fansite, "this ancient Gypsy curse, invented by scriptwriter Curt Siodmak for the *Wolf Man* (1941) pretty much sums up what we think werewolves are." http://wolfden.critter.net/interest/bizarre.htm. In its review of the film another site says: "The Werewolf suffered a gypsy's curse." http://blogcritics.org/video/article/dvd-review-the-monster-squad/.

38. *Thinner*, DVD, directed by Tom Holland (1996; Republic Pictures, 2001). *Drag Me to Hell*, DVD, directed by Sam Raimi (2009; Universal Studios, 2009).

King's film is based on his 1984 novel of the same name. Although he starts the novel version of *Thinner* using the inaccurate/problematic term five times in the first few pages, he does use the term Rom in later chapters, including a reference to "Rom Justice." (In the film this phrase uses the inaccurate/problematic term.) See Richard Bachman, *Thinner* (New York: Penguin, 1985), 200–201. In the novel, the Romani characters speaking what appears to be a gibberish version of Swedish, with at least one word from Yiddish, dybbuk, thrown in. On page 197, a character translates what she has just said (*"Ta mig Mamma! Va dybbuk! Ta mig inte till mormor! Ordo! Vu'der-lak!"*) as "I say to my old-papa that you killed my old-mamma! I say you are a demon and we should kill you!" Google Translate identifies this as Swedish, but translates it as *Take me mommy Va dybbuk Take me to your grandmother Ordo Vu'derlak*. Richard Bachman, *Thinner* (New York: Penguin, 1985), 197.

39. *The Hunchback of Notre Dame*, DVD, directed by Gary Trousdale and Kirk Wise (1996; Walt Disney Studios Home Entertainment, 2002).

40. Goran Gocić, *Notes from the Underground: The cinema of Emir Kusturica* (London: Wallflower Press, 2001), 93.

41. "Angel," *Buffy the Vampire Slayer* 1.7, DVD, written by David Greenwalt, directed by Scott Brazil (1997: Twentieth Century Fox, 2006)); "Surprise" *Buffy the Vampire Slayer*, 2.14, DVD, written by Marti Noxon, directed by Michael Lange (1998: Twentieth Century Fox, 2006).

42. See, for example, Wilcox, *Why Buffy Matters*, 46–65.

43. "Faith, Hope & Trick," *Buffy the Vampire Slayer* 3.3, DVD, written by David Greenwalt, directed by James A. Contner (1998: Twentieth Century Fox, 2002).

44. Wilcox, *Why Buffy Matters*, 46.

45. "Angel," *Buffy the Vampire Slayer* 1.7, DVD, written by David Greenwalt, directed by Scott Brazil (1997: Twentieth Century Fox, 2001). There are sometimes differences between the original shooting scripts and the episodes as first aired (and as released in the DVD boxed sets). These differences will be noted, if relevant to the focus of this essay. For a discussion suggesting the importance of shooting scripts in determining the Whedonverse canon, see Kevin K. Durand "Cannon Fodder: Assembling the Text," *Buffy Meets the Academy: Essays on the Episodes and Scripts as Texts*, ed. Kevin K. Durand (Jefferson, NC: McFarland, 2009), 9–16. For a discussion of how

the writing process with multiple scripts happens from a writer's perspective, see Espenson's comments in Kaveney "Writing."

46. This episode initiates what Stacey Abbott calls the "epic narrative" of Angel's life (Stacey Abbott, *Angel*, Detroit: Wayne State University Press, 2009, 24). Abbott locates the beginning of the epic arc in the penultimate episode of Season Two ("Becoming, Part 1," *Buffy the Vampire Slayer* 2.21, DVD, written by Joss Whedon, directed by Joss Whedon (1998: Twentieth Century Fox, 2002), but it clearly originates here.

47. *Buffy*, "Angel," 1.7.

48. *Ibid.*

49. *Ibid.* The spelling "Romani" is found in "Angel," *Buffy the Vampire Slayer* 1.7, Shooting Script, written by David Greenwalt (November 13, 1996) in *Buffy the Vampire Slayer: The Script Book: Season Two, Volume Two* (New York: Simon, 2001), 53. According to Ian Hancock (*We Are the Romani People*, xxi), this spelling is the one used by the United Nations, the Library of Congress and most Romani organizations. According to Hancock, the alternative spelling, Romany, although still found in literature, is starting to be seen as an older style. In the broadcast version Angel stresses the middle syllable of the word, which, according to Hancock (*ibid.*, xxi), is not the standard pronunciation, where the stress should fall on the initial syllable.

50. *Buffy*, "Angel," 1.7. In the shooting script the time frame of these crucial events is set explicitly in a line just before this one that didn't make it into the broadcast version: "It was just before the turn of the century." See "Angel," *Buffy the Vampire Slayer* 1.07, Shooting Script, written by David Greenwalt (November 13, 1996) in *Buffy the Vampire Slayer: The Script Book: Season One, Volume Two* (New York: Simon 2000), 53. Alert viewers may have caught reference to the time of Angel's punishment, in an earlier conversation between Darla and Angel that was preserved in the broadcast version, where she says, "For a hundred years, you've not had a moment's peace..." *Buffy*, "Angel," 1.7 (DVD) and *Buffy*, "Angel," 107 (Shooting Script) in *Buffy: Script Book*, 47. The specific year, 1898, is only revealed in the original broadcast version of the series in the penultimate episode of the season, Buffy, "Becoming, Part 1," 2.21.

51. Hancock, *We Are the Romani People*, xix.

52. *Buffy*, "Angel," 1.7. Nikki Stafford, *Bite Me!: An Unofficial Guide to the World of* Buffy the Vampire Slayer: *The Chosen Edition* (Toronto: ECW Press, 2007), 137 lists this in her "Oops" category in her description of the episode, saying, "Romani is the gypsy language, not the name of the clan."

While the word Romani (Romany) is frequently defined in English dictionaries as only the language, it is originally a feminine adjective that can be combined with any feminine noun in the Romani language. The noun meaning language is feminine, creating the phrase, Romani čhib. The noun apparently dropped out of use in English, allowing Romani to turn into an all purpose modifer, used with any noun, as in Romani Studies, Romani Voice, etc.

For more information on the Romani language, see Ian Hancock, *A Handbook of Vlax Romani* (Columbus, OH: Slavica, 1995), Peter Bakker, Milena Hübschmannová, Valdemar Kalinin, Donald Kenrick, Hristo Kyuchukov, Yaron Matras and Giulio Soravia, *What Is the Romani language* (Hatfield, England: University of Hertfordshire Press, 2000), Yaron Matras, *Romani: A Linguistic Introduction* (Cambridge: Cambridge University Press, 2002), O Yanko le Redjosko (Ian Hancock), *American Romani Cultural Vocabulary*, online resource (University of Texas at Austin: Romani Archive and Documentation Center 2007–2008), http://www.radoc.net/radoc.php?doc=art_c_lan guage_glossary&lang=en&articles=true.

53. "Angel," *Buffy* 1.7.

54. *Ibid.* The Whedonverse is not alone in this. A similar pattern can sometimes be found even in Romani Studies where either the scholars (or possibly the publishers) seem to feel the need to use the inaccurate/problematic term to clarify the topic: Thomas Acton and Gary Mundy, ed., *Romani Culture and Gypsy Identity* (Hatfield, England: University of Hertfordshire Press, 1997); Donald Kenrick, *The Historical Dictionary of the Gypsies (Romanies)* (Lanham, MD: Scarecrow, 1998), Walter Weyrauch, *Gypsy Law: Romani Legal Traditions and Culture* (Berkeley: University of California Press 2002).

55. "Angel," *Buffy* 1.7.

56. James Marsters, quoted in Stafford, *Bite Me*, 66.

57. "Surprise," *Buffy the Vampire Slayer* 2.13, DVD, written by Marti Noxon, directed by Michael Lange (1998: Twentieth Century Fox, 2002).

58. In "Surprise," *Buffy the Vampire Slayer*, Shooting Script, written by Marti Noxon (November, 17, 1997) in *Buffy the Vampire Slayer: The Script Book: Season Two, Volume Three* (New York: Simon 2001), Uncle Enyos is called only "Gypsy Man." His name is not actually used until a later episode, "Passion," *Buffy the Vampire Slayer*, DVD, written by Ty King, directed by Michael E. Gershman (1998: Twentieth Century Fox Century Fox, 2002).

59. "Surprise," *Buffy* 2.13.

60. *Ibid.*

61. "Surprise," *Buffy* 2.13. Although viewers could not know it, in the shooting script for "Surprise," *Buffy* 2.13 (Script Book, 21) in contrast to the shooting script for "Angel," *Buffy* 1.7 there is no upper case "G," as should be afforded to any ethnicity name in English. See Endnote 17 for more discussion on this issue.

Stafford, *Bite Me*, 175, in a section called "Nitpicks" wonders, "Why does Jenny's tombstone read 'Jennifer Calendar'? They all know that's not her real name."

The show calls her Janna and places her in the Kalderash group of Roma. This has led some who write on *Buffy* (in the popular realm, as well as scholarship) to assume that her name must be Janna Kalderash. See, for example, Christopher Golden, Stephen R. Bissette, and Thomas E. Siegoski, Buffy the Vampire Slayer: *The Monster Book* (New York: Pocket Books, 2000), 180; Jowett, *Sex and the Slayer*, 175, 235; and Wilcox, *Why Buffy Matters*, 115. The anàv rromanò, the traditional Romani naming system, as described in O Yanko le Redjosko (Ian Hancock), *American Romani Cultural Vocabulary*, is quite different from that found in the Anglo-American tradition. It is unlikely that Joss Whedon or the other writers would have been familiar with it.

62. Kalderash was originally "an occupational label, meaning 'maker of (copper) kettles,'" Hancock, *Handbook of Vlax Romani*, 31. It was one of the occupations forced on the Roma during slavery. For further discussion see Hancock, *We Are the Romani People*, 18–20.

63. David Bianculli "*Fresh Air* Interview with Joss Whedon," in *Joss Whedon: Conversations*, ed. David Lavery and Cynthia Burkhead (Jackson: University Press of Mississipppi, 2011), 4.

64. Kaveney, *Critical Companion*, 2.

65. *Buffy*, "Angel," 1.7; *Buffy*, "Surprise," 2.13.

66. *Buffy*, "Surprise," 2.13.

67. *Buffy*, "Angel," 1.7; *Buffy*, "Surprise," 2.13.

68. Rhonda V. Wilcox and David Lavery, "Introduction," in *Fighting the Forces: What's at Stake in* Buffy the Vampire Slayer, ed. Rhonda V. Wilcox and David Lavery (Lanham, MD: Rowman & Littlefield, 2002), xxiii–xxiv.

69. *Ibid.*, xxiii.

70. *Ibid.*, xxiii.

71. "Five by Five," *Angel* 1.18, DVD, written by Jim Kouf, directed by James Contner (2000: Twentieth Century Fox 2002).

72. *Buffy*, "Angel," 1.7.

73. *Angel*, "Five by Five," 1.18.

74. *Ibid.*

75. *Ibid.*

76. *Ibid.*

77. *Ibid.* Note that the script (found as an extra in the DVD boxed set), uses upper case "G" for the flashback scenes and lower case "G" for the scene set in the present. As discussed in Endnotes 17 and 61, the use of the lower case letter suggests that the Roma are not an ethnicity. "Five by Five," *Angel* 1.18, Script, written by Jim Kouf (2000: Twentieth Century Fox 2002).

78. *Buffy*, "Passion," 2.17. In David Bianculli's "*Fresh Air* Interview with Joss Whedon," Whedon explains his penchant for killing off important characters, "I want people to understand that not everything is perfectly safe."

79. *Buffy*, "Passion," 2.17.

80. "Buffy vs. Dracula," *Buffy the Vampire Slayer* 5.1, DVD, written by Marti Noxon, directed by David Solomon (2000: Twentieth Century Fox 2003).

81. For an erudite and entertaining discussion of Spike's role as the "self conscious performer of and spectator on the aesthetics of the *Buffy*verse," see Cynthea Masson and Marni Stanley, "Queer Eye of That Vampire Guy: Spike and the Aesthetics of Camp," *Slayage: The Online International Journal of Buffy Studies*, 6, no. 2 (Winter 2006).

82. *Buffy*, "Buffy vs. Dracula" 5.1.

83. *Buffy*, "Passion," 2.17.

84. *Buffy*, "Buffy vs. Dracula" 5.1.

85. Ono, "To Be a Vampire on *Buffy the Vampire Slayer*," 175.

86. *Buffy*, "Passion," 2.17; *Buffy*, "Buffy vs. Dracula" 5.1.

87. Pateman, *The Aesthetics of Culture in* Buffy the Vampire Slayer, 189.

88. Colin Clark, "'Severity has often enraged but never subdued a gipsy,'" 233. See also 226–246 for discussion.

89. "Inca Mummy Girl," *Buffy the Vampire Slayer* 2.4, DVD, written by Matt Kiene and Joe Reinkemeyer, directed by Ellen Pressman (1997: Twentieth Century Fox, 2002).

90. *Ibid.*

91. *Webster's New World Dictionary*, 648, lists the term as "probably from gypsy."

92. Whedon, "A Personal Message from Joss Whedon," (April 23, 2003) http://www.digitalbits.com/mytwocentsa72.html, used the term in his reply to *Buffy* fans who were disappointed that the DVD release of Season Four was not in the widescreen format. "No doubt you are looking over this scrumptious BUFFY package and exclaiming 'No @#$%ing letterboxing? Whutzat? GYPPED!' Possibly you are breaking things. Please calm down..."

93. See Hancock, *Pariah Syndrome*, 145–162, for examples of overtly pejorative usage, like that in a Detroit newspaper headline: "It's Gypsy Season, So Don't Get Gypped!" that clearly make the connection.

94. "The Girl in Question," *Angel* 5.20, DVD, written by Steven S. DeKnight and Drew Goddard, directed by David Greenwalt (2004: Twentieth Century Fox, 2004).

95. *Ibid.*

96. *Ibid.*

97. *Ibid.*

98. *Ibid.* For a discussion of the use of repetition in this episode, see Cynthea Masson, "What the Hell? *Angel*'s 'The Girl in Question,'" presented at *SC3: The Slayage Conference on the Whedonverses* (Henderson State College, Arkadelphia, Arkansas, June 2008).

99. *Angel*, "The Girl in Question," 5.20.

100. Bianchi's outburst parallels, both emotionally and linguistically, the earlier utterances of Darla, Angelus's vampire "sire." Besides the quote from *Angel*, "Five by Five" (1.18) where she tells Angel, "They gave you a soul. A filthy soul!" in addition Darla orders Jenny's ancestors to "remove that filthy soul…" in "Darla," *Angel* 2.7, DVD, written by Tim Minear, directed by Tim Minear (2000: Twentieth Century Fox, 2003).

101. Kenrick and Puxon, *Gypsies Under the Swastika*, 12.

102. See Hancock, *We Are the Romani People*, 75–76 for a brief outline of the pollution/purity (Marimè) system in traditional Romani culture. For an extremely detailed introduction to Marimè among the American Kalderash, see Anne Sutherland, *Gypsies: The Hidden Americans* (Prospect Heights, IL: Waveland Press, 1986), 255–274.

103. *Buffy*, "Inca Mummy Girl," 2.4; *Angel* "The Girl in Question," 5.20.

104. *Buffy*, "Passion," 2.17; *Buffy*, "Buffy vs. Dracula," 5.1.

105. *Ibid.*

106. *Buffy*, "Surprise," 2.13.

107. *Buffy*, "Innocence," 2.14; *Buffy*, "Becoming, Part 1," 2.21.

108. *Buffy*, "Becoming, Part 1," 2.21.

109. *Ibid.* If this episode shows the locale in which Jenny Calendar's ancestors are found is Romania, it is odd that the shooting script for "Surprise" (2.13) indicates that Jenny Calendar's uncle "speaks with a DISTINCT YUGOSLAVIAN ACCENT." ("Surprise," *Angel* 2.13, Shooting Script, written by Marti Noxon, November 17, 1997). It's possible that changes were made between episodes. However, indifference toward matching language and culture is not unusual in cinematic and televisual characters from Eastern Europe. For example, in *Chicago*, directed by Rob Marshall (2002; Miramax Home Entertainment, 2003) a character who is supposed to be Hungarian is speaking Russian. In an episode of *Night Court* a character who is supposed to be Russian is speaking Bulgarian. "Dan's Escort," *Night Court* 3.12, written by Bob Stevens, directed by Jeff Melman (1986; Warner Home Video, 2010).

110. Clark "'Severity has often enraged but never subdued a gipsy,'" 232.

111. For a summary of the belief system, see Fraser, *Gypsies*, 242–246. For a detailed discussion of imagined spirituality, see Ian Hancock, "Romance vs. Reality: Popular Notions of the Gypsy," *Roma*, 2, no. 1 (1976), 7–23. http://radoc.net/radoc.php?doc=art_d_identity_romancevsreality&lang=en&articles=true.

112. Kenrick, *The Historical Dictionary*, 90; Hancock, *We Are the Romani People*, 103.

113. Stafford, *Bite Me!*, 179.

114. "Innocence," *Buffy the Vampire Slayer* 2.14, DVD Commentary by Joss Whedon (1998: Twentieth Century Fox, 2002). Perhaps Whedon's ironic stance stems from his realization that he is merely invoking the cinematic trope? Is he referencing Shakespeare's Hamlet? Wouldn't Oedipus be a better example of a classic curse?

115. Hancock, "Romance vs. Reality."

116. http://forum.dvdtalk.com/movie-talk/561229-gypsy-curse-movies.html.

117. *The Wolf Man*, written by Curt Siodmak, directed by George Waggner (1941; Universal Studio, 1999).

118. *Drag Me to Hell*, DVD, directed by Sam Raimi (2009; Universal Studios, 2009).

119. *Buffy*, "Innocence" 2.13.

120. *Buffy*, "Innocence," 2.13, DVD Commentary.

121. Dina Iordanova, "Mimicry and Plagiarism," 306.

An Inevitable Tragedy

The Troubled Life of Charles Gunn as an Allegory for General Strain Theory

Rejena Saulsberry

"You expecting somebody else?"[1]

From the first time we meet Charles Gunn in Season One of *Angel*, we are told unequivocally that this is not the usual Sunnydale transplant trying to find his way in Los Angeles like the rest of our regular cast. Gunn appears as a glowering, lanky figure teasingly reminiscent of the show's hero, Angel, but clothed in what has become the urban uniform of baggy jeans, hooded sweatshirt and chunky boots.[2] He, along with a racially diverse group of twenty-something followers quickly become embroiled in a street fight, complete with a growling jeep fitted with thick wooden stakes in order to become a more efficient vampire killing machine. Some of the vampires are killed while others escape by retreating, and Gunn's group suffers a poignant loss in the form of a young man who dies still questioning the reason his attacker so easily overpowered him. It is here, in the aftermath of a tragedy, that the viewer is given a glimpse into Gunn's motivations. His sister, Alonna, is quickly silenced when she attempts to confront him about their friend's murder. Gunn has moved on. "Everyone dies," is his response to her attempt to grieve.[3] His meaning is clear. Any expectation of a long happy life is futile. They're all destined for a young death, so the point is to put it off as long as possible and "stay dead," once it happens.[4]

Born in Los Angeles, Charles Gunn exemplifies the often-used trope of an African American male from the inner city, with few family ties and a belief in an inevitable violent death.[5] Despite these obstacles, Gunn continually attempts to create a better life, forming ties with the core cast of *Angel* characters and contributing more to the group's mission than brute force.

The conclusion of Gunn's story is more tragic than heroic, a common fate for many modern African American male characters. But instead of dismissing Gunn's story as a shallow attempt to diversify *Angel*'s Caucasian cast, his struggle to obtain respect and legitimacy in the eyes of his friends and society in general may be seen as an allegory for the external pressures that often lead young men into lives of crime and violence.

Gunn's initial fatalistic view of his future aligns with the attitude of many young, African American men in urban, impoverished areas. Though the show portrays Gunn as a modern day Robin Hood, he rationalizes the dangerous and criminal nature of his actions with the belief that he will die at a young age. Though Gunn becomes a welcome member of Angel's group, he continually struggles to fit into their world and is eventually forced to compromise his integrity in an attempt to receive respect from his peers by entering into a morally questionable bargain for the sort of intellect and education he was unable to achieve through legitimate means. Based on the work of Émile Durkheim, Robert King Merton, Albert K. Cohen, and Robert Agnew, this essay will examine the storyline and characterization of Charles Gunn as an allegory for the strain theory of deviant behavior, and why it ultimately leads to Gunn's status as an outsider for the duration of the show's canon. For purposes of this essay I will examine Gunn's storyline during Seasons One through Five and the additional canon established by the *Angel: Only Human* comic book series. I will begin by explaining strain as developed by four major contributors to the theory and applying the concept to the storyline of Charles Gunn. I will then examine two specific sources of general strain for Gunn, his race and lack of education, in order to explain why despite his acceptance by the show's core cast of characters, he remains isolated by his failure to truly overcome these obstacles. Finally, I will argue that as opposed to creating an offensive, stereotypical black male character in Gunn, the show's strict adherence to the core nature of Gunn as an outsider is actually a step forward for the portrayal of black characters in that it avoids the post-racial, color-blind, class-blind narrative that is more prevalent and problematic.

A Brief Introduction to Classical Strain Theory

> No living being can be happy or even exist unless his needs are sufficiently proportioned to his means.[6]

According to strain theory, deviant behavior is caused by the pressures that individuals face from various social structures within society. The theory originated from Émile Durkheim, who argued that when a society undergoes significant economic changes, a discrepancy develops between ideological values and what is realistically obtainable for individuals. He called this discrepancy anomie.[7] An anomic society develops in an environment of normlessness. Norms are rules of action adhered to by members of society that guide acceptable behavior. Anomie develops when the norms that once applied to success and achievement in the society have been compromised. In the United States, the idealized American Dream becomes impossible for certain segments of society to attain because the traditional methods of obtaining success are no longer guaranteed predictors of whether the individual will achieve that success. The dwindling importance of a four-year college education is a modern example of this phenomenon. Despite the continued push for high school students to obtain a bachelor's degree, it is becoming less of a predictor of career success, which can be a source of strain for those who depend on this method of social mobility.[8]

In his introductory episode, the Los Angeles that Gunn calls home is poor and violent, a sharp contrast to the affluent, decadent party attended by the core cast.[9] The people in his neighborhood have a deeply ingrained distrust of authority, likely born from the powerlessness and fear to which they were subjected at an early age. This lack of power will be discussed at length in the racial strain section of this essay, but here it is a logical result of the sort of normless environment that surrounds Gunn. In order to reach the universal goals of a capitalistic society, there must be a clearly ascertainable path to follow, steps that each individual regardless of their race or economic class can take to achieve whatever quality of life that society equates with success. In poor, crime-ridden areas like that surrounding Gunn, the steps are merely a theoretical path for those who manage to overcome a variety of obstacles. Young people must contend with the institutional failure of schools that lack effective teachers or safe learning environments. They must also cope with personal challenges such as the negative influence of peers or family members. The presence of vampires in *Angel*'s LA compounds these challenges, in that young people who live in communities where both formal and informal methods of social control have broken down are more vulnerable to victimization; in this case, easy prey for predatory monsters.[10] In the face of such obstacles, the theoretical path to the American Dream becomes obstructed and in some cases disappears altogether. Gunn, with his lack of education or stable home life, falls into this category of youth.

Robert Merton expanded this lack of opportunity into a new criminological theory to explain why certain individuals resort to deviant behavior in an attempt to gain what they cannot gain through legitimate means. Merton believes that every society creates its own cultural aspirations or benchmarks for measuring the success of its citizens. In the United States this is typically defined by the middle class ideal of wealth, power and respectability. However, coupled with these aspirations are rules; acceptable and unacceptable methods of attainment.[11] When an individual attempts to achieve these goals through legitimate means and fails, a social frustration develops.

The character Charles Gunn is, at his core, an extremely frustrated young man. Though he is physically strong, that strength is consistently tested by obstacles such as poverty or homelessness and supernatural threats like the vampires that have infested the city of Los Angeles. Though he has no supernatural powers or divine mission to motivate him, Gunn's impetus for action arises from his constant anger at the forces that threaten his existence and his inability to do anything to stop them.

Merton divides the possible reactions to this type of frustration into four categories: conformity, innovation, ritualism, and rebellion. A conformist will settle into whatever form of the American Dream he or she can attain. The ritualist will seek success through membership in small groups such as churches and fraternities, shifting the focus from society's approval to the approval of a discrete group of individuals. The rebel will redefine what it is to be successful, effectively rejecting the norms of society. Finally, the innovator will create a new path to success, even if it means violating institutional norms. This final individual is most likely to resort to criminal behavior.

Gunn falls into multiple categories. He is a conformist because his goals align with those of society in general in that he desires a home, a family, and validation for his professional contributions in the form of praise and power. Merton blames the American class system for creating the strain that occurs when someone who has internalized the desire for wealth, power and success is unable to compete "in terms of conventional standards of achievement."[12] Simply stated, an African American male with little education will have a difficult time receiving recognition for those skills he does possess because of the value placed on white-collar, professional positions that he will be unlikely to obtain. This lack of recognition does not insulate this hypothetical worker from the belief that success is only realized through the obtainment of wealth and status. Though the conventional response is to encourage hard work and personal responsibility, obstacles such as a lack of financial resources, a family support system, or a strong primary education could act as barriers to any attempt he would make to improve his situation. The neglect of these realities by mainstream media has historically been blamed for causing unrealistic expectations in young people regarding their potential for social mobility. A particularly relevant example would be the widespread backlash against the 1980s African American sitcom, *The Cosby Show*, which featured a black, upper middle class family who appeared to easily navigate the path to success in America by simply obtaining a college education and adhering to widely accepted moral values.[13] While the portrayal of a functional, two-parent household on network television has been widely credited with instilling a sense of pride in black families, it has also been blamed for lulling blacks into "the image dream world that nobody profits from, except the network and its advertisers."[14] A narrative focusing solely on the successful obtainment of the American Dream, with periodic allusions to a vague history of higher education, provides the impetus for a dream without a realistic roadmap tailored to overcome the individual's personal obstacles. The resulting frustration is a perfect example of the sort of strain that Merton argues leads to deviant actions.

When the path to achieving these goals is largely blocked for Gunn, he responds by becoming an innovator. Prior to joining Angel Investigations, Gunn's home is the street and whatever abandoned building he can find. He does attempt to create a safe space for his sister Alonna and the members of his gang by molding himself into a surrogate father for the group he has put together. This is exemplified by his insistence "Everybody eats," despite the protests of his second in command that "they don't take squatters."[15] However, in order to maintain this lifestyle, Gunn innovates in the form of violence and theft as opposed to what society would consider a legitimate path of education.

Once Gunn joins Angel Investigations, he becomes a ritualist, seeking the approval of his newly found friends and coworkers. His motivation for working for Angel has more to do with the man himself than the desire for any financial gain. This is demonstrated by Gunn's willingness to help the group before the subject of financial compensation was ever mentioned.[16] His migration away from being the reluctant employee to becoming part of the gang is complete in Season Two's aptly named "Redefinition" (2.11), when he joins Cordelia and Wesley at Caritas, a club frequented by humans and demons seeking insight into their fate, despite initially characterizing his work with them as a "side gig."[17] At this point, Gunn's worldview has clearly aligned with this small group and their immediate needs and conflicts. This transition is an apt example of a ritualist's response to strain.

In 1965, Albert K. Cohen attempted to move toward a general theory of deviant behavior by expanding on Merton's theory of anomie. He defined strain as "a function of the degree of disjunction between goals and means or of the sufficiency of means to the attainment of goals."[18] Though he agrees with Merton in certain aspects, he argues that Merton's theory attempts to examine individuals as though they were "in a box."[19] The impact of others on the individual is largely ignored. What happens when a person sees similarly situated individuals failing to achieve their goals through legitimate means? What happens if that same person observes an individual who achieves his goals through illegitimate means? "What effect does the propinquity of the wicked have on the peace of mind of the virtuous?"[20]

The effect on Charles Gunn is the creation (at least in the character's inception) of a myopic, utilitarian view of crime and justice. Utilitarianism is the belief that actions should be evaluated by their tendency to produce advantage, pleasure and happiness and to avoid mischief, pain, evil, or unhappiness.[21] Under this doctrine, actions are not judged by their nature but by their outcomes. There are no universally moral actions, only advantages and results. Gunn is taught at the age of twelve by his grandmother to protect himself and those he loves by any means necessary. His first encounter with a vampire is a violent confrontation that culminates in his grandmother staking the creature in front of him. She then calms his fears by telling him to sleep and that "there'll be time enough for nightmares later."[22] This brief, nurturing moment is then followed by a brutal lesson in hand to hand combat, followed by his grandmother's stern warning that failure to do exactly what she tells him could end in his death. Gunn observes his grandmother's any-means-necessary attitude towards survival until she dies of old age in a hospital bed. According to his grandmother, it is the best end either of them could ask for.[23] Watching such an influential person in his life succeed at surviving through the use of violence and a no-nonsense attitude would likely influence Gunn for the rest of his life. Gunn determines to achieve just outcomes through any means necessary, which, based on utilitarian ideals, could include criminal or immoral behavior. Again, it is the end result, not the means of obtaining this result, which establishes the morality of a given action under this ideology.

Observing others succeed through illegitimate means also influences Gunn's willingness to resort to violence or dishonesty in order to achieve his goals. Cohen hypothesizes that the virtuous may experience strain by the constant presence of norm-violating behavior being rewarded while others are denied access to the American dream. This engenders a "why bother" attitude towards legitimate work. However, success through illegitimate means would create additional strain for the virtuous, in that the immoral nature of their actions would conflict with their virtuous nature. In the end, both paths create a form of societal strain.

Before Gunn joins Angel Investigations, he is never seen working a minimum wage job to feed his family and friends. There are no discussions about his failure to fill out job applications or to apply to college as an alternative to squatting in abandoned buildings for shelter. The implication is that Gunn's apathy toward traditional means of survival is a "why bother" response to observing the continued triumph of the wicked (in this case vampires) over the virtuous (their victims). In later seasons, though Gunn receives compensation for his work with Angel, it is his desire to belong and not his need for financial compensation or social mobility that seems to be the motive for his continued employment.[24] However, despite being constantly surrounded by monsters and demons taking advantage of the weak in order to survive, Gunn manages to resist the temptation to abandon his convictions for the majority of the show's canon.

When People Get Mad, They Act Bad: Robert Agnew and General Strain Theory

Following criticisms of classic strain theory, sociologist Robert Agnew introduced the concept of general strain theory in 1985, in order to account for factors such as social class, individual expectations and the influence of personal relationships to determine the likelihood of criminality. Agnew believes that in addition to frustration caused by the failure of an individual to meet certain goals, a person may become angry and frustrated by the inability to escape an adverse situation as well. Responses to this type of strain may be shaped by different factors, such as the duration of the strain, the emotions that the strain elicits in an individual, the ability of the individual to cope with that strain and/or the environment in which the sources of strain occur.[25] For example, adolescents who are dependent on financially stable yet emotionally abusive parents may find themselves in possession of the tools needed to obtain the American Dream, yet also lacking the ability to escape a situation that threatens their immediate happiness. This creates a feeling of powerlessness and anger that may result in deviant behavior.[26] It also explains the aging-out phenomenon (the tendency of delinquent adolescents to cease criminal behavior once they reach the age of majority) by crediting the additional freedom that comes with adulthood for reduced frustration, anger and the resulting strain. When adults fail to reach this level of independence, their reactions can mimic that of adolescents, and their criminal behavior may continue.

Like many other young people that come of age in a poor, violent environment, Gunn's focus is initially on the day-to-day survival of street living. He sells his soul to a demon in exchange for a truck at the age of 17 because he considers the immediate need more pressing than any fate he may encounter in the afterlife.[27] The impact of this revelation on the viewer is likely disbelief that a younger, less worldly version of the character they've come to respect can be so careless with something so important. However, at the time he makes this trade, Gunn is sure of his fate. Death is all around him, a constant threat that he assumes will catch up to him eventually. His situation is one that would likely result in the individual feeling powerless, frustrated, and angry—three emotions Agnew believes are likely to result in deviant behavior. In "First Impressions" (2.3), Cordelia quickly realizes that Gunn's recklessness, and not a demon attack as she initially believed, is the source of the danger she sensed.[28] Gunn's willingness to die is a consistent theme that follows the character for the duration of his character's life.

Gunn's lack of hope for the future feeds into his willingness to risk his life for the small comfort of a night of safety and a warm meal for his friends during Seasons One and Two. The stress caused by the constant threat of death is one of what Robert Agnew refers to as a negative affective state. Negative affective states are caused by disruptive or stressful social interactions and tend to precipitate criminal activity.[29] In this case, Gunn's helplessness with regard to his own destiny results in a continued state of frustration and anger, the latter of which, according to Agnew, are the most destructive emotions for those at risk of criminality. Anger prevents the individual from controlling impulses and using rational thinking. This is best illustrated through Gunn's dilemma in Season Three's "Old Gang of Mine" (3.3), which begins with an aggressive dream sequence reliving the death of his sister.[30] Not only does the episode explicitly deal with Gunn's transition away from his original life on the streets into Angel's business, it shows how despite the presence of stabilizing structures (i.e., his job, coworkers and steady income) the frustration and powerlessness Gunn experienced during most of his life has not gone away. The plot of this episode challenges Gunn's utilitarian worldview in that he's forced to reject his black and white view of good and evil. He becomes mired in a conflict of loyalties between his new friends and his old crew, to the point of lashing out at Angel and Wesley during various parts of their investigation. In the end, Gunn's resulting anger at being taunted about his new life explodes with the murder of a demon in Caritas, something expressly forbidden and a good example of the sort of strain Agnew blames for destructive behavior.

Agnew's expansion of strain theory connects factors such as self-esteem, intelligence, lack of opportunity, and disorganized neighborhoods with the likelihood of strain to result in deviant behavior. Unlike Merton, who focused solely on financial strain caused by a capitalist society, Agnew argues that criminal behavior occurs in individuals for reasons beyond the failure to obtain material wealth. In the case of Charles Gunn, two such factors that distinguish him from the other members of the core group of *Angel* characters are his race and lack of education. Both are major factors that cause the type of strain that Gunn lacks the tools to cope with.

Charles Gunn and Racial Strain

"I don't need advice from some middle class white dude that's dead. You don't know what my life is."[31]

Not every person who experiences social strain will engage in criminal behavior. Different people have different methods of coping with frustration, some of which enable them to lead well-adjusted lives. Agnew states that the impact of strain on an individual is affected by several different factors, such as whether the strain can be blamed on some entity other than the individual, whether that person has reliable support in the form of family and friends, and what tools, if any, the individual may have for coping with societal strain.[32]

Since African Americans are disproportionately affected by strain that is easily attributable to external sources, based on general strain theory, they are more likely to engage in deviant behavior as a result.[33] A recent poll by the Pew Research Center found that the racially based wealth gap between black or Hispanic Americans and white Americans is at an all time high.[34] Economic strain is more likely to lead to crime when individuals are surrounded by others who are similar in many ways (such as age or goals) but are privileged differently than them. Applying this real world income disparity, the fictional Los Angeles of *Angel* provides insight into Gunn's resentment of people like Angel, Fred, Cordelia and Wesley during Seasons One and Two. Though they live in the same city and, in the case of Cordelia and Fred, are similar in age, their lives are vastly different.

Gunn's first encounter with Angel is contentious and resentful. Gunn's assertion that he doesn't need help from "some middle class white dude," shows that he sees Angel as a privileged outsider invading the small section of Los Angeles that Gunn considers home.[35] The labeling of Angel based on his class and race is particularly telling. In that instant, Gunn establishes a clear divide between the two men, branding Angel as the oppressing Other and unworthy of his respect. Othering occurs when the perceived weaknesses of another group is emphasized to stress the strength of those in power.[36] Angel, both an affluent, educated white man and an immortal, bloodthirsty vampire, is the living embodiment of the societal strains that have been placed on Gunn. The acceptance of assistance would be seen as a weakness, particularly when offered by an outsider. Angel's race and class are negatives in Gunn's world, handicaps that blind him to the realities of living on the streets. Of course, Angel eventually overcomes this objection by revealing his compassion for Gunn's plight, but the fact remains that the mere presence of those outside his immediate community, whether affluent white men or bloodthirsty vampires, threatens Gunn's way of life. This is shown in Season Three's "Old Gang of Mine" (3.3), when Gunn inadvertently reveals his true feelings about Angel by stating that they could never be friends, "on account of who [Angel] is."[37]

Victimization can also cause the type of strain that leads to criminal actions. Because African Americans are more likely to live in high crime neighborhoods, this places them at a greater risk for this type of strain.[38] Gunn's neighborhood is riddled with crime and has become infested with vampires preying on the weak and helpless. It is safe to assume that the majority of Gunn's family and friends have been victims of strain at some point in their lives. When Gunn's sister is killed and turned into a vampire, it is the catalyst for his amenability to accepting Angel's help. Angel has no official legal authority and doesn't offer legitimate work for Gunn until later seasons, but the strain of seeing yet another person he cares about victimized by this outside force pushes Gunn into a mutually beneficial relationship with the same type of creature that killed his sister, as opposed to turning to a source of legitimate legal authority, such as law enforcement.

It could be argued that both of these instances of strain can be attributed to other factors besides race. All races sometimes "Otherize" outsiders in an attempt to maintain a position of power. All racial groups are sometimes victims of violent crime. However, Gunn's race is a constant source of strain in that he's identified by it, judged by it, and at times negatively stereotyped for being an African American male. In Season Two's "Judgment" (2.1.), Cordelia and Wesley meet Gunn's appearance at her apartment with awkward discomfort, despite the fact that Angel has told them about his existence. Their initial exchange is tense solely because of his race and clothing style, which causes them to behave as though they are stumbling through a broken English conversation with a new foreign exchange student. This is exemplified by Cordelia's fumbling use of slang, misidentifying Gunn's last name as a "really fly street tag."[39] Gunn's reaction is one of hostile apathy. He doesn't expect to be treated any differently by Wesley and Cordelia, and yet resents them both for confirming that assumption. When Gunn and Cordelia track down Angel's stolen car in Season 2's "First Impressions" (2.3), she responds to his disbelief that she doesn't have the car keys by asking him to hotwire it. Gunn's response is a bitter "just because I know some car thieves, doesn't mean I am one."[40] In "The Thin Dead Line" (2.14), Gunn explains to Anne that all they have to do is walk down the street and wait for the police to stop them for "walking while black."[41] For Gunn, the very nature of being a black man in the presence of white individuals has created the type of frustration and strain that typically leads to the rejection of traditional social norms in favor of a more deviant path.

In Season Three, Gunn embarks on a sincere if ultimately tragic romantic relationship with Fred Burkle. This relationship is arguably the largest example of Gunn's commitment to his life with the Angel Investigations group, in his willingness to extend their influence to one of the most private aspects of his life. The difference in race between Gunn and Fred is not an explicit issue for the characters. The viewers are not treated to random people hurling insults or awkward *Guess Who's Coming to Dinner* moments between families, but Gunn's race is the ultimate reason behind their breakup. Race is a contributor to strain and Gunn's strain has led to his willingness to use violence in order to achieve a just result. In "Supersymmetry" (4.5), Gunn stops Fred from murdering a professor who victimized her by killing the professor himself.[42] The race of the actors playing Gunn and Fred makes this sacrifice problematic on the surface, despite the fact that protecting Fred from the realities of violence and death is a recurring theme in the show.[43] However, when examining the impact of Gunn's race on this decision, strain theory argues that his comfort with this sacrifice is born out of an acceptance of the violence around him and the belief that his choices are irrelevant to how he is viewed by the world. It is not a leap in logic to say that the strain caused by being a black man in a society dominated by a white patriarchy plays a very large part in this fatalistic view.

Charles Gunn and Educational Strain

Over the course of Seasons One through Four, Gunn manages to overcome the differences between himself and the other members of Angel's gang to the point of considering them his friends and family. However, Season Five shifts the show from the streets of Los Angeles where Gunn grew up and where his combat experience was necessary and appreciated, to the corporate world of Wolfram & Hart, a law firm teeming with formally trained foot soldiers and with little need for any additional muscle. Fred fits comfortably in this professional world, despite her initial insecurities about running such a large lab.[44] Angel, though struggling with the morality of joining the firm, has adapted to these types of changes for centuries. Gunn, however, is an uneducated, unskilled worker who struggles to find a place in this strange new environment.

Amuzie Chimezie characterizes education as a "potent standardizer of culture."[45] He argues that education communicates the cultural norms of the majority to the minority, develops the cognitive process by which members of a privileged group change their values and lifestyles, and raises income potential and contributes to social stratification. A lack of education deprives an individual of this crucial knowledge, prohibiting their mobility into that privileged group and causing frustration and shame. Gunn's lack of higher education is clearly established in the show's canon and based on his long history of living on the streets, as it is unlikely that he completed much education at the secondary level either.[46] A recurring theme throughout Gunn's story is his self-deprecating references to being "the muscle" of the group during Season 4, which talent he implies is inferior to the talents of the other characters (i.e., Fred's intellect and Angel's leadership) by stating that his physical strength is "all that's left."[47]

The firm of Wolfram & Hart personifies the unattainable American Dream of power and financial success, so that when confronted with his inability to achieve those goals, Gunn innovates once again. Instead of enrolling in college and seeking an advanced degree, or becoming one of the many other enforcers for the firm, he agrees to a surgical procedure performed by the firm's medical department to improve not only his intellect, but his diction as well.[48] This is one of the more telling changes Gunn undergoes as a character. His transition into this culture is not only about what he knows, but how he speaks and dresses. He lets his hair grow longer and wears expensive suits while handling the firm's legal affairs. And when his newfound abilities begin to diminish, he agrees to sign for a mysterious package in exchange for a permanent upgrade to his intellect, which ultimately results in the death of Fred Burkle.[49]

The death of Fred is a catalyst for Gunn's downward and (arguably backward) spiral into the anger and powerlessness that characterized his actions earlier in the series. Gunn kidnaps Knox, the lab assistant responsible for Fred's death, brutally beats him and ponders torture as punishment for his crime.[50] This course of action directly contradicts his legal knowledge, which at this point in the narrative, he still possesses. Gunn deliberately ignores the norm enforcing rule of law and resorts back to a utilitarian, outcome based view of right and wrong; that if Knox, who is responsible for Fred's death, is made to suffer that means justice has been served, regardless of how it was accomplished.

Gunn is at his most vulnerable during Season Five. In earlier seasons, though he was constantly in physical danger, his place at Angel Investigations was stable and easy to navigate. The knowledge he gained on the street translated well to the more legitimate, but still legally questionable casework they engaged in. Wolfram & Hart places Gunn in free fall, with little in the way of rules or guidance on how to navigate such a world without bargaining away integrity. In the end, Gunn rejects the new life that leads to the death of another loved one and returns to the violent, black and white view of justice he adopted on the street.

Gunn's subsequent actions are the prime examples of Cohen's belief that the profiting of the wicked can create strain for the virtuous. Gunn's static definition of good and evil, though constantly challenged, is never quite eroded throughout his storyline. Gunn judges the morality of actions via their outcomes, and in this case, his actions led to the death of a loved one. Therefore, in order to atone for this injustice, Gunn sacrifices himself in "Underneath" (5.16), by switching places with the exiled ex–Wolfram & Hart employee Lindsey in a hell dimension, where Gunn's memory of his life is erased, save for the conviction that he is "where he belongs."[51] Though he is eventually saved by Illyria, Gunn's quest for redemption never leaves him, as he spends the rest of the series and the subsequent comic book continuation atoning for his crimes and mistakes.[52]

"Sayin' people are free don't make 'em free"[53]

When examining *Angel* through the lens of strain theory, the ultimate question when facing a character like Charles Gunn is whether the characterization is honest, transcends traditional stereotypes, and succeeds in whatever the creator's goal might have been in creating the character. While it is difficult to guess what individual writers of separate episodes might have been thinking whenever they each slipped into Gunn's mind, the trajectory of his character arc does succeed in portraying the very real difficulties an individual with Gunn's identity and background might face when confronted with the narrative that plays out in *Angel*. While there may be no shortage of young black men from rough neighborhoods on American television, they are typically superficial stories, told from a safe distance, with endings that are either swiftly and predictably tragic, or unrealistically optimistic. With Gunn, the audience is allowed to see his evolution from beginning to uncertain ending with all the emotional highs and lows that accompany his journey. As exemplified by the preceding analysis of strain theory, a man with Gunn's background would not slip seamlessly through the obstacles constantly placed in his path by the show. Gunn faces strain from the structure of American society itself, in its glorification of an American Dream that few have the tools to obtain. The pursuit of those tools can ultimately end in frustration, because the rules for achieving that dream are constantly shifting, changing too quickly for someone coping with violence, poverty and social isolation to keep up with. This is eloquently summarized by Gunn's tearful confession that he took the actions that ultimately resulted in Fred's death, "Because I was weak. Because I wanted to be somebody that I wasn't. Because I don't know where I fit. Because I never did."[54] Not only does strain theory explain Gunn's reckless and at times irrational responses to the changes in his life, it also gives insight into the apparent contradiction between his resentment of societal norms and his desire to be accepted by *Angel*'s core group of characters. He is at times frustrating and endearing, stubborn but accepting of the worst in people, all of which make him a well-rounded and well-realized character.

Just like many minority characters written as the single source of diversity in a show ensemble, Gunn does suffer from the burden of the token character. As the sole black character regularly featured on the show, his use of urban slang, lack of education, and broken home become problematic in light of the show's failure to provide any alternative to the characterization. This leads to the question of whether it would be better to forego characters such as Gunn altogether, since their stories have been told to the point of being a negative stereotype. Did *Angel* really need to introduce another violent black man living on the streets of Los Angeles into the Joss Whedon universe? I believe the answer is yes. What the show did not need was another carbon copy of its core characters, with similar backgrounds and challenges only with darker skin.

In her essay "From Rogue in the Hood to Suave in a Suit: Black Masculinity and the Transformation of Charles Gunn," Michaela D.E. Meyer argues that the most problematic aspect of Gunn's character is not his black, urban characterization, but rather what she describes as his racial passing, or whitening that is harmful to the representation of black men on television.[55] She views Gunn's attempts to change his life as a desire to shed his blackness via an interracial relationship with Fred Burkle, changing his speech patterns to mimic that of his white peers and obtaining legal knowledge at Wolfram & Hart. Though Meyer accurately points out some of the more troubling racial implications of Gunn's seemingly innocuous choices, this analysis carries with problematic implications of its own. Tokenism often creates this problem when addressing race in popular media and the Whedonverses in particular. As the lone character of color regularly featured in *Angel*, Gunn's story becomes *the* black experience instead of *his* black experience, problematizing storylines that would normally be a natural progression for the character. This is exemplified by Meyer's dismissal of Gunn's decision to save Fred from the burden of a vengeance-fueled act of murder by committing the deed himself as the preservation of her whiteness, while this evil is absorbed by his blackness.[56] The presence of other black major characters would have muted the racial implications of such a sacrifice and allowed it to be seen as a selfless sacrifice consistent with the character's history instead of the personification of interracial power dynamics in a narrative otherwise devoid of such interactions.

Meyer also believes that the transition of Gunn represents a flight from blackness by the character which is inevitably rewarded with white privilege (i.e., a white girlfriend and an education).[57] Aside from the dangerous precedent set by deeming an education and speech devoid of street slang as "whiteness," Gunn's attempts to reshape his identity are constantly thwarted (his education is a brief and costly bribe from Wolfram & Hart) or ultimately result in loss (his sacrifice for Fred ends their relationship.) It is difficult to view Gunn's ultimate fate as a reward for his choices in any light. The idea of societal strain as a catalyst for deviant behavior is one that can be difficult for the viewer or reader in a consumer culture that idealizes individualism and class mobility over the moral obligations of citizenship inherent in the concept of democracy. The American Dream tells us that whatever we want is within our grasp and we need only opportunity to achieve it. *Angel's* strain allegory undermines such a fallacy eschewing Gunn's fairy tale ending in favor of a frustrating, sometimes hopeful, but ultimately tragic story that teaches us the danger in measuring every life by an objective set of standards for success or failure.

Race is a subject that is rarely dealt with in the Whedonverses. It would be easy to criticize Whedon's works for this omission, and to a certain extent criticism is well deserved. But there is also a polarizing effect that comes with explicit racial discourse that obscures the deeper, insidious nature of the type of barriers young people face in their attempts to assimilate into the American ideal. Gunn's story is the story of many young, African American men in urban settings and his struggle to find a place in American society is a story that is rarely told over the span of five seasons with continuing comic book story arcs. By allowing us to watch his rocky navigation of a white, middle class environment, we the viewers learn more about the realities of social mobility and stratification than we ever anticipated when choosing an escapist fantasy like *Angel* for an hour of television entertainment. In the end, Gunn's life is not measured by his career, education or appearance. It is his constant search for justice in what he continues to learn is a grossly unjust world that makes up who he is as a character.

NOTES

1. "War Zone," *Angel*, 1.20, DVD, written by Gary Campbell, directed by David Straiton (2000: Twentieth Century Fox, 2003).

2. See John A. Rich, *Wrong Place, Wrong Time: Trauma and Violence in the Lives of Young, Black Men* (Baltimore: Johns Hopkins University Press, 2009) in which Rich refers to this as the new "urban uniform" a phrase coined by sociologist Elijah Anderson.

3. "War Zone," *Angel*, 1.20, DVD, written by Gary Campbell, directed by David Straiton (2000: Twentieth Century Fox, 2003).

4. *Ibid.*

5. This trope can be traced to the 90's popularity of the urban crime drama, initiated in large part by the 1991 film *Boyz n the Hood*, DVD, John Singleton, 1991, United States, Sony Pictures Home Entertainment, 1998. For a discussion of films using this trope see R. Corliss and P. Coates, "Boyz of New Black City." *Time* 137, no. 24 (June 17, 1991): 64. *Academic Search Complete*, EBSCOhost.

6. Émile Durkheim, "On Anomie" in *Criminological Theory: Foundations and Perceptions*, ed. Stephen Shafer, Richard D. Knudten (New York: Lexington Books, 1977), 192.

7. *Ibid.*

8. Hope See Yen, "New College Graduates Facing Bleak Employment Landscape." *Community College Week*, 24, no. 20 (May 14, 2012): 10.

9. *Angel*, "War Zone," 1.20.

10. For a discussion of victimization and income levels, see Steven Levitt, "The Changing Relationship Between Income and Crime Victimization," *Economic Policy Review*, 5 (1999): 87–98.

11. Robert K. Merton, "Social Structure and Anomie." *American Sociological Review*, 3, no. 5 (October 1938): 672–682.

12. *Ibid.*

13. Linda Fuller, *The Cosby Show: Audiences, Impact and Implications* (Westport, CT: Greenwood Press, 1992): 136.

14. *Ibid.*

15. "War Zone," *Angel*, 1.20, DVD, written by Gary Campbell, directed by David Straiton (2000: Twentieth Century Fox, 2003).

16. "Untouched," *Angel*, 2.04, DVD, written by Mere Smith, directed by Joss Whedon (2000: Twentieth Century Fox, 2003).

17. "Redefinition," *Angel*, 2.11, DVD, written by Mere Smith, directed by Michael Grossman (2000: Twentieth Century Fox, 2003).

18. A. K. Cohen (1965). "The Sociology of the Deviant Act: Anomie Theory and Beyond," *American Sociological Review*, 30(1), 5–14.

19. *Ibid.*

20. *Ibid.*

21. Jeremy Bentham, *An Introduction to the Principles of Morals and Legislation* (Oxford: Clarendon Press, 1907), p. 3, Library of Economics and Liberty.

22. Lobdell, Scott (w), David Messina (p), *Angel: Only Human*, #3, IDW Publishing (October 2009).

23. *Ibid.*

24. Gunn's response to Angel's offer to pay him for his services is met with a dismissive, "Cool," in "Untouched," *Angel*, 2.4.

25. Lisa M. Broidy, "A Test of General Strain Theory," *Criminology*, 39.1 (2001), 9–36.

26. Agnew, "A Revised Strain Theory of Delinquency," 152.

27. This is also an example of Gunn's utilitarian nature, in that his focus is on the outcome of this exchange (the possession of a truck) rather than the moral implication of selling his soul for a material possession.

28. "First Impressions," *Angel* 2.3, DVD, written by Shawn Ryan, directed by James A. Contner (2000: Twentieth Century Fox, 2003).

29. Robert Agnew, Helene Raskin White, "An Empirical Test of General Strain Theory," *Criminology* 30 (1992): 475–499.

30. Old Gang of Mine," *Angel*, 3.03, DVD, written by Tim Minear, directed by Fred Keller (2001: Twentieth Century Fox, 2006).

31. *Angel*, "Warzone," 1.20.

32. Joanne M. Kaufman, Cesar J. Rebellon, Sherod Thaxton and Robert Agnew, "A General Strain Theory of Racial Differences in Criminal Offending," *The Australian and New Zealand Journal of Criminology*, Vol. 41, No. 3 (2008): pp. 421–439.

33. For an analysis of race, crime and general strain theory, see Anthony Hoskin, "Explaining the Link Between Race and Violence with General Strain Theory." *Journal of Ethnicity in Criminal Justice*, 9, no. 1 (January 2011): 56–73.

34. Rakesh Kochhar, Richard Fry and Paul Taylor, *Wealth Gaps Rise to Record Highs Between Whites, Blacks and Hispanics*, http://pewresearch.org/pubs/2069/housing-bubble-subprime-mortgages-hispanics-blacks-household-wealth-disparity. July 26, 2011.

35. "Warzone," *Angel*, 1.20.

36. Edward Said, *Orientalism* (New York: Random House, 1979): 3.

37. "That Old Gang of Mine," *Angel*, 3.3.

38. Steven Levitt, "The Changing Relationship Between Income and Crime Victimization," *Economic Policy Review*, 5 (1999): 87–98.

39. "Judgment," *Angel*, 2.1, DVD, written by Joss Whedon and David Greenwalt, directed by Michael Lange (2000: Twentieth Century Fox, 2003).

40. "First Impressions," *Angel*, 2.3, DVD, written by Shawn Ryan, directed by James A. Contner (2000: Twentieth Century Fox, 2003).

41. "The Thin Dead Line," *Angel*, 2.14, DVD, written by Jim Kouf and Shawn Ryan, directed by Scott McGinnis (2001: Twentieth Century Fox, 2003).

42. "Supersymmetry," *Angel,* 4.5, DVD, written by Elizabeth Craft and Saraj Fain, directed by Bill L. Norton (2002: Twentieth Century Fox, 2004).

43. Angel stops Fred from killing a member of Gunn's old gang in "That Old Gang of Mine" (*Angel* 2.3).

44. Conviction," *Angel*, 5.1, DVD, written by Joss Whedon, directed by Joss Wehdon (2003: Twentieth Century Fox, 2005).

45. Amuzie Chimezie, *Black Culture: Theory and Practice* (Shaker Heights, OH: The Keeble Press (1984).

46. See "Spin the Bottle," *Angel*, DVD, written by Joss Whedon, directed by Joss Whedon (2002: Twentieth Century Fox, 2004), in which a spell reverts the characters back to their teenage selves. Gunn responds to Wesley's question, "What school do you attend," with a dismissive eyeroll.

47. *Ibid.*

48. "Conviction," *Angel*, 5.1.

49. "A Hole in the World," *Angel*, 5.15, DVD, written by Joss Whedon, directed by Joss Whedon (2004: Twentieth Century Fox, 2005).

50. "Shells," *Angel,* 5.16, DVD, written by Steven S. DeKnight, directed by Steven S. DeKnight (2004: Twentieth Century Fox, 2005).

51. "Underneath," *Angel*, 5.16, DVD, written by Elizabeth Craft and Sarah Fein, directed by Skip Schoolnik (2004: Twentieth Century Fox, 2005).

52. See generally Scott Lobdell (w), David Messina (p), *Angel: Only Human*, IDW Publishing (October 2009).

53. "There's No Place Like Plrtz Glrb," *Angel* 2.21, DVD, written and directed by David Greenwalt (2001: Twentieth Century Fox, 2005).

54. "Shells," *Angel*, 5.16.

55. Michaela D.E. Meyer, "From Rogue in the 'Hood to Suave in a Suit: Black Masculinity and the Transformation of Charles Gunn," *Reading Angel: The TV Spin-Off with a Soul*, ed. Stacey Abbott (London: I.B. Tauris, 2005): 180–183.

56. *Ibid.*

57. *Ibid.*

PART III

Firefly/Serenity and Dollhouse

Examining Race and Ethnicity at the Margins of the 'Verses

Race, Space and the (De)Construction of Neocolonial Difference in *Firefly/Serenity*

BRENT M. SMITH-CASANUEVA

In the wake of the significant social, political, and economic shifts engendered by the processes of late capitalist globalization, an increasing number of science fiction texts have engaged with the shifting power structures of a "globalized" world. In fact, it might be argued that the characteristics of science fiction as a genre render it uniquely capable of engaging with the realities of the current global order. Fredric Jameson speaks to this capability in his suggestion that "the representational apparatus of Science Fiction [sic] ... is sending back more reliable information about the contemporary world than an exhausted realism."[1] In particular, the historical development and present iterations of the genre make it a potent forum for the exploration of neocolonial power structures within neoliberal globalization.[2]

Science fiction's engagement with colonial and neocolonial ideologies throughout its history has, however, been markedly ambivalent. This ambivalence has manifested itself in such contrasting representations as those of a benevolent and disinterested imperialism in the *Star Trek* franchise to the sympathetic portrayal of the Martian Others in Ray Bradbury's *The Martian Chronicles*.[3] This ambivalence is no less evident in recent science fiction films and television series that have explored the questions generated by the intensification of neocolonial power structures under the conditions of neoliberal globalization. Almost all of these texts have engaged in some way with the problem of Otherness raised by the opposition of First/Third World or core/periphery produced within dominant neocolonial discourse. Many recent series (notably the *Star Trek* and *Stargate* franchises), however, have tended to reproduce the essentialized and depoliticized imagining of this opposition through employing race (either different human races or the opposition of human/alien races) as a signifier of neocolonial difference and by recycling the racist tropes of colonial discourse. In its construction of neocolonial difference, however, Joss Whedon's *Firefly/Serenity*[4] provides an alternative to these essentializing representations, illuminating and subverting the Eurocentrism that naturalizes neocolonial power structures. In this essay, I argue that *Firefly*, unlike other contemporary science fiction series that employ race as a signifier of difference, rejects the racialization of neocolonial discourse and instead politicizes and de-essentializes neocolonial difference through foregrounding the political and economic forces inherent in its construction—specifically the diffuse and pervasive mechanisms of neocolonial power structures. Furthermore, I suggest that *Firefly* also celebrates new modes of resistance against these mechanisms and embodies these modes in its visual aesthetics.

Race, Neocolonial Difference and Global Capitalism

My interest in this essay is not in *Firefly*'s representation of any particular racial group but rather more broadly in the construction—and specifically the *racialization*—of political and cultural difference between the "First" and "Third World" within dominant discourses and the ways in which we can understand *Firefly* as destabilizing these constructions and challenging the Eurocentric power structures that produce them. Such an approach necessitates an understanding of race not as a fixed category but, as Stuart Hall has suggested, a "floating signifier" that is historically contingent and discursively constructed within particular power/knowledge regimes.[5] Race is, as Hall argues more generally of cultural identities, "far from being fixed in some essentialised [sic] past" but is instead "subject to the continuous 'play' of history, culture and power."[6] To understand more precisely the specific relations of history, culture and power involved in the construction of racial difference and *Firefly*'s challenge to this construction, we must consider the political, economic and social colonization of the "Third World" by Europe and the United States—both in its historical development and in its persistence in the present in the form of U.S.-led global neoliberalization. The use of race as a signifier of difference is a central feature of colonial discourse and is deeply embedded within the power structures and historical development of colonialism. As Anibal Quijano argues, the Spanish colonization of the Americas inaugurated a new model of global power, "one of the fundamental axes... [of which] is the *social classification of the world's population around the idea of race*, a mental construction that expresses the basic experience of colonial domination and pervades the more important dimensions of global power, including its specific rationality: Eurocentrism."[7] The development of a system of social classification based on the idea of race was thus fundamental to the construction of European identity and to the legitimatization of colonialism.

Racism as a "classifying matrix" does not, however, operate solely on the basis of skin color but also, as Walter Mignolo points out, "extends to the realm of human activities like religions, languages … and geopolitical classifications of the world"; thus, "racialization is applied not only to people, but to language, religions, knowledge, countries, and continents as well."[8] Central to this expansive process of racialization has been the operation of a Eurocentric colonial discourse—a broad intertextual network of images, ideas, and stereotypes produced in Western cultural texts that have represented the peoples, cultures, landscapes, etc., of the world outside of Europe and North America—a discourse that has constructed what Edward Said terms an "imaginative geography" of the world.[9] As we will see, *Firefly*'s engagement with this imaginative geography through its politicization of the opposition between the "core" and "border" planets is crucial to the series' deconstruction of racialized difference. Within colonial imaginative geographies, the difference between colonizer and colonized is conceived not as one produced through historical relations of power but as one naturally existing between (superior and inferior) races inhabiting different spaces. Contemporary science fiction series have too often tended to reproduce these dominant imaginative geographies through their representations of alterity (most often between human and alien) within the spatial constructions of their narrative universe that displace global geographies onto an interplanetary stage. In series like *Star Trek* and *Stargate SG-1*, the societies discovered on other planets are often either represented as "primitive" and their technological underdevelopment naturalized in the terms of an evolutionary anthropological perspective, or they are "advanced" but shown as tyrannical and undemocratic or in some other way, lacking the moral qualities that characterize the explorers from Earth.[10] In this way, neocolonial difference is constructed as a natural product of either societal development along a linear timeline—there is, to borrow Johannes Fabian's phrase, a "denial of coevalness"—or of an essential moral deficiency or inferiority. It is here where *Firefly* departs significantly from many previous engagements with neocolonial power structures.

In employing the term "neocolonial difference" within my discussion of contemporary hegemonic imaginative geographies and *Firefly*'s destabilization of these geographies, I am borrowing from Mignolo's concept of "colonial difference": the irreducible difference within modernity/colonialism that has structured knowledge and power globally along the lines of center/periphery.[11] I add the prefix "neo" not to suggest the existence of any historical rupture between colonialism and neocolonialism or to deemphasize the continuities between the two, but rather simply to draw attention to the new global politico-economic structures under which colonial power relations persist in the neocolonial present, as these structures are especially evident in the narrative universe of *Firefly*. In particular, the transglobal order under the hegemony of the Alliance decidedly represents the current transnational order of late capitalist globalization that Michael Hardt and Antoni Negri have termed Empire. Two of the most important (and interrelated) developments in the transition to this new order have been the shift Hardt and Negri identify from an imperialist to an imperial mode of power[12] and the emergence of neoliberalism as the dominant economic logic of this new global order.[13] Together these two developments have created the conditions under which the expansion of global capitalism has effectively intensified the divisions in the distribution of wealth between the center and periphery. In *Firefly*, this center/periphery division is allegorized in the opposition between the core and border planets. As we learn in the pilot, the core planets are those under tighter Alliance control, enjoying great material wealth and advanced technology while the border planets, those who resisted unification by the Alliance, suffer from poverty and underdevelopment.[14] This opposition between core and border becomes, as we will see, central to *Firefly*'s politicized and de-essentialized construction of difference.

De-racializing Difference, Destabilizing Eurocentrsim

Perhaps more important than *Firefly*'s commentary on the diffuse power structures and insidious economic logic of late capitalist globalization is its destabilizing of the Eurocentrism that continues to subtend these realities. Eurocentrism has been, as I have argued above, essential to the construction of neocolonial difference within the current global order. In contrast to the Eurocentric perspective offered to viewers by series like *Star Trek* and *Stargate SG-1*,[15] the narrative identification in *Firefly* centers on Mal—a former soldier who fought against the Alliance with the Independents—and his crew of outlaws that includes two fugitives, Simon and River, on the run from the Alliance. The association with lawlessness and the specter of vanquished revolution clearly situate these characters on the margins of transglobal society and in opposition to the panoptic authority of the Alliance. The crew of Serenity's association with the border planets as opposed to the core planets (with the exception of Simon and River) further confirms the marginality of the central characters.

Unlike many other contemporary science fiction series, which employ race as a signifier of difference, either in constructing Otherness through an opposition of human/alien races or through the deployment of racial signifiers to establish distinctions between groups of humans, *Firefly* eschews neocolonial discourse's racialization of difference. In *Firefly*, neither the core nor border planets are racially marked, either by skin color or cultural association. In terms of skin color, the populations of both core and border planets appear racially mixed (although it could be noted that both tend to be predominantly white), as does the crew of Serenity. There is also no significant difference in culture (at least in terms of racialized difference) between the two sets of planets; both exhibit a mix of Anglo-American and Chinese cultural influences. Both the bustling markets on the central planets, such as the one we see in "Serenity" (1.1) and the kitsch-filled gift shops on the border planets showcase a mix of Americana and Asian styles in their merchandise. This cultural blend is, however, not suggested as a product of innocuous mixing and thus does not fit within a depoliticized neoliberal multiculturalist framing but is instead explicitly connected to the political and economic hegemony of the United States and China on "Earth that was" and the persistence of these power structures under the transglobal order of the Alliance. *Firefly* also, rather than employing the familiar science fiction trope of using alien races as representations of Otherness, provides a universe inhabited solely by humans. As Judith Leggatt notes, presenting a human, rather than extraterrestrial, Other in science fiction texts "emphasizes the similarities between ... conflicting societies, rather than their differences."[16] The humanizing of Otherness in *Firefly* allows the series, in contrast with other contemporary science fiction texts, to construct the difference between groups as a function of political and economic forces rather than a product of essentialized racial and cultural oppositions.[17]

Firefly's destabilization of racialized neocolonial discourse, however, is most clearly demonstrated in its representation of the group that most embodies absolute alterity: the Reavers. Again, rather than employing race as a signifier of difference in its representation of this absolute Other, *Firefly* instead politicizes and de-essentializes the difference through foregrounding the political and economic forces inherent in its construction, highlighting in *Serenity* that the Reavers were produced through the actions of the Alliance. The Reavers are neither racially marked (either by skin color or cultural/religious association) nor of extraterrestrial origin. While some scholars have argued that the Reavers can be read as American Indian, and there are certainly specific elements of the Reavers' appearance and the mythology surrounding the Reavers that support this view, I would argue that rather than representations of a particular group, the Reavers can be read as allegorical of the absolute Otherness that colonized populations are often made to embody.[18] The tropes self-consciously referenced in *Firefly*'s depiction of the

Reavers point to the discursive production of various colonized groups (the cannibalism of the Reavers, for instance, suggests colonialist imaginings of Indigenous Caribbean and Brazilian populations) rather than that of an actual single group. This allegorical function of the Reavers, along with the humanization and absence of specific racial signification in *Firefly*'s representation of them, allows the series to construct the violent and savage actions of the Reavers not as essentialized characteristics of their racial origin but as the product of particular political forces, specifically the Alliance's neocolonial expansion and attempts at "civilizing" the inhabitants of the outer planets. In *Serenity*, Mal and the crew discover, through a video communiqué they find on the abandoned border planet of Miranda, that the Reavers are the result of an Alliance experiment gone awry. The Alliance, the video reveals, released a sedative into the planet's atmosphere in an attempt to create a peaceful, well-adjusted society and workforce. While the sedative had the desired effect on most of the population, it had the reverse effect for a small portion that became ultra-violent and murdered many of the other inhabitants. The Reavers then left the planet, traveling through the outer reaches of the system and preying on and pillaging ships they encounter.[19] Thus, the existence of the Reavers is de-essentialized, presented as an adverse product of the neocolonial power relationships embodied by the intertwined political and economic interests of the Alliance and their attempts at control over the subjectivity of the population.

Firefly also exposes the obscuring of these global power relations in colonial discourse through its seemingly self-conscious invocation of colonialist tropes in earlier references to the Reavers. When Simon is asked whether he has ever heard of Reavers, he responds that he has only heard "campfire stories" that, in a manner that evokes the spatial imaginary of Joseph Conrad's *Heart of Darkness*,[20] told of men losing their minds and turning savage on the edge of the universe, a narrative echoed in Mal's comment that the Reavers, existing so long in nothing, became nothing.[21] In *Serenity*, during a flashback in which River is a young student in an Alliance classroom, a teacher lectures to the students about the uncivilized and barbaric inhabitants of the outer planets, some of whom, she tells them, are even cannibals.[22] Here, the warnings about cannibals recall early colonial stories about the indigenous inhabitants of the Americas. Both of these instances present the essentializing tendencies of (neo)colonial discourse—in Simon and Mal's comments, the edge of the universe, like Conrad's Africa, is essentialized as a space of savagery and in the classroom lecture the inhabitants of these spaces, like the indigenous Americans, are essentialized as savages. The revelation of the Reavers' true origins as a product of the Alliance's expansion, however, subverts these colonial discursive constructions through exposing the political and economic interests they obscure.

(Outer) Spaces of Conflict

Crucial to *Firefly*'s politicization and de-essentialization of neocolonial difference is the series' geographic imaginary. As John Rieder notes, science fiction has been "shaped throughout its history by the imaginary relationship of the European (and later American) economic core to the periphery or 'contact zone' between capitalist and non-capitalist economies and western and non-western cultures."[23] This "imaginary relationship" is central to the spatio-temporal geographies of *Firefly*, and the disparity in the distribution of technology across these geographies is a pivotal feature of the series' spatial and temporal imaginaries. While other science fiction series—and here again *Stargate* and *Star Trek* provide instructive examples—reify technological development through essentializing representations of other cultures and the spaces they inhabit and code "the uneven distribution of technology across a spatial geography … as a temporal one,"[24] *Firefly* politicizes and historicizes the spatial disparity in technology as a product of global economic power structures. In other words, *Firefly* departs from most science fiction in that rather than depicting differences in the level of technological advancement between planets as a result of natural characteristics of a particular culture or a culture's temporal separation along a linear timeline of historical development, it highlights the political and economic processes through which this difference is produced. Thus, in *Firefly*, the relationship between core and periphery is imagined as one produced through capitalist globalization's "uneven geographical development," to borrow David Harvey's phrase.[25] In particular, the series highlights the way in which capitalism articulates all historical forms of labor in the pursuit of profit.

In "Jaynestown" (1.7) we are exposed on one of the border planets to the "Mudders," workers who exist in a semi-feudal labor relationship with Higgins, the local magistrate.[26] As the foreman explains to Simon, the workers are "mostly indentured" and are paid "next to nothing."[27] The Mudders' labor is inserted into the interglobal circuits of capitalist exchange as Mal explains to the crew that the mud mined by the workers is purchased by businessmen from the central planets. The local economic power relationships such as those between the Mudders and Magistrate Higgins are a central feature of the peripheral spaces of the border planets, where a small economic elite (often only one individual) holds control over the planet's economic resources while the rest of the population lives in abject poverty. In "Heart of Gold" (1.13) for example, Ranse Burgess's lavish wealth, exemplified by his ultra high-tech weaponry, is counter-posed to the relative poverty of the bordello and the citizens of the local town.[28] As Nandi tells Mal, Ranse has enough money to vastly improve the condition of the town, but he instead keeps it all to himself. In these planetary economic power relationships, we can see an allegory for the state of many postcolonial nations, in which a small national economic elite—most often with close ties to U.S. and European economic interests—holds control over the vast majority of the nation's resources. The resonance of this allegory is quite powerfully attested to by the recent global spread of the Occupy movement and its rhetoric of the 99 percent and 1 percent, which evinces a growing consciousness of global conditions of inequality. While the economic elite of the border planets in *Firefly* are not always directly part of the Alliance, they nevertheless serve as a kind of stand-in for the power of the Alliance and its economic and political oppression of the citizenry. In this way, figures like Burgess, Higgins, and Saffron's former husband Durran—who although not explicitly part of the alliance, lives in extreme wealth and with the dedicated protection of the Alliance[29]—embody what Quijano terms the "coloniality of power" to situate the power of the postcolonial national elite within the larger power structures of global capitalism.[30]

The border planets also, however, become spaces of potential resistance to the power represented by the Alliance and the local economic elite, as we see in both "Jaynestown" (1.7) and "Heart of Gold" (1.13). In "Jaynestown," (1.7) the arrival of Jayne—who we discover became an unlikely folk hero to the workers after he, several years prior, unintentionally dumped money he had stolen from Magistrate Higgins over the Mudders' village—inspires a worker uprising against Higgins.[31] In "Heart of Gold" (1.13), the crew joins Nandi and the other men and women of the bordello in an ultimately successful battle against Ranse and his posse.[32] The narrative's construction of the border planets as spaces of conflict is affirmed in the visual representation of these spaces, representations that frequently deny the spectator any privileged standpoint from which to observe and possess these spaces. In other words, the rare visual glimpses we are given of the border planets affirm their construction as sites of conflict through refusing the viewer a placid "god's-eye view."

Firefly's neocolonial landscapes thus exist always as sites of potential resistance that constantly threaten to elude the panoptic gaze of the Alliance and that de-center the privileged gaze of the European or North American spectator dominant in visual representations of colonized landscapes.[33] This is particularly evident during a standoff on the border planet of Whitefall between Mal and Constance, the local "mayor" who has double-crossed Mal.[34] The standoff is captured almost entirely through tight shots that alternate between Mal's and Constance's point of view. Even the shots from the perspective of Jayne, who is hiding above in the hills with a sniper rifle, are restricted to Jayne's view through the scope of the rifle and are followed by reverse-shots that reveal Jayne's position, thus drawing attention to the embodiment of this perspective. The spectator's gaze, then, is mostly limited to the narrow perspective of the different characters in the scene, all but denying the spectator a sense of spatial mastery and visual possession of the foreign landscape.

Firefly's employment of the generic conventions of the Western genre is also of particular importance to the series' construction of the border planets as spaces produced through capitalist globalization, particularly in allegorizing the centrality of the market in determining relations between individuals under neoliberalism, and in gesturing towards new forms of social organization within these conditions of possibility. While the Western has traditionally functioned as a predominately conservative genre, Daniel Worden notes that the genre has produced, in recent years, texts that engage in a more complex way with the contemporary realities of neoliberal globalization. In his reading of the HBO series *Deadwood*, Worden notes the way in which the series "allegorize[s] the impact of neo-liberalism upon subjects and social organization"[35] through its depiction of a town in which the only order is an economic one and the "residents relate to one another strategically and are quick to sever ties and create new ones as social and economic situations shift."[36] *Firefly* presents a very similar allegorization in its representation of social relationships on the border planets as determined by their economic necessity and characterized by their contingency. This is particularly evident in Mal's relationships with the various individuals he and the crew perform jobs for—Constance and Badger are two notable examples— as well as in the relationship between Jayne and the rest of the crew, as these relationships quickly shift when the situation provides more profitable possibilities for either party.[37] However, *Firefly* also points towards possibilities for the formation of new collectivities within this neoliberal system and outside of the traditional liberal framework of government intervention. Here again, Worden's analysis of *Deadwood* is instructive. Worden argues that "the show gestures to possibilities for the redirection of neo-liberal effects"[38] in the formation of "strategic alliances that break the very logic of the free market from within. By acting as self-interested agents, individual neo-liberal actors can form collectives that place limits on the free market."[39]

In *Firefly*, the crew of Serenity represents exactly this sort of "strategic alliance" as it is formed under the conditions of the free market—the primary purpose for the formation of the crew is, after all, to make a living—but in its collectivity presents an alternative logic to that of the neoliberal global order. This collectivity is one, furthermore, that encompasses individuals representing a relatively broad diversity in terms of race, religion, class, and even sexual orientation: markers typically employed in homogenizing constructions of neocolonial difference. Thus, the dynamics of the crew are a product of contingent and strategic alliances rather than of essentialized racial difference.

Mobility and Resistance

Beyond mapping the social and economic relations of uneven geographical development produced within neoliberal globalization, *Firefly* valorizes new forms of resistance that also take on a distinctly spatial character. From the position of marginality in which they are situated and in the face of an oppressive transglobal order, the crew of Serenity does not attempt to directly confront the Alliance or to engage in revolutionary violence against the representatives of its order. The defeat of the Independents at the Valley of Serenity clearly marks the impossibility of traditional revolutionary action in the present global order.[40] Instead, the transgressive acts of the crew of Serenity are to be found in their affirmation of a strategic and liberatory mobility.[41]

Within the context of a decentralized network of power, the mobility of Mal and his crew takes on a particularly subversive and liberating character. As Hardt and Negri argue, mobility represents an especially potent form of resistance against the current global order, one that "always express[es] a refusal and a search for liberation: the resistance against the horrible conditions of exploitation and the search for freedom and new conditions of life."[42] In *Firefly*, the spaceship Serenity itself becomes a central symbol of this liberating and transgressive mobility. In "Out of Gas" (1.5) Mal flashes back to the moment, shortly after buying Serenity, that he showed the ship to Zoe. Mal shares with her his vision for their nomadic life aboard the ship with a "small crew, them as feel the need to be free. Take jobs as they come—and we'll never be under the heel of nobody ever again. *No matter how long the arm of the Alliance might get ... we'll just get us a little further.*"[43] For Mal, the ship and the mobile existence it affords him and his crew thus become a response to the power of the Alliance, a response characterized by agility and elusiveness rather than violent confrontation. The ship holds a similar symbolic meaning for Simon and River, as the constant movement of the ship allows them to stay always just beyond the reach of the Alliance operatives hunting them. The connection between the ship as a signifier of mobility and opposition to the Alliance is further established through the addition of Shepherd Book to the crew. Book, who was an operative for the Independents and became a Shepherd (i.e., pastor) after the defeat by the Alliance,[44] tells Kaylee that he is more interested in the ship than the destination.[45] Just as it does for Mal, the ship symbolizes for Book mobility as a form of resistance against a power that he was unable to defeat through participation in traditional revolutionary activity. As Matthew Hill notes, the mobility embodied by Serenity is also communicated visually through the use of handheld cameras for interior shots of the ship and their opposition to the static shots in scenes occurring on the core planets.[46] Perhaps the most powerful visual evocation of the ship's interior as a space of mobility is the opening of *Serenity*, a four-minute long tracking shot that takes us with Mal on a fluid tour of the ship.[47]

Firefly does not, however, simply and unproblematically celebrate free movement. It also, through highlighting the barriers to mobility imposed on the crew of Serenity and those living on the border planets, exposes the dissonance between neoliberal globalization's promise of uninhibited movement for both goods and people and the restrictions on the movement of those on the margins of global society. The necessity of avoiding the grasp of the Alliance in order to maintain mobility often places the crew of Serenity in perilous situations, forcing them into Reaver territory or leaving them at the mercy of ruthless outlaws on the border planets. This is nowhere more evident than when Serenity breaks down on the outer reaches of the galaxy in "Out of Gas" (1.5); as Wash points out, Mal's insistence that they stay off the grid has left them stranded far away from any ships that might receive their distress signal.[48] Thus, the barriers to the free movement of Serenity ultimately threaten not only the crew's continued mobility but also their very lives. This perilous and restricted mobility—analogous to the dangerous journeys of undocumented immigrants across national borders—stands in sharp contrast to the free and uninhibited movement of goods throughout the universe. When, in "Ariel" (1.8) the crew discusses a possible job in which they would steal medicine from an Alliance hospital, Kaylee protests that the patients would need the medicine. Mal reassures her by pointing out that, since it's an Alliance hospital, the drugs would be replaced immediately.[49] The barriers to the movement of Mal and his crew are thus opposed here to the instantaneous flow of goods across space through the Alliance-controlled distribution channels.

Despite the importance of mobility for the crew of Serenity, the series also suggests the refusal to move as an equally valid and potentially effective response to power. In "Heart of Gold" (1.13) for example, the crew helps the inhabitants of a bordello on one of the border planets in their fight against the local strongman Ranse Burgess. Worried that they would be outgunned by Ranse and his men, Mal suggests that the inhabitants run away, escaping the planet with them aboard Serenity. However, Nandi, the owner of the bordello, refuses, responding that this is their home and that she isn't going to let Ranse take it away from them. The ensuing defensive battle is, despite claiming several casualties including Nandi, ultimately successful and Ranse is killed.[50] Here, we see that rejection of mobility can constitute an equally potent stance of being-against as does Mal and the crew's constant movement. Or, perhaps more precisely, rather than rejecting mobility, *Firefly* here valorizes mobility at another level, that of strategy. In other words, a mobile and agile strategy of resistance contingent on the given conditions within a particular situation is affirmed over a totalizing and prescriptive strategy of resistance.

Science Fiction and the "Cognitive Mapping" of Difference

In considering the potential of science fiction to provide a critical engagement with the realities of a world increasingly shaped by "globalizing" flows of capital, knowledge, technologies and people, I find it fruitful to return to Jameson, who has suggested that one of the primary problems of late capitalism is the inability of the individual to locate herself or himself within a "mental map of the social and global totality."[51] While Jameson's conceptualization of a "totality" is certainly problematic,[52] I find his gesture towards the need for an aesthetics of "cognitive mapping" productive. Furthermore, I would agree with Phillip E. Wegner's suggestion that science fiction is especially capable of engaging in such an aesthetic practice.[53] In *Firefly's* politicized spacescape, structured as it is by the complex political and economic forces that the series strives to make visible, we can, I think, see a glimpse of science fiction's capacity to produce a complex spatial image of our present global reality. *Firefly* moves beyond just providing the individual a way in which to locate herself or himself within a diffuse network of global power relations. *Firefly's* geographic imaginary destabilizes the hegemonic racialized imaginative geographies of neocolonial discourse through politicizing and de-essentializing neocolonial difference. The series allows the individual to locate *both self and other* within complex global, social, and economic power structures, providing a way of cognitively mapping difference that deconstructs the racialized and de-politicized imaginaries that remain dominant within the current global order. In addition to constructing a politicized map of difference within a complex social reality, *Firefly* also suggests a way of acting spatially, one emphasizing mobility and agility to subvert and resist the hegemonic logic of this global order. As the ideological struggles of our present moment continue to play out in the ambivalent imaginary of science fiction, one can hope that the potential within the genre to which *Firefly* points for a critical engagement with the complex realities of late capitalist globalization and neocolonialism is one that will increasingly be realized.

NOTES

1. Fredric Jameson, ""Fear and Loathing in Globalization," in *What Democracy Looks Like: A New Critical Realism for a Post-Seattle World*, eds. Amy Schrager Lang and Cecila Tichi (New Brunswick, NJ: Rutgers University Press, 2006), 123.

2. By "neocolonial" I mean the continuation of colonial political and economic relationships of power between "First World" and "Third World" nations following the end of most forms of direct colonialism. In relation to this understanding, "neoliberalism" refers to the economic ideology underpinning the efforts of transnational organizations like the WTO, IMF, and World Bank to open "Third World" labor and commodity markets to Western corporations.

3. Ericka Hoagland and Reema Sarwal, "Introduction," in *Science Fiction, Imperialism and the Third World: Essays on Postcolonial Literature and Film*, eds. Ericka Hoagland and Reema Sarwal (Jefferson, NC: McFarland, 2010), 7–11.

4. From this point forward, I will use *Firefly* to refer collectively to both *Firefly* and *Serenity*.

5. Stuart Hall, "What Is This 'black' in Black Popular Culture?" *Social Justice*, 20, no. 1/2 (1993): 111.

6. *Ibid.*, "Cultural Identity and Cinematic Representation," *Framework* 36 (1989): 70.

7. Aníbal Quijano, "Coloniality of Power, Eurocentrism, and Social Classification," in *Coloniality at Large: Latin America and the Postcolonial Debate*, eds. Mabel Moraña, Enrique Dussel, and Carlos A. Jáuregui (Durham, NC: Duke University Press, 2008), 181 (my emphasis).

8. Walter Mignolo, *The Idea of Latin America* (Malden, MA: Blackwell, 2005), 17.

9. On the concept of 'imaginative geographies,' see Edward Said, *Orientalism* (New York: Random House, 1979).

10. On neocolonialism and neocolonial discourse in *Stargate* and *Star Trek*, see Scott Simpson and Jessica Sheffield, "Neocolonialism, Technology, and Myth in the Stargate Universe," in *Siths, Slayers, Stargates, and Cyborgs: Modern Mythology in the New Millenium*, eds. David Whitt and John Perlich (New York: Peter Lang, 2008) and Kent A. Ono, "Domesticating Terrorism: A Neocolonial Economy of Différance," in *Enterprise Zones: Critical Positions on Star Trek*, eds. Taylor Harrison, Sarah Projansky, Kent A. Ono, and Elyce Rae Helford (Boulder, CO: Westview Press, 1996).

11. Walter Mignolo, "The Geopolitics of Knowledge and the Colonial Difference," in Moraña, Dussel and Jáuregui, 229–231.

12. See Michael Hardt and Antoni Negri, *Empire* (Cambridge, MA: Harvard University Press, 2000).

13. On the historical development of neoliberalism, see David Harvey, *A Brief History of Neoliberalism* (Oxford: Oxford University Press, 2005).

14. "Serenity," *Firefly* 1.1, DVD, written and directed by Joss Whedon (2002: Twentieth Century Fox, 2008).

15. In *Star Trek*, viewer identification is aligned with the Federation, a transglobal governmental organization with origins in the United States. In *Stargate SG-1*, narrative identification centers on Stargate Command, a U.S. military organization dedicated to defending Earth and less developed alien civilizations. In both cases, the center of narrative identification is with organizations that mirror Eurocentric transnational networks of power in the contemporary era.

16. Judith Leggatt, "Critiquing Economic and Environmental Colonization: Globalization and Science Fiction in *The Moons of Palmares*," in *Science Fiction, Imperialism and the Third World: Essays on Postcolonial Literature and Film*, eds. Ericka Hoagland and Reema Sarwal (Jefferson, NC: McFarland, 2010), 132.

17. I do not mean to suggest here that the use of alien races as representations of Otherness necessarily always reproduces Eurocentric conceptions of difference. Furthermore, the absence of alien cultures in *Firefly* could alternatively be read as an example of human exceptionalism, in which case it could be understood as reinscribing the humanist ideology that underpins neoliberalism. However, the Reavers—as human figures turned, as a result of neocolonial expansion, into figures no longer recognizable as human—problematize the boundaries of the "human" and thereby complicate, even if they do not entirely subvert, neoliberal humanist ideology.

18. See Agnes B. Curry, "'We don't say "Indian"': On the Paradoxical Construc-

tion of the Reavers," *Slayage: The Online International Journal of Buffy Studies*, 25, no. 1 (2008) and J. Douglas Rabb and J. Michael Richardson, "Reavers and Redskins: Creating the Frontier Savage," in *Investigating Firefly and Serenity: Science Fiction on the Frontier*, eds. Rhonda V. Wilcox and Tanya R. Cochran (New York: I.B. Tauris, 2008), 127–38. While Rabb and Richardson argue that *Firefly* deconstructs and subverts stereotypical images of American Indians, Curry suggests that the series ends up in fact resinscribing these stereotypes. However, if we understand the Reavers as allegorical of colonial Otherness in general, as I suggest here, the discussion shifts beyond this disagreement over questions of stereotyping to an interrogation of whether or not *Firefly* reproduces or subverts the essentializing and depoliticizing operations of colonial and neocolonial discourse.

19. *Serenity*, DVD, Joss Whedon (2005, Universal City, CA: Universal Studios, 2007).

20. On colonial discourse and Conrad's *Heart of Darkness* see Edward Said, *Culture and Imperialism* (New York: Alfred A. Knopf, 1993).

21. "Bushwacked," *Firefly* 1.2, DVD, written and directed by Tim Minear (2002: Twentieth Century Fox, 2008).

22. *Serenity*.

23. John Rieder, "Spectacle, Technology and Colonialism in SF Cinema: The Case of Wim Wenders' Until the End of the World," in *Red Planets: Marxism and Science Fiction*, eds. Mark Bould and China Miéville (Middletown, CT: Wesleyan University Press, 2009), 85–86.

24. *Ibid.*, 86.

25. On the notion of "uneven geographical development" in neoliberal globalization, see Harvey, *A Brief History*.

26. "Jaynestown," *Firefly* 1.4, DVD, written by Ben Edlund, directed by Marita Grabiak (2002: Twentieth Century Fox, 2008).

27. *Ibid.*

28. "Heart of Gold," *Firefly* 1.12, written by Brett Matthews, directed by Thomas J. Wright (2003: Twentieth Century Fox, 2008).

29. "Trash," *Firefly* 1.13, written by Ben Edlund and Jose Molina, directed by Vern Gillum (2003: Twentieth Century Fox, 2008).

30. On the "coloniality of power" see Quijano, "Coloniality of Power" and Mignolo, *The Idea*.

31. *Firefly*, "Jaynestown," 1.4.

32. *Firefly*, "Heart of Gold," 1.12.

33. On the colonial gaze in visual culture see W. J. T. Mitchell, "Imperial Landscape," in *Landscape and Power*, ed. W. J. T. Mitchell (Chicago: University of Chicago Press, 2002) and Ella Shohat and Robert Stam, *Unthinking Eurocentrism: Multiculturalism and the Media* (London: Routledge, 1994).

34. *Firefly*, "Serenity," 1.1. It is interesting to note here that this view of the border planets is established in the pilot episode (or what was supposed to be the pilot episode), thus foregrounding their role as allegorical of neocolonized spaces at the beginning of the series.

35. Daniel Worden, "Neo-Liberalism and the Western: HBO's Deadwood as National Allegory," *Canadian Review of American Studies*, 39, no. 2 (2009): 224.

36. *Ibid.*, 228.

37. We see the crew's interaction with Badger in both "Serenity" (1.1) and "Shindig" (1.6). *Firefly*, "Serenity," 1.1 and "Shindig," *Firefly* 1.6, written by Jane Espenson, directed by Vern Gillum (2002: Twentieth Century Fox).

38. Worden, 226.

39. *Ibid.*, 235.

40. *Firefly*, "Serenity," 1.11.

41. Matthew Hill has similarly noted the significance of mobility in *Firefly*. However, he suggests understanding the series as a post–9/11 national allegory, in which the mobility of the crew (and Mal in particular) serves as a response to the sense of immobilizing national trauma brought on by the events of 9/11. While I would agree with Hill's suggestion that *Firefly* "is the story of the defeated, survivors who linger at the margins of a dominant culture and must find a way to survive in the wake of traumatic defeat," I would suggest that the crew of Serenity embodies the globally, rather than simply the nationally, marginalized. The power structures signified by the Alliance are not state-centered and exclusionary but transnational and expansive. Matthew B. Hill, "'I am a leaf on the wind': Cultural Trauma and Mobility in Joss Whedon's Firefly." *Extrapolation*, 50, no. 3 (2009): 485.

42. Hardt and Negri, 212.

43. "Out of Gas," *Firefly*, 1.5, written by Tim Minear, directed by David Solomon (2002: Twentieth Century Fox, 2008).

44. This element of Book's backstory, only vaguely intimated in the series, is explained in the graphic novel *Serenity: The Shepherd's Tale.* Zack Whedon and Joss Whedon, *Serenity: The Shepherd's Tale* (Milwaukie, OR: Dark Horse, 2010).

45. *Firefly*, "Serenity," 1.11.

46. Hill, 493.

47. *Serenity*, DVD, Joss Whedon (2005, Universal City, CA: Universal Studios, 2007).

48. *Firefly*, "Out of Gas," 1.5.

49. "Ariel," *Firefly* 1.8, written by Jose Molina, directed by Allan Kroeker (2002: Twentieth Century Fox, 2008).

50. *Firefly*, "Heart of Gold," 1.12.

51. Fredric Jameson, "Cognitive Mapping," in *Marxism and the Interpretation of Culture*, eds. Cary Nelson and Lawrence Grossberg (Urbana: University of Illinois Press, 1988), 353.

52. On this point see Cornell West's response to Jameson in *ibid.*, 360.

53. Phillip E. Wegner, "Soldierboys for Peace: Cognitive Mapping, Space, and Science Fiction as World Bank Literature," in *World Bank Literature*, ed. Amitava Kumar (Minneapolis: University of Minnesota Press, 2003), 284.

Mexicans in Space?

Joss Whedon's Firefly, Reavers and the Man They Call Jayne

DAOINE S. BACHRAN

Critics have lauded Joss Whedon's work for its remarkable and transgressive treatment of gender.[1] However, his work's interaction with race is far more complicated. Jeffrey Middents notes that the *Buffy*verse is a white, middle-upper class space, where images of blackness are few and often tied to evil or demons.[2] Images of brownness—or more specifically images of Mexicans and Chicanas/os—are even fewer. For a world set in southern California, the absence of the area's largest ethnic group is problematic. Whedon's series do engage issues of immigration, even as Mexicans are missing from the overt plots and casting. Jane Stadler points out that "Buffy's task was to protect her home from savage 'aliens' spilling over the border. *Angel* is set in an actual city located near the Mexican border," and the problems with immigration faced by people in Los Angeles are articulated on a continuum ranging from human (good) to demon (evil).[3] There are scant literal representations of Mexican-Americans or Mexico in both series. The actress who plays Kennedy, Iyari Limon, is Mexican-American, but cultured as a lesbian instead of a woman of color, a move which marginalizes possible considerations of ethnic identity to focus on issues of gender and sexuality. *Angel* devotes an episode—"The Cautionary Tale of Numero Cinco" (5.6), perhaps the only one of Whedon's to deal with immigrant humans directly—to a broken Chicano man who, alongside his four brothers, has a wrestling mask for a face and a number for a name.[4] Though engaging in the tradition of lucha libre, the representation of the series' scant Mexican subjects as faceless numbers hearkens to a cinematic and televisual history of omitting the Mexican presence from productions filmed and staged in southern California.[5] Though Numero Cinco is literally figured as Mexican, he is symbolic of the absence of *Mexicanidad* in Whedon's work, an absence reflective of ignored and feared Mexican immigrants, faceless and numerous, in California specifically and the Southwest generally.

Given the dearth of Mexican and Chicana/o characters in Whedon's initial series, it's not surprising that this chronic absence continues into Whedon's space Western, *Firefly*. This trait appears to be further confirmed when one considers the position of Mexico within the Western genre itself: representing what is not visible in the camera's frame, but threatens the subjects being filmed nonetheless.[6] This invisibility is doubled with the conspicuous absence of Mexicans in the very science fiction genres Whedon sought to humanize and personalize with *Firefly*, such as *Star Trek* and *Babylon 5*.[7] In the realm of televisual studies, according to the logic of representation, that which is most hidden is often most pressing. Whedon's chronic lack of Chicanas/os or Mexicans in his southwestern productions, coupled with his choice of genres, makes *Firefly* a space in which U.S./Mexico border issues are central; they are worked on, but not worked out. In *Firefly*, the space beyond the rim and the Reavers are representative of Mexico and social fears of immigration. Jayne Cobb, marked as a Mexican cowboy, a vaquero, enables issues of immigration to frighten the viewer, but defuses these fears with humor and allows us to be assured that the "threat" posed by Mexicans is under control. Simultaneously, the faceless, countless immigrants still in Mexico are subsumed within the image of the "savage" Reavers and the empty space beyond the rim.[8]

Theorizing Absence: Mass Culture, Westerns and Science Fiction

Fredric Jameson heavily theorized issues of representation in film and other forms of mass culture, arguing that "mass culture entertain[s] relations of repression with the fundamental social anxieties and concerns, hopes and blind spots, ideological antinomies and fantasies of disaster."[9] Historically present social anxieties are both expressed and repressed in popular culture, allowing films to displace fear, rage, and anxiety onto similar objects and to "project a 'solution' to social contradictions."[10] Issues of social fragmentation, such as the Vietnam War, Civil Rights Movement, and Mexican immigration, get repressed in the collective social unconscious, and emerge in mass cultural production in a veiled form. "Mass culture [is ...] a transformational work on social and political anxieties and fantasies" allowing historically present hopes and fears "to be 'managed' or repressed."[11] Watching contemporary social issues play out safely on the small screen and seeing issues metaphorically represented and transposed onto other forms provides a safe venue for viewers to process these fears and gain a sort of catharsis through the film's projection of solutions.

For Jameson these are capitalist fears, fears of a bourgeois class concerned about losing their economic security. Clyde Taylor contests that in American culture, it is a racialized fear as well. In fact, it is a fear that is always primarily racial, even when financial. Master narratives, mass culture's texts, (re)create racial hierarchies in their subtext and subsume fear of the racialized "Other" in figures marked as black, dark, alien, or otherwise not-white. Challenges to these master narratives take place in the text only to be resolved with the reapportioning of whiteness as the controlling force.[12] Hollywood provides white, American culture a venue for coding figures as racial "Others," allowing these figures status to evoke fear in the viewer and then be repositioned within the dominant culture's idealized framework.

This covering of issues, or converting images to symbols, can be brought to the surface by looking for incongruities in the text, such as inaccuracies in history or time, "empty" or polysemous objects and subjects that "absorb and organize [...] distinct anxieties together" and permit "essentially social and historical anxieties to be [...] recontained in what looks like a conflict with other forms of biological existence."[13] In addition to incongruities and "empty" metaphoric objects, strategic shifts in genre and changes in material as medium shifts (i.e., from novel to film) provide fertile ground for digging up a film's repressed content. Looking for these inconsistencies or signs of a hidden subject allows the viewer to unearth the social and historical content the text represses, and point to the subsumed meaning therein.

In Whedon's first *Firefly* genre, science fiction, it's all about looking for signs and traces of what is suspiciously absent. For example, Daniel Leonard Bernardi's *Star Trek and History* notes that "science fiction tends less to imagine the future than to 'defamiliarize and restructure our experience of our own present.' Aliens, for example, can be said to be always already real world peoples—signifiers of nations, cultures, and identities—simply because there are no real space-time referents for living and embodied extraterrestrials."[14] In other words, aliens don't exist. They are imagined based on something concrete, on people and cultures already existent. The very presence of aliens indicates there is a hidden subject.

The Western genre has built in empty signifiers as well. Agnes B. Curry's "We Don't Say Indian" makes a clear connection between Whedon's depictions of Reavers and Hollywood's representation of "Indians."[15] Curry argues that although Whedon claims to have removed all racial coding from the Reavers, in reality he has failed to "deracialize" what he considers symbols of "humanity's darkness" because he uses the tropes and iconography of Hollywood Indians. For example, the Reavers have war paint on their ships, and they "raid" colonial settlements.[16] Curry argues that the Reavers, much like

"Indians" in the Western genre, provide "a frame for working out other problems of national self-identity" as representations of something else, much as aliens do.[17] But what is being represented and "worked out" through the Reavers, and where are the absences providing venues for discussions of repressed anxieties in *Firefly*?

Holes in the 'Verse

The first place to look for holes is in the ground: the foundation of the "imagined" world. The series is structured on a continuum from insider to outsider reflected in the universe's geography. The Alliance is the ultimate insider in the show: the "beacon of civilization."[18] The people of the core are well-adjusted capitalists, those who live highly structured lives, lives the crew of Serenity see as stagnant and fake. In the central planets, Reavers are fairy tales and fantasies designed to frighten children. The core planets, comfortably situated within the Alliance's economic stability, seem to be the more "civilized" places in Whedon's universe. Persephone is "almost like a second home" to the crew, and the trappings of the core's uniformity give way to more diversities and individualism, similar to Hollywood's characterizations of the "settled" parts of the West.[19] The planets and moons that sit *on* the rim remove most of the vestiges of "civilized society," and represent the contested frontier—the places said civilization has not yet reached. People are "dumped on the world with barely enough to make it."[20] They balance on the edge, between violent raids by Reavers and richer worlds that exploit their natural resources.

So what lies beyond the rim? Structurally located on the borderlands between safety and nothing, inside the series and outside the camera's lens, beyond the rim and narrative, is a place in Westerns typically occupied by Mexico. This trope of Mexico as the space beyond the camera's lens shows up in countless Western films, a structure that posits the space outside the narrative as Mexican: for example the "bad Indians" of *Broken Arrow* are led by Geronimo out of the plot to Mexico, and *The Searchers* begins with a civil war veteran (sound familiar?), Ethan, returned from putting down a rebellion in Mexico before the camera begins filming.[21] Whitefall, Persephone, and most of the other border planets we see look strangely like Southern California specifically, and the Southwest in general. It's not John Ford's Southern Utah big sky, but rather, the sagebrush and prickly pear growing in the areas of the United States most fully representative of border problems with Mexico. All of the terraformed planets in the 'verse were made, as Zoe puts it, "as close to Earth-That-Was as we can make 'em" suggesting that even their mythic homeworld (arguably our planet) looked like the U.S./Mexico border.[22]

Couple the series' sets with Whedon professing one of his biggest inspirations was *Stagecoach*—a film whose hero and heroine, Ringo Kid and Dallas, ride out of the film to Mexico and freedom—and you have a clear connection to a different kind of border world.[23] The series, much like most science fiction tales of space exploration and Western films of manifest destiny, focuses on survival and settling the wild. This myth, however, is always at the expense of the bodies being displaced, pushed further out. For example, *Star Trek* "perpetuates the longstanding myth of the natural and humane right of white rule and occupation into and beyond the final frontier. In what amounts to a white future-time, these films participate in longstanding myths fundamental to the persuasiveness of white common sense in United States culture and history."[24] *Star Trek* promulgates the myth of justified social and technological supremacy of the United States' ruling class and dominant culture— the Prime Directive sees to that. Much as *Star Trek* reifies manifest destiny, *Firefly*'s 'verse focuses on the Alliance spreading its influence outward, pushing marginalized figures further toward the rim. But it's not empty space they're occupying.

In Westerns, Mexico acts as an unfriendly barrier that pushes back. In *Star Trek* it is alternately the Klingons (who Bernardi reads as black) and the violent Romulans looming over the border.[25] Although it is the Alliance that Whedon consciously connects to *Star Trek*'s Federation, the communal culture Mal fights to save on the rim is just as much a facet of whiteness as the domineering empire.[26] Instead of the Federation, a massive socialist formation vying for colorblindness in the Regan era, the Alliance seems to be more connected with *Star Wars*' Galactic Empire, and Mal's intrepid crew with Hans Solo and the Millennium Falcon—misfits just trying to live their lives as war rages around them, a war "between the malevolent, materialist Empire and the Jedi Knights for the Third World, that is, 'the universe.'"[27] Westerns use geographical emptiness to represent Mexico. *Star Trek* and *Star Wars* use borders and absence to represent the United States' struggle both internally and externally with people of color. Whedon's 'verse functions similarly.

In fact, the ubiquitous of whiteness in science fiction has led to several productions that self-consciously engage this lack.[28] The 2004 film *A Day Without a Mexican* is a science fiction parody where Los Angles wakes up to find all of the Mexicans gone for several weeks. The city becomes surrounded by an impenetrable fog and slowly falls into chaos as the film plays with California's unwillingness to see its exploited workforce. The 2008 film *Sleep Dealer* similarly "gives the U. S. what it always wanted: all the work without the workers"[29] when it creates a set of maquiladoras where Mexicans are cybernetically hooked up to robot workers across an impassible border. Rosaura Sanchez and Beatrice Pita's 2009 novel *Lunar Braceros* engages the exploration and exploitation of space, and the use and abuse of Mexican workers on the moon, because even in the future there are unsafe and undesirable jobs. It is improbable that a series focused on finding jobs, any jobs, filmed in the early 2000s in California could be as unaware of migrant labor as *Firefly* seems to be.

The Present in the Future

Following the premise that aliens represent an actual human corollary, that "savages" are placeholders for the fears that are too great for film to engage openly, as well as the idea that the space beyond the camera's lens is just as important as what lies in front of it, what does that say about the actual time and place (California, 2002) where *Firefly* "took place?" In the series, hordes of savage aliens swoop into civilized space, raping and cannibalizing decent folk, destroying whole towns and cities in quick, unexpected attacks. The fear of outsiders (especially racially–Othered ones that characterize the United States protectionist philosophy post–9/11) and California's staunch anti-immigrant sentiments ooze through the edges of the narrative. California has a long history of conflicted relations with Mexico. From taking land from newly citizenized Mexicans, to newer anti-immigrant sentiments, California has had mixed relations with those of Mexican descent both living within borders and moving across them.

During *Firefly*'s conception, filming, and airing, the issue of Mexican immigration loomed large in California generally, and southern California specifically, gaining national attention through legislation concerning immigration. In 1994, amidst huge political and social turmoil, California passed Proposition 187, a bill denying undocumented immigrants health care and public education, and requiring that public officials report to the Immigration and Naturalization Services (INS) anyone that they suspected might be undocumented. Robert Dale Jacobson calls the Proposition "a watershed in contemporary race relations."[30] In fact, more recent anti-immigration bills in Arizona and Minnesota reflect the same language of Proposition 187, even though its most controversial tenets were overturned in court. As Jacobson notes, "Proposition 187 generated lasting schemas that criminalized Mexican migration and highlighted Mexican cultural and political threat to democracy."[31] Two years later California passed Proposition 109, the "California Civil Rights Initiative" which prohibited public institutions from considering race, age, or ethnicity, trying to effectively end affirmative action in the state. In 1998 Proposition 227 was passed, the "English Language in Public Schools Initiative," which ended bilingual education in public schools. Beginning in 1996, the United States Army supplanted civilian policing of the border, a task supported by California's anxiety about its shift to the first United States "minority majority" state in 2000, where whites were outnumbered by people of color. Post–9/11, immigration issues exploded as the country's fear of outsiders and racial "Others" inflamed. *Firefly* was filmed only two years before the infamous Minuteman Project began recruiting, and four years before the "Secure Fence Act" was enacted, though miles of border fence was constructed in the late '90s. Recalling Jameson and Taylor's theories about cultural repression, it is possible to read traces of these anxieties in *Firefly*, revealing that the series, though clearly focused on our intrepid crew of spacefarers, is also conversing with the country's anxiety about Mexico and Mexican immigration.

Here There Be Reavers

Beyond the borders of the United States lies Mexico. Beyond the rim of the *Firefly/Serenity* 'verse, Reavers dominate. At the end of space (an astronomic impossibility) are savage creatures referred to as "nothing—got out to the edge of space and saw nothing, so that's what they became."[32] The "nothing" beyond the rim (coded as blackness) is the same as the nothing the Reavers signify. In addition to Whedon's attempt to absent race from the Reavers, Whedon absented the Reavers bodily, physically removing them from the frame.[33] Mal argues that "Reavers ain't men. Or they forgot how to be. Now they're just ... nothing."[34] No body. No soul. No solidness at all. In the logic of representation, this tells us that they are *everything*—the repressed content of the series. Additionally, Jayne, confounded with the appearance of the Reaver-ravished survivor in "Bushwacked" (1.3) remarks that the colonist "looked bigger when I couldn't see him."[35] As do Reavers. As do the faceless, countless numbers of Mexicans across the border, outside the camera's lens. Everything looks bigger when you can't see it. Undocumented immigrants are more frightening because they are literally unwritten and perceived as uncountable, invisible, and in *Firefly*, continually tied to the galaxies beyond the colonized 'verse. California's longstanding conflict between its "invisible" and all too visible Mexican worker population and its desire for a less "overrun" homeland is touched on and manipulated in the series via another traditional Western, colonial sign: cannibalism.

According to Rebecca M. Brown, "Reavers encompass the overlapping colonial fears of cannibals ... murderous thugs ... and a wider mythos of sexual violence by 'black men' against 'white women.'"[36] This history of cannibalism in Western cultural production (as well as tales of being "attacked by savages") is always laced with racial tones, referents to "Other" people. But no matter how inhuman the cannibals are, the very act of cannibalism makes them the same species as those who they eat—an "Other" that is the same.

Cannibals are a population dehumanized via the insult of cannibalism, and simultaneously humanized by that same insult. Although it is the Reavers who practice literal cannibalism, it is the dwellers of the core worlds that are obsessed with it, even as it acts as a cautionary tale against the "unknown" wilds and dangers of the frontier. As children, River and Simon play war in their aristocratic home, and River quickly decides that they're "going to have to resort to cannibalism" and "eat the men."[37] Even (especially) in the cultures which do not interact with Reavers other than through myths and legends, the fetishistic need for cannibalism connects the economic structure of Whedon's universe to colonial appropriation and devouring. The Core devours the space around it.

The series' use of cannibalism works in several registers. In "Bushwhacked" (1.3), Reavers are not interested in goods or services, just people—their cannibalism is literal. The crew, however, is engaged in economic cannibalism. Mal et al. are entirely focused on the food and supplies that would have created a new civilization for the colonists, as are the Alliance when they say Mal and the crew are scavengers "picking the flesh off the dead."[38] Reavers don't care about goods. What makes the Reavers so frightening is that they are outside of manifest destiny, the American Dream, and the mythic quest for the lost city of gold. Because they are interested in flesh and the body rather than money, the Reavers' value system is foreign to the Alliance, Serenity's crew, and the viewer. The horror of their cannibalism is in its distance from contemporary economics. It is akin to accusations that Mexican immigrants won't learn English, maintain extended family structures, and "refuse" to accept the "white" American lifestyle. White Americans fear immigrants will devour their culture and country. The Reavers are a projection of contemporary North American economic and social strife; anxieties about the United States' border and racial composition bleed through.

The Man They Call Jayne

There is one point at which the cannibalism becomes more complex. In "Bushwhacked" (1.3) when the crew boards a derelict ship floating in space and discovers a group of potential colonists' remains, there are shots of Jayne gorging on leftover food in the ship's galley intercut with images of pale, white, bloated bodies suspended from the ceiling. By layering shots of cannibalized white humans with close-ups of Jayne stuffing his mouth with food, Whedon links Jayne to the Reavers via his flesh-eating tendencies, and contrasts the deathly whiteness of the colonists with his vibrant living color. Jayne is distanced from the crew's focus on goods and economic cannibalism, and linked to a more bestial, savage, and literal consumption as Reavers are.

Jayne is also the character most affected by the "emptiness" of the Reavers, alternately denying their personhood and denying the existence of *anything* beyond the rim more forcefully than the rest of Serenity's crew. Jayne acts as an intermediary between the darkness of the rim, the simulations of the Reavers, and the border-crossing Serenity. This continues beyond *Firefly* through *Serenity*. When the crew is making their last stand against the Reavers, Zoe implies that there's no hope anyone will survive the onslaught. Jayne replies "I might …" again making himself distinct from the rest of the crew and demonstrating a different relationship to the incoming Reavers than they have.[39] We are shown bits and pieces of what the dominant culture fears through Jayne: through glimpses beyond the rim, and through the crew, we are allowed to interact with the emptiness and control it.

Jayne is never explicitly referred to as Mexican in *Firefly*; after all, there are no countries under the Alliance. However there are traces and touches that link him with the Mexican migrant culture of 2002. His vaquero links are most evident in the scene replaying his acceptance onto the crew of Serenity, shown in the episode "Out of Gas" (1.8).[40] Jayne's soon to be former crewmates are short, dirty, bandolier-wearing, mustachioed men who resonate with images of Mexicans in Western films such as the racially-mixed bandits in *The Outlaw Josey Wales*. These men fit cleanly into Hollywood's Mexican bandito stereotype.[41] Jayne may not look like a Mexican, but the company he keeps is unquestionably coded as vaquero.

On top of Jayne's obvious connection to banditos, other elements of the show mark him as a migrant in ways no other crewmember is (although technically the ship migrates constantly). In "The Message" (1.12), the viewers find out that Jayne is sending money home to his mother and family, and his mother has knitted him a hat to keep him warm in the cold of space. This very move echoes an immigrant identity, one which other crewmembers could easily take part in, but don't. Mal and the crew are at home on Serenity; they don't send out messages, send money home, or otherwise indicate there is anywhere they'd rather be. In fact, the series trumpets that "There's no place I can be / Since I found Serenity."[42] Which is odd, as Kaylee, for example, has a poor mother and father at home that we know of, and shows no indication of sharing her loot with them. Jayne's home is grounded elsewhere—literally grounded, in that home is not the flying ship, and figuratively grounded, as we know he has no loyalty to Mal or the crew. In a show centered on finding and keeping work, the figure who sends his money elsewhere, into a different economy, is suspect.[43] Even Jayne's "cunning" hat, designed to keep him warm, lets the viewer know that he is not to be trusted as it also demonstrates that Jayne's mother envisions his life as a colder one than he would have at home.[44] This life runs parallel with migrant farm workers: heading further North, getting colder, and going where the work of picking takes them. Worker loyalty lies not with American bosses, but with families back home in Mexico. Jayne is the only member of the crew not at home.[45] Moreover, the poverty and sickness back home makes Jayne's financial assistance not just welcome, but necessary, as we learn that Jayne's brother Matty is "sick with the Damp-lung," and they are worried about his father being laid off from his welding job (a lifestyle resonant with the so-called Third World and Mexico).[46] Jayne's travels while working are not for himself or his love of freedom, as they are for Mal, but for his kin, again echoing an immigrant sentiment. In addition, Jayne stumbles through his mother's simplistic letter, revealing his difficulties with the written word and literacy, specifically written English. Not just a marker of class, letters to and from home while traveling were a common part of the Mexican migrant workers' lives and demonstrate connections to family.

Another glimpse into Jayne's past happens in "Jaynestown" (1.7). When he leaves the ship to go into Canton, he disguises himself ridiculously, trying (and failing) to remain inconspicuous because he "crossed the magistrate of this company town."[47] In "Jaynestown" (1.7), viewers are given a clearer connection between Jayne and the border through the folk ballad we hear. "The Man We Call Jayne" follows the tradition of the Mexican border folk hero ballad, such as written for Gregorio Cortez or Joaquín Murrieta, but made comedic. Border heroes were the people who are remembered as standing up for the "common" Mexican against Spain, and later against the United States, particularly in California and Texas. The border folk hero is often connected to the time when newly minted citizens of the United States (courtesy of the treaty of Guadalupe Hidalgo) were deprived of their life, liberty, and property, among other things, in the name of colonial expansion. These and many other border folk heroes are remembered through song, further cementing a reading of Jayne as linked to immigration.

Américo Paredes argues that the Mexican border hero is a man who's "a good shot and a superb rider, a man of nerve, ingenuity and endurance."[48] Jayne fits this description, as he's definitely a good shot, especially with Vera; we've seen him ride horses and a moving train; he is flexible, quick to (re)act, and vigilant. And he is remembered through the ballads, or *corridos,* that memorialize Mexican border heroes. For example, Gregorio Cortez's legend is based on a historical figure remembered through "The Ballad of Gregorio Cortez." Paredes remarks that "it is the legend that has developed the heroic figure which the ballad keeps alive."[49] Joaquín Murrieta was vilified in California newspapers, then valorized in a novel of the same name by John Rollin Ridge, and kept vibrant in *corridos* on both sides of the border. Murrieta inspired Zorro's creation, another bandit Robin Hood.[50] "The Ballad of Jayne" (1.7) fulfills the same function, keeping Jayne's deliverance (albeit unwitting) of money to Canton's residents alive past what the crew believes is appropriate. However, unlike Murrieta and Cortez, Jayne is a figure unworthy of his own ballad, and the series undermines the tradition of the border hero to disempower Jayne, much as the tradition of lucha libre is used to both represent and hide the people across the U.S./Mexico border, focusing on the "Minis" division (shorter wrestlers) to make the threat seem smaller and more comedic.

Jayne's accomplishment of giving the Mudders money is marginalized because he acted out of greed instead of nobility, ignorant of the effects of his actions: "Look, Mal, I got no ruttin' idea. I was here a few years back, like I said. Pulled a second-story, stole a lotta scratch from the Magistrate up on the hill. But things went way south, and I had to high-tail it. They don't put you on a pedestal in town square for that."[51] Cortez is remembered because of his actions, not motivations—he does not fight for "the people," though that is what he is remembered for, but avenges his brother, unjustly shot by a Texas sheriff. Murrieta's tale is one of personal vengeance, not concern for poverty. Jayne fights against the magistrate and inadvertently helps the Mudders. All three heroes are remembered for harming unjust rulers, but *Firefly* doesn't let Jayne be a vaquero *and* a hero. The ballads of Murrieta and Cortez function as rallying points, strengthening the marginalized Chicana/o or Mexican communities in the United States. Harry Love and the California Rangers cut off Murrieta's head, displaying it throughout California as a warning to the new Mexican citizens of the United States. But instead, like the *corrido*, this act just fueled his legend.[52]

These men became myths. Jayne undergoes the opposite. *Firefly* disempowers Jayne far more successfully, leaving him in pieces, able to be the Mudders' symbol, but ineffective as a 21st-century Mexican border hero. The series undercuts Jayne's valiant possibilities and refigures the mythic Mexican hero as a harmless, comedic sidekick.[53] The mystique of the bandit hero is removed and we are left not with a song-worthy man, but an amoral thief who is too stupid to initially grasp the social relations between him and the town. Jayne makes the border hero ridiculous because the viewer is given the dominant culture's perspective on Jayne's actions, one that consciously undermines and refigures his thrilling heroics to comedic mistakes. His power is continually undermined: the crew uses Jayne's status as hero in Canton to get stolen goods back to the ship, in "Objects in Space" (1.14) Jayne sleeps through the entire invasion of the ship by Jubal Early, and any praise he might earn through his actions is always undermined by his "amoral" motivations. Jayne can't win.[54] Even when he succeeds in helping people, such as the Mudders' successful revolts in Canton, or when he fires off the shot that saves the day in "The Train Job" (1.2), he isn't taken seriously.[55] The use of comedy to undercut Jayne's heroic potential echoes the marginalization of those to whom he is figuratively and cinematically tied: the current Chicano/a, Mexican American, and Mexican residents of North America.

Jayne is a joke in the series, much as the "hero" Numero Cinco and his brothers were in *Angel* (5.6).[56] If one were to take seriously the threats that Jayne represents, both within the series' content and structure, he would far outweigh any evil the Reavers or Alliance might muster. Jayne is a muscled mass of barely-contained violence on the ship, not distanced from it. In "Jaynestown," (1.7), he is thrilled that the Mudders riot because of him. Border violence bubbles up through Jayne. It is only through the constant vigilance of Mal that he is kept in check. A perfect example of this is the moment in "Our Mrs. Reynolds" (1.6) where Jayne confronts Mal, feet spread apart, massive body blocking Mal's path, cocking his rifle, explaining "six men came to kill me one time, and the best of them carried this. It's a Callahan fullbore autolock, customized trigger and double cartridge thorough-gage."[57] For a few seconds, Jayne is terrifying. You see just what might happen if Mal were to lose his hold on the ship. Then the situation is defused when apparently Jayne wants sex, not a revolt, further disempowering the border legend, and deconstructing the possibility of immigrants as people with power in California.

In "Ariel" (1.9), Jayne finally shows agency apart from the crew by turning in the *actual* illegal immigrants, River and Simon.[58] However, a certain bias reveals itself insofar as these white characters and the fallen bourgeoisie they represent—welcome additions to the 'verse—are rescued. Mal is able to easily detect Jayne's duplicitous act without evidence, catching the vaquero. However he cannot eject Jayne from the ship and series, much as the United States cannot summarily eject its undocumented immigrants. Even when Jayne puts himself in charge of the ship in "The Train Job" (1.2), threatening to leave the captain and Zoe behind, Simon (the least physically capable of the characters), is able to "tranquilize" Jayne, overpowering him physically, setting him up, yet again, as the butt of a joke. Simon, the "dandy," the rich, white doctor is capable of taking down the threat to civilization and social order.[59] Jayne's menace is flashed at the viewer just enough so we understand that Jayne is very dangerous. Jayne is a snake in the grass. He, especially as a representative of migrant Mexicans in California, is a *real* threat to the wellbeing of the crew, and a threat to the viewers should the sleeping giant of Mexico awake. All of these parallels evince a culturally selective mode of representation, eliding the very issues of immigration and whiteness at the heart of the series' anxieties.

Through Jayne, the viewer is allowed to face the fear of border violence and insurrection and laugh at it, knowing that Mal will be there to hold it off. Like Numero Cinco, Jayne's purpose seems to be largely to act as a comedic foil. Although he may explode at any time, he still has a purpose that outweighs the danger he represents. Laughing at their fear allows the viewer some sort of limited catharsis, allows us to in some measure mentally process the sociological and political issues surrounding us as we watch *Firefly*. The Reavers are not so easy to fit into the narrative. They claw at the edges of space, threatening the very insurgence to which Jayne inspired the Mudders. The unknown that lurks in the dark of space sidles into the series through Jayne, and it is in his character that we see the potential conflict on the rim of the 'verse. We see the results of conflict in Reaver-wrecked towns and ships, but *we never see the conflict in process in the television show*. Just as we hear about but never see the Reavers' acts of violence, we never see Jayne mounting the takeover he so often threatens. The U.S./Mexico border is too volatile to be held within the series and shown in full-scale motion. It is mediated for the viewer through the Western and science fiction genres.

Much as Gene Roddenberry, born in El Paso and living in Los Angeles, created a series without Mexicans in an act of dismissal, whether willful or not, Whedon's border series continually invokes Mexico as it deliberately refuses to see Mexico in California, demonstrating that space's repressed content, at least imaginatively, is the existence of Mexico. California's anxiety over immigrants and Chicana/os enveloping the 20th and 21st centuries is projected onto the Reavers clawing at the edges of the rim, allowing the dominant culture a safe venue with which to engage those fears. Jayne's character allows for a "guest worker program," in the series, providing a venue for the country's need for workers in the show's unconscious. As a representative of immigrants, Jayne is controlled in the series through comedy, his violent and threatening nature kept under constant watch by Mal and by his own continual mistakes. By representing Jayne as a border hero, the series infuses him with the representative power of other border heroes, such as Murrieta or Cortez, then argues that "every man ever got a statue made of him was one kind of sumbitch or another," not only disempowering Jayne, but the others by extension.[60] Jayne is a demonstration of how to control a minority/migrant population in the United States. He can come into the visible and known 'verse as long as he obeys the economic and social tenets, registers himself, and remains useful. The absence of Mexicans and Chicana/os in Whedon's *Firefly* reaffirms an Anglo-centric hierarchy in the United States through Jayne, as it bolsters the fear of Mexico and undocumented immigration through the Reavers.

NOTES

1. For examples of critics' responses to Whedon's treatment of gender, see Gwenyth Bodger, "Buffy the Feminist Slayer? Constructions of Femininity in *Buffy the Vampire Slayer*," *Journal of Entertainment Media*, 2 (2003), http://blogs.arts. unimelb.edu.au/refractory/; Holly Chandler, "Slaying the Patriarchy: Transfusions of Vampire Metaphor in *Buffy the Vampire Slayer*," *Slayage: The Online International*

Journal of Buffy Studies, 3, no. 1 (2003), http://www.slayageonline.com/essays/slayage9/Chandler.htm; Lorna Jowett, *Sex and the Slayer: A Gender Studies Primer for the Buffy Fan* (Middleton, CT: Wesleyan University Press, 2005); Gwyn Symonds, "Solving Problems with Sharp Objects: Female Empowerment, Sex and Violence in *Buffy the Vampire Slayer*," *Slayage: The Online International Journal of Buffy Studies*, 3, no. 3–4 (2004), http://www.slayageonline.com/essays/slayage11_12/Symonds.htm; and Sherryl Vint, "'Killing us Softly': A Feminist Search for the 'Real' Buffy," *Slayage: The Online International Journal of Buffy Studies*, 2, no. 1 (2002), http://www.slayage.tv/essays/slayage5/vint.html.

For a consideration of *Firefly*, race, and gender see Amy-Chinn, Dee. "'Tis Pity She's a Whore." *Feminist Media Studies*, 6, no. 2 (June 2006): 175–189.

2. Jeffrey Middents, "A Sweet Vamp: Critiquing the Treatment of Race in *Buffy* and the American Musical Once More (With Feeling)," *Slayage: The Online International Journal of Buffy Studies*, 5, no. 1 (2005), http://slayageonline.com/EBS/buffy_studies/scholars_critics/k-n/middents.htm.

3. Jane Stadler, "Becoming the Other: Multiculturalism in Joss Whedon's *Angel*," *Flow TV* 7, no. 4 (2007), http://flowtv.org/?p=997.

4. "The Cautionary Tale of Numero Cinco," *Angel*, 5.6, DVD, written by Jeffery Bell, directed by Jeffery Bell (2005: Twentieth Century Fox, 2005).

5. See Charles Ramirez Berg, *Latino Images in Film: Stereotypes, Subversion, and Resistance* (Austin: University of Texas Press, 2002).

6. See Edward Buscombe, *"Injuns!": Native Americans in the Movies* (Bodmin: MPG Books Ltd, 2009); Richard Slotkin, *Gunfighter Nation: The Myth of the Frontier in Twentieth-Century America* (Norman: University of Oklahoma Press, 1998), 231–346; and Will Wright, *Sixguns and Society: A Structural Study of the Western* (Berkeley: University of California Press, 1975).

7. See: "Director's Commentary," *Serenity*, directed by Joss Whedon (2005: Universal City, CA: Universal Pictures, 2006), DVD.

8. I'd like to note that I am not looking at *Serenity* for this discussion because first, I feel that the representations of television networks and personal networking in *Serenity* displace the signified presences I'm discussing. The cancellation of *Firefly* by Fox impacted the subtext of the movie, especially when paired with Whedon's next major project, *Dr. Horrible's Sing-Along Blog*. In *Serenity,* the Alliance becomes a media-controlling force, a network (like, say, Fox), the Reavers transform to Alliance-brainwashed consumers of television, making the crew of Serenity agents in consumer-controlled mass media. The past is represented by Mr. Universe sitting inside the panopticon, watching, until Mal takes control and reverses the feed, sending instead of receiving, re-creating the medium with his message. And secondly, as Agnes B. Curry, J. Douglas Rabb and J. Michael Richardson mention, the Reavers of *Firefly* (disembodied presences) and the Reavers of *Serenity* (fully bodied monsters) are not the same.

9. Fredrick Jameson, *Signatures of the Visible* (New York: Routledge, 1992), 25–26.

10. *Ibid.*, 32.

11. *Ibid.*, 25.

12. Clyde Taylor, "The Master Text and the Jedi Doctrine," *Screen*, 29, no. 4 (1988): 97.

13. Fredrick Jameson, *Signatures of the Visible*, 26–27.

14. Daniel Leonard Bernardi, *Star Trek and History: Race-ing Toward a White Future* (New Brunswick, NJ: Rutgers University Press, 1999), 12.

15. Agnes B. Curry, "'We don't say "Indian"': On the Paradoxical Construction of the Reavers," *Slayage: The Online International Journal of Buffy Studies,* 7, no. 1 (2008), http://slayageonline.com/EBS/buffy_studies/scholars_critics/a_e/curry.htm.

16. *Ibid.*

17. *Ibid.,* 22.

18. *Serenity,* directed by Joss Whedon, 2005.

19. "Shindig," *Firefly* 1.4, DVD, written by Jane Espenson, directed by Vern Gillum (2003: Twentieth Century Fox, 2003).

20. "Serenity," *Firefly* 1.1, DVD, written by Joss Whedon, directed by Joss Whedon (2003: Twentieth Century Fox, 2003).

21. See Richard Slotkin, *Gunfighter Nation,* 231–346 and Will Wright, *Sixguns and Society.*

22. *Serenity,* directed by Joss Whedon, 2005, DVD.

23. *Ibid.*

24. Bernardi, *Star Trek and History,* 23.

25. *Ibid.*

26. For a discussion of the "oriental" cultural presentations in the series, see: Rebecca M. Brown, "Orientalism in *Firefly* and *Serenity,*" *Slayage: The Online International Journal of Buffy Studies,* 7, no. 1 (2008), http://slayageonline.com/PDF/Brown. pdf.

27. Clyde Taylor, "The Master Text and the Jedi Doctrine," 100.

28. Whedon does populate his worlds with black people, but rarely out of stereotypical roles. For example, Zoe is a soldier, Book is a preacher, Jubal Early is a bounty hunter, and *Buffy*'s Kendra is an African in need of education about the glory of white, middle-class life.

29. *Sleep Dealer,* directed by Alex Rivera (2008: New York, NY: Likely Story, 2008), DVD.

30. Robin Dale Jacobson, *New Nativism: Proposition 187 and the Debate Over Immigration* (Minneapolis: University of Minnesota Press, 2008), 15–16.

31. *Ibid.,* 165.

32. *Firefly,* "Serenity," 1.1.

33. Curry, "We Don't Say 'Indian.'"

34. "Bushwhacked." *Firefly* 1.3, DVD, written and directed by Tim Minear (2003: Twentieth Century Fox, 2003).

35. *Ibid.*

36. Brown, "Orientalism in *Firefly* and *Serenity.*"

37. "Safe," *Firefly* 1.5, DVD, written by Drew Z. Greenberg, directed by Michael Grossman (2003: Twentieth Century Fox, 2003).

38. *Firefly,* "Bushwhacked," 1.3.

39. *Serenity,* DVD, directed by Joss Whedon, 2005.

40. "Out of Gas," *Firefly* 1.8, DVD, written by Tim Minear, directed by David Solomon (2003: Twentieth Century Fox, 2003).

41. See Charles Ramirez Berg, *Latino Images in Film: Stereotypes, Subversion, and Resistance.*

42. "Serenity," *Firefly* 1.1; (theme song).

43. "Director's Commentary," *Serenity,* directed by Joss Whedon, 2005, DVD.

44. "The Message," *Firefly* 1.12, DVD, written by Joss Whedon and Tim Minear, directed by Tim Minear (2003: Twentieth Century Fox, 2003).

45. Book is also not at home on Serenity, but he is seeking a new home, or peace within a conflicted world. He does find that home in the space between the show and

film, and leaves the ship. Jayne always had a home, and his exploits in the broader world are to support that home.

46. "The Message," *Firefly* 1.12.

47. "Jaynestown," *Firefly* 1.7, DVD, written by Ben Edlund, directed by Marita Grabiak (2003: Twentieth Century Fox, 2003).

48. Américo Paredes, *"With His Pistol in His Hand": A Border Ballad and Its Hero* (Austin: University of Texas Press, 1958), 114.

49. *Ibid.*, 108.

50. Robert McKee Irwin, "The Many Heads and Tales of Joaquín Murrieta," *Bandits, Captives, Heroines, and Saints* (Minneapolis: University of Minnesota Press, 2007), 38–90.

51. "Jaynestown," *Firefly* 1.7.

52. Robert McKee Irwin, "The Many Heads and Tales of Joaquín Murrieta," *Bandits, Captives, Heroines, and Saints.*

53. *Ibid.*

54. "Objects in Space," *Firefly* 1.14, DVD, written by Joss Whedon, directed by Joss Whedon (2003: Twentieth Century Fox, 2003).

55. "The Train Job," *Firefly* 1.2, DVD, written by Joss Whedon and Tim Minear, directed by Joss Whedon (2003: Twentieth Century Fox, 2003).

56. *Angel*, "The Cautionary Tale of Numero Cinco," 5.6.

57. "Our Mrs. Reynolds," *Firefly* 1.6, DVD, written by Joss Whedon, directed by Vondie Curtis-Hall (2003: Twentieth Century Fox, 2003).

58. "Ariel," *Firefly* 1.9, DVD, written by Jose Molina, directed by Allan Kroeker (2003: Twentieth Century Fox, 2003).

59. "The Train Job," *Firefly* 1.2.

60. "Jaynestown," *Firefly* 1.7.

Zoe Washburne

Navigating the 'Verse as a
Military Woman of Color

MAYAN JARNAGIN

How does one successfully implement a balanced character while at the same time avoid problematic racial stereotypes? It is no easy task, as critics and the public are all too willing to analyze and dissect an artist's creation. Zoe Washburne, stalwart second-in-command from Joss Whedon's science-fiction series *Firefly*, can in some ways be seen as problematic for the modern African American woman. On the surface, the character as portrayed by Gina Torres and written by Tim Minear and Joss Whedon could easily be viewed as yet another example of the culturally, psychologically, and physiologically debilitating Strong Black Woman stereotype. At the extreme, the Strong Black Woman can be defined as an African American woman who has been systematically indoctrinated by society to "remain one without pause or rest until the grim reaper relieve[s] [her] of the burdens of [her] mortality."[1] In its most ordinary of forms, the Strong Black Woman is any woman of African descent who is seen as the solitary provider, defender, or nurturer of her family or community. In an ironic twist, the Strong Black Woman (hereafter referred to as SBW) is a figure who represents a certain pinnacle of second wave white-feminism; she does not conform to the post–World War II nuclear Caucasian family "in which the mothers [and wives wear] high heels, dresses and pearls to cook dinner and never [have] outside employment."[2] Not bound by white, patriarchal ideas of soft femininity, she is self-sufficient, self-controlled, and empowered. Yet as a woman of African lineage, the SBW, having never been *allowed* her femininity by said white male patriarchy, must eschew vulnerability by taking the burdens of the world upon her shoulders while never asking for help. The Strong Black Woman is not descended from the cloistered white woman who "would be freed from dependency on men and the family and be involved in 'productive' labor," she is descended from slaves who never had the opportunity to be "dependent" on others, but were always forced into "productive labor," be it work in the master's fields and home, or as reproductive breeders of new slaves.[3] As Sojourner Truth said, "Nobody ever help[ed] [her] into carriages, or over mud puddles"; society forced her into a life where she "ploughed and planted [...] and no man could head" her as a result.[4] The Strong Black Woman can and *must* do it all: she must be indefatigable, stoic, maternal, loyal and hard-working to a fault, always in danger of being the "mule of [her] world."[5]

This essay examines how and to what extent the character of Zoe Washburne does, and does not, fall victim to SBW categorizations. I argue that appearances are deceiving and the creators and writers of the show balance the fine line between creating a heroine and a stereotype. Significantly, the dynamic family environment rooted in filial and military social structures used to characterize Zoe helps her avoid falling into the pitfalls of the SBW, allowing for one of the more complex representations of a female of color in modern science fiction. In the end, Zoe Washburne's character represents a gestalt of characteristics that demonstrate great flexibility in navigating the feminine and masculine, civilian and military, stoic and sensual aspects of the life of a modern woman of color.

Defining the Strong Black Woman and the Problem Therein

The Strong Black Woman is a problematic representation in modern culture that can be understood as any characterization of an African American female in which she is challenged to face insurmountable odds without the aid of others; through indoctrination or internalization of patriarchal expectations, she either does not, cannot, or will not consider her situation as out of the ordinary.[6] As with any classification, variations on the theme exist. This essay is concerned with two forms of SBW: the provider or caregiver (The Mammy) such as Hattie McDaniel's eponymous character in the 1939 film *Gone with the Wind*, and the hyper-professional woman (The Black Lady) such as Captain Victoria Gates from the 2009 television show *Castle*. Whether the Mammy or the Black Lady, the SBW faces her life's adversities day in and day out without relief and is encouraged "to embrace struggle as [her] hallmark."[7] The SBW is either not allowed or unwilling to find succor amongst her friends and family lest she show vulnerability she can ill afford to have. Such a tactic inevitably leads to a culture-wide phenomenon of martyrdom encouraging undue emotional and physiological stress on the black female. Worse, African American society becomes loath to address the issue, and Caucasian society remains either willfully or unintentionally ignorant of these negative consequences.[8]

Thus, to quote Tamara Beauboeuf-Lafontant, "[b]ecause the Strong Black Woman discourse is upheld both within and outside of the Black community, there is very little resonance for any African American woman who acknowledges or desires to speak about her weaknesses, pains, and frustrations."[9] The iconic SBW is so pervasive in American culture at large that from an early age African American women "hop[e] to become strong—that is, to suppress feelings of uncertainty and to project a façade of calm" to the point where culturally, there is even a definitive "lack of patience with young black girls who acknowledg[e] physical and emotional hurts."[10] By and large, the cultural mentality for this behavior is rationalized as a form of life training which operates under the basis that "societal respect and concern given to white girls and women" will not be subsequently offered to Black girls and women.[11] Such a bleak (and likely all too familiar) outlook on future opportunity and hardship helps illuminate both the history of the stereotype, as well as the need for pop culture representations of women of color to be more varied.

The idea of the Strong Black Woman stems from the days of slavery in early colonized Americas and has persisted to modern times, tracing its roots to what is called the Mammy figure. The Mammy was arguably "created to justify the economic exploitation of house slaves" by introducing a compliant, "contented" female servant emblematic of the "supposed humanity of the institution of slavery."[12] The Mammy was both "desexualized" and unquestionably loyal to her white master's family due to the class and race hierarchical distinctions of the day.[13]

The Mammy stereotype masks the plight of the African American domestic slave and servant who in reality was often sexually exploited by her owners. The myth of the Mammy has been propagated and the echoes of the (often) large, cheerful, black domestic female can be seen even in today's media, most recognizably in the corporate Aunt Jemima logo. The Mammy can be seen as a figure either designed or appropriated with the intent to "reconstruct race relations along the line of pre–[Civil] War south" in order to persuade African American women to realign themselves with conservative white mentalities that force the black woman to choose between their family and that of their master or employers.[14] This of course forces the African American female into a position that is simultaneously in conflict with both her own culture and that of white America. As such, the majorities of older Strong Black Women roles consist of "portraying African American women as stereotypical mammies, matriarchs, welfare recipients [which] help justify U.S. Black women's oppression" and are still highly relevant in today's pop-culture awareness.[15] Thus, the Mammy figure is an origin of the modern Strong Black Woman that is caught in an interstitial tug of war having to manage two sets of competing cultures, families, and paradigms, leading to further expectations to adjust, adapt, and overcome without much in the way of guidance, sympathy, and understanding from inner and outer circles.

Yet another form of the SBW exists that can be in many ways even more insidious. This is the seemingly commendable character type that Patricia Hill Collins calls "the Black Lady."[16] The Black Lady is in theory a successful woman: she has made her way in life by getting her degree, and she has climbed the corporate ladder and/or conquered her chosen profession. The Black Lady at least on the surface appears to be a pinnacle of second wave feminist goals. However, there is much more to the characterization than that. What Beauboeuf-Lafontant claims of the SBW in general is doubly true for Hill-Collins' Black Lady: "One reason for persistence of the image […] is that [for] both [b]lack women and white women the image is often viewed as a refreshingly 'unfeminine' and therefore more empowering alternate to the dominant construction of white womanhood."[17] Of importance here are the terms "unfeminine" and "white" which connote the goals of second wave white feminists who desired to be viewed as more capable in the work force and less subjugated by the perceived notions of weakness inherent to constructions of femininity.

The Black Lady exists as an "image" whose career has become "so all consuming that [she] has no *time* for men [or women for that matter] or [has] forgotten how to treat them [with respect]," which leads to an interesting case of masculinization suggesting the successful African American woman is inherently flawed as a female.[18] The Black Lady is a hard woman who has no time for herself, fun, pleasure or romance; she is married to her job and must take on a persona that allows her to survive in a (white) man's (and woman's) world. A good example of this would be Captain Victoria Gates of the series *Castle* who insists on her subordinates calling her "sir," never refers to a lover, and caries herself perpetually stone-faced. The Black Lady cannot allow any displays of personal weakness or insecurity. She is left to eventually collapse in on herself, because she, like her predecessors, must be a form of superwoman who needs no other support system beyond her own force of will, yet another form of a problematic stereotype. As seen in the examples of the SBW, being viewed as unfeminine and hyper self-reliant is precisely the concern African American feminists have with this depiction, leading to inherent problems in many characterizations of black women in popular fiction.

Zoe Washburne: Navigating the Critical 'Verse

These theories, then, apply to *Firefly/Serenity*'s second-in-command Zoe Washburne in a number of ways. Zoe is first and foremost Mal Reynold's second in command throughout both the *Firefly* (2002–3) series and *Serenity* (2005). Making Zoe (a woman of African descent) subordinate to Mal (a man of Caucasian origin) creates complications. Africa and Europe, both as concepts and as geographical realities, are as chronologically and astronomically distant as the chaotic fringes of non–Alliance space seems compared to the orderliness of Earth-That-Was. Nonetheless, viewers who interact with science fiction today are consequentially very much part of physical realities which the show, through plot, has left behind; modern consumers will judge their entertainment based on modern sensibilities. *Firefly* posits an African female in a secondary role, subordinate to a Caucasian male, and therefore propagates modern and historical race and gender power structures. Examining Zoe's interactions with Captain Reynolds and the rest of the crew, one sees a deeply complicated set of interpersonal relationships that, by nature, must carefully balance chain of command, family life, and personal voice.

Zoe's introduction features her warning then–Sergeant Reynolds of the dangers of his current tactical plan; for Zoe, the "high-ground" they have claimed is "death with that skiff in the air," with Mal's response agreeing "that's our problem," and thanking Zoe for "volunteering" ("Serenity" 1.1).[19] The order is implicit: Zoe is to join Mal in an attempt to intercept the enemy airship thereby placing the two of them in the most immediate danger. This interaction is a common occurrence throughout the series: Mal gives orders, Zoe follows them. This pattern does not go unnoticed by those around her and evolves into a minor subplot in a few episodes culminating in a flashpoint during "War Stories" (1.10).[20] This interaction eventually creates a division in the crew when Zoe's husband Wash declares to Mal "I'm the one she swore to love, honor, and obey […] well… no… not [obey] but […] you she obeys! There's obeying going on right under my nose," suggesting that Zoe's obeisance constitutes a SBW betrayal of family for work.[21]

The conflict between Mal and Wash over perception of control of Zoe also emerges elsewhere in the series. Zoe and her husband discuss the potential for a small vacation after their latest adventure with the intent to engage in intimate affairs like "you with the bathing and me with the watching you bathe."[22] While Zoe shows she clearly desires such a respite, she responds to her husband's offer with "if the captain says it's all right," showing the complications of a military woman's need to balance home and work life.[23] Two men are placing Zoe in a hypothetical Mammy-esque position to choose between her loyalty to her military patriarch and her family. More importantly, this conflict is a classic dilemma for the Strong Black Woman: she has no choice but to sacrifice home-life for her work.

Another complication with Zoe's portrayal within the pilot episode is her mistreatment by the minor antagonist known as Badger. Badger, a small time criminal middleman, challenges Zoe by insisting on referring to her as a "little girl," while referring to Mal and Zoe's war regiment as a "balls and bayonets brigade," two sets of phrases that simultaneously infantilize and masculinize her, the latter of which carries intimations of the Black Lady.[24] Arguably, in the episode "Bushwacked," (1.3) her masculinization is taken further by her own husband as he proudly describes her as a "warrior woman."[25] Moreover, Zoe could be seen as de-feminizing herself as she declares a dress in a window as having "too much foof-a-rah" in "Shindig," (1.4) and in the same episode she seemingly emasculates the ship's muscle Jayne twice by first dismissing his concern about the near Lovecraftian Reavers with "Jayne, you'll scare the women," and the deadpan retort "I can hurt you" after he volunteers to help buy her a dress.[26]

In addition to Zoe's arguable masculinization, one of the more important group interactions occurs during the pilot episode when she defuses a hostile situation between two male secondary characters, Jayne and Shepherd Book, as they argue over the fate of an infiltrator. Zoe responds to their standoff by taking both the physical and moral higher ground, ordering Jayne to tie the Alliance agent up while she cocks her gun to cover any potential surprises from the wounded enemy (1.1).[27] This characterization persists through the series, since generally speaking Zoe tends to act as a mediator among the other shipmates, usually when neutralizing male to male conflict, and somewhat problematically by utilizing her hardened persona and proficiency with a rather phallic weapon. Zoe's "mare's leg" rifle is the second largest personal weapon after Jayne's "Vera." In summary, Zoe is a female character of color who is masculinized by her sense of duty to her job, her own projected persona, and the judgments of peripheral characters so that she's torn between work and home, despite the two being, in her case, so inseparable as to be nearly the same thing.

This characterization paints a fairly grim and stereotypical portrait of a workaholic Strong Black Woman with characteristics of both the Mammy and Black Lady archetypes. However, as Zoe's characterization extends beyond these problematic tropes, she arguably offers a subversion of these detrimental characterizations, insofar as her characterization also contains a complex weave of traits that complicates one-sided readings of her subject position: namely, the fact that she is a distinctly empathetic realization of a female military leader who very much knows when to be a soldier and when to be a civilian.

Washburne, Zoe: One Each

Zoe Washburne's military status (and warrior persona) has been one of her most touted, and in certain cases, most criticized aspects. But what does such a status actually entail?

It can be assumed that Zoe Washburne held a rank equivalent to either Corporal or an entry level Sergeant during her military career as evidenced by her ability to give and receive orders during combat as well as take part in mission planning as seen in flashbacks during the episodes "Serenity" (1.1) and "The Message" (1.12). Whedon critic Tanya Huff estimates that "Zoe was very likely also a sergeant during the war. There's no other explanation for the way she responds in 'The Message' [calling Tracey 'Private'] ... corporals just don't take that tone."[28]

Indeed, Zoe's military career helps in subverting the pitfalls and label of Strong Black Womanhood, due to the oaths and regulations governing the enlisted leadership body. In summary, the United States Army Non-Commissioned Officer Creed states "No one is more professional than I [...] Competence is my watchword [...] My [...] responsibilities [are] accomplishment of my mission and the welfare of my soldiers [...] I will be loyal to [...] seniors, peers, and subordinates [and] I will not forget, nor will I allow my comrades to forget that we are professionals."[29] If Zoe exemplifies any part of this code, she embodies competence and ensures her fellows never forget their professionalism. The military structure as seen in the various flashback sequences throughout the series indicates a derivation or continuation of our contemporary military culture on Earth (specifically North-American military culture), so one can assume both Malcolm Reynolds and Zoe would have been expected to adhere to similar non-commissioned officer creeds and mentalities. Thus, the very dictates of her former profession seem to be the foundation in which Zoe approaches her work-life throughout the series. There is arguably no one more professional than Zoe when it comes to the crew of *Serenity*. Whenever Mal or others ask if she is prepared, her answer is always "ready" (1.1).[30]

As for loyalty, competence, and the concern for her crew's welfare, her exploits particularly highlight her outstanding dedication to these principles during the hostage scenario in "War Stories" (1.10).[31] During this episode, Zoe makes a number of highly qualified decisions that exemplify the aforementioned ideals of military leadership. In the position of command while Malcolm Reynolds is on a mission, Zoe utilizes a specialist crewmember to confirm her suspicions of Malcolm's and her husband's capture. Through conference with said specialist Jayne, she is able to determine the most likely suspect. She then pools available resources, commits herself to an attempt at a peaceful resolution through payment for the return of the hostages, and when her negotiations do not achieve all of her goals (i.e., both prisoners), she returns with the full support of her crew, assigns them their positions and duties, and proceeds to successfully extract her last missing crewmember.[32] Or, as Natalie Haynes summarizes: "[s]he tried negotiation, and got half of what she wanted, so then she returned, using force—she is both a consummate soldier and diplomat."[33] As such, Zoe's ability to navigate between communicator (a commonly held female role in Western culture: see *Star Trek's* Uhura, 1966) and hero (the white, male standard in Western culture) reveals her to be a woman who is not as constrained by race/gender roles as previously thought.

To further explore Haynes's soldier-diplomat label, Zoe's ability to lead the entirety of her crew to victory is clearly shown to be based on certain admirable traits that stem from both her own personal charisma and her military bearing. First, through her professionalism and competence, she has gained the respect of her compatriots, even ones with authority issues like Jayne. In the episode "Shindig," (1.4) Zoe is able to refocus Jayne's inappropriate and crude jest with her deadpan response "I can hurt you," to which Jayne half nods in agreement, showing that Jayne understands Zoe's power, physical or otherwise, and furthermore respects her for both her ability and authority.[34] For Tanya Huff, this scene solidifies Zoe not only as a successful warrior woman (an archetype that Huff normally takes issue with, due to persistent one-dimensional stereotyping of such characters in media) but also as an effect that "lifted the ordinary television portrait of a beautiful woman" as well.[35] Zoe's ability to diffuse potential conflict on the ship, as mentioned, also goes a long way toward earning the support of her crew. Her ability to terminate Jayne and Shepherd Book's standoff as well as her ability to navigate interpersonal disputes between both Mal and Wash, and Mal and Simon, show how Zoe consistently helps maintain morale, and thus helps maintain the welfare of the crew, which in turn shows both Zoe's dedication to her non-commissioned officer oath and her care for a crew she sees as family.

To balance family and military, Zoe makes repeated efforts to explain the concept of rank structure to her husband, such as reminding him that she can take leave "if the Captain says it's alright" and "[he's] the Captain, Wash."[36] These failed attempts to get through to her husband shows that Zoe is far from a superwoman and does not always win, subverting the Black Lady aspect of the Strong Black Woman. She uses unsuccessful tactics such as attempting to convince her husband by deferring to Mal, but what is important is that she makes the attempt. In the latter example with Mal and Simon, she reminds her captain that he has a responsibility to his crewmembers (and to humanity in general) no matter how much they may aggravate him by insisting that he weigh the options: "No, I think things will go a helluva lot smoother without [Simon and River] on board, but how long do you think they'll survive?"[37] Such advice demonstrates a strong sense of practicality, a grasp of tactical and logistical threats to overall efficiency, and the competing desire to ensure the safety and wellbeing of her entire crew.

When a leader projects such wherewithal and concern, superiors, subordinates and peers quickly develop loyalty toward such an individual. Examining Mal's interactions with his First Mate demonstrates this. There is rarely, if ever, a time when Mal commits to an act without first ensuring that Zoe, at minimum, is able to voice her dissent or approval. In "Out of Gas" (1.8) Mal is concerned, if not disheartened, at Zoe's initial disapproval over both the acquisition of the ship Serenity, and the choice of hire for the ship's pilot (ironically her future husband).[38] Zoe's opinions matter to her Captain and as Huff states, "In 'Trash' […] it was perfectly clear that [Mal's] decision would [not] be made until after Zoe had her say."[39] Thus, Zoe's input is viewed as significant if not vital to those who interact with her, which in turn shows the mutually beneficial relationship she has with her command structure. This relationship is born of equality and respect, qualities that are not seen together in the world of the SBW who would be forced into a situation where she alone made decisions without the benefit of council.

Her ability to communicate is part of what makes Zoe Washburne a successful, fully developed character, rather than a stereotype. One can see this within the context of both her friendships and her marriage. With Jayne, as seen above, Zoe understands how to speak and affect an aggressive posture that demands respect and acquiescence. With characters like Simon Tam, her communication skills are more nuanced. As seen in "The Message" (1.12), Zoe witnesses the aftermath of one of Simon's failed attempts to connect romantically with Kaylee. Initially, Zoe starts off with a gentle verbal ribbing by dropping her arm around Simon's shoulder and asking "scare her away again did ya?"[40] Her smile is wry and her intent clearly not malicious. In fact, she begins to transition rather smoothly into commiseration with Simon by leaning her head in to rest on his until she is taken aback by her own husband's non-sequitur commentary of a carnival attraction. What the viewer can see between Simon and Zoe is a clearly defining filial moment between an adoptive younger brother and his understanding older sister. In contrast, the Strong Black Woman is not allowed such reciprocal intimacy; she must always show more parental or detached modes of expression.

We see throughout the series that these familial support structures have always been pivotally available for Zoe; the series itself is arguably about family. Time and time again the heart of the ship proves to be the dining area; countless joys, sorrows, and bonding take place with the crew seated in its warm glow. In the episode "Out of Gas" (1.9) much of the episode happens around the table with individuals telling amusing stories to both pass the time and to forge stronger interpersonal relationships, a scene that leads to Simon's being surprised with a birthday cake.[41] In "The Message" (1.13), Zoe and Mal work through their sorrow over the supposed passing of an old war buddy by honoring his memory with tales of his impish pranks.[42] The ship itself is a safe haven for Zoe, one that allows her to emotionally and physiologically unwind during times of respite; inside its halls she actively pursues her sex life with her husband. During moments like these, in "Shindig" (1.4) for example, husband and wife satisfy one another and let their normal barriers down while physically and verbally teasing one another as part of their post-coital interactions.[43] In doing so, their bonds are further reinforced and their love for one another reaffirmed. She is loved and takes part in a home, both physically and emotionally. Thus, Zoe is seen as a functional member of the family and not simply a beloved servant (Mammy) or loyal worker (Black Lady).

Zoe and Wash's marriage is another relationship built on communication and is in fact noted as one of, if not the strongest, interpersonal relationships found within the *Firefly* universe. Michelle Sagara West notes that "[Zoe and Wash] treated each other seriously, let their anger show; they offered each other this much respect" which in turn allows their relationship to weather internal and external pressures encountered throughout their respective worlds.[44] There are times when Zoe is less than open with her husband (specifically when it concerns Mal) but these issues are always brought to bear and eventually organically worked through. In the episode "War Stories" (1.10), which deals primarily with the Zoe-Wash-Mal work-family tangle, Wash and Zoe find themselves in a marital argument: Wash is concerned that his wife does not respect him because of her tendency to prioritize Mal's viewpoints when it comes to work, and Zoe wants for her husband to understand that, as an ex-sergeant who lives in constant peril, the military chain of command presents a reliable and sure way to deal with the unique stresses of the *Firefly* 'verse. While they argue with one another on the ship's bridge, Zoe begins to see Wash's side of the argument responding "is there any way I'm gonna get out of this with honor and dignity?"[45] Wash however oversteps his bounds by pressing the issue and questioning her familial loyalty earning him the remonstrance "you're losing the higher ground here sweetcakes."[46] This exchange does not initially solve the problem but it helps to open the doors to future reconciliation and is representative of their consistent back and forth of honest emotional discourse.

Yet, Zoe and Wash are more often seen as tender and nurturing to one another. During the events of the movie *Serenity*, Wash and Zoe are often seen looking, touching, and consoling each other for support during the movie's high and low points, most notably during the aftermath of the post bank-robbery Reaver chase scene when they embrace one another and are both near tears, and when Wash consoles Zoe after Jayne crudely calls up what appear to be troubling memories for her while questioning how only she, Mal and very few others of their platoon survived the battle of Serenity Valley. Their closeness is also highlighted prior to this, as during the aforementioned Reaver chase, Zoe is never out of contact with Wash while they respectively pilot the getaway skiff and ship to coordinate their rescue and flight from the enemy. Their mutual communication and reliance on one another literally save the entire crew from certain death.[47] The complexity of their relationship is best summed up once again by West: "The marriage of Wash and Zoe is an *adult* marriage ... they don't agonize about it ... it's a choice they've made, aware of who the other person is, and it's founded on respect, on communication and ... affection and consideration" (emphasis in the original).[48] This emotional support Wash provides, and more importantly Zoe accepts and seeks, goes a long way to ensure that Zoe does not fall victim to the trappings of Strong Black Womanhood.

Zoe maintains a balanced characterization by being part of something greater than herself and allowing others to effect her as much as she affects them. This reinforces her professional military personality by harmonizing work and home, private and public, which lets her achieve what Mercedes Lackey refers to as a "Zen" state of being: "If there is a single person in the crew who has a real grasp on the situation, I suspect it is Zoe. I do not believe she harbors any illusions with respect to freedom or anything else in her life. She seems to have come to a ... state of acceptance of whatever enters her world; it is not good, it is not bad, it merely is, and she will deal with it."[49] Zoe does her best to deal with her situations by relying not only on herself, but on her family, her friends. She takes life as it comes, unlike the SBW who will bottle up her feelings and either not think to, or not be able to, gain help from others.

Lackey elaborates in the above quote what many other anlyses of Zoe's character have intimated or outright stated. Robert B. Taylor unabashedly claims that while Zoe is "a hard woman" she is also equally "loving, sexy as hell" and "occasionally a smart ass."[50] Tanya Huff states succinctly that Zoe "knows where she stands" which arguably differs from the core of Strong Black Woman vulnerability, in which women like the Black Lady and the Mammy are never fully aware of how or where they stand in their worlds.[51] The Mammy and her derivatives are torn between multiple worlds which inevitably force a persistent favoring of either the establishment or their own careers while excluding their communities. Power is not shared, and since the Black Lady stands alone with subordinates below and superiors above, she has no real peers and thus cannot know equality as she has no point of reference other than herself. Yet Zoe, through her blending of her personal authority with her embracing of her crew as a family of equals, helps ensure that the "power structure" of the ship *Serenity* is anything but "pyramidical."[52]

However, one scene seems to present Zoe as becoming victim to Strong Black Woman characterization, namely, when Wash is slain by Reavers during the events of *Serenity*. With only a moment to process, not even to truly grieve for the death of her husband, she finds herself cast back into the role of taking orders from Mal.[53] Once the crew is in place for their final stand against the Reaver horde, Zoe becomes distracted and loses Lackey's Zen-like state of awareness carelessly pushing forward into the oncoming enemy mass. She effectively forgets her compatriots fighting for survival behind her and presses on without regard for her own safety. The overall impression is that of a woman succumbing to a death wish, "remain[ing] one without pause or rest until the grim reaper relieve[s] [her] of the burdens of [her] mortality"[54]; she'll continue killing until either they or she stops moving.

Yet this moment of despair actually acts as both a criticism and deconstruction of the Strong Black Woman. While acting on her own, single-mindedly gunning down Reavers, she is gravely wounded, a physical representation of the psychological dangers of Strong Black Womanhood. The wound is a violent gash down her spine, a parallel, if one will, to the broken backed African American woman who after years of hardship can go on no longer, but is expected to persevere alone nonetheless, forever scarred. It is apparent that if Zoe continues on without the support of her comrades, she will die broken, mentally and physically. However, Zoe is not going to be that ill-fated stereotype, as her crewmates pull her out of immediate danger and return to their fortifications to be patched up by Simon who declares the wound to have left her spine intact.[55] She is not truly broken, and her community does not give up on her even when she despairs; they risk themselves to bring her back from the states of mental and physical oblivion.

With this kind of support system in place, Zoe is able to rebalance herself and regain her position as a responsible and effective leader, as seen in the denouement of the film where the crew honors both the dead and Zoe, as well as when Mal ultimately addresses Zoe in the cargo bay of their newly reconstructed ship. Mal asks of his second in command "think she'll hold together?" to which Zoe replies "She's tore up plenty, but she'll fly true."[56] Mal's use of "she'll" denotes the ship, but the look of concern on his face suggests he is using the conversation as a way to get Zoe to talk about her own emotional and physical well-being. Her subsequent responses reveal that Zoe understands what Mal is attempting to do and respects his choice of communication. Mal's next request is that Zoe should "make sure everything's secure," implying that her physical state as a person is nothing without her own emotional security. Mal's addendum "...it could be bumpy," and Zoe's final words "always is," clarify their mutual respect, caring, and understanding of one another.[57]

Yes, Zoe is still clearly in pain from her loss but her Captain and by his proxy the entire crew is there to remind her of those who will always care. Zoe is allowed to be strong yet vulnerable, professional yet sensual, beautiful yet down to earth. Her character accomplishes this by being both as interstitial as she needs to be, and by having a familial society actively encouraging and supporting her multi-faceted needs. She takes care of them and they in turn take care of her; she is no one's Mammy, no one's Black Lady, but rather she is a wife, widow, sister, executive officer, friend, and loved one. Most importantly, she is her own woman. This representation of a mutually beneficial support system by necessity grounded in military core values paves the way for the collective acceptance of a truly complex woman of color who pushes the boundaries of both science fiction and cultural narrative consciousness.

Notes

1. Wambui Mwangi, "Black Women Mythology," *The New Black Magazine.* http://www.thenewblackmagazine.com/view.aspx?index=50.

2. Wilfred L. Guerin, Jeanne C. Reesman, Earle Labor, et al., "First, Second, and Third Wave Feminisms," *A Handbook of Critical Approaches to Literature* (New York: Oxford, 2011), 255.

3. Charlotte Kroløkke, Ann Scott Sørenson, *Gender Communication Theories and Analyses: From Science to Performance* (Thousand Oaks, CA: Sage 2006), 10.

4. Sojourner Truth, "Ar'n't I a Woman? Speech to the Woman's Rights Convention in Akron, Ohio," *Norton Anthology of African American Literature.* Eds. Henry Louis Gates, Jr., and Nellie Y. McKay (New York: Norton, 2004), 246–249. (Diction removed for clarification.)

5. Zora Neale Hurston, *Their Eyes Were Watching God* (New York: Harper Collins, 1937), 14.

6. Mwangi, "Black Women Mythology."

7. Tamara Beauboeuf-Lafontant, "Keeping Up Appearances, Getting Fed Up: The Embodiment of Strength Among African American Women," *Meridians: Feminisms, Race, Transnationalism,* 5, no. 2 (2005): 104–123

8. Mwangi, Beabouef-Lafontant, and Collins all intimate and or declare as much in their respective articles.

9. Tamara Beabouef-Lafontant, "Strong and Large Black Women? Exploring Relationships between Deviant Womanhood and Weight," *Gender and Society,* 17, no. 1 (2003): 111–121.

10. Beauboeuf-Lafontant, "Keeping up Appearances," 110.

11. Beauboeuf-Lafontant, "Keeping up Appearances," 112.

12. Patricia Hill Collins, "Mammies, Matriarchs, and Other Controlling Images," *Black Feminist Thought: Knowledge, Consciousness, and the Politics of Empowerment* (New York: Routledge, 2000), 69–96; *Jim Crow Museum of Racist America,* Ferris State University. "The Mammy Charicature," last modified 2012. http://www.ferris.edu/htmls/news/jimcrow/mammies/.

13. *Jim Crow Museum of Racist America, ibid.*

14. M.M. Manning, *Slave in a Box: The Strange Career of Aunt Jemima* (Charlottesville: University Press of Virginia, 1998).

15. Collins, "Mammies, Matriarchs, and Other Controlling Images," 69.

16. Collins, "Mammies, Matriarchs, and Other Controlling Images," 81.

17. Beauboeuf-Lafontant, "Keeping up Appearances," 108.

18. Collins, "Mammies, Matriarchs, and Other Controlling Images," 81.

19. "Serenity," *Firefly*. 1.1, DVD. Dir. Joss Whedon (2002: Twentieth Century Fox, 2002).

20. "War Stories" *Firefly*.1.10, DVD. Written by Cheryl Cain, Dir. By James Contner (2002: Twentieth Century Fox, 2002).

21. *Firefly*, "War Stories," 1.10.

22. *Ibid.*

23. *Ibid.*

24. *Firefly*, "Serenity," 1.1.

25. "Bushwhacked," *Firefly*. 1.3, DVD. Written by Tim Minear, Directed by Tim Minear (2002: Twentieth Century Fox, 2002).

26. "Shindig," *Firefly*. 1.4, DVD. Written by Jane Espenson, Directed by Verne Gillum (2002: Twentieth Century Fox, 2002).

27. *Firefly*, "Serenity," 1.1.

28. Tanya Huff, "'Thanks for the Reenactment Sir' Zoe: Updating the Woman Warrior," *Finding Serenity: Anti-Heroes, Lost Shepherds and Space Hookers in Joss Whedon's Firefly*. Ed. Jane Espenson (Dallas: Benbella, 2004), 105–112.

29. "NCO Creed," *Army Values*. http://www.army.mil/values/nco.html.

30. *Firefly*, "Serenity," 1.1.

31. *Firefly*, "War Stories," 1.10.

32. *Ibid.*

33. Natalie Haynes, "Girls, Guns, Gags: Why the Future Belongs to the Funny," *Serenity Found: More Unauthorized Essays on Joss Whedon's Firefly Universe*. Ed. Jane Espenson (Dallas: Benbella, 2007), 27–36.

34. *Firefly*, "Shindig," 1.4.

35. Huff, "Thanks for the Reenactment Sir," 107.

36. *Firefly*, "Serenity," 1.1.

37. Joss Whedon, *Serenity* Directed by Joss Whedon. DVD (2005; Universal Studios Home Video 2005).

38. "Out of Gas," *Firefly*, 1.8, DVD, written by Tim Minear, directed by David Solomon (2002: Twentieth Century Fox, 2002).

39. Huff, "Thanks for the Reenactment Sir," 108.

40. "The Message," *Firefly*, 1.12, DVD, written by Joss Whedon and Tim Minear, directed by Tim Minear (2002: Twentieth Century Fox, 2002).

41. *Firefly*, "Out of Gas,"1.8.

42. *Firefly*, "The Message," 1.12.

43. *Firefly*, "Shindig," 1.4.

44. Michelle Sagara West, "More than a Marriage of Convenience," *Finding Serenity: Anti-Heroes, Lost Shepherds and Space Hookers in Joss Whedon's Firefly*. Ed. Jane Espenson (Dallas: Benbella, 2004), 97–104.

45. *Firefly*, "War Stories," 1.10.

46. *Ibid.*

47. Whedon, *Serenity* (2005).

48. West, "More Than a Marriage of Convenience," 99–100.

49. Mercedes Lackey, "*Serenity* and Bobby McGee," *Finding Serenity: Anti-Heroes, Lost Shepherds and Space Hookers in Joss Whedon's Firefly*. Ed. Jane Espenson (Dallas: Benbella, 2004), 63–74.

50. Robert B. Taylor, "The Captain May Wear the Tight Pants, but It's the Gals Who Make *Serenity* Soar," *Finding Serenity: Anti-Heroes, Lost Shepherds and Space Hookers in Joss Whedon's Firefly*. Ed. Jane Espenson (Dallas: Benbella, 2004), 131–138.

51. Huff, "Thanks for the Reenactment Sir," 107.

52. Haynes, "Girls, Guns, Gags," 27.
53. Whedon, *Serenity* (2005).
54. Mwangi, "Black Women Mythology."
55. *Ibid.*
56. *Ibid.*
57. *Ibid.*

Programming Slavery
Race, Technology and the Quest for Freedom in Dollhouse

Brandeise Monk-Payton

> ECHO: I have 38 brains. Not one of them thinks you can sign a contract to be a slave. Especially now that we have a black president.
>
> CAROLINE: We have a black president? I am missing everything.[1]

In "Omega" (1.12), Season One's penultimate episode of Joss Whedon's science fiction series *Dollhouse*, the body of protagonist Echo comes into immediate contact with the mind of Caroline, her own previous self residing in a different body. Conversation between the two concludes with Echo's attempt to convince Caroline to return to her original corporeal self, thereby breaking the five-year contract that Caroline has signed with the Rossum Corporation's elusive Dollhouse, an organization that recruits lost souls and erases these individuals' personalities with the aid of advanced technology. Effectively *tabulae rasae*, these "Dolls" or "Actives" (as they're called) sign contracts in which they agree to be imprinted with different memories for a wealth of powerful clients in order to complete various types of engagements in exchange for a substantial financial award after the five-year time period is up. As demonstrated by the exchange between Echo and Caroline quoted above, the discourse of enslavement figures prominently in the series. Yet the acts of slavery that the Dollhouse is frequently charged with committing are situated within the realm of the potential exploitative nature of sex work. As such, much commentary on *Dollhouse* highlights the program's representation of prostitution and the controversial issue of human trafficking. However, the scene above is a curious moment in the show which links the eradication of the Dollhouse's participation in what the character of FBI agent Paul Ballard designates as "consensual slavery" to the historical overcoming of racial slavery exemplified here by the election of Barack Obama, the first African American President of the United States.[2] Thus, racial rhetoric is utilized to denote the progressive quality of the current U.S. sociopolitical climate that can allow Caroline to liberate herself from the self-imposed slavery of the Dollhouse.

In this essay, I seek to explore *Dollhouse*'s parallel investment in both racial progress, which is to say, the progress associated with the transition of blacks from slavery to citizenry, and in technological progress. In other words, I argue that while the Dollhouse is marketed as technologically sophisticated, the organization's practices, whether intentional or not, also reflect the sociohistorical trajectory of African Americans from slavery to citizenry, i.e., freedom. Freedom here is registered on two different levels: first, the freedom associated with Barack Obama's presidency that has come to epitomize a "post-racial" moment in the United States[3]; and second, the freedom that emerges from Dollhouse technology in which Dolls can potentially traverse the line between inhuman and posthuman status. However, this dual investment in racial and technological progress is complicated by the televisual and narrative logic of the series, which is predicated on a continual process of remembering and forgetting. Under the careful watch of their personal Handlers, the Dollhouse programs its Actives by providing them with memories as information and then removing the data once an assignment is fulfilled, reducing the Active to a primitive state of subjugation once again. This vexed relationship between remembering and forgetting contributes to Caroline's confusion in the opening quotation that discusses the current election of a black president. Indeed, how can Caroline be "missing everything" concerning the racial progress being experienced by the country and manufactured by Rossum if she is simultaneously participating in it as a Doll? Thus, as the show operates under the auspices of progress, it is simultaneously always under the threat of regression in both its racial and technological discourse.

The dichotomy between progression and regression is fully realized in the relationship between Active Echo and her African American Handler-turned-Dollhouse Head of Security, Boyd Langton. While their relationship begins with Boyd routinely serving as Echo's faithful conduit for the Dollhouse's business transactions, it culminates in a shocking reversal that pits Echo against Boyd when he is revealed to be one of the founders of the Rossum Corporation and the harbinger of the slave-making machine. The implications of such a role reversal are immense, as Boyd's identity as a black man is in direct conflict with his reliance on a historically white European ideal of domination predicated on the enslavement of others. The fact that he eschews any racial politics in favor of increased corporate power is tragic and ultimately leads to his demise. Furthermore, the irony of Boyd's downfall lies in his defeat by the enslaved white woman. Indeed, by the series' end, Echo's posthuman "ascension" to enlightened composite of multiple identities frees her from the Dollhouse's practices of slavery; in rupturing the system, she challenges Boyd's desire for the technological advancement of society, which is conflated with the imagined progressive quality of a "post-racial" America. In this way, the characters of Echo and Boyd are the key to understanding the show's complex and arguably regressive racial politics, particularly as this relates to a re-telling or televisual reprogramming of black history—past, present, and future.

Fantasizing Race

"The Dollhouse deals in fantasy. That is their business, but that is not their purpose," says Echo in "Man on the Street" (1.6).[4] This recurring cryptic mantra used to describe the function of the organization speaks to the way in which the series, through its task to fulfill multiple desires, engages in its own generic promiscuity. While it offers fantastical elements, *Dollhouse* is also in part a crime/detective procedural, action-adventure, drama, and science fiction program, showing how while the show is in the business of providing fantasies, its purpose goes beyond this designation. Rhonda Wilcox puts forth an interesting amalgamation of these genres through her concept of unreal television. Unreal TV emphasizes the use of metaphor and symbolism to highlight the thematic elements of a series, and in particular, to comment on the social issues represented in the text.[5] One such symbolic register functions on the level of race and race relations.

Conventional unreal television texts frequently utilize supernatural or fantastical effects as allegories for racial politics. For example, Whedon's *Buffy the Vampire Slayer* (1997–2003) inscribes the trope of racial Otherness onto the multitude of vampires, demons, monsters, and disenfranchised creatures that inhabit the whitewashed fictional Sunnydale, California. Here, any figure existing outside of the human norm is deemed aberrant and potentially dangerous.[6] When such racialized metaphors of Otherness are not utilized and replaced by actual characters of color, these figures are often racially essentialized such as Kendra the Slayer of Caribbean ancestry, Nikki Wood the Blaxpoitation era Slayer, and The First Slayer, a primitive African woman. All provide a foil to Buffy, the blonde-haired heroine of the show. In contrast to the racial tokenism of worlds like *Buffy*, *Dollhouse* provides a somewhat different perspective on issues of race. First, the show's focus does not concern the representation of blackness or African American expressive culture, but rather the progressive erasure of these signifiers. Second, the Dollhouse's processes of enslavement are created and cultivated through the utilization of computer programming. In other words, the show's exploration of what can be considered technological slavery both directly and indirectly hearkens to racial slavery.

Extensive theoretical analysis of the relationship between race and technology has only recently been done.[7] The concept of race *as* technology necessitates a detailed understanding of both terms in this equation. While the analysis of race as a social construct has been widespread, race in the digital age offers up new paradigms of thinking about such identity politics predicated on its emerging relationship to codes, networks, and advanced computer information technology.[8] The connection between technology and the etymologically similar term technique is of great importance because it highlights race's potential function as a strategy, which "shifts the focus from the *what* of race to the *how* of race, from *knowing* race to *doing* race by emphasizing the similarities between race and technology."[9] *Dollhouse* cleverly employs race through its implementation of specific technology that becomes a tool for slavery and subjugation.[10] As discussed briefly earlier, the Dollhouse imprints information into Actives in the form of a "wedge" (a type of storage device) in order for them to embody another individual and complete a certain task. Once the engagement is fulfilled, the Active is wiped of the memory entirely and returns to a benign state of being. The technological and eerily ritualistic procedure is done by technician Topher Brink and is called a "treatment." These treatments can be thought of as a profitable technique by which the Doll is positioned as a slave to a dominant power. Indeed, the creation of Dolls is a tactical endeavor for the Rossum Corporation as the technological manufacturing of such individuals with flexible identities to be bought and sold is depicted to be a lucrative business model within the show. Thus, the highly sophisticated process of enslavement that the Dollhouse practices highlights how the fusion of race and/as technology has profound ethical implications.[11]

The show tackles these ethical conundrums by presenting them reflexively in the much-discussed Season One episode, "Man on the Street" (1.6).[12] This episode begins as a television news investigative piece that frames the Dollhouse as an urban legend and explores multiple opinions from Los Angeles citizens on the conspiracy, and in doing so addresses the public's (and by extension, the viewer's) relationship to the Dollhouse as an organization shrouded in mystery and intrigue. In addition to contextualizing the Dollhouse as an illegal for-profit establishment that programs people, man-on-the-street interviews are conducted and interstitially placed within the episode and woven through the primary plot. The testimonials about the

Dollhouse run the gamut from lauding the technology as the harbinger of romantic (not to mention physical) love to condemning it as dystopian nightmare. While the general consensus still remains that Dolls are "mindless whores" sold into sex work, one reaction alludes quite explicitly to the function of the Dollhouse in terms of racial slavery.[13] An African American woman's interview in this episode is particularly revealing in this regard. When the reporter prompts her to comment on the veracity of the Dollhouse and its practices, she eagerly replies, "Oh it's happening. There's one thing people will always need is slaves [sic]."[14] In response to a follow-up question that highlights the voluntary nature of becoming a Doll, the woman states that "there's only one reason someone would volunteer to be a slave is if they is one already. Volunteers. You must be outta yo [expletive] mind [sic]."[15] The vernacular in which she speaks coupled with her gestures code her within an expressive black culture and ultimately, the moment reveals how a discourse of racial slavery is embedded into the series. It is clear that the entire episode attempts to obtain diverse perspectives on the controversial organization from various populations and yet the frankness and conviction with which the black female figure speaks stand out as a manifestation of the underlying racially charged dynamics of the Dollhouse operation that linger on the fringes of the show's narrative up until this point.

Indeed, racial enslavement is not a topic that is frequently taken up in television programming: The miniseries *Roots* (1977) became the first prolonged popular historical engagement with the topic of U.S. slavery for a mass audience. *Roots* was a critical and commercial success, and, as Herman Gray states, the program "contributed quite significantly to the transformation, in the popular imaginary, of the discourse of slavery and American race relations between blacks and whites."[16] While *Dollhouse* did not make nearly the same impact during its short stint on air with less-than-stellar reviews and ratings, it is an imagined representation of slavery that distances the oppressive practice from its socio-historical and racial determinants while simultaneously reinforcing those determinants through the narrative, effectively depicting a distinct iteration of slavery based on programmability.[17] In other words, it brings a fantastical element to U.S. racial slavery that is predicated on the use of digital technology.

Programming Slavery

Dollhouse is a series that directly comments on the notion of programming as it relates to both technology and television as a medium. Since the entire Dollhouse operation rests on the ability to program people by stripping individuals of their memory and inserting new memories, the show is predicated on a logic of amnesia that also pervades televisual practice itself. As film theorist Stephen Heath suggests, "television produces forgetfulness, not memory, flow, not history."[18] Television thrives on repetition and *Dollhouse* incorporates this component of the medium through its process of simultaneous narrative progression and regression. Each episode highlights the technological procedure that the Dolls endure for the organization, which sees their passive disposition be transformed quite literally into Active status, only to be returned to a state of equilibrium. Therefore the show continually undermines its own seriality by placing such impermanent figures as Dolls at the forefront of each episode. The fragmentation and continual disruption of the narrative creates a circularity to the program in its negotiation to become a composite; in effect, to remember. This call to remember not only refers to the actual series as a whole but also to the Dolls who do not recall their identity after engagements, as well as to the audience of such a high-concept show that must retain information concerning lead characters despite being introduced to their "new" personas every week.

Indeed, *Dollhouse* exhibits what some scholars have argued is the television medium's privileging of immediacy and liveness that has served to destroy its memory and evacuate it of history.[19] However, *Dollhouse* becomes increasingly invested in its own history throughout the program's two seasons, especially in the Dolls' past lives that constantly serve to evade them. This makes it all the more interesting that the show attempts to narrate a discourse of progress reflected by the historical trajectory of African Americans from slavery to Barack Obama's presidency in the pivotal scene between Caroline and Echo discussed earlier. Coupled with the show's emphasis on the recovery of memory, *Dollhouse* is particularly ripe for analysis through a racial lens. Michel Foucault states that, "Since memory is actually a very important factor in struggle, if one controls people's memory, one controls their dynamism. And one also controls their experience, their knowledge of previous struggles."[20] The Dollhouse's practice of enslavement is fundamentally dependent on this control and ultimate loss of memory that contains a previous identity with a history. In the case of *Dollhouse*, African American identity is always under the threat of erasure in Whedon's world in its continual displacement of racial politics. Therefore, the Dollhouse could be conceived as a racist operation that capitalizes on rendering the past invisible. Drawing on Saidiya Hartman's discussion of racial subjection during slavery, Lisa Nakamura and Peter A. Chow-White note that, "If racism is a technology, or rather, a systematic way of doing things that operates by mediating between users and techniques to create specific forms of oppression and discrimination, then enforced forgetting of the familial or historical past is surely a key part of its workings."[21] By requiring individuals to succumb to amnesia in order to become Dolls, the Rossum Corporation negates prior exposure to trauma and the subsequent suffering inflicted, both of which serve to produce human subjectivity, in favor of a cyclical practice of domination that perpetuates nonhuman status; put differently, Actives are simultaneously rendered *in*Active in this iteration of slavery. Therefore, Echo's admission to Caroline that she cannot *voluntarily* sign a contract to be a slave by virtue of the existence of a black President, calls attention to the show's parallel commentary on racial and technological advancement via the programming of enslavement.

The nature of complicity is an issue that is brought up frequently in the series and most importantly, in the idea that individuals consent to become Dolls through their own volition and thus cannot truly be seen as slaves.[22] However, to suggest such a voluntary enslavement predicated on the coercive ability of technology is to elide the actual experience of becoming a Doll.[23] The first shot in the televised pilot of *Dollhouse* ("Ghost" 1.1) comes from the high angle of a security camera, the grainy surveillance video allowing viewers to witness a scene between Los Angeles Dollhouse Director, Adelle DeWitt, and new recruit, Caroline Farrell.[24] In the exchange, DeWitt attempts to get Caroline to sign up as a Dollhouse participant. When DeWitt explains that becoming part of the Dollhouse is an opportunity for a clean slate, Caroline retorts, "You ever try and clean an actual slate? You always see what was on it before," acknowledging that she doesn't have a choice in the matter of serving the Rossum Corporation.[25] Thus, Caroline becomes a Doll in a scheme to erase her past indiscretions. In this way, DeWitt is able to frame the relationship between a Doll and the Dollhouse as a "mutual transaction" which allows for the Dolls to retain a false sense of agency.[26] The methods by which the Dollhouse manipulates the Dolls into subjugation (where Dolls are considered physically and mentally fragile, less-than human entities that are lost without the Dollhouse) are reminiscent of a traditional scene of slavery on the plantation in which the paternalism espoused by slaveholders becomes the justification for oppression. In addition to paternalistic gestures, slaveholders often relied on the production of slave performance as a means of subjection. As Hartman comments, "The innocent amusements and spectacles of mastery orchestrated by members of the slaveholding class to establish their dominion … were significant components of slave performance."[27] This is particularly salient and exemplified in *Dollhouse* through the programmed theatricality of Dolls who don costumes and accents to depict various characters. Indeed, there is even the utilization of deceivingly open-ended questions that are actually scripts to further program the Actives. This includes Handlers asking, "Are you ready for your treatment?"[28] as a trigger to end an engagement and most notably, the infamous "Did I fall asleep? For a little while" exchange that Topher has with each Doll in order to complete the wiping process.[29] These types of call and response interactions increase Doll docility by lulling them into a sense of security. Yet, the Dolls are frequently put in dangerous or unstable conditions while on engagements.[30] Indeed, even the act of imprinting and wiping is a semi-violent act, as Topher quips, "This is going to pinch a bit" in the series premiere.[31] As programmer, he has the ability to alter the mind and body through neurological manipulation, sometimes (eventually) leading to disastrous results. Thus, despite the Dollhouse's efforts to represent its practices as consensual, the acts involved in the process of identity transformation call into question the degree to which the Doll is actually able to agree to being programmed.

Yet still the relative ease with which Actives can be programmed to every client's whims foregrounds the degree to which they are seen as commodities to be sold. The Dollhouse economy consists of the production and consumption of constructed individuals. They are packaged and marketed for specific occasions, transforming into the ideal person for a given circumstance. Due to the practice of forgetting involved in the activities of the Dollhouse, Dolls can be seen as being estranged from their labor in Marxist terms. Much like black bodies being bought and sold during slavery, the Dolls' bodies are also utilized for the same purpose within a capitalist system of exchange, thus becoming an iteration of slave labor.[32]

However, it is Echo who ruptures the Dollhouse economy as she begins to remember her past life as Caroline. Indeed, her resistance to being completely wiped after each engagement provides an avenue for liberation. Lisa K. Perdigao notes that because Echo is "programmed with multiple narrative threads and character arcs, she transcends her role as the most recent Whedonbot to become a symbol of television, or at least a composite."[33] Echo reflects the inherent destabilization of television as a medium. Her advancement or "ascension" beyond Dollhouse technology, ultimately having the capacity to reprogram herself at will, highlights Echo's fluidity and ability to be fully awakened from her subjugation as a Doll. While on the surface this narrative of liberation is progressive, given the discourse of racial slavery that I have shown permeates the television text, *Dollhouse* alters the African American historical experience of enslavement by representing it through the struggles of a young white woman. As we shall see, this ultimately mutes the radical quality of Echo's insurgent act as a "runaway slave."

Liberation and the Runaway Slave

Julie L. Hawk notes that a theme in the Whedonverses consists of designating certain characters as game-changers in their ability to make choices that alter the narrative of the series. For example, both Buffy and Echo are chosen, but while Buffy's status as the Chosen One is one of inheritance based on a historical lineage of Slayers, Echo is "chosen" because of a "microbiological predisposition on the part of the body of Caroline."[34] At the end of the first episode of the series, a recording is shown of Caroline as a fresh-faced idealistic college student in which she addresses the camera noting that, "The world is in need of some serious saving."[35] She alludes to her role in this task of changing the world due to her liberal politics, and as the series continues, Caroline is revealed to be a renegade who is committed to debunking the system at any cost. In fact, in the episode "Getting Closer" (2.11), prior to becoming a Doll, Caroline breaks into DeWitt's office with an unwitting man in order to investigate, stating, "Relax, I'm not a thief. I'm a terrorist."[36] When her plan to expose the Rossum Corporation goes awry, she is enlisted (read: blackmailed) by the Rossum Corporation to become a participant in the Dollhouse. Caroline is stored on a wedge while her corporeal self becomes known as Echo. Echo's unique ability to "ascend" by remembering the multiple selves that have been programmed to inhabit her, as well as her power to be able to control them, makes her an asset in the eyes of the Rossum Corporation. However, Echo's consciousness of her function within the Dollhouse also makes her a threat because she has the potential to overthrow the establishment. Within a framework of race relations in the United States such a resistance to change by those in power and the possibility for activism against oppression can be directly seen in the Civil Rights Movement of the 1950s and 1960s. By giving voice to struggle, African Americans during this era paved the way for equality as U.S. citizens. In a different vein, with her memories intact , Echo is able to recognize the unethical practices of the Dollhouse and thus can be the harbinger of a revolt through her own enlightenment and awareness of herself as subject.

Indeed, as Echo transforms into a composite of various personalities, she comes to understand her own self as an independent entity. This paradoxical realization allows her to become an agent of change, a runaway slave within the Dollhouse-as-plantation. However, Echo's potential escape is hindered by not only the overall power structure of the Rossum Corporation, but also by her personal Handler, Boyd Langton. The Dollhouse employs individuals known as Handlers in order to monitor Actives, particularly when they are involved in engagements. The Handler, though conceptualized as a benign conduit between Doll and Dollhouse, holds a certain degree of control over his assigned Doll and can assert his dominance through unethical practices.[37] In such a master/slave relationship, Boyd provides an interesting subversion of this power dynamic in his function as Echo's African American protector and surrogate father figure. Yet, this subversion is called into question later on in the series as his attempts to gain power are predicated on maintaining the Rossum Corporation's success through oppressive Dollhouse acts.

Boyd is first presented on the show as an ex-cop who replaces Echo's former Handler who was killed by an Active named Alpha during his murderous rampage in the Dollhouse. Boyd is initially depicted as the moral center of *Dollhouse*, the one character that actually has scruples concerning Dollhouse practices. This is intriguing in itself because the Dollhouse exists as a private corporation outside of the purview of the law as a public service. Yet the former law enforcement official continually scrutinizes and attempts to monitor and regulate Dollhouse operations; in particular, he is very wary of the commonly held belief that individuals volunteer to become Dolls. When Topher insists that people have volunteered to become Dolls in order to downplay his own involvement with the system, Boyd quips, "So we're told."[38] Despite the organization's questionable practices, Boyd sees it as his duty to be responsible for Echo, as Season One's "The Target" (1.2) depicts the story of their bond and his devotion to her.[39] The connection between Handler and Active is unique and predicated on technological programming that forces Actives to unconditionally trust their Handlers. In this way, Handlers become the most crucial aspect of an individual's stint as a Doll, positioned between the external world of the engagements and the internal world of the Dollhouse. Thus the show re-envisions what can be seen as the master/slave paradigm between the Handler and Active and transforms it into a necessary bond for the arrangement and completion of tasks. Though the Handler still holds power over the Doll, it is a power that is founded on contingency and not force. This element of contingency fuels the argument concerning the consensual nature of Dollhouse practices. However, as I have indicated previously, an insidious type of force (enacted by the removal of inhibitions through a techno-drug, so to speak) is still utilized that operates under the auspices of a mutual interaction and affection between Doll and Active. While this relationship is optimal for the vast majority of Dolls, Echo is special. Boyd originally conceives of Dolls as helpless children that are incapable of resistance and Echo ruptures those assumptions. Indeed, at a certain point in her journey, Echo begins to make her own decisions irrespective of her mission parameters. In her creation of new approaches to a particular problem she becomes increasingly unpredictable and adaptable in her actions. Therefore, it is not surprising that Echo ultimately arrives at a point where she no longer adheres to her Handler's directives; though Boyd receives a promotion at the Dollhouse from Handler to Head of Security towards the end of the first season ("Spy in the House of Love" 1.9), he still has interactions with Echo in which she is both endeared to him and wary of the Dollhouse system.[40] Her commitment to Boyd (i.e., a technologically programmed connection) stands in conflict with her increasingly deprogrammed Doll status and produces an emotional fissure, which affects the power dynamic between her and her former Handler that disrupts the master/slave paradigm.

Echo's growing ability to resist control or containment, in other words, her status as a disobedient slave on the Dollhouse-as-plantation, makes her a prime candidate for liberating herself from the constraints of the Dollhouse. As an interesting foreshadowing of future events in the series, when transformed into a back-up vocalist for a pop artist, Echo sings in her audition: "I've gotta find the freedom that's promised me / Freedom from our struggles and our misery / Freedom is all we need to heal the pain of history."[41] Her soulful expression of the possibility of emancipation from slavery puts the issue of resistance at the forefront of the narrative. Like Caroline, Echo desires to mobilize a movement against injustice and in this case, the removal of basic human rights from Dollhouse participants. Indeed, in the episode "Needs" (1.8), Echo channels Caroline in her insistence on making a difference by releasing everyone captured in the Dollhouse.[42] Though her carrying out of this feat in this episode is revealed only to be a test, a simulation exercise constructed by Dollhouse management, it indicates how Echo's "ontological awareness transforms into an epistemological drive to know."[43] Echo's journey to gain knowledge of herself as a subject is inextricably intertwined with her quest for freedom. Thus, her official composite event at the end of Season One is crucial and highlights Hawks' argument that Echo "becomes able to use the technology subversively and to create a posthuman subjectivity that is both at odds with and in debt to the technological tampering that at first rendered her powerless."[44] Echo's final status as a figure that is seen to be *more* than human is directly related to the paradox that exists between the progressive and regressive character of race and technology in *Dollhouse*.

Being Post-Human, Becoming Post-Race

One of the primary themes in *Dollhouse* relates to the question of the human. "We're great humanitarians," Topher comments.[45] In this way, the Dollhouse believes that it is providing a service to society through the programming of people. In the unaired pilot ("Echo"), DeWitt states that "An Active is the truest soul among us" providing the "purest, most genuine human encounter" of one's life.[46] Yet though the Dolls supply this service, they are not recognized as people. Memory wipes evacuate an individual of his or her history, a technological feat that is not unlike the process of dehumanization that the slave undergoes. Dolls are treated as less than human (they are even referred to as mindless herding animals in "Gray Hour" (1.4) because they are believed not to have the necessary neurological capacity to function as enlightened people.[47] They are primitives, in all senses of the term, pre-cognitive entities that are allowed to be imprinted which gives them a sense of identity however fleeting it may be.

Despite the inherent lack of consciousness needed to become a human, Actives are constantly told to "be their best." This impetus towards enhancement and optimization hearkens back to the rhetoric of eugenics. Conceived by Charles Davenport, eugenics is predicated on the improvement of the human population and it ultimately served as a tool of racism through its emphasis on the science of breeding, and fittingly, "the term *breeding* exemplifies human races as technologically manipulable."[48] The Active goal of becoming better (indeed, of even being "number one") reflects the show's emphasis on technological advancement that is then programmed onto its underlying conception of African American racial progress. This is exemplified by Boyd's existence and role in the Dollhouse. As mentioned earlier, though *Dollhouse* has recurring black characters, their racial identity is rarely remarked on or expressed explicitly.[49] Boyd appears on screen bearing a stark resemblance to President Barack Obama in skin tone, stature, and voice.[50] He is calm, cool, and collected as an authoritative and wise figure, frequently serving as a confidante to various characters. Similar to how Anna Everett discusses President Obama, Boyd maintains a "careful cultivation of a race-neutral or transcendent political persona"[51] as a diligent observer of Dollhouse practices who successfully "passes" as an employee of the Rossum Corporation. Wilcox notes that Boyd's disposition makes it all the more unsettling that he is revealed to be the Founder of Rossum as the viewer realizes that "the person we thought he was, never existed."[52] In racialized terms, this indicates that Boyd's status as an African American man is called into question when he is revealed to be the dominant oppressive force within the Dollhouse-as-plantation and not the representative of the struggle against slavery or racial activism for civil rights. His acceptance of the technology's inevitable ability to imprint and enslave gives him the desire to create a vaccine against imprinting for a select few, his "family."[53] This paternalistic gesture highlights his investment in technological innovation as a post-racial patriarchal figure. In effect, he becomes the epitome of a narrative of racial progress from slave to societal leader, from inhuman to superior specimen of the human race. However, so constructed, he renders ahistorical his identity as a black male in order to become a dominant oppressive figure within a liberal humanist project. In other words, an African American character's "progress" is ultimately to become a master who enslaves others. There are troubling implications for this type of reliance on hegemonic power; implications equally troubling in how they are "solved" in the narrative, because as noted previously, the white female Echo is the one to punish Boyd for such a strategy of control.

Indeed, Echo foils Boyd's plan through her ability to be posthuman. In N. Katherine Hayles' formulation, "the posthuman subject is an amalgam, a collection of heterogeneous components, a material-informational entity whose boundaries undergo continuous construction and reconstruction."[54] Hayles privileges the notion of embodiment in the posthuman and the potential to include those marginalized from conceptions of the liberal humanist subject; namely, anyone who could be identified as a non-white European male. In this way, the posthuman designation can account for race and gender difference through its construction of a flexible identity. Echo's posthuman nature calls attention to her status as both an evolutionary and a *re*volutionary subject. Her ascendance to composite status allows her to become a subject and rebel against the powerful forces that seek to control her. Because of Caroline's genetic coding, Echo is able to become a person, and even further, a person capable of housing multiple personalities, histories, and memories. She is awakened in this process and her refusal to return to sleep as well as her drive to rescue other Dolls from the slumber of subjugation ultimately allows her to defeat Boyd. When Topher wipes him remotely, Boyd transforms into an Active and Echo becomes his Handler. When she directs him to commit suicide, his last words are, "I try to be my best."[55] This is a symbolic reversal on many different levels. Not only is the relationship between master and slave deconstructed in this instance, but the moment also speaks to the potential ramifications of such perceived racial progress aligned with an advanced technological project.[56] Boyd's faith and trust in Echo to be the key to the Rossum Corporation's liberal humanist interests is undercut precisely because she breaks the mold and uses the advanced technology of the Dollhouse against him by the end of the series. While Echo is constructed as a slave within the Dollhouse-as-plantation who ultimately defeats Boyd-as-Master in her quest for freedom, the show can be interpreted as what Hartman calls a "resubordination of the emancipated."[57] In other words, Boyd's status as what I call a "(doll)house negro" backfires to the point where he ironically becomes re-enslaved as a black man (despite his denial of a racial identity and heritage) by a white woman through the Rossum Corporation's privileging of technologically programmed posthumanism as power.[58] The demise of the African American man in the narrative reifies certain tropes in U.S history, namely the preservation of a racial hierarchy of white dominance whereby existing prejudices against African American progress and citizenry are reaffirmed.

Dollhouse, in many ways Whedon's most complicated and most misunderstood series, provides a commentary on televisuality and the crisis of historical memory in the navigation of its own narrative stakes. Therefore, it seems crucial to analyze the imperfect series as a working-through of larger issues concerning programming itself. In this piece, I have begun to do the work of analyzing such a nuanced Whedon text by looking at the show's use of racial and technological programming as both a progressive and regressive act. In contrast to how the series positions the Dollhouse as an ethical conundrum dealing with human trafficking and sexual slavery, I suggest that *Dollhouse* is doing more provocative work in its articulation of racial slavery. The argument that Dolls are technologically programmed contemporary slaves can be gleaned from the show's conflation of freedom from enslavement with Barack Obama's current Presidency. *Dollhouse*'s evocation of the Dolls as slave labor foregrounds a historical remembering of racial oppression in America. Simultaneously the show emphasizes the implications of a crisis in memory; thus, as *Dollhouse* engages with its own textual history (and even future), it is also involved in a constant process of forgetting. Echo and Caroline's dialogue which foregrounds this essay is a particularly reflexive moment that exemplifies the paradoxical quality of the show, which creates complex identity politics through its post-racial and posthumanism rhetoric.

To be imprinted is to be enslaved, which is to lack consciousness of one's own identity. The Dollhouse functions as an inhibitor of identity through the multiplication of selves. However, Echo's unique ability to "evolve" or transcend this restraint—in effect, to remember—renders her the epitome of technological progress. However, the show complicates these issues by revealing Boyd Langton to be one of the founding fathers of the Rossum Corporation. By furthering Rossum's liberal humanist endeavors, Boyd's amnesia lies in seldom acknowledging or deliberately misremembering the struggles of African Americans during slavery, hiding from his racial past, and therefore wielding corporate power to enslave individuals in the Dollhouse-as-plantation. Providing this close reading of the relationship between Boyd-as-master and Echo-as-slave demonstrates the program's use of race as well as narratives of progress within a dialectic of remembering and forgetting identity both in *Dollhouse*'s construction of history and its own televisual logic.

By articulating a concept of freedom that becomes the implicit driving force of the show, we can observe how *Dollhouse* reprograms the function of slavery and by extension, race, perhaps in order to liberate itself from narrative inhibition as a televisual product. Indeed, the underlying series' problematic is Echo's increasing rogue status as a Doll who implements an emancipatory project because, as she states in the first episode of Season Two ("Instinct" 2.1), "No one is their best in here."[59] Boyd's defeat by Echo changes how freedom is conceived and highlights its limitations. In particular, the representation of an African American man as an oppressive force whose power is undermined by a white female heroine renders the show a complex depiction of vicitimization predicated on the entanglement of race and technology. Therefore, *Dollhouse* can be seen as a cautionary tale of confinement that utilizes concepts of racial progress and technological advancement in parallel to shed light on its instability as a televisual text by reprogramming narratives of racial history and liberation.

NOTES

1. "Omega," *Dollhouse* 1.12, DVD, written by Tim Minear, Tracy Bellomo, Andrew Chambliss, Maurissa Tancharoen, and Jed Whedon, directed by Tim Minear (2009: Twentieth Century Fox 2009). This episode was televised as the season finale, while the DVD release of Season One included the final 13th episode of the season because Fox counted the unaired pilot, "Echo," as part of the 13-episode contract. The actual season finale, "Epitaph 1" (1.13) is set in the future and is drastically different in setting, tone, and narrative from the previous episodes.

2. "Briar Rose," *Dollhouse* 1.11, DVD, written by Jane Espenson, Tracy Bellomo, Andrew Chambliss, Maurissa Tancharoen, and Jed Whedon, directed by Dwight Little (2009: Twentieth Century Fox 2009).

3. Anna Everett, "Have We Become Postracial Yet?," in *Race After the Internet*, ed. Lisa Nakamura and Peter A. Chow-White (New York: Routledge, 2012), 146–167. For Everett, there is a correlation between the Internet boom of the late 1980s and early 1990s with its cultivation of "the nation's desire to imagine and construct colorblind or hyper-tolerant virtual communities and digital public spheres" (165) and Barack Obama as the first President who fully embraced digital media that contributes to current post-racial ideology.

4. "Man on the Street," *Dollhouse* 1.6, DVD, written by Joss Whedon, Tracy Bellomo, Andrew Chambliss, Maurissa Tancharoen, and Jed Whedon, directed by David Straiton (2009: Twentieth Century Fox 2009). This mantra is most notably seen in "Man on the Street," though other characters utter it as well in future episodes.

5. Rhonda Wilcox, "Unreal TV," in *Thinking Outside the Box: A Contemporary Television Genre Reader*, ed. Brian G. Rose and Gary R. Edgerton (Lexington: University Press of Kentucky, 2005), 201–225.

6. Cynthia Fuchs, "Did Anyone Ever Explain to You What 'Secret Identity' Means?" Race and Displacement in *Buffy* and *Dark Angel*," in *Undead TV: Essays on Buffy the Vampire Slayer*, ed. Elana Levine and Lisa Parks (Durham, NC: Duke University Press, 2007), 96–115. Importantly, when different "races" of beings come into contact, there is always the threat of miscegenation, a crucial issue during the period of U.S. slavery.

7. Martin Kevorkian, *Color Monitors: The Black Face of Technology in America* (Ithaca, NY: Cornell University Press, 2006); Wendy Chun, *Control and Freedom: Power and Paranoia in the Age of Fiber Optics* (Boston: MIT Press, 2006); etc.

8. Lisa Nakamura and Peter A. Chow-White, "Introduction," *Race After the Internet*, ed. Lisa Nakamura and Peter A. Chow-White (New York: Routledge, 2012), 5.

9. Wendy Hui Kyong Chun, "Introduction: Race and/as Technology; or, How to Do Things to Race," *Camera Obscura*, 24.1 (2009): 8.

10. Kevorkian, *Color Monitors*, 119. Here, he notes that technological labor can be considered a legitimate and prominent form of slavery.

11. Chun "Introduction: Race and/as Technology; or, How to Do Things to Race," 9.

12. *Dollhouse*, "Man on the Street," 1.6.

13. *Ibid.*

14. *Dollhouse*, "Man on the Street," 1.6.

15. *Ibid.*

16. Herman Gray, *Watching Race: Television and the Struggle for "Blackness"* (Minneapolis: University of Minnesota Press, 1995), 78.

17. Michael Ausiello, "This Just In: *Dollhouse* Axed," last modified Nov. 11, 2009, http://insidetv.ew.com/2009/11/11/this-just-in-dollhouse-axed/.

18. Stephen Heath, "Representing Television," in *Logics of Television*, ed. Patricia Mellencamp (Bloomington: Indiana University Press, 1990), 279.

19. Mary Ann Doane, "Information, Crisis, Catastrophe," in *Logics of Television: Essays in Cultural Criticism*, ed. Patricia Mellencamp (Bloomington: Indiana University Press, 1990), 222–239. In particular, Doane suggests that "Television thrives on its own forgetability," relying upon "the annihilation of memory, and consequently of history, in its continual stress upon the 'nowness' of its own discourse." (226, 227).

20. Michel Foucault, "Film and Popular Memory," *Radical Philosophy*, 11.11 (1975), 22.

21. Nakamura and Chow-White, "Introduction," 3.

22. Rhonda V. Wilcox, "Echoes of Complicity: Reflexivity and Identity in Joss Whedon's *Dollhouse*," *Slayage: The Online International Journal of Buffy Studies*, 30–31 (2010), 1. Wilcox brings up complicity, also on the part of the actors; for her, the show is a meta-narrative of the Whedonverse navigation of the medium of television and by extension, the entertainment industry.

23. Shelley S. Rees and Tom Connelly, "Alienation and the Dialectics of History in Joss Whedon's *Dollhouse*," *Slayage: The Online International Journal of Buffy Studies,* 30–31 (2010), 5.

24. "Ghost," *Dollhouse* 1.1, DVD, written by Joss Whedon, directed by Joss Whedon (2009: Twentieth Century Fox 2009).

25. *Dollhouse*, "Ghost," Episode 1.1.

26. Connelly and Rees, "Alienation and the Dialectics of History in Joss Whedon's *Dollhouse*," 8.

27. Saidiya Hartman, *Scenes of Subjection: Terror, Slavery, and Self-Making in Nineteenth Century America* (New York: Oxford University Press, 1997), 8.

28. *Dollhouse*, "Ghost," Episode 1.1.

29. *Ibid.*

30. Most notably, Echo is put at risk when she takes part in a mission where her lover hunts her for sport in "The Target" (1.2).

31. *Dollhouse*, "Ghost," Episode 1.1.

32. Connelly and Rees, "Alienation and the Dialectics of History in Joss Whedon's *Dollhouse*," 8.

33. Lisa K. Perdigao, ""This One's Broken": Rebuilding Whedonbots and Reprogramming the Whedonverse," *Slayage: The Online International Journal of Buffy Studies*, 30–31 (2010), 12.

34. Julie L. Hawk, "Hacking the Read-Only File: Collaborative Narrative as Ontological Construction in *Dollhouse*," *Slayage: The Online International Journal of Buffy Studies*, 30–31 (2010), 12.

35. *Dollhouse*, "Ghost," Episode 1.1.

36. "Getting Closer," *Dollhouse* 2.11, DVD, written by Tim Minear, directed by Tim Minear (2009: Twentieth Century Fox 2010). In particular, Caroline is against scientific testing on animals and breaks into the Rossum Corporation's building on her college campus to take photos of the animal cruelty and incriminate the conglomeration.

37. For example, Hearn, Sierra's Handler, is accused and found guilty of sexually assaulting her multiple times in "Echoes" (1.7), which interestingly goes along with the abundance of rape within such historical master/slave narratives.

38. "Gray Hour," *Dollhouse* 1.4, DVD, written by Sarah Fain, Elizabeth Craft,

Tracy Bellomo, Andrew Chambliss, Maurissa Tancharoen, and Jed Whedon, directed by Rod Hardy (2009: Twentieth Century Fox 2009).

39. "The Target," *Dollhouse* 1.2, DVD, written by Steven S. DeKnight, Tracy Bellomo, Andrew Chambliss, Maurissa Tancharoen, and Jed Whedon, directed by Steven S. DeKnight (2009: Twentieth Century Fox 2009). In particular, when Boyd comes to rescue Echo from a maniacal client in the woods, he tells her "everything's going to be alright." When Boyd is injured and Echo has to fend for herself, she asks Boyd, "Do you trust me?" to which he replies, "With my life."

40. "The Spy in the House of Love," *Dollhouse* 1.9, DVD, written by Tracy Bellomo, Andrew Chambliss, Maurissa Tancharoen, and Jed Whedon, directed by David Solomon (2009: Twentieth Century Fox 2009). Previous Head of Security Lawrence Dominic gets sent to the Attic after he is found out to be a spy for the National Security Agency and Adele promotes Boyd to the position.

41. "Stage Fright," *Dollhouse* 1.3, DVD, written by Tracy Bellomo, Andrew Chambliss, Maurissa Tancharoen, and Jed Whedon, directed by David Solomon (2009: Twentieth Century Fox 2009).

42. "Needs," *Dollhouse* 1.8, DVD, written by Tracy Bellomo, Andrew Chambliss, Maurissa Tancharoen, and Jed Whedon,, directed by Felix Alcala (2009: Twentieth Century Fox 2009).

43. Julie L. Hawk, "Hacking the Read-Only File: Collaborative Narrative as Ontological Construction in *Dollhouse*," 12.

44. *Ibid.*, 1.

45. *Dollhouse*, "Ghost," Episode 1.1.

46. "Echo," *Dollhouse* unaired pilot, DVD, written by Joss Whedon, directed by Joss Whedon (2009: Twentieth Century Fox 2009).

47. *Dollhouse*, "Gray Hour," Episode 1.4. Specifically, Topher calls them bison that instinctively flock together when he and Boyd notice that Echo, Sierra, and Victor repeatedly eat lunch together in the Dollhouse.

48. Chun, "Introduction: Race and/as Technology; or, How to Do Things to Race," 17.

49. In fact, the only moment in the entire series in which Boyd is referred to as a "Black guy" is in the episode "True Believer" (1.5).

50. Julian Sancton and Tim Heffernan, "White House Casting: Who *Should* Play the President?," http://www.esquire.com/the-side/feature/movie-president-look-alike-2011-44. Indeed, even popular media has noticed the resemblance between Barack Obama and Boyd's portrayer, Harry Lennix, choosing Lennix as the actor who would play President Obama in a film.

51. Everett, "Have We Become Postracial Yet?," 157.

52. Wilcox, "Echoes of Complicity: Reflexivity and Identity in Joss Whedon's *Dollhouse*," 14. She earlier comments in the essay that Boyd's "persona is no more real than a doll's imprint" (12). Indeed, it is quite feasible that Boyd has taken on numerous bodies in the past and his current racial demarcation (a "virtual blackness") is inconsequential because his true identity is a mystery. This is a provocative question, particularly in terms of the relationship between posthumanism and the ideology of a post-racial society.

53. "The Hollow Men," *Dollhouse* 2.12, DVD, written by Michele Fazekas, Tara Butters, and Tracy Bellomo, directed by Terrence O'Hara (2009: Twentieth Century Fox 2010). Boyd's plan is to inoculate Echo, Adele, Topher, Paul and others close to him because he considers them his family, telling them charmingly, "I love you guys."

54. N. Katherine Hayles, *How We Became Posthuman: Virtual Bodies in Cybernetics, Literature, and Informatics* (Chicago: University of Chicago Press, 1999), 3.

55. *Dollhouse*, "The Hollow Men," 2.12.

56. Clyde Randolph (known as Clyde 2.0) and his arguably more sinister mission of weaponizing the Dollhouse technology is still enacted in the dystopic future of "Epitaph 1" (1.13) and "Epitaph 2" (2.13). However, Echo and the Resistance Effort are able to restore all personalities to original selves.

57. Hartman, *Scenes of Subjection*, 116.

58. Malcolm X, "Twenty Million Black People in a Political, Economic, and Mental Prison," *Malcolm X: The Last Speeches,* ed. Bruce Perry (New York: Pathfinder Press, 1989), 27. The "house negro" is a largely pejorative term for a particular type of black slave who was able to work in the Master's house instead of on the plantation as a "field negro." Frequently it was predicated on issues of colorism, as lighter skinned blacks were more prone to occupying this position during slavery and therefore seen as bourgeois.

59. "Instinct," *Dollhouse* 2.2, DVD, written by Michele Fazekas and Tara Butters, directed by Marita Grabiak (2009: Twentieth Century Fox 2009).

"Memory itself guarantees nothing"
Dollhouse, *Witnessing and "the jews"*

SAMIRA NADKARNI

History repeats itself. A great deal of *Dollhouse*'s (and indeed, of most contemporary sci-fi shows') power and appeal lies in the fact that despite the show's supposed futuristic technology, the ideas being expressed aren't really all that far from our own current (and past) obsession with power.[1] The series' narrative is complicated by questions of authenticity, identity, slavery, consumerism, technology, and freedom, and it is the interplay of these various tropes that leads one into Whedon's exaggerated version of postmodern society—a world in which humanity is the product, engineered like any other, even if it harms the smooth functioning of consumer capitalism to think of ourselves this way, with the means and signs of production having been made invisible.[2] The viewer is presented with an ideological critique of power that evades any attempts at simple rationalization, unmasking the hidden realities of a situation in order to allow the marginalized or ignored subject to be given voice. Furthermore, *Dollhouse* explicitly makes its own historical parallels, most notably to the events of the Holocaust—such as Echo and Alpha's confrontation regarding their potential as *Übermensch* in "Briar Rose" (1.11) or Boyd Langton's speech about the "deserving few" in "The Hollow Men" (2.12)—in order to underscore the fact that memory in and of itself isn't enough.[3] And each time these parallels present themselves, Echo voices her (and the audience's) concerns. As the main staging of an amalgamation of memory, she remembers the events of the past that are presenting themselves now, only vaguely altered. But few are willing to hear what she has to say. Nothing really changes; the show ends on its post-apocalyptic note with Adelle DeWitt and the others facing the challenge of rebuilding the world, but nothing guarantees that these events will not repeat themselves or that similar events, only slightly altered, will not come to pass.

Dollhouse articulates a contemporary concern with the problematic nature of identity. The show focuses on the difficult nature of memory and recall, as well as on hierarchies of power and the rewritings of history.[4] Viewers are often led to question not only the identities constructed within the purview of the show, but also those without.[5] However, while this focus on memory and its importance in the construction of a personal and social identity is at the forefront of any discussion of *Dollhouse*'s significance, it remains a fact that access to memory, at its core, is not the real issue at hand. After all, we see Echo slowly begin to collate her various identities and begin remembering fairly early into Season One. Despite the missing piece of Caroline in her psyche (up until the end of the Season Two), no one can doubt that Echo remains a repository of knowledge. And yet, more is required of her—the simple fact remains that access to memory in and of itself is not enough.

This essay makes explicit the series' evocation of the events of the Holocaust in order to contextualize its appropriation of and commentary upon contemporary Jewish cultural identity. This is justified by a consideration of *Dollhouse*'s appropriation of the golem narrative, suggesting that the show, which lacks any explicitly Jewish characters, moves beyond an ethnically specific theorizing of race to a theorizing that encompasses not only contemporary Jewish identity, itself affected by the events of the Holocaust (a formative event in Jewish history), but also the cultural debt felt by the world in the aftermath of such an event. As such, there will be a consideration of Jean-François Lyotard's theorizing of "the jews" as per his work *Heidegger and "the jews,"* as well as an attempt to interpret what part the series' conclusion plays in this commentary.

The series' reinterpretation of the events of the Holocaust is subtle but unmistakable, particularly given the fact that *Dollhouse* situates itself within an ongoing discourse regarding complicity and responsibility.[6] We are repeatedly confronted with the understanding that the Actives are denied any true form of consent; as Echo succinctly puts it, "you can't sign a contract to be a slave" ("Omega" 1.12).[7] The viewer is made aware that these supposedly consenting Actives have often entered into these contracts in extreme situations that easily preclude any question of true consent. And most damning of all, in the final vision of this world as depicted in "Epitaph One" (1.13) and "Epitaph Two" (2.13), consent is made moot with wiping and imprinting occurring without the need for contracts or even face-to-face interaction. Lisa K. Perdigao notes that "because the Dolls are imprinted and subjected to memory wipes, their identities are transient, changeable, and interchangeable."[8] The Actives are not individuals, merely the bodies once occupied by those individuals. Denied their individuality and reduced to shells of themselves, the Actives effectively become dehumanized upon their entry into the Dollhouse, unable to access memories from their (or the) past.[9] Due to having been wiped, only the experience of the present moment registers for most Dolls. In this, only Echo and Alpha stand apart.

Consider these facts: the Actives have their identity removed and become simply one in an endless series of Sierras, Victors, Alphas and Echos—as a disguised Alpha puts it, "we're all just cells in a body.... We're all just Adams in the big continuous universe" ("Briar Rose" 1.11). They are treated like and referred to as animals rather than human beings.[10] All of this occurs in secret locations hidden from the general public, and the results are intended to benefit the "deserving few" (as Boyd Langton, the father figure and primary orchestrator of events through the series, puts it).[11] In addition, the series explicitly references its link to Nazism in the episode "Briar Rose" (1.11) wherein the term "*Übermensch*," taken from Nietzsche's work *Thus Spoke Zarathustra,* is used by Alpha in his attempt to convince Echo of their supposed supremacy in having experienced composite events.[12] He terms her and himself "*Übermensch*," clearly asserting a stance of superiority much in the manner that Nazism adopted the term to declaim racial superiority. Echo's reply then places this in historical context once more: "new, superior people. With a little German thrown in. What could possibly go wrong?" ("Omega" 1.12).[13] This quote demonstrates that the series evokes themes in line with the events of the Holocaust, although perhaps not as clearly as would merit the viewer's immediate dismissal; if the viewer was informed explicitly at the outset of the show that the Rossum Corporation is to be equated with Nazism, there would be no way in which he or she would be drawn into its push and pull of supply and demand versus memory and individuality. Rather, the series reels the viewer in with soft lighting, yoga classes and swimming pools, every appearance of comfort and elegance, a direct contrast to the stark images of camps such as Auschwitz or Buchenwald. We're told that the Actives chose to be here, will be released after five years and given generous compensation, and will have no memory of their time in the Dollhouse to live a better (and considerably richer) life. The contrast is compelling. And yet, if the eventual outcome is to be considered, the premise brought to its logical conclusion, there isn't much difference at all. The Actives aren't really seen or treated as human within the Dollhouse, they are never really going to be freed once their time is served, and perhaps most chillingly, there's always the chance that they could be sent to a space from which they cannot return, i.e., the Attic.

Added to the mix is the show's method of raising questions regarding complicity and responsibility. However, these questions are not restricted only to the events presented in the course of the series. The viewer is also made complicit in some manner by simply viewing these events, by finding them interesting or titillating. As Wilcox puts it, "whether we are *examining* exploitation or *participating* in it is part of the question Whedon and Dushku put to us."[14] The viewer is positioned as an onlooker, simultaneously aware of the incidents occurring and yet remaining inactive, maintaining his or her distance.[15] And while the viewer's complicity and responsibility are problematic enough, the fact that the various Dollhouses are hidden from the general public in the series but remain visible to the viewer simply emphasizes the viewer's role as onlooker, as witness. But this witnessing is complicated by a sensation of culpability, a knowing of what these events portend; the viewer becomes witness, but also in some manner, perhaps due to their (complicit) inaction, could feel culpable for the events that unfold. The viewer's potential knowledge and inaction, their implicit culpability once again invites a comparison to the Holocaust, in that it mirrors the implied inaction and culpability of the inhabitants of the villages located near the concentration camps, whose possible witnessing left them in an untenable position: either to assist the prisoners which would certainly be courting death, or to do nothing in the face of a vastly sinister force.[16] In a similar vein, consider the reaction of the average person in "Man on the Street" (1.6), who halfway believe that the Dollhouse is a myth, floundering their way through rumor, and those who believe in its possibility display nothing so much as opinion coupled with inaction—it seems possible that this reference could parallel the implicit knowledge held by many of the people at the time of the Holocaust who viewed the rounding up of Jewish families, who understood what that probably meant but dismissed it as hearsay.[17]

Dollhouse is not the first among Whedon's series to make a link between the events of World War II and America's role as a global power. As Cynthea Masson has noted in her essay "'Evil's Spreading, Sir—and It's Not Just Over There!': Nazism in *Buffy* and *Angel*," the *Buffy*verse has numerous examples of this very link, undercutting the supposedly explicit binary of good and evil exhibited in popular historical memory.[18] Masson closely examined the *Angel* episode "Why We Fight" (5.13) , quoting Henry Giroux's statement that "[w]hile it would be ludicrous to suggest that the United States either represents a mirror image of fascist ideology or mimics the systemic racialized terror of Nazi Germany, it is not unreasonable … to learn to recognize how different elements of fascism crystallize in different historical periods into new forms of authoritarianism."[19] In a similar manner, the Initiative in Season Four of *Buffy the Vampire Slayer* draws strong parallels between the *Buffy*verse and the events of World War II, with its hidden location, experimentation on demons, and eventual intention to "better" the human race. Whedon's work displays a pattern of recurring engagement with neo-fascist elements that can be traced back to *Buffy the Vampire Slayer* with the Watchers' Council and the Initiative, through *Angel* in the episodes "Hero" (1.9), "Why We Fight" (5.13) and through the Wolfram & Hart storyline, through *Firefly* with the Alliance's experiments on River, as well on Miranda in *Serenity*, and through to his latest work in the 2012 blockbuster *The Avengers* where a single old man in Germany dares to stand against Loki because "there are always men like you."[20] His constant re-appropriation of the World War II narrative suggests an attempt to grapple with an ongoing concern with power, responsibility, complicity and subjugation. *Dollhouse* continues within this preoccupation, but in a manner that seems far subtler than previously displayed in the Whedonverses. The series functions as a commentary on the aftermath of the events of the Holocaust, its final outcome not just suggesting an augmented interpretation of witnessing and memorializing, but also reminding the viewer that despite the fact that history presents a record of these events occurring, their effects are still felt and still present themselves within our amalgamations of personal and cultural identity. As such, both the characters within the series and the viewer without are positioned inside what Lyotard refers to as a "singular debt of an interminable anamnesis."[21] We all have a shared obligation to a memory that cannot be represented, memorialized, or made concrete and presentable because it is unimaginable in its magnitude. It's a debt that cannot be repaid. As such, we are all, in some manner, caught in the aftermath of the event, and we become what Lyotard terms "the jews," a phrase that is not connected to a nation, an ideology, or a concept, but is both part of and apart from Jewish identity. The debt felt could not be present without taking into consideration the Jewish experience of the time, but does not restrict itself to Jewish identity; "the jews" is intended to be considered as apart from Jewish identity but related to aftermath of the Holocaust experience.

In many ways making a claim of this nature can seem reductive, forced, and rather unnecessary. After all, *Dollhouse*'s links to questions of transgression, violence and identity allow it to function as commentary on any number of historical events. Added to this is the fact that the show is set primarily in Los Angeles and concerns itself less with a single race of people and their history, and more with contemporary society's obsession with mass production and consumerism. However, the series' explicit references to the events of the Holocaust suggest that a focused reading might prove fruitful in articulating the essential problem at the close of the series and in the aftermath of events of this nature: the fact that remembering the past is no guarantee that these events will not repeat themselves in some manner in the future. Rather, as David Carroll notes, "memory in itself guarantees nothing; it all depends on what kind of memory and how, within memory, one goes about combating the revenge the memory of injustice often calls for."[22] At its close, *Dollhouse* isn't giving us what might be misunderstood as an easy solution on the writers' part, i.e., re-setting the world to where we began.[23] There is a more complex issue at play. The Actives, and Echo in particular, remain largely the focus of the show and given the events that occur, appear to be positioned as representations of Jewish identity in this process, particularly given the series' appropriation of the modern golem narrative. The term "golem" comes from the Hebrew word "*gelem*," signifying raw material, something that is unformed or imperfect, and it is this position of the Actives as golem figures that allows for the series to articulate a novel theorizing of witnessing, a further commentary on the representation of Jewish identity and our own identity as "the jews" in the world today. Thus, while none of the characters within *Dollhouse* are depicted as Jewish themselves, this does not preclude their depiction as "the jews" of Lyotard's description, thereby both linking them to and separating them from Jewish identity itself.

Dollhouse's evocation of the golem legend is made explicit in the episode "Getting Closer" (2.11) wherein Caroline meets with the head of the Rossum Corporation.[24] Expecting to meet a Mr. Rossum, she's confused when the man present states that there is no such person and that the name of the corporation was taken "from a play. Although technically you're not robots, it seemed to fit."[25] This clear reference to Karel Čapek's 1921 play *R.U.R.* (or *Rossum's Universal Robots*) suggests the Rossum Corporation's own acknowledgement of the implicit (or rather, fairly explicit) slavery, mass production, and consumerism at the heart of their endeavor. Čapek stated of his play that "*R.U.R.* is in fact my own rendering of the legend of the golem in modern form ... the robot is the golem made flesh by mass production."[26] The play opens on a world in which robots are mass-produced in order to follow humanity's commands.[27] At its outset, the main characters appear to display utopian ideals, intending the manufacture and use of robots to carry out all necessary work, thereby eradicating hunger and poverty. And like most utopian ideals, these rapidly degenerate into war, chaos, and eventually, the robots' rising up against humanity and killing their creators en masse. Čapek offers hope at the close of the play, albeit not hope for humanity, but rather for their creation. The robots Primus and Helena are seen as capable of love, homunculi with souls that distinguish them from the other apparently soulless masses. Čapek presents the possibility of the birth of a new race of robots, with Primus and Helena depicted as Adam and Eve, respectively, on an island that both presents and subverts the notion of Eden (depending upon the individual viewpoint). Viewers familiar with *Dollhouse*'s narrative arc will no doubt see the obvious parallels.[28]

Čapek's vision of a consumerist future relies quite heavily upon one of the best-known golem legends, that of Rabbi Judeh Loew ben Benzalel, the Maharal of Prague (1513–1609) in the 16th Century. The Jewish folklore tradition depicts the golem as an artificial creature, shaped in the manner of a large man, yet without will, intellect or personality, brought to life by the addition of the name of God through a mystic process, either by calling out God's real name, or by writing this name on parchment and placing it in the golem's mouth. Initially created in order to assist the local populace and save them from persecution, the golem eventually runs amok and threatens innocent lives. The tale ends differently as per various interpretations, either with the golem rendered lifeless by the removal of the divine name, or by going mad and running away.[29] Thus, the original golem narrative suggests a link to the Jewish faith, while Čapek's own interpretation presents and subverts an association with religion, choosing instead to focus on the effects of consumerism and mass production.[30] Both versions present a link to Jewish cultural identity, even if the link to Jewish faith is removed in later adaptations.

As Dale Koontz has noted, Čapek's vision of a consumerist future is reinterpreted in *Dollhouse*.[31] Much like Čapek's *R.U.R.*, the series opens on a utopian premise, with Adelle DeWitt, the head of the Dollhouse in Los Angeles, stating "I know you've heard colorful rumors about what an Active is. Robots, zombies, slaves—they are, of course, quite the opposite. The Active is the truest soul among us" ("Ghost" 1.1). Therefore at the very outset of the narrative, the Actives in the series are indicated as constructed subjects, but with souls, very much in the manner of the robots, Helena and Primus, at the close of Čapek 's play. However, Whedon's figuring and use of the trope of the modern golem does not lend itself well to easy categorization. In terms of a broad, over-arching narrative, it refigures the creation of beings that appear at the outset of the series to have been stripped of their will, their intellect and personality, and these beings are then made to serve. As per the original narrative of the golem figure, these beings eventually rise up against their creator. All three narratives—the Maharal of Prague, *R.U.R.* and *Dollhouse*—share in common the basic premise that the homunculi, robots or Actives were intended to make things easier, to make lives better, to give people what they thought they needed. And all three end in a version of Iris/Caroline's statement: "kids playing with matches. And they burned the house down" ("Epitaph One" 1.13).[32] And yet the series makes itself distinct from these previous representations.

Dollhouse responds to the evolution of thought from the original golem legend through to *R.U.R.* by refusing to engage in the question of divinity at all, moving instead to a questioning of systems of belief. While the series is concerned with the same hubristic subverting of the natural order that characterizes other representations of the golem narrative, *Dollhouse*'s version displays a further evolution with regard to the body/mind (or soul) divide. The golem narrative presumes the construction of the body to be within man's purview, whereas the construction of the soul or the mind occurs in a manner that is more organic, outside of man's control. However, in *Dollhouse* we see Claire Saunders realize that her entire existence has been constructed. She states explicitly that although she's not real, she doesn't want to die.[33] She's the equivalent of a made-up person walking around in someone else's body. Upon considering this, Saunders does not function within the traditional theorizing of the golem figure, but rather straddles the boundary of constructed subject and evolving mind. Her entire reality has been constructed by Topher—who is positioned early on in the series as Young Rossum from *R.U.R.*, unconcerned with questions of religion or souls and more interested in streamlining the process, making production convenient—but this constructed subjectivity has elements he never intended. With Saunders' constructed subjectivity evolving outside of Topher's frame of reference as creator, the question of what led to this evolution is left unanswered. And potentially, all that is seen to matter is her own belief in her identity, her own fears and the need to overcome them.[34] The establishment of her identity forms its own paradox in that it falls neither entirely within her own purview, nor Topher's. And most notably, divinity is never factored in as any form of agency in this setting.

Moreover, *Dollhouse*'s concern with constructed and original identities somewhat returns the viewer to early versions of the golem legend wherein the golem's figure requires the addition of the divine name in some manner in order for the creature to be brought to life.[35] In the nightmarish scenes of "Epitaph One" (1.13) and "Epitaph Two" (2.13), the viewer is informed that in order to identify and confirm their identity as "Actuals," or people who have not yet been printed, people tattoo their names on their body—specifically on their backs where they would be unable to easily see it and fake their response. The viewer is led to understand that if the name a person gives doesn't match up with their tattoo, the person will be killed in order to ensure the survival of the remaining Actuals. Life being dependent upon this name, the golem legend presents itself once more within the purview of *Dollhouse*, although again without its links to the divine.

Interestingly, the show's parallel and integrated references to the golem and the Holocaust narratives suggest a further reading of these tattooed names.[36] Upon entry to Auschwitz, prisoners were provided with a tattoo of a number by which they would then be referred to, often placed on their forearm. These numbers were intended to provide easy identification of bodies, often after the person's death in the gas chambers whereupon clothing would have been removed, making other identification problematic.[37] These tattoos were not provided to inmates directly intended for the gas chambers, and therefore could be considered to be a demarcation between life and death similar to the provision of tattooed names upon Actuals' bodies in *Dollhouse*. However, rather than functioning as a dehumanizing mechanism as per Auschwitz, the emphasis in *Dollhouse* is upon a named identity, subverting the Holocaust narrative. However, although the tattooed name provides what one might term an affirmation of the individual, it remains that its use as a border between life and death links it strongly back to the events of Auschwitz.

It appears that the constantly shifting boundaries within the series present this modified golem narrative but without the clean distinctions that the viewer may have come to expect upon identifying the tropes in question. The framework of any moral judgment that the viewer might seek to simplify the series is constantly shifting, even as the characters themselves evolve from their original characterization. Thus we see Topher, the primary figure of creator (although not one with absolute control over the events), move from his label of "sociopath in a sweater vest" to Christ-figure at the close of Season Two.[38] Agent Paul Ballard moves from his original position of "white hat" to a slightly more questionable association as Handler and back again, becoming first another golem and then eventually, at the close of the series, ghost.[39] Adelle DeWitt fluctuates between being portrayed as reprehensible and as trustworthy (her eventual position at the series' close.) And then there's Boyd Langton who, at the close of the series, is creator, protector, villain and (once wiped) golem. Specifically in this case, the golem narrative is refigured to suggest a notion of subjecthood that has identity and voice, even if these are constantly put in question or subverted by events that unfold. Echo, as primary protagonist, constructs her identity not only from the various constructs that she is programmed with over the course of the series, but also from her own understanding of her position as Active; her identity configures itself at various points as an empty (or temporarily inhabited) Doll, a modern golem figure, the tool of a consumerist future, *Übermensch*, postmodern Eve, or any or all of these.

Arguably, it is primarily Echo's position as golem figure or Active that allows her to be configured within the series narrative as all of these. And the links between Echo as modern golem and her identity as post-modern Eve are further underlined by the fact that according to Jewish Talmudic legend, Adam is referred to as "golem," meaning "body without a soul," for the first twelve hours of his existence.[40] This is borne out by the depiction of the Dolls in their non–Active state as child-like, innocent, defenseless and serene, willing to be "created" or imprinted by Topher who stands in place of the modern God of consumerism, i.e., the Rossum Corporation, who watch from above. The series makes direct references to its link as potential parable, the disguised Alpha informs Paul Ballard that Eden was a prison, since "the apples were monitored" ("Briar Rose" 1.11).[41]

The Dollhouse as Eden is devoid of divine presence, its inhabitants rising from their original unaware states to rebellion and awareness. Whedon both presents and collapses any attempts to read *Dollhouse* as a parable, in that the series positions Echo as the postmodern Eve, and Alpha acting as the snake to seduce her, to confirm what she herself has only begun to suspect: they are not just simple humans anymore, as she has evolved beyond any original self and there is no going back for either Alpha or her. Paul Ballard enters the narrative strain as a possible Adam figure, following Caroline/ Echo into her world and abandoning his innocence at the entrance to the Dollhouse, banished from his previous existence as a federal agent. And, at the close of the tale, Echo returns to the Dollhouse to make a stand, metaphorically eating once more of the tree and imprinting her love, the now deceased Paul Ballard, into herself and thus adding him to her legion of selves. Adam and Eve collapse back into the same body (although it is Eve's body in this tale), a return in theory, even if it is not a return to innocence. The conclusion undermines our positing of the tale as a parable, even as we begin to accept its construction. Innocence has no place in this work, and Echo herself rejects any return to a state of unknowing subservience, as seen, for example, when Ballard suggests finding a way to wipe her completely and she responds: "Feeling nothing would be worse. It would be like before—asleep. I'm awake now. I don't want to go back to sleep ("Instinct" 2.2).[42]

Echo's development throughout the series from uninhabited Doll to revolutionary self-awareness parallels the golem legend, although the series' revolutionary element occasions a notably sinister tone; Alpha suggesting that the Actives are not simply golem figures, but rather herald the arrival of *Übermensch*, stating that they're no longer just humans or multiple personalities but have evolved into something perfected, something new. Echo then explicitly links Alpha's use of the *Übermensch*, itself benign in its original incarnation in Nietzsche's text, to its use as German propaganda during World War II.

The series' combination of the modern golem narrative and eugenics propaganda strongly associated with Nazism suggest a collapse of the traditional moral binaries within depictions that draw on the events of the Holocaust.[43] The binary of Jewish cultural identity and Nazism, of good and bad, cannot be seen to hold in this representation. Alpha is originally a victim of the authoritarian and capitalistic Dollhouse, and yet he is no longer simply victim by the time the viewer is introduced to him. The question arises of whether he ever was. Alpha assumes both roles—the golem figure, as well as potential *Übermensch*—collapsing them into the same identity. The good versus evil distinction is no longer absolute, and one cannot posit a potential victim or abuser as easily in this scenario. There is no easy answer and nuance becomes the name of the game. The series underlines this fact by displaying a lack of resolution with regard to this collapsing of identities; despite Echo's rejection of the *Übermensch* identity, the fact remains that Echo and Alpha retain their position as evolved at the series' close. The viewer is led to question whether this is the heralding of a new future—Echo is displayed as the new Eve, with all the potentiality that entails.

Dollhouse's depiction of Echo and Alpha's continued potentiality as both golem and *Übermensch* points towards a problematic correlation with regard to an evolving Jewish identity in the aftermath of the Holocaust. While it may seem reductive to suggest that Jewish identity is now permanently defined in some manner by the events that took place, it does appear to be inextricably linked to the aftermath.[44] The collapsing of the supposed binaries that occurred during that time within Echo and Alpha, the two "evolved" Actives over the course of the series, suggests a distinct acknowledgement of this effect. That Echo and Alpha see themselves as potentially evolved, that they are golem figures, and that they survive in the aftermath of a war for survival, all point towards a melding of what might be seen as conventionally antithetical identities.

Alpha's collation of these two identities suggests another possibility—that the golem figure, previously disregarded or seen as inferior, is now the superior figure, is now the *Übermensch*.[45] There is no doubt that to consider this inversion wherein a traditional representation of Jewish identity is elevated in this manner is dubious at best, reprehensible at worst, especially considering the parallels being drawn. And yet *Dollhouse* takes this element on as well. The tech-heads seen in "Epitaph Two" (2.13) explore this supposed racial superiority, embracing their golem status and viewing themselves as superior to the Actuals under their care. However, once again this thought process is firmly nipped in the bud—Tony refuses temptation in much the same manner as Echo originally refused her status as *Übermensch*. But problematically, while Tony is capable of returning to his status as Actual once the tech is removed, Echo cannot do so. Despite her outright refusal to view herself in this manner, this aspect remains unresolved. Echo's fragmented self retains all the angles of the narrative and becomes our central focus: as Caroline, she is both freedom fighter against and complicit in her contract with the Rossum Corporation. As Echo she is golem, *Übermensch*, and postmodern Eve, due to a confluence of factors: the access to a historical past, both in terms of her ability to remember and reference past events, as well as the fact that her spinal fluid is an inoculation against the dystopian reality at the close of the show.

Perhaps most important at the close of the series is the question that opened up this essay, that of memory, of remembering, or of memorializing. In the aftermath of the Holocaust, "witnessing" became a charged word. In his book *The Drowned and the Saved*, Primo Levi suggests the inadequacy of any account provided by a survivor of the Holocaust, stating "we the survivors, are not the true witnesses…. We are those who by their prevarications or abilities or good luck did not touch bottom. Those who did so … have not returned to tell about it or have returned mute ... the submerged, the complete witnesses, the ones whose deposition would have a general significance. They are the rule, we are the exception."[46] In a similar vein of thought, Jorge Semprun writes in the final scenes of *Le Grand Voyage*, a fictionalized account of his deportation and incarceration in a concentration camp, of the death of a compatriot on his journey known only as "the guy from Semur." As Ofilia Ferràn and Lawrence Langer surmise, the guy from Semur functions within the narrative as a link to the narrator, the part of him that dies upon arriving at the camp. Gérard (Semprun's fictional self in the novel) is no longer a whole self speaking, and is fragmented. Witnessing becomes impossible in some manner because to witness requires a self, and Semprun appears to evoke Robert Antelme's argument that the loss of name and therefore of identity was necessary for the dehumanizing mechanism of the camps to function.[47] In other words, the camps' aim was to destroy the possibility of a self who could bear witness.

Given *Dollhouse*'s use of similar themes, witnessing once again becomes problematic in light of how the Actives are effectively stripped of self and identity. Even when these are restored, their memories and therefore their identities will always be potentially malleable, in doubt. Those that retain their memory without becoming golem figures, such as Adelle and Topher, cannot bear witness to what they have not experienced. However, Echo once again stands apart in this theorizing. Her position arising from the collation of her role as *Übermensch* and golem figure allows her the possibility of witnessing, of speaking for those marginalized. After all, Echo's singular identity is constructed by her amalgamation of these various selves that she has been programmed with. She contains not only her original self (Caroline is reintegrated amongst Echo's amalgam of selves, although she's no longer the primary persona), but also the now deceased Paul Ballard who has been person, golem, and victim. Echo is both victim and survivor. She has amongst her various personalities both the living and the dead; as she puts it, "we're not anybody because we're everybody."[48]

Arguably, Echo's position as potential witness places her outside of conventional restrictions, her ability to remember and speak for the living and the dead, the golem and the *Übermensch*, suggests a fully rounded testimonial. Furthermore, the importance of her testimonial is emphasized by the destruction of the memorial at the top of the Rossum tower; Topher's memories of the events leading up to the Dollhouse before Caroline's entry, his own work in creating and streamlining the Doll technology, as well as the actual artifacts (i.e., photographs) placed under the slogan 'To Remember' are all erased by the reversion to a pre-wiped world.[49] And perhaps this is why Whedon closes the series with Echo choosing to remain in the Dollhouse, falling asleep in her bed without reintegrating amongst the reawakened masses. The show refuses us the possibility of this final answer, even refuses to close the viewer to the very possibility of the question. As "the jews," we are all present in the aftermath, all attempting to come to terms with this formless, impossible debt and to present us with an easy answer would be, inevitably, a failure to respond adequately to this demand. The series' return from a post-apocalyptic future to a world slowly awakening to itself places us once more in the aftermath of the event with the knowledge that simply remembering the past gives us no guarantee against its repetition. And choosing to forget, as the series shows, is not the easy solution it appears to be. So the real question remains: where do we go from here?

NOTES

1. Further examples of science-fiction shows that emphasize an obsession with power and re-writings of history would include shows such as *Doctor Who, Warehouse 13, Fringe,* and *Eureka,* to name a few.

2. I owe parts of this analysis to Alyson Buckman (CSU, Sacramento). I am also extremely grateful to Tamy Burnett (University of Nebraska-Lincoln), Anne Jamison (University of Utah) and Matthew Pateman (Kingston University, London) for their extensive involvement in the theorizing and reviewing of this essay. I am also deeply indebted to my editors, Mary Ellen Iatropoulos and Lowery Woodall, III, for their time, effort, and insightful comments.

3. "Briar Rose," *Dollhouse* 1.11, DVD, written by Jane Espenson, Tracy Bellomo, Andrew Chambliss, Jed Whedon, and Maurissa Tancharoen, directed by Dwight H. Little (2009: Twentieth Century Fox, 2009); "The Hollow Men," *Dollhouse* 2.12, DVD, written by Michelle Fazekas, Tara Butters, and Tracy Bellomo, directed Terrence O'Hara (2009, Twentieth Century Fox, 2010).

4. See for example, "The Left Hand," *Dollhouse* 2.6, DVD, written by Tracy Bellomo, directed by Wendy Stanzler (2009: Twentieth Century Fox, 2009). This episode is a significant example of the problematic core of *Dollhouse*'s re-writings of history. In the episode, Senator Daniel Perrin makes an announcement regarding the death of his wife/Handler as well as Madeline Costley's own personal history. The viewer knows (as do Echo and the others) that this announcement is completely fabricated, and yet it will be the version remembered and articulated in the future unless it can be disproved. And within the series itself, his statement is never challenged publicly.

5. For more in this vein, see Madeline Muntersbjorn, "Disgust, Difference, and Displacement in the *Dollhouse,*" *Slayage,* 8.2–3 (2010), http://slayageonline.com/essays/slayage30_31/Muntersbjorn.pdf.

6. For more information on these elements, please refer to Rhonda V. Wilcox, "Echoes of Complicity: Reflexivity and Identity in Joss Whedon's *Dollhouse,*" *Slayage,* 8.2–3 (2010), http://slayageonline.com/Numbers/slayage30_31.htm; or see Madeline Muntersbjorn, "Disgust, Difference, and Displacement in the *Dollhouse,*" *Slayage,* 8.2–3 (2010), http://slayageonline.com/essays/slayage30_31/Muntersbjorn.pdf.

7. Echo is not the only one who makes this link explicitly. Other examples would include "Briar Rose," *Dollhouse* 1.11, DVD, written by Jane Espenson, directed by Dwight Little (2009: Twentieth Century Fox, 2009); "Man on the Street," *Dollhouse* 1.6, DVD, written by Joss Whedon, directed by David Straiton (2009: Twentieth Century Fox, 2009). In "Briar Rose," Paul Ballard strongly emphasizes that contractual

slavery is a problem, and an African American woman in "Man on the Street" states, "Only one reason someone would volunteer to be a slave is if they is one already."

8. Lisa K. Perdigao, "'This One's Broken': Rebuilding Whedonbots and Reprogramming the Whedonverse," *Slayage*, 8.2–3 (2010), http://slayageonline.com/essays/slayage30_31/perdigao.pdf.

9. In addition, their experiences within the Dollhouse become essentially interchangeable. They experience treatments, return and repeat their mantra of having fallen asleep and questioning whether they can now leave. Nothing really sets one Active apart from another.

10. Bennett Halverson makes reference to the Actives in the Los Angeles Dollhouse as "free range chickens" and likens the D.C. Dollhouse's own Actives to "veal." In terms of the latter, it is perhaps more clear than ever that what is being referred to here is not a living being but explicitly its flesh. She does not refer to them as living (as cattle), but rather to their flesh, the product that they reflect ("Getting Closer" 2.11).

11. "Getting Closer," *Dollhouse* 2.11, DVD, written and directed by Tim Minear (2009: Twentieth Century Fox, 2010).

12. "Briar Rose," *Dollhouse*, 1.11.

13. *Ibid.*

14. Rhonda V. Wilcox, "Echoes of Complicity: Reflexivity and Identity in Joss Whedon's *Dollhouse*," *Slayage*, 8.2–3 (2010), http://slayageonline.com/Numbers/slayage30_31.htm, 4.

15. It is possible to suggest that *Dollhouse* evokes a notable parallel here in terms of a distanced and problematically complicit viewing experience. In the American propaganda documentary film by Billy Wilder, entitled *Death Mills*, the viewer watches as residents of the village of Weimar located approximately 8 kilometers from the Nazi camp, Buchenwald, were made to bear witness to the events that had occurred so close to their city. As such, *Death Mills* carries with it a fairly explicit suggestion of the residents' complicity in allowing the events to take place, or, at the very least, is a disavowal of any lack of knowledge on their part. This event as well as the rebuttal provided by the residents of Weimar is discussed in Klaus Neumann's *Shifting Memories: The Nazi Past in the New Germany* (Ann Arbor: University of Michigan Press, 2000), pp. 181–2. However, while complicity is impossible to truly determine in the aftermath of such events, it is interesting to note a particular parallel: that of the Americanization of World War II in the aftermath of the event. In large part, the production of these propaganda documentaries was intended to educate the German public about the Nazi atrocities that occurred at the time, but they also functioned in producing a distinct narrative regarding the American presence in World War II and their role as "liberators." As such, if *Dollhouse* is in fact making a similar reference to the viewer's complicity, it is interesting to note that the complicity this time occurs once again within a narrative that appropriates these stories and re-presents them with a distinctly American emphasis. And perhaps the intended emphasis this time is that the big evils are American corporations like Rossum that would reduce us all either to Dolls who do their bidding, or complicit viewers/onlookers.

16. There are numerous accounts of these confrontations in the literature produced in the aftermath of the Holocaust. Jorge Semprun makes reference to an event in the fictionalized account of his own incarceration, *Le Grand Voyage*, in which Gérard, his fictional self, walks into a house located near the camp where he was held and confronts the old woman living there whose bedroom overlooks the courtyard of the camps. When he confronts her with her knowledge of the atrocities inflicted

in the camps, she responds simply that she lost two sons to the wars. Jorge Semprun, *Le Grand Voyage* (Paris: Gallimard, 1963), 183–184.

17. This is not to say that it is really possible to equate the viewing of a fictional TV series with the personal events of the people who at that time watched their friends and neighbors being rounded up. Rather, this is meant to suggest a possible parallel that is far less demanding within the situation implied, but nonetheless equitable when taken to an extreme.

18. Masson uses the term *"Buffyverse"* to refer to both *Buffy the Vampire Slayer* and its spin-off series *Angel*.

19. Henry Giroux, 2006, quoted in Cynthea Masson, "'Evil's Spreading, Sir— and It's Not Just Over There!': Nazism in *Buffy* and *Angel*," *Monsters in the Mirror: Representations of Nazism in Post-War Popular Culture*, ed. Sara Buttsworth and Maartje Abbenhuis (Oxford: Praeger, 2010), 179–99, 181.

20. For a close analysis on World War II imagery in *The Avengers*, it's worth reading Ensley F. Guffey's essay titled "Avengers Assembled: Joss Whedon Throws Down His Mighty Shield," in *A Joss Whedon Reader*, ed. David Lavery, Rhonda Wilcox, Tanya Cochran, and Cynthea Masson (Syracuse University Press, 2014). I would also recommend Ensley F. Guffey's essay titled "War in the Whedonverses: Iconic World War Two Imagery in *Angel* and *Firefly*," presented at *The 5th Biennial Slayage Conference on the Whedonverses* in Vancouver, British Columbia, July 2012.

21. Jean-François Lyotard, as quoted in David Carroll, "Foreword: The Memory of Devastation and the Responsibilities of Thought: 'And let's not talk about that,'" *Heidegger and "the jews,"* trans. Andreas Michel and Mark Roberts (Minneapolis: University of Minnesota Press, 1990), vii–xxix, xii.

22. David Carroll, "Foreword: The Memory of Devastation and the Responsibilities of Thought: 'And let's not talk about that,'" in Jean François Lyotard, *Heidegger and "the jews,"* trans. Andreas Michael and Mark Roberts (Minneapolis: University of Minnesota Press, 1990), ix.

23. I mean this in the sense that the close of the series features a re-setting the world in terms of the technology for imprinting being lost and everyone being re-wiped and imprinted with their original identities. This does not erase the events that have occurred, but does suggest a new beginning at a point comparable to the past.

24. "Getting Closer," *Dollhouse*, 2.11.

25. *Ibid.*

26. Karel Čapek, Comrada 251, as seen in Nicola Morris, *The Golem in Jewish American Literature: Risks and Responsibilities in the Fiction of Thane Rosenbaum, Nomi Eve and Steve Stern* (New York: Peter Lang Publishing, 2007), 119.

27. It is worth noting that Čapek's use of the term robot does not have the same connotations as current use of the term; the robots indicated here were created as homunculi from organic matter, and brought to life by a scientific formula in order to perform their master's commands.

28. If not, it's well worth reading K. Dale Koontz, "Czech Mate: Whedon, Čapek, and the Foundations of *Dollhouse*," *Slayage*, 8.2–3(2010), http://slayageonline.com/essays/slayage30_31/koontz.pdf.

29. Alden Oreck, "The Golem," http://www.jewishvirtuallibrary.org/jsource/Judaism/Golem.html.

30. This occurs through the characters of Old Rossum and Young Rossum, the former attempting to create beings in order to subvert and supersede God as creator, whereas the younger endeavors only to streamline the process to speed production.

It is possible to read this as religion being in the past and taking a back-seat to the more recent obsession with consumerism, an idea repeated in Topher Brink's own stance wherein he mocks any theorizing of imprinting the Actives as having to do with their souls, and is clearly responsible for streamlining the process of imprinting.

31. K. Dale Koontz, "Czech Mate: Whedon, Čapek, and the Foundations of *Dollhouse*," *Slayage*, 8.2–3(2010), http://slayageonline.com/essays/slayage30_31/koontz.pdf.

32. "Epitaph One," *Dollhouse* 1.13, DVD, written Maurissa Tancharoen and Jed Whedon, by directed by David Solomon (2009: Twentieth Century Fox, 2010).

33. "Vows," *Dollhouse* 2.1, DVD, written and directed by Joss Whedon (2009: Twentieth Century Fox, 2010). Claire realizes: "I'm not even real. I'm in someone else's body and I'm afraid to give it up."

34. Editors' note: Claire Saunders' arc almost defies linear interpretation, as the role of self-determination in her fate is vexed by the under-explained circumstances prompting her to shoot Bennett Halverson, then disappear and reappear with Clyde Randolph's brain installed in her body in "The Hollow Men" (2.12). Complicating things further is the fact that, once Randolph-in-Saunders exits the "Hollow Men" narrative, the next time we see the former Dr. Saunders she has reverted to a Doll state, as Whiskey keeps watch over the abandoned Dollhouse in "Epitaph One" (1.13) and "Epitaph Two" (2.13).

35. I use the terms here as per the series itself to indicate the original subject-minds of each body and did not intend the statement to be seen as disputing identity's essential nature as constructed.

36. I owe this analysis to Lowery Woodall, III.

37. "Tattoos and Numbers: The System of Identifying Prisoners at Auschwitz," in the Holocaust Encyclopedia, available at http://www.ushmm.org/wlc/en/article.php?ModuleId=10007056.

38. "Vows," *Dollhouse* 2.1.

39. Ballard originally sees the events at the Dollhouse as repugnant, yet at the start of Season Two we see him hiring Echo in order to accomplish one of his own goals, i.e., bringing down Martin Klar. His original hard and fast lines no longer appear to be in effect. When I use the word "ghost," I mean this in terms of the fact that he's not integrated into Echo's melange of identities out of which she views herself as "Echo" in total, but rather remains Paul Ballard *with* Echo in her mind ("Epitaph Two" 2.13).

40. Sanhedrin 38b, in Alden Oreck, "The Golem," http://www.jewishvirtual library.org/jsource/Judaism/Golem.html.

41. "Briar Rose," *Dollhouse*, 1.11.

42. "Instinct," *Dollhouse* 2.2, DVD, written by Michele Fazekas and Tara Butters, directed by Marita Grabiak (2009: Twentieth Century Fox, 2010).

43. The *Oxford English Dictionary* defines eugenics as the science of improving a population by controlled breeding to increase the occurrence of desirable heritable characteristics. Eugenics propaganda promoted by the Nazis during the Second World was a racially-based system wherein the promotion of the Aryan race was at the centre of the Nazi agenda. A number of their policies were adopted from the policies carried out by California eugenicists. For more information, see Michael Berenbaum and Abraham J. Peck's *The Holocaust and History: The Known, the Unknown, the Disputed and the Re-Examined* (Bloomington: Indiana University Press, 1998).

44. It is impossible to be unaware of how problematic this statement is. However

it remains a fact that cultural memory has inscribed itself in such a manner; the Holocaust is a formative event in Jewish cultural history. This is acknowledged by Ronit Lenin in her book *Israel and the Daughters of the Holocaust: Reoccupying the Territories of Silence* (New York: Berghahn Books, 2000), 1. My argument here is not that there are not other events in Jewish history that are not just as formative in terms of persecution, or that Jewish history is defined by numerous instances of persecution, but rather that the series appears to be alluding to a specific parallel here that would entail a reference to Jewish identity in the manner that Lyotard defines "the jews" in his work *Heidegger and "the jews."*

45. I owe parts of this analysis to Tamy Burnett.

46. Primo Levi, *The Drowned and the Saved*, trans. Raymond Rosenthal (New York: Vintage Books, 1989), 83–84.

47. Brett Ashley Kaplan, "'The Bitter Residue of Death': Jorge Semprun and the Aesthetics of Holocaust Memory," *Comparative Literature*, 55: 4 (2003), 320–337, 322.

48. "Omega," *Dollhouse* 1.12, DVD, written and directed by Tim Minear (2009: Twentieth Century Fox, 2010).

49. "Epitaph Two," *Dollhouse* 2.13, written by Maurissa Tancharoen, Jed Whedon and Andrew Chamblisss, directed by David Solomon (2009: Twentieth Century Fox, 2010).

PART IV

It's a Play on Perspective

Long Views and Deep Focus on Race in the Whedonverses

On Soldiers and Sages

Problematizing the Roles of
Black Men in the Whedonverses

CANDRA K. GILL

Race and gender are common topics in Whedon scholarship, yet essays discussing these themes mainly focus on either race or gender, and many are concerned with one show or one character at a time.[1] This paper takes a composite view of characters across Whedon productions, specifically the ways in which characters who are black and male are portrayed on *Buffy the Vampire Slayer*, *Angel*, *Firefly*, *Serenity*, and *Dollhouse*.[2] This discussion focuses on characters who are human or formerly human—characters who, because of their appearance, are read by us, the audience, as black men rather than as demons or other fantastical creatures.[3] This overview approach is necessary as it helps reveal patterns in the depiction of black male characters in Joss Whedon productions.

Black Masculinity and Multidimentionality

Race and gender complicate each other. Intersectional theory, which has its roots in black feminism, offers a way of interrogating both race and gender together.[4] This is an "and" rather than an "or" approach. To look at characters in terms of both race and gender allows for a more complete understanding than looking at just race or just gender.

Multidimentionality, which evolved from intersectionality, provides a way of complicating identities in a contextual, situational manner. Where intersectionality deals with the ways in which race and gender complicate each other, multidimentionality provides further context. Athena D. Mutua describes three key "insights" that multidimentionality affords. Firstly, people

253

have "many dimensions," some of which are "embodied" (e.g., features such as "skin color, earlobe length, and eye color") and some of which are "expressive" (e.g., religion or political affiliation). In addition, some of these features are "materially relevant"—that is to say that societal privilege and status can be afforded or denied based on these dimensions. Finally, these privileges and other societal forces "interact with one another and are mutually reinforcing."[5] As a result of this, "the intersection of two or more systems of disadvantage may produce unique categories and experiences."[6] I seek to be multidimentional in the exploration of black, male characters in Whedon productions and argue that being black and being male together results in a unique category of experience for these characters that being black alone or being male alone does not.

Patricia Hill Collins observes that, "Definitions of black masculinity in the United States reflect a narrow cluster of controlling images situated within a broader framework that grants varying value to racially distinctive forms of masculinity."[7] She discusses a continuum of representations. "One end of the continuum contains images of black men as beasts who pose varying degrees of threat to white society…. The other end of the continuum holds representations of safely tamed Negroes who pose little threat to white society."[8] Touchstone black male characters on these shows can all be described as some kind of warriors, or teachers or other learned, guiding men—soldiers and sages. Some can be described as both. While this describes these men in terms of professional roles or skills, it is also important to discuss them in terms of how they relate to other characters. To do this, I have divided them into antagonists and allies. While sometimes complicated, these characters mostly fit into one or the other category. In terms of Collins' continuum, antagonists can be situated as threats, and allies can be situated as non-threats, which often plays out in terms of how black male characters interact with white women on these shows. This is not to say that these interactions are of exclusive import. They are not. But they do need to be explored, especially since white women are so often symbols of empowerment in the Whedonverses. Black male characters can usually be said to assist or infringe on that empowerment, but it's rarely, if ever, about empowering themselves.

Black men as allies are placed in auxiliary roles. These characters are not the center of the story. They are not protagonists. To discuss black male allies in the Whedonverses, we have to first look at the repeated theme of found and chosen families. In his study of found families, Jes Battis observes "both *Buffy* and *Angel*, if they can be said to embody any 'theme' other than media deconstruction, are shows about the production, maintenance and disruption of families—families we're born with, families we choose and families we stumble upon."[9] This is significant to the discussion of black male allies in the Whedonverses, as these characters do not become integrated into these families. They assist with the struggle and are often cast in roles as protectors (particularly of white women), but they are also held at metaphorical arm's length from the central characters. Black male antagonists are situated as threats to these found families.

This essay discusses Whedon's media output in a way that assumes basic familiarity with their premises. I will first discuss characters from *Buffy the Vampire Slayer* and *Angel*. I will then discuss characters from *Firefly* and *Serenity*. Finally, I will discuss *Dollhouse*'s Boyd Langton, whose character arc makes him difficult to discuss as just an antagonist or just an ally *or* as just a soldier or as just a sage.

Black Men in Buffy *and* Angel

Black men in antagonist roles on *Buffy the Vampire Slayer* are fairly straightforward. Mr. Trick, Forrest Gates, and The Shadow Men either work for the villains or are villains themselves.[10] This is embodied in the first touchstone black male character we encounter in the Whedonverses, the vampire Mr. Trick. Trick is interesting because he voices race as an issue in Sunnydale for the first time, famously declaring it's "admittedly, not a haven for the brothers—strictly the Caucasian persuasion" ("Faith, Hope, and Trick," 3.3).[11] Notably, though Trick is a vampire—and therefore arguably beyond human concerns or definitions—he identifies as a Black man. This approach to race continues to matter in his unlife even though he is no longer human. Beyond this, Trick is a foot soldier. He works for others—first Kakistos and then Sunnydale's evil mayor—having little agency until he's killed by Faith (a white woman) to save Buffy (another white woman) in "Consequences" (3.15).[12]

Forrest Gates is a professional soldier, enlisted in the U.S. Army, and a member of The Initiative, a clandestine group tasked to capture and experiment on supernatural beings. Throughout his run on the show, he repeatedly voices his belief that Buffy is a threat to Riley Finn, especially once Riley and Buffy become involved in a relationship and when it is revealed that Buffy is the Slayer. His role is almost solely to express mistrust of Buffy until he is killed. This mistrust is particularly shown in a scene in "The Yoko Factor" (4.20).[13] Forrest and Buffy run into each other while patrolling. Forrest is angry with Buffy because Riley, who is now her boyfriend, has left The Initiative, which means he has deserted his military post. When Buffy comments on Forrest patrolling alone, Forrest replies that his military family is "tearing apart." Buffy replies, "Family? What kind of family are you? Corleone?" Forrest then tells Buffy that she is the first of Riley's girlfriends to "get him to commit treason."[14] Forrest's mistrust of Buffy is interesting here in that it is framed in terms of the found families narrative common in Whedon shows.

The Initiative is Forrest's family of choice. The Initiative is also Buffy's enemy. In order for Buffy to triumph and protect her own found family, Forrest's family must be defeated.

The Shadow Men are some of the only antagonist characters that fit the role of sages. They are also some of the only black male characters that are presented as having a significant amount of agency. They use their arcane knowledge to create the first Slayer. In a scene in "Get It Done" (7.15), they forcefully try to make Buffy accept the same dark essence into her body that they used to give the first Slayer her power until Buffy overcomes them.[15] They say they cannot give Buffy knowledge—only power. But it is knowledge that they ultimately give her in the form of a glimpse of what she faces in her coming battle with the First Evil.[16] The Shadow Men represent patriarchy and are ultimately revealed to be the precursors of the Watchers. They have far more agency than Mr. Trick or Forrest Gates. They are decision makers whose actions influence the world for centuries. They also are the first of several black male characters who threaten white female characters with sexual (or sexualized) assault.[17] The image of black men as sexual threats to white women has a much-explored, involved cinematic history, from *The Birth of a Nation* on.[18] That the majority of black men on *Buffy* are antagonists—threats to be overcome—situates black men outside of any kind of empowerment narrative to be found in *Buffy*.

The sole black male ally in *Buffy the Vampire Slayer* is Season Seven's Robin Wood. In his essay "The Caucasian Persuasion" that discusses *Buffy* as a text concerned with construction of whiteness, Ewan Kirkland suggests that Robin Wood undergoes an ethnic erasure due to his Beverly Hills roots and a lack of racial markers. Kirkland states that Wood's ethnicity is attributable to his "maternal parentage, son of Slayer Nikki from "Fool for Love" (5.7) whose racial coding functions largely as kitsch shorthand locating Spike's narration temporally and geographically in 1970s New York via the Blaxploitation film cycle."[19] However, to read Wood as whitewashed both ignores the existence of black people of middle class backgrounds and erases his connection to his mother, who, as a direct reference to Blaxploitation film, cannot be read as white. This is a connection that Wood asserts in "First Date" (7.14) when he reveals that he knows about vampires and knows how to fight them.[20] In "Lies My Parents Told Me" (7.17), Wood tries to kill Spike to avenge his mother's death.[21] Wood also tries to reclaim his mother's coat from Spike, who, after having killed Nikki, claimed it as a trophy. When Wood is unable to kill Spike, Buffy chastises him for trying, saying, "The mission is what matters," echoing something Nikki says at the beginning of the episode in a flashback to Wood's childhood.[22] He is unable to reclaim his biological heritage—a heritage that is a connection to the legacy of the Slayer. At the same time, he is unable to fully become a part of the found family of the Scoobies, a marginalization Lorna Jowett notes in *Sex and the Slayer*.[23] In this way, even black male allies are left out of the empowerment narrative.

In contrast to *Buffy the Vampire Slayer*, which did not see a black male character in an ally role until its seventh and final season, *Angel* introduced Charles Gunn at the end of its first season. Michaela D.E. Meyer's insightful "From Rogue in the 'Hood to Suave in a Suit" argues that the representation of *Angel*'s Charles Gunn "is ultimately problematic. Gunn comes from the street literally, is taken in by his white counterparts and ultimately does what he can to 'whiten' himself throughout the series."[24] She discusses Gunn's arc starting from his Season One role as leader in his neighborhood to his Season Five position as a lawyer by means of mystically gained knowledge. The problem is not by any means that Gunn becomes a lawyer. The problem is how this is framed, especially when Gunn loses his knowledge and makes a Faustian bargain to retrieve it—a bargain that results in Fred Burkle's death. Meyer observes that Gunn does not want to return to who he was when we first meet him, as Gunn is repeatedly described as "the muscle" of the group. In "Shells" (5.16) when Gunn is confronted about his role in Fred's death, he says, "I couldn't go back to being just the muscle."[25] Meyer discusses the way in which Gunn's arc is racially coded and says, "The narrative frequently emphasizes Gunn's physical strength over his emotional or intellectual abilities."[26]

To expand on Meyer's essay, I would add that the show continually downplays the intelligence it took to be the community organizer Gunn was when first introduced. During his initial appearance in "War Zone" (1.20), we find that Gunn was a character who kept a group of people fed and clothed and protected them from vampires.[27] He organized patrols, found shelter, and made connections with other community groups. Angel acknowledges that Gunn "put a lot of work into this" and that it's "clever, really." But he also immediately tells Gunn, "I have a few suggestions."[28] Gunn's actions in and for his community are depicted as "less-than"—less expert and less effective—than what Angel Investigations does. This is a pattern that continues for Gunn, particularly in terms of how he sees himself in relation to the rest of the Angel Investigations team.

Throughout the show Gunn continues to be "the muscle" until he becomes a lawyer. In "Shells" (5.16), it is revealed that Gunn has had "knowledge and deductive reasoning" implanted in his brain, expertise Gunn describes as, "everything that made me different. Special."[29] Gunn doesn't feel worthy of the Angel Investigations team without this special knowledge, despite the fact that he's been an effective member of the team for years. In order to make the implantation permanent, Gunn agrees to help Wolfram & Hart with a legal hang-up, an act that unwittingly sets into motion the events that result in Fred's death.[30] The cost of him staying a lawyer is a white woman's life—a woman he previously acted against his own interests to save—which keeps him from fully being a part of the Angel Investigations family. To be fair, at this point, the entire Angel Investigations family is falling apart, not just Gunn's positioning in it. Gunn is punished for this in several ways, notably when Wesley Wyndham-Pryce uncharacteristically stabs him in retribution for Gunn's role in Fred's death.[31] In "Underneath" (5.17), Gunn volunteers to have his heart ripped out on a daily basis in pursuit of "atonement" for his role in Fred's death.[32] Gunn's reasons for enduring this punishment are noble, and he is eventually rescued.[33] But it is telling that a character whose strengths were logistics, group coordination, and tactics when we first met him endures torture to atone for his artificially gained intelligence as the show neared its end.

Black Men in Firefly and Serenity

The short-lived television series *Firefly* and its movie sequel, *Serenity*, collectively Joss Whedon's take on a space Western, offer three significant black male characters. Two soldiers fill antagonist roles: the bounty hunter Jubal Early in the episode "Objects in Space" (1.14) and the unnamed Alliance Operative in *Serenity*.[34] Derrial Book, a sage with hints of a soldier's past, is an ally.

Perhaps more than any other character in the Whedonverses, Jubal Early presents the image of the black male body as a threat. This is a powerful image that has a long history in United States culture. In his fascinating discussion of the music that accompanies Early, Neil Lerner writes that "Objects in Space" "brings questions of representation of race squarely into view, ironically by way of our ears."[35] "[The] highly effective musical score reinscribes some rather old—and traditionally racist—musical codes onto the character of Jubal."[36] Lerner compares the score with that from *The Birth of a Nation* and other racist texts.[37]

Lerner's discussion of the music is effective, but it is important to talk about Early's body as well. From the moment he sneaks onto Serenity to the moment that Mal casts him off into the void of space, Jubal Early is shown to be an invader through his actions and words—an invader who specifically threatens white women on the ship. We first see Early listening in on the crew, spying on them to determine their weaknesses. He is also shown to stealthily infiltrate Serenity. He physically incapacitates Mal and Book on screen, but it is his interaction with Kaylee that is most chilling. In it, between musing aloud to her about how he got on the ship, he asks her calmly if she has ever been raped. At one point, he tells her that if she makes a "ruckus," then her "body is forfeit. Ain't nothing but a body to me, and I can find all unseemly manner of use for it." He later manipulates Simon Tam into assisting him by again threatening to rape Kaylee, telling him, "She will die weeping if you cross me."[38] Like Buffy's Shadow Men, Jubal Early threatens a white woman with sexual violence in pursuit of his goals. Unlike the Shadow Men, however, there is not even a pretense of those goals benefitting anything other than him. Early makes threats in pursuit of his bounty because of the pleasure he takes in harming others.[39]

Lerner suggests that "while Whedon indulges in cinematic codes long associated with white racism against blacks, he complicates these by fusing the character of the bounty hunter Jubal Early with the historical figure of [Confederate] General Jubal Early."[40] The implication here is that the racist coding of Early's portrayal is tempered in some way by naming him after a Confederate general, given the anti-black racial history of the Confederacy. I would argue that if Whedon is complicating a discussion of race through Early, then he isn't complicating it enough to avoid engaging in racist or racially problematic portrayals himself. In his discussion of black people in science fiction film, Adilifu Nama observes that "black corporeality remains a source of visual spectacle and cinematic titillation in American culture."[41] While Nama suggests that portrayals of black bodies are not as extreme in their stereotypes as in the past, "American SF film still provides a representational space for repressed racial anxieties associated with black physicality as a source of revulsion, fascination, phallic fear, and desire."[42]

Though Nama deals with film, it's appropriate to apply these observations to *Firefly*, especially when taking the show's cinematic style into account. Early's body is without question a source of racialized anxiety that is also informed by gender, through both actual and threatened action. His intellectual, existentialist musings throughout neither change nor mitigate this, nor does naming him after a Confederate soldier. Early's very body is a threat, which is only overcome when Early is tricked by River into leaving Serenity, after which he is cast out into space to his death by Mal—a potent image that is contrasted by the exuberant embrace with which Mal receives River back onto the ship.[43] This moment is made all the more powerful by what it represents in the larger context of the episode. "Objects in Space" (1.14) opens with a series of discussions with Serenity's crewmembers talking about the ways in which River scares or concerns them.[44] Jubal Early's bodily threat serves to provide a common enemy against which the crew can unite. River and her strangeness may be scary, but Early is scarier. He is so scary, that, as River reveals, even his own mother rejected him for his violence.[45]

Like Early, *Serenity*'s Operative is another threatening figure, also intent on capturing River Tam. Unlike Early, however, the Operative does not pursue River for a bounty, and he does not threaten sexual violence. The Operative is sent by the Alliance to hunt River down and will stop at nothing until he captures her. When Mal confronts him about his relentlessness, specifically condemning him for murdering children, the Operative simply states, "I am a monster."[46] The Operative has so subsumed his identity into his role for the Alliance that he has no name—no identity other than his role. When asked for his rank and name, The Operative says, "I have neither." He is described by two characters as "a believer," which is the source of his motivation. Book tells Mal, "The sort of man they like to send believes hard. Kills and never asks why." Inara tells Mal, "Because he's a believer. He's intelligent, methodical, and devout in his belief that killing River is the right thing to do." The Operative confirms this himself: "I believe in something greater than myself. A better world." It is a world he's willing to sacrifice for, to commit monstrous acts for, even though "There's no place for me there."[47]

The Operative does not waver until he is confronted with video evidence that the Alliance is responsible for creating the terrible Reavers by experimenting on their own citizens. At the end of the video, the woman narrating is tortured by Reavers, with the audience only hearing her screams. It is obviously supposed to be the information about the Reavers that causes the Operative to finally act against his Alliance orders, but it is especially telling that the result of Alliance action that inspires his change of heart involves seeing a white woman tortured.[48]

In his discussion of American racialized constructions of masculinity in the context of the Civil War, Christopher Looby states that "Manhood in America is crucially dependent upon a dialectic of racial difference; categories of gender and sexuality are inextricably entangled with racial identities."[49] He goes on to discuss the ways in which white masculinity is defined against black masculinity, situating black men as Other.[50] Jubal Early and The Operative fill the role of the Other against which Mal is defined. Early and The Operative are both physical threats to Serenity and its crew. From the first scene in which we encounter The Operative, he kills with elegance and precision. He is equally comfortable killing face-to-face or attacking from a distance. He kills with a purpose, as a means to an end.[51] We never see Jubal Early kill, though we have no reason not to believe he is capable of doing so. He uses threats to manipulate the crew, most notably, the repeated threat to rape Kaylee. In both cases, these are physical threats that Mal, the white male protagonist, must physically overcome to protect his crew in general and specifically white women Kaylee and River. The nature of the threat matters here. Early, the sexual threat, is left to drift in space with only his space suit—a death sentence.[52] The Operative, the killer who has a change of heart, is allowed to live.[53]

Of *Firefly*, Jes Battis says, "The idea of choosing a support system rather than relying on a biological family is, I think, more apparent from the beginning in *Firefly* than it ever was in *Buffy* and *Angel*."[54] *Serenity* continues to explore Mal Reynolds' crew as a chosen family. Shepherd Derrial Book, a black male ally, is featured in both. Book is a member of a Christian monastic order that informs his character throughout the TV show and film. In this role, he often makes it a point to protect vulnerable (or perceived to be vulnerable) people, especially white women such as River and Saffron. Saffron, of course, does not need protecting, but that doesn't keep Book from warning Mal of condemnation in a "special hell" if Mal consummates the marriage he unwittingly entered into with her ("Our Mrs. Reynolds" 1.6).[55]

It is worth noting that in direct contrast to Early and The Operative, Book is clearly presented as not being a physical threat to the crew of The Serenity. This is not to say that he is *not* a physical threat. Early considers Book to be enough of a threat to incapacitate him without a word when he infiltrates Serenity, for example.[56] But when it comes to Book's interaction with the crew, the most notable instance where Book's body is a factor in *Firefly* is played for laughs. In humorous scenes in "Jaynestown" (1.7), River is frightened when she sees Book's long, natural hair let out, rather than pulled back as he usually wears it.[57] His body is literally a joke. Book's beliefs complicate his relationship with Mal. In "Serenity Part 1 & 2" (1.1), Book states that he is not sure he is in the right place on Serenity.[58] He is a monk amongst smugglers and thieves. Mal has no time for religion, yet still he often listens to Book's council. Throughout *Firefly* and *Serenity*, there are also hints of Book's military background, making him a sage and a likely former soldier.[59]

Between *Firefly* and *Serenity*, Book leaves the ship. Shortly after we meet him again in *Serenity*, Book is killed in a raid authorized by The Operative. In his essay "The Good Shepherd," Eric Greene notes that Book's death galvanizes Mal, "shows him that he cannot remain just an observer, that he cannot forever run."[60] Book becomes an inspiration for Mal, but having left Serenity, he isn't part of the family (something Greene also observes[61]). Book says as he dies, "I'm not one of your crew."[62] Mal answers that he is, but Book's dying moments later would seem to negate that.[63] Like Wood and Gunn, Book gets close to the core group but is not wholly a part of it.

The Strange Case of Boyd Langton

Dollhouse's Boyd Langton embodies multiple roles. We see him as an ally and as an antagonist. A helper and a threat. A soldier and a sage. This is unique in all of the portrayals of Black men on Whedon's shows. Up until this point, we have seen Black male characters as clear allies or as antagonists. To see these roles presented in one person is an invitation to explore the contextual strategies of the overall positioning of black men in Whedon productions.

Up until the last few episodes of *Dollhouse*, Boyd Langton's role as Echo's Handler seemingly embodies the same positioning of other black male allies on Whedon shows. He is extremely protective of Echo and later of Claire Saunders and even Adelle DeWitt. He is given a backstory that puts him in the role of a soldier, specifically as a law enforcement officer. This is later emphasized on the show when he is promoted to Head of Security of DeWitt's Dollhouse. Throughout the series, he appears to be uncomfortable with the Dollhouse and with using people as living Dolls. He makes comments that reveal that he is skeptical about the Dollhouse's claims. In "Ghost" (1.1), Langton states, "I've been here long enough to know that you like to tell yourself what we do helps people."[64] This is not the comment of a true believer, especially when taking into account how Harry Lennix delivers the line. This is the comment of a skeptic. Langton constantly asks questions of DeWitt, Topher Brink, and other characters running the Dollhouse but he seems to never fully accept what they do. He also seems to try to get them to ask questions. In "Gray Hour" (1.4), when Topher says of the Dolls, "They volunteered for this," Langton replies, "So we're told."[65] At this point, Topher doesn't have any reservations about his work at the Dollhouse, but Langton appears to want Topher to examine more closely what he does. Langton's apparent questioning of and skepticism about the Dollhouse continue throughout the series.

Everything changes at the end of "Getting Closer" (2.11) when Langton is revealed to be the mysterious—and until that point anonymous—head of the Rossum Corporation.[66] He moves from protector to threat and, interestingly, from soldier to sage. Re-watching the series knowing Langton is the founder of the Rossum Corporation reframes his questioning as a kind of almost Socratic inquiry that allows him to assess DeWitt, Brink, and others who all thought of Langton as a subordinate. He fills the role of a learned man who wants to see if others are worthy of his vision for the world.

When Langton reveals himself to DeWitt, Brink, and Caroline in "The Hollow Men" (2.12), he tells them that he chose them, saying, "You're here 'cause you're my family. I love you guys."[67] When they reject this, Langton orders Caroline's spinal fluid to be forcefully taken from her with a harvesting machine that entraps her, penetrates her with needles, and causes her great pain. He does this in order to make a vaccine against imprinting. This is another example of a black male character assaulting a white female character in a sexualized manner in order to make use of her body. This also reframes Boyd's protectiveness of Echo/Caroline—it is literally her body that he needs and therefore needs to protect, not her personality. Echo/Caroline is ultimately rescued from Boyd's harvesting machine by Priya, another Doll. When she thanks Priya, Priya replies, "We're family." Echo rejects this, saying, "Call us whatever you want, just not family."[68] Not only is Langton not accepted into a found family here, but Langton's claim of family taints the very term for Echo.

Langton is arguably Whedon's most complex black male character. He has the most power and agency since *Buffy*'s Shadow Men. And like the Shadow Men, he uses his power in a way that endangers the white, female protagonist by violating her body. Unlike the Shadow Men, who transformed the original Slayer by giving her power and sought to force a certain kind of power on Buffy, Boyd seeks to take power from Caroline.

It matters that the most powerful black men in Whedon productions use that power in service of patriarchal control. A simple way to look at this is to see these men as emblematic of patriarchy in the ways that many men in general are portrayed in Whedon productions. But if we look at these portrayals from a multidimensional perspective, we see that the kinds of oppression black men can face are rarely if ever explored here. They are portrayed as threats to white female protagonists using the language and imagery of racialized anxiety, or they are portrayed as helpers, but only if their own needs are put aside.

With Whedon, critics often argue that there is more going on than what is on the surface. This is especially true when discussing portrayals that can be interpreted in a way that shows Whedon as less than progressive. Perhaps Whedon and his collaborators mean for these depictions to be more complicated than they appear. That said, the surface images, complicated or not, are powerful and are imbued with deep cultural history that may require more time and effort to effectively interrogate. Black men in Whedon productions are situated along a continuum of antagonist to ally. The story is rarely about them, but rather about the ways in which they impact other characters who are usually white and often female.

Each of the productions discussed is closed—the series have all ended. They may continue in other media, such as comic books, but as televised documents they are complete. So where does this leave us? In terms of Joss Whedon productions, it remains to be seen if Whedon is capable of offering a more complex take on race in general and black men in particular. There is already more to explore. Since *Dollhouse* was canceled, there have been other Joss Whedon productions that have featured black male characters including *Cabin in the Woods*, a film which Whedon co-wrote, and *The Avengers*, a film which he wrote and directed. Both feature black male characters who, interestingly enough, can be defined as soldiers and sages. Given that Nick Fury is a character that Joss Whedon did not create, it would be particularly interesting for someone to take the analysis laid out here and apply it to Whedon's version of *The Avengers*' Nick Fury. But that is a discussion for another paper. For now, it remains to be seen if black men can have a place in the center of Joss Whedon's empowerment narratives.

NOTES

1. Several examples of such essays are discussed in this essay. Some that are not particular to this paper, but are worth reading include two early works in Whedon scholarship: Frances Early's "Staking Her Claim: Buffy the Vampire Slayer as Transgressive Woman Warrior," which explores Buffy's warrior role in terms of her being a female character, and Kent Ono's "To Be a Vampire on *Buffy the Vampire Slayer*: Race and ('Other') Socially Marginalizing Positions on Horror TV," which explores the role of race in early seasons of *Buffy*. Frances H. Early, "Staking Her Claim: Buffy the Vampire Slayer as Transgressive Woman Warrior" in *Journal of Popular Culture* 35, no 3 (2001): 11–27; Kent Ono, "To Be a Vampire on *Buffy the Vampire Slayer*: Race and ('Other') Socially Marginalizing Positions on Horror TV" in *Fantasy Girls: Gender in the New Universe of Science Fiction and Fantasy Television*, ed. Elyce Rae Helford (Lanham, MD: Rowman & Littlefield, 2000), 163–186.

2. The scope of this essay does not include works in other media, such as tie-in novels or comic book series.

3. Consider this in contrast to a character like Sweet, the villain from the *Buffy the Vampire Slayer* episode "Once More with Feeling" (6.7). Sweet is portrayed by a black actor, Hinton Battle, and the character has a number of racial markers; however, he is also clearly a demon without a human face or background. In the world of the show, he is not a black man. For the purposes of this discussion, the focus is on characters who are or have been black men within the worlds of the shows. "Once More with Feeling," *Buffy the Vampire Slayer* 6.7, DVD, written by Joss Whedon, directed by Joss Whedon (2001: Twentieth Century Fox, 2006).

4. Kimberlé Williams Crenshaw, a legal scholar and one of the preeminent figures attached to the Critical Race Theory movement is widely credited with the creation of the term "intersectionality." If you are interested in further reading related to intersectional theory, please see the following: Kimberlé Williams Crenshaw, "Demarginalizing the Intersection of Race and Sex: A Black Feminist Critique of Antidiscremination Doctrine, Feminist Theory and Antirasicist Politics," *University of Chicago Legal Forum*, Vol. 139, 1989, and Kimberlé Williams Crenshaw, "Mapping the Margins: Intersectionality, Identity Politics, and Violence Against Women of Color," *Stanford Law Review*, Vol. 43 (6), 1991, pp. 1241–1299.

For a history of black feminist thought/theory development please see: Patricia Hill Collins, *Black Feminist Thought: Knowledge, Consciousness, and the Politics of Empowerment* (London: Routledge, 1999) (Revised 10th Edition). bell hooks, *Ain't I a Woman: Black Women and Feminism* (Cambridge, MA: South End Press 1999).

For more on interrogating race and gender together, please see Athena D. Mutua, "Theorizing Progressive Black Masculinities," in *Progressive Black Masculinities*, ed. Athena D. Mutua (New York: Routledge, 2006), 21–22.

5. Athena D. Mutua, "Theorizing Progressive Black Masculinities, 22–24.

6. *Ibid.*, 22–24.

7. Patricia Hill Collins, "A Telling Difference: Dominance, Strength, and Black Masculinities," in *Progressive Black Masculinities*, ed. Athena D. Mutua (New York: Routledge, 2006), 75.

8. *Ibid.*, 75.

9. Jes Battis, *Blood Relations: Chosen Families in* Buffy the Vampire Slayer *and* Angel (Jefferson, NC: McFarland, 2005), 17.

10. I explored these characters specifically in terms of race in a previous essay: Candra K. Gill, "'Cuz the Black Chick Always Gets It First: Dynamics of Race in *Buffy*

the Vampire Slayer," in *Girls Who Bite Back: Witches, Mutants, Slayers and Freaks*, ed. Emily Pohl-Weary (Toronto: Sumach Press, 2004), 39–55.

11. "Faith, Hope & Trick," *Buffy the Vampire Slayer* 3.3, DVD, written by David Greenwalt, directed by James A. Contner (1998: Twentieth Century Fox, 2006).

12. "Consequences," *Buffy the Vampire Slayer* 3.15, DVD, written by Marti Noxon, directed by Michael Gershman (1999: Twentieth Century Fox, 2006).

13. "The Yoko Factor," *Buffy the Vampire Slayer* 4.20, DVD, written by Doug Petrie, directed by David Grossman (2000: Twentieth Century Fox, 2006).

14. *Ibid.*

15. "Get It Done," *Buffy the Vampire Slayer* 7.15, written and directed by Douglas Petrie (2003: Twentieth Century Fox, 2004).

16. *Ibid.*

17. *Ibid.*

18. For example, in his book *Black Space*, which is cited later in this essay in the section on *Firefly*, Adilifu Nama discusses *The Birth of a Nation*'s depiction of black men as rapists of white women and the way in which the racial anxieties encoded in this depiction play out in science fiction film. Adilifu Nama, *Black Space: Imagining Race in Science Fiction Film* (Austin: University of Texas Press, 2008), 43.

19. Ewan Kirkland, "The Caucasian Persuasion of *Buffy the Vampire Slayer*," *Slayage: The Online International Journal of Buffy Studies*, 5, no. 1 (2005), http://slayageonline.com/Numbers/slayage17.htm.

20. "First Date," *Buffy the Vampire Slayer* 7.14, DVD, written by Jane Espenson, directed by David Grossman (2003: Twentieth Century Fox, 2004).

21. "Lies My Parents Told Me," *Buffy the Vampire Slayer* 7.17, DVD, written by David Fury and Drew Goddard, directed by David Fury (2003: Twentieth Century Fox, 2004).

22. *Ibid.*

23. Lorna Jowett, *Sex and the Slayer: A Gender Studies Primer for the* Buffy *Fan* (Middleton, CT: Wesleyan University Press, 2005), 142; *Buffy the Vampire Slayer*, "Lies My Parents Told Me," 7.17.

24. Michaela D.E. Meyer, "From Rogue in the 'Hood to Suave in a Suit: Black Masculinity and the Transformation of Charles Gunn," in *Reading* Angel: *The Spin-Off with a Soul*, eds. Rhonda V. Wilcox and Tanya R. Cochran (London: I.B. Tauris, 2005), 177.

25. "Shells," *Angel* 5.16, DVD, written by Stephen S. DeKnight, directed by Stephen S. DeKnight (2004: Twentieth Century Fox, 2004).

26. Meyer, "From Rogue in the 'Hood to Suave in a Suit," 182–183.

27. "War Zone," *Angel* 1.20, DVD, written by Garry Campbell, directed by David Straiton (2000: Twentieth Century Fox, 2002).

28. *Angel*, "War Zone," 1.20.

29. *Angel*, "Shells," 5.16.

30. *Ibid.*

31. *Ibid.*

32. "Underneath," *Angel* 5.17, DVD, written Sarah Fain & Elizabeth Craft, directed by Skip Schoolnik (2004: Twentieth Century Fox, 2004).

33. Illyria rescues Gunn at the beginning of "Time Bomb" (5.19), which is significant for two reasons: (1) she is powerful enough to rescue Gunn where others in the group could not. (2) Illyria is the entity that took over Fred's body, killing Fred, and who continues to inhabit Fred's body. Gunn is therefore rescued by the being who killed Fred, the death for which Gunn was seeking atonement. "Time Bomb,"

Angel 5.19, DVD, written by Ben Edlund, directed by Vern Gillum (2004: Twentieth Century Fox, 2004).

34. "Objects in Space," *Firefly* 1.14, DVD, written by Joss Whedon, directed by Joss Whedon (2002: Twentieth Century Fox 2003); *Serenity* Collector's Edition, DVD, Joss Whedon (2005; Universal City, CA: Universal Studios Home Entertainment, 2007).

35. Neil Lerner, "Music, Race, and Paradoxes of Representation: Jubal Early's Musical Motif of Barbarism in 'Objects in Space,'" in *Investigating* Firefly *and* Serenity: *Science Fiction on the Frontier*, eds. Rhonda Wilcox and Tanya R. Cochran (London: I.B. Tauris, 2008), 183.

36. *Ibid.*, 184.

37. *Ibid.*, 186–188.

38. *Firefly*, "Objects in Space," 1.14.

39. *Ibid.*

40. Lerner, "Music, Race, and Paradoxes of Representation," 189.

41. Adilifu Nama, *Black Space*, 95.

42. *Ibid.*, 95.

43. *Firefly*, "Objects in Space," 1.14.

44. *Ibid.*

45. *Ibid.*

46. *Serenity* Collector's Edition.

47. *Ibid.*

48. *Ibid.*

49. Looby offers a fascinating discussion of the white male gaze on black male bodies, specifically situating it in Civil War military interactions between a white commanding officer and the black soldiers he commands. Christopher Looby, "'As Thoroughly Black as the Most Faithful Philanthropist Could Desire': Erotics of Race in Higginson's *Army Life in a Black Regiment*," in *Race and the Subject of Masculinities*, eds. Harry Stecopoulos and Michael Uebel (Durham, NC: Duke University Press, 1997), 71.

50. *Ibid.*, 71.

51. *Serenity* Collector's Edition.

52. *Firefly*, "Objects in Space," 1.14.

53. *Serenity* Collector's Edition.

54. Battis, *Blood Relations*, 160.

55. "Our Mrs. Reynolds," *Firefly* 1.6, DVD, written by Joss Whedon, directed by Vondie Curtis Hall (2002: Twentieth Century Fox, 2003).

56. Early also notably says "That ain't a shepherd" when another character asks him why he attacked Book. *Firefly*, "Objects in Space" (1.14).

57. "Jaynestown," Firefly (1.4), DVD, written by Ben Edlund, directed by Marita Grabiak (2002: Twentieth Century Fox, 2003).

58. "Serenity Part 1 & 2," *Firefly* (1.12), DVD, written by Joss Whedon, directed by Joss Whedon (2002: Twentieth Century Fox, 2003).

59. *Firefly* often hinted at Book's backstory, but we were never given definitive details about his past. Given *Firefly's* short run, it is reasonable to believe that more of his history might have been explored in later seasons of the show if the show had lasted longer. It is also reasonable to believe that Book was meant to remain a mysterious figure on the show. Comic books are outside of the scope of this essay, but readers may be interested in a *Serenity: The Shepherd's Tale*, a single-issue comic that depicts Book's life before he joined the crew of Serenity. Joss Whedon, Zack Whedon,

and Chris Samnee, *Serenity: The Shepherd's Tale* (Milwaukie, OR: Dark Horse Books, 2010).

60. Eric Greene, "The Good Book," in *Serenity Found: More Unauthorized Essays on Joss Whedon's* Firefly *Universe*, ed. Jane Epenson (Dallas: BenBella Books, 2007), 88.

61. Greene, "The Good Book," 92.

62. *Serenity* Collector's Edition.

63. *Ibid.*

64. "Ghost," *Dollhouse* 1.1, Netflix, written by Joss Whedon, directed by Joss Whedon (2009: Twentieth Century Fox).

65. "Gray Hour," *Dollhouse* 1.4, Netflix, written by Sarah Fain & Elizabeth Craft, directed by Rod Hardy (2009: Twentieth Century Fox).

66. "Getting Closer," *Dollhouse* 2.11, Netflix, written by Tim Minear, directed by Tim Minear (2010: Twentieth Century Fox).

67. "The Hollow Men," *Dollhouse* 2.12, Netflix, written by Michele Fazekas, Tara Butters, and Tracy A. Bellomo, directed by Terrence O'Hara (2010: Twentieth Century Fox).

68. *Ibid.*

The Godmothers of Them All

*Female-Centered Blaxploitation Films
and the Heroines of Joss Whedon*

MASANI MCGEE

For all his nuanced portrayals of concepts like women's issues and adolescent coming-of-age, Joss Whedon has frustratingly relied on caricature
when it comes to the subject of race. *Buffy the Vampire Slayer* villain Mr.
Trick or even major characters like *Angel*'s Charles Gunn are at least in part
defined by racial clichés such as the thug or the streetwise con-man. An interesting example comes in the case of minor character Nikki Wood, a deceased
Slayer that is the mother of *Buffy* character Robin Wood. During her first
appearance in the episode "Fool for Love" (5.7), she is initially shown as little
more than an ersatz for the Blaxploitation heroines popularized by Pam Grier
during the 1970s.[1] Though she is merely a plot point within the series, Wood
is presented in a way that has interesting repercussions, both for Whedon's
problems concerning race and the portrayal of women in the series as a whole.
For all this talk of caricatures, it is strange that Nikki Wood is treated in such
a dismissive way—especially given that much of the Whedonverses, specifically the female heroines that populate them, would not exist in their current
state without the efforts of women like Grier and the genre they helped define.

During the 1970s, the influence of the Black Power movement led to a
surge of African American centered films called "Blaxploitation" for their
stereotypical depictions of the minority group. For the most part, Blaxploitation concerned the tales and battles of male protagonists; however, a particular subset of the genre contained the first portrayals of black women in
dominant, action-oriented roles. With characters such as Foxy Brown, Cleopatra Jones, and T.N.T. Jackson, the films were often as famous for the hypersexuality of their protagonists as they were for portraying strong leads, which
led to frequent criticism. Nonetheless, these films are credited by some schol-

ars with reshaping both the action film and the expectations of how women could be portrayed in film. Recent scholarship has seen serious consideration of the impact female-centered Blaxploitation films have on the modern action heroine. Stephane Dunn's *"Baad Bitches" and Sassy Supermamas: Black Power Action Films*, and Yvonne Sims' *Women of Blaxploitation: How the Black Action Film Heroine Changed American Popular Culture* are especially thorough in explaining how each deals with the lasting effects of the genre on popular culture, African American womanhood, and sexuality. However, with the exception of occasional references to *Buffy the Vampire Slayer*, there is no current scholarship that specifically explores the connection between Blaxploitation and the women at the center of Whedon's series.[2]

Though Whedon's creations and Blaxploitation each originated from very different sets of circumstances, they both are concerned with very similar subjects at heart, specifically the expression of sexuality, power, and identity. The original cycle of Blaxploitation films was developed and released during a time of considerable political and social upheaval, which had a strong impact on how gender and race were portrayed within them. Whedon's series, on the other hand, tend to avoid direct political commentary, meaning any discussion there is will be cloaked by metaphor or the tropes of whatever genre he happens to be working in. The pressing issue here, then, is how those subjects are characterized, and what it means for Whedon to appropriate the ground that was originally laid by female-centered Blaxploitation films. This essay will explore the legacy of female-centered Blaxploitation as characterized by the works of Joss Whedon, with a specific focus on how his work appropriates the ground laid by this genre and what it means for primarily white characters to interpret and claim concepts that have their basis in African American culture.

Sexuality

The physical appearance of women that was so essential to the original cycle of female-centered Blaxploitation films also contributes to the popularity of modern-day action heroines, if only for the practical purpose of attracting a larger male audience. Dunn argues that the sexual allure of the protagonists in Pam Grier's films is connected to the characters' agency; they gain power through their sexuality.[3] Foxy Brown and Coffy are in many ways defined by their ability and willingness to use their physical appearance to tempt and deceive their enemies, with both posing as prostitutes in order to gain information about the adversaries they face. In the former film, the protagonist has no problem using her body to humiliate a city judge who has paid for her services, and it is made clear by his and the audiences' gaze on her semi-nude body that he will do little to resist. Modern action heroines find similar ways for their sexuality to benefit them, yet it can also be seen that ways of thinking about sex are confronted in ways that Blaxploitation did not have the opportunity to explore. As an inheritor of the concepts established by Blaxploitation, Whedon's heroines find ways to address, challenge, and in some cases uphold how sexuality was explored within the genre.

The sexual power of physical appearance often extends to what characters wear; *Buffy the Vampire Slayer* and Blaxploitation films both demonstrate that how female characters dress is connected to their agency. Clothing can allow these women to assume multiple identities, subvert the expectations of others due to pre-conceived notions about femininity, and make an individualized declaration of the authority they possess. Grier's undercover work as a prostitute in both *Coffy* and *Foxy Brown* is characterized by her dress, which serves as something akin to a superhero's costume. For example, in the former film she uses her wig as a weapon by hiding razor blades within it to fell a prostitute competitor. The film *Cleopatra Jones* uses clothing to demonstrate the protagonist's power, with the often-outlandish costumes signifying her refusal to bow to anyone's standards other than her own. While Whedon does not place the same type of emphasis on his heroines' clothing, apparel still plays a significant role in their characterization. Buffy Summers' love of clothing connects her to the "normal" teenage life she's lost, in addition to functioning as a comment on the discrepancy between her appearance as a "girly-girl" and the immense power she possesses as a warrior.[4] And much like Grier before her, she uses her appearance as a weapon by playing on her enemies' expectations about what femininity encompasses.

With that in mind, Whedon's *Dollhouse* could be seen as a continuation and perhaps deconstruction of how clothing and appearance function as tools to achieve one's goals and as markers of personal identity and power. The protagonist Echo lives in the Dollhouse, an underground facility that imprints their "Dolls" with various identities for the pleasure of paying clients. The imprinted personalities (in addition to the inevitable clothing changes they require) could be seen as a type of "costume" that protagonist Echo assumes. Unlike the representation provided by *Cleopatra Jones*, however, Echo does not (initially) have agency in her actions, as her ability to assume these different personas is controlled by others. Echo's exploitation is not only perpetrated by the Dollhouse itself but by her original identity of Caroline Farrell. The crimes that Caroline has committed in the past working as a terrorist against the Rossum Corporation haunt Echo in the future. Ironically, the technology that has oppressed Echo and the rest of the Dolls is also the key to her salvation, as a "composite event" that allowed Echo to contain multiple personalities inside her mind also allows her to form an identity that is uniquely hers. This process ensures that the "clothing" she wears is no longer a façade, and each fractured personality becomes a distinct part of a cohesive whole that has sole determination over her actions.

Because of the way Blaxploitation used appearance to accomplish personal goals, Whedon's series have not only been able to continue that tradition, but they have found ways to critique and challenge the tactic on their own terms. Yet these shows also do not have to face the stigma that is often associated with African American female sexuality. As Gwendolyn D. Pough asserts, "black women ... cannot opt to leave their peculiarities at the door. They are physically marked as Black and female, and these are two sources of their oppression."[5] Echo may have the ability to be whoever she wants and Buffy can play with the expectations of others, but having those choices is a luxury—no matter how many disguises Coffy or Foxy Brown puts on, they are still African American women and that will affect every social interaction they have with others. Despite the power they can gain over others from their appearance, they will inevitably operate at a disadvantage.

Whedon has improved upon how heroines use their physical appearance to their advantage in ways that Blaxploitation films could not have accomplished due to both structural and cultural factors. In other areas, however, there are some disturbing trends regarding women's sexuality. Many of his characters have some measure of sexual agency, but some consider those depictions to be narrow, especially in the case of characters like Buffy and Faith.[6] Buffy experiences feelings of shame and disgust for transgressing outside of sexual norms with Spike. Likewise, Faith is characterized as the "bad girl" for her enjoyment of fetishistic sex. The tendency for Whedon's characters to be "punished" in some way for their sexual behavior in many ways mirrors the same type of criticism directed at Blaxploitation heroines and their actresses, who were often condemned for playing overtly sexual characters.[7] This condemnation rarely seems to extend to his male characters, who are typically free to engage in various sexual activities with little or no repercussion.

Female characters in Whedon's series are punished for their sexual behavior, but in comparison to Pam Grier's characters, their treatment lacks the same type of social framework. In *Coffy*, for example, the protagonist is forced to grovel at the feet of a racist mob boss; she begs to "have his precious white body" before he spits in her face.[8] Even though Coffy is attempting to use this situation to her own advantage, Vitroni himself is intent on humiliating her for her sexuality and her race. Given the similar events that happen later in the film, there is a sense that Coffy is continually being punished for those aforementioned traits. *Foxy Brown* is perhaps even more extreme in its approach to castigating Foxy's sexuality, as this time the main character is actually raped. Dunn argues that incidents like these bring up the specter of slavery and the abuses committed against black women, but do not truly address them.[9] The punishment that women receive for their sexuality in

Blaxploitation is always situated within the context of African American history. Whedon's heroines, however, are in many cases very detached from the social and political contexts of their sex.

Rather than the physical abuse suffered by Coffy and Foxy Brown, Whedon's heroines are often forced to suffer emotional pain. The most obvious example here would be Buffy's relationship with Spike, which is characterized by sadomasochistic activities. When she finally admits that she is sleeping with Spike, for whom until this point she felt mostly contempt and disgust, she has this reaction: "It's wrong. I'm wrong. Tell me that I'm wrong, please… (6.13)."[10] Other candidates include Faith, who is exceedingly promiscuous and often unapologetic about being so. But after sleeping with Buffy's then-boyfriend Riley Finn during a body-switch mishap, she is visibly distressed that he is actually in love with Buffy, and was not solely interested in her for sex. Gwyn Symonds argues that "we need to consider whether the show is in danger of promoting the disempowering message that indulging in sexual pleasure inevitably leads to some form of penalty and that the expression of desire always threatens life, self-esteem, and one's sense of self."[11] The anguish that female characters are made to feel about their sexuality is certainly not the same as the repeated sexual assault that Pam Grier's characters experienced, but it does leave a lasting impact on the viewer. Characterizing female pleasure as something to be punished creates many problematic implications for a supposedly feminist text.

Portrayals in Blaxploitation and Whedon are torn between encouraging and condemning sexual behavior in women. It's important to note that all of these texts are created by white men; one wonders how much that encourages various depictions of sexuality. Dunn writes that Jack Hill, the writer and director of *Coffy* and *Foxy Brown*, gives often-contradictory views on the portrayal of race and gender in his films, which could possibly explain why there are discrepancies between the characters' status as strong women and the often-degrading treatment they suffer in their respective films.[12] His views on who those characters should be were determined not only by his status as a white male, but as a result of how African Americans were viewed during the seventies.

As for Whedon, Jennifer Crusie offers an interesting perspective on the characterization of sex within *Buffy* that could apply to all of Whedon's series—she frames the issue as being partially a result of reader versus authorial interpretations: "The continued insistence throughout Season Six that this relationship is wrong, unhealthy, symbolic of something evil and immoral is not only inexplicable but annoying, which is probably why so many viewers are unhappy with the direction the series takes in the sixth season: they were reading a different metaphor than the writers intended."[13] From this standpoint, the viewer can choose to read Buffy and Spike's relationship as something ultimately positive. Given some of the events of the series, that may be difficult to accomplish, but it does say something about who has authority in the relationship between creator and viewer. The concept of power—who has it, and how it is used—is significant to understanding the connections between Blaxploitation and Whedon.

Power

The relationship that the women of Blaxploitation and Whedon's heroines have to power is often related to fighting those who abuse it. Certain examples, such as Cleopatra Jones and Buffy do fight for a greater good; though they use vastly different methods, each of these women believes in a sense of equity and does her utmost to see that it is upheld in her respective sphere. Some have a more personal outlook in regard to unfair treatment; Coffy does see the institutionalized abuse within her city in a broad sense, but is primarily concerned with avenging her younger sister, who was preyed on by the drug dealers in their neighborhood.[14] Other protagonists have a more ambiguous relationship with injustice, such as *Firefly*'s Zoe Washburn; they desire to see the wrongs done to them corrected, but they also must consider the needs of others and their own personal values. The methods used by action heroines to redress injustices have become increasingly nuanced as action films have moved from Blaxploitation to modern day works. And in each case but the last, the character's race has a significant impact on their ability to fight against abuses of power.

In most Blaxploitation films featuring Pam Grier, revenge has been at least a partial motive for the protagonist's actions, and her characters often find themselves operating outside of the law in order to accomplish their goals. Critic Hilary Neroni emphasizes that female Blaxploitation heroines, unlike their male counterparts, still operate on the side of the law even if they are not explicitly associated with it.[15] While it is true that the motivations of protagonists similar to Grier's tend to be based in a desire to help family or loved ones, it would be inaccurate to say that female heroines are completely aligned with the interests of the law. The film *Coffy* depicts the main character as having an antagonistic if not outright abusive relationship with authority figures; for example, police officer McHenry is not only corrupt, but is also prepared to stand by while the protagonist is injected with a (supposedly) fatal amount of heroin and almost raped. The cultural background of the Black Power movement ensures that the audience will sympathize with Coffy, seeing the criminal and political forces she must face as another example of how African Americans of the period were beset on all sides by institutions that sought their continued marginalization. The idea of vengeance in Pam Grier's Blaxploitation films is very closely tied to race and discrimination. Conversely, the portrayal of fellow heroine Cleopatra Jones can be correlated to a desire to see a strong black woman depicted as not only an agent of justice, but also as a legally-recognized figure of authority.

Unlike the majority of Blaxploitation protagonists, Cleopatra Jones works within the context of a legal institution designated to dispense justice.[16] Dunn characterizes her as a genuine "crime fighter" who does not fit into the traditional depictions of female Blaxploitation heroines.[17] Critics consider her to be a representation of a positive black role model that still maintains her racial identity.[18] While Cleo is depicted as caring deeply about her community, it is still significant that she is a part of an established system. Because she is not working against that system of authority, she maintains a level of respectability that eludes other Blaxploitation heroines as well as the protagonists of Whedon's series. Sims highlights the character's ability to challenge convention, stating "Cleo's authority and sexuality dominate the screen and represent a significant redefinition of racial and gender roles because her occupation … is one that has been traditionally reserved for white men."[19] Jones radiates an almost regal sense of command because she understands the authority she possesses as a black woman within a traditional power structure. She is an authority figure in the most traditional sense, making the power she wields an oddity within both Blaxploitation and Whedon's works.

If Coffy, Foxy Brown, and Cleopatra Jones cannot escape the fact that their race defines their relationship to power, then *Firefly*'s Zoe might demonstrate a different relationship with the institutions she encounters. While skin color may influence definitions of the previously mentioned characters, in *Firefly* it becomes a non-issue—race is not just downplayed for certain characters, it is arguably ignored for everyone. As a result, Zoe can engage with power structures in a way that reflects all of the heroines before her. Removing race from Zoe's equation allows her to use both vengeance and justice-aligned models of action when dealing with institutions in the series. While she never explicitly seeks revenge against the Alliance, it is also clear that she still harbors a great deal of resentment towards them. Even as an outsider within the system the Alliance has created, she and her crew have developed a distinct code of morality that determines how, when, and on whom they pass judgment.

A prime example of Zoe's ethical code comes in the film *Serenity*, where she is prepared to question her own Captain Malcolm Reynolds, when he proposes unsavory methods to fight the Alliance: "Sir, do you really mean to turn our home into an abomination so that we can make a suicidal attempt at passing through Reaver space?"[20] Zoe is willing to follow Mal through almost anything, but because he is proposing to violate the code of ethics they have always shared as soldiers, she has no problem calling him out on his actions. Rarely will Zoe engage in any action that is merely revenge for the sake of revenge; the needs of her crew and the moral rectitude of the situation are always considered first. She follows a justice-based moral code that, while not a part of a recognized institution (or even legal at times), is very much concerned with fairness for all parties.

While Zoe can be said to benefit from the erasure of race within *Firefly*, it is still important to consider whether or not it's valid to create a world where race is a non-issue. While the characters appear to live in a culturally-plural universe with little or no trouble, it is still inevitable that skin color will be noticed by viewers at some point. This brings attention to the tendency of science fiction to showcase utopian situations within its texts: while *Firefly* is mostly dystopian in form and structure, the idea of making race irrelevant is a utopian gesture. Toni Morrison argues that "the habit of ignoring race is understood to be a graceful, even generous liberal gesture. To notice is to recognize an already discredited difference. To enforce its invisibility through silence is to allow the black body a shadowless participation in the dominant cultural body."[21] Creating a world where race is unimportant is a grand gesture, but as it stands, race is too significant to the viewer to completely ignore how it might affect Zoe's life and how she engages with power structures. This is especially jarring considering that she is involved in an interracial relationship with her husband Wash. Dismissing this aspect of their relationship out of hand without offering a better explanation in the series' short life is rather unrealistic. It is possible that Whedon might have gone on to explain race relations within the show had it continued, but given his track record up until that point, this seems unlikely.

Both Whedon's heroines and the women of Blaxploitation tend to operate at a disadvantage when it comes to power, and even Cleo with her government clearance is not infallible. However, Blaxploitation heroines, as well as many of the minority characters within Whedon's series have more difficulty gaining access to the influence and clout they need in order to accomplish their goals. In his discussion of *Buffy*, Ewan Kirkland argues that there is a sense of whiteness that is embedded into both the structure of the series and its genre; this would likely prevent non-white persons from gaining an overly large amount of personal power.[22] If this tendency can be seen as prevalent throughout Whedon's series, then it would also warrant a discussion of how race is tied to the formation of identity, and how it determines ties to one's community.

Identification and Community

Blaxploitation heroines formed much of their identity through their race, and in many respects Whedon's heroines are no different. Yet while race was always in the foreground of the previous generation of films, Whedon never truly acknowledges how the skin color of his characters allows them to form their respective identities, not to mention the advantages they gain as a result. This can be seen as a rejection of how identity was characterized for the heroines of Blaxploitation; race in Whedon is typically ignored or downplayed. Black female characters in *Buffy* are some of the most prominent victims here. While black males, though few, have played important roles within Whedon's series, black women's voices are often suppressed in some way. This is accomplished through their deaths (Kendra, Nikki Wood), their removal from the series (Olivia), or by ignoring, stifling, or their inability to express themselves (Kendra, Olivia, the First Slayer). In describing the First Slayer, for example, Cynthia Fuchs argues that "she also can be read as an ignorant (not to say racist) image of a primitive black character being bested by a white girl's "modern" know-how and training."[23] Privileging this white, youthful character over other minority women does little to help Whedon's presentation of Buffy as a feminist icon.

If Buffy (and Whedon's other heroines) are meant to be figures women can identify with, how does his portrayal of race within his series conflict with that goal? For Blaxploitation heroines, Sims argues that the genre, while problematic, allowed young black women to redefine their femininity in a way that suited them personally.[24] Characters like Buffy do possess traits that women (and men) regardless of race or background can identify with; however, for minority audiences the overwhelming lack of diversity is bound to affect their viewership on some level. Arguably, this is true for European-American audiences as well. Kirkland argues that *Buffy* is characterized by an overwhelming sense of whiteness, one that not only erases race, but other ethnic and social distinctions such as religion or social class.[25] While television and film may favor white perspectives, no white person is completely ignorant of the diversity around them. Having such minimal representation of other races and backgrounds can be as distancing to the majority as it is to minorities.

Whedon's way of linking race with identity has diverged rather greatly from Blaxploitation; the concept of community that can be found within the genre, particularly how heroes are shown to have a responsibility to the well-being of that community, is ambiguous within the auteur's series. In *Coffy*, the protagonist's anger towards the corrupt system that destroyed her sister's life is also grounded in the knowledge that the lives of her friends and neighbors are being similarly devastated. Even Howard, Coffy's boyfriend and a villainous politician, talks with reporters (rather hypocritically) about the damage being done to the black community by big business and the government. A more positive connection can be seen in *Cleopatra Jones*, in which the aforementioned heroine is shown to be personally involved in fighting drug use in her community, despite also being a globetrotting government agent. Cleo immediately responds to an unfair raid on a rehabilitation center run by her boyfriend, demonstrating that her commitment to her home is equal to her governmental responsibilities. She is also able to call on multiple friends within her old neighborhood (including her boyfriend and sparring partners) not only to supply her with information, but also to eventually aid her in a showdown against the villain Mommy. Because she continues to maintain these personal connections, she is able to eventually defeat Mommy and her cadre of drug dealers. *Cleopatra Jones* depicts a strong, confident hero—but also emphasizes the concept that communities must band together in order to solve far-reaching problems such as drug abuse.

The focus on individualism in *Buffy* runs in direct contrast to the mindset found within *Cleopatra Jones* and in some cases characterizes the notion of community in a negative light. Buffy, for instance, struggles to remain connected, often feeling isolated from both the world at large and even those close to her. Her frequent wishes to feel normal are in opposition to temporary co–Slayer Kendra, who explains "that's how seriously the calling is taken by my people…. My mother and father gave me to my Watcher because they believed they were doing the right thing for me … and for the world (2.13)."[26] Kendra's beliefs about being the Slayer are grounded in a sense of the greater good, and though it is implied that she sometimes wishes for the life of a normal teenage girl, she refuses to feel sorry for herself. In another series, this might be considered ennobling; in the context of Buffy's then-teenage environment, however, it is viewed as odd or even freakish. Buffy makes frequent comments that disparage Kendra's dedication to her work, and the character ultimately leaves Sunnydale at the end of the episode. Her upright values regarding a Slayer's role do not and cannot have a place in the protagonist's adolescent conception of reality, where the focus on self-actualization is of far greater importance.

Buffy does not completely reject the idea of community; the core-Scooby group and others associated with them become what Vivien Burr and Christine Jarvis describe as an alternative family, one that is "based upon non-hierarchical structures and individual freedom of choice."[27] While Buffy and her friends' sense of community differs from that which is established in Blaxploitation film, their idea of family is remarkably similar to that of many African American households; while families in general within the United States are reflecting this model more and more, African American family structures have traditionally been "less kin-based, less specific to childrearing, less permanent, more permeable, and more flexible."[28] Whedon's heroines draw from Blaxploitation not only for their strength and sexuality, but also for their interpersonal relationships as well. With that in mind, it is all the more confusing that Nikki Wood, the character most associated with

Blaxploitation, rejects a concept of family originating in African American culture.

Though she explicitly embodies the stereotypical Blaxploitation heroine, Nikki Wood does not inherit the belief in community that her forebears share. Wood constantly insists on the importance of the mission, which is tellingly depicted in a scene from Season Seven: "But remember, Robin, honey what we talked about. Always got to work the mission. Look at me. You know I love you, but I got a job to do. The mission is what matters ... right? (7.17)."[29] Her tone and demeanor here indicate that her work as a Slayer comes even before being a mother. The scene demonstrates that isolation is antithetical to a Slayer's success in the fight against evil, yet it does so by bringing up uncomfortable issues surrounding black motherhood.[30] Bette J. Dickerson insists that a variety of myths circulate about black single mothers, particularly that their families are "dysfunctional" and "inferior" to nuclear white families.[31] Characterizing Wood in this manner is especially jarring given the fact that Buffy herself is raised by a single mother, who, while largely ignorant of her daughter's mission, is still portrayed as being devoted to her well-being.

In a sense, Nikki Wood is an extreme symbol of the behavior that Buffy increasingly displays over the seven seasons. The focus on her relationship with fighting evil stems more from personal choice, rather than a responsibility to her community and the people within it. Rather than act inclusively and engage with the town she has sworn to protect, Buffy distances herself from the other inhabitants of Sunnydale and her friends. This culminates in Season Seven, where Buffy admits why she has begun to distance herself: "They don't know. They haven't been through what I've been through. They're not the slayer. I am. Sometimes I feel—this is awful—I feel like I'm better than them. Superior (7.07)."[32] The detachment that Wood manifests and Buffy inherits is significant from a narrative standpoint, but it comes at the cost of divorcing each of them from their cultural background.

What does it mean for Nikki Wood to, in a sense, subvert one of the hallmarks of Blaxploitation film (having strong ties to the black community)? It seems unlikely that the intent was to deliberately criticize that particular feature of the genre; instead it's more feasible that this signals a lack of understanding of the importance of racial ties within these films. While it is true that Blaxploitation was primarily driven by the desire of white-owned studios to make money off of the untapped black market, the response that the African American community had to these films was palpable.[33] Superficial though it may have been, Blaxploitation was to some extent a place of cultural understanding. Though the genre was harshly critiqued and still is today, it must be acknowledged that it allowed African Americans to be portrayed in ways they never had before, for better or worse. The shallow use of Nikki

Wood in this manner ignores many of the social and political issues that African Americans brought with them when viewing these films.

To find the sense of community that both supported and motivated Blaxploitation heroines, the best place to look in Whedon's productions is at the men. In male-led series like *Angel* and *Firefly*, there is a clear sense that not only are characters interacting with the community beyond their social group, but that doing so defines who they are as people. Angel's journey begins as something very personal and singular, but over time, he broadens his focus to the wider community within Los Angeles where he works as a private investigator. An even better example is *Firefly*, where Malcolm Reynolds portrays someone who began fighting for the people, loses his way, and must begin again. Though he lost his faith in working for freedom for those the Alliance oppressed, over the course of the series and in the film *Serenity*, he finds his way back to being the man who believed in defending the rights of his fellow citizens. This culminates in the climactic speech at the end of *Serenity*, where he argues his reasons for bringing the crimes of the Alliance to light:

> Y'all got on this boat for different reasons, but y'all come to the same place. So now I'm asking more of you than I have before. Maybe all. Sure as I know anything, I know this— they will try again. Maybe on another world, maybe on this very ground swept clean. A year from now, ten? They'll swing back to the belief that they can make people ... better. And I do not hold to that. So no more runnin'. I aim to misbehave.[34]

The sense of duty that could be found in *Cleopatra Jones*, or even in more revenge-focused pieces like *Coffy* and *Foxy Brown* is present here, more than anywhere else in Whedon's series. Rather than being grounded in the collective experiences of one group of people, Mal's desire to defend his community is born out of the same impulse that was present for many characters in Blaxploitation. Of the many tropes and concepts that found their way into Whedon's work, this one is perhaps the most successful in not only communicating the individual message of the text itself, but in displaying the ideals that could be found within Blaxploitation's stories.

It is possible that depicting men as the shepherds of their communities is deliberate. If Whedon consistently attempts to subvert traditional expectations regarding femininity by having women be the ones who fulfill the function of warriors, then it is also possible that he intentionally sets up at least some of the men in his series as nurturing figures. Here again they reflect aspects of Blaxploitation; in *Cleopatra Jones*, the protagonist's boyfriend ran a rehabilitation clinic for recovering drug addicts. But while Cleo, Coffy, and Foxy could at least appreciate the importance of engaging with one's community, for many of the women in Whedon's series, this proves to be a difficult concept to approach. Though it is understandable that Whedon attempts to distance his heroines from more feminine roles, their lack of involvement with their communities makes their roles as protectors somewhat empty—

how can they fight for a cause when they have little or no connection to the people they are fighting for?

Whedon's heroines are the beneficiaries of power and agency that their forebears in Blaxploitation could not enjoy within or without the films that made them famous. Blaxploitation died out after 1975, and Sims mentions that most of the actresses that populated these roles had difficulty finding work in more mainstream films.[35] The action heroines that sprang up their wake were not only able to enjoy the use of tropes that characterized women as strong, competent, and physically capable, they were also able to erase the fact that their stories originated in African American culture. Blaxploitation films, and particularly those featuring female protagonists, are now met with derision by the general public; because these films are dismissed, it will likely prevent many from seeing the connection between the genre and the modern action heroine.

All this is not to say that all of Whedon's work is either racist or guilty of intentional theft in some way. Nor is it saying that Blaxploitation was completely without flaw—many of the scenes within Pam Grier's films especially are difficult to watch because of their pronounced level of racist and sexist imagery. However, to neglect consideration of the influence of Blaxploitation on Whedon arguably would do a disservice to both sets of work; concepts that were developed through this period have become normalized within female-dominated action film, and ignoring that fact would erase cinematic, social, and political history. For all of his significant work to increase the visibility and development of female characters within television, Whedon strangely falls back on many of the tendencies of second-wave feminism by focusing his gaze on the white middle-class. Cristina Lucia Stasia also considers this type of trend, asserting that "my concern is that these new female action heroes provide images of an equality that has not been achieved, and that they mitigate their viewers' interests in exploring inequalities. It is easy to be seduced by images of strong women fighting, but these images capitalize on a basic belief in feminism evacuated of any consciousness of why girls still need to 'kick ass.'"[36] In the rush to show the strong, capable women that populate his series, Whedon has left many behind, creating unbalanced and distorted view of women in the process. Blaxploitation, though imperfect, proved that African American women could be engaging characters that were just as fierce as male protagonists, if not more. It would be nice to see creators like Whedon not only acknowledge this but incorporate these types of portrayals into future work.

NOTES

1. "Fool for Love," *Buffy the Vampire Slayer* 5.7, DVD, written by Douglas Petrie, directed by Nick Marck (2000: Twentieth Century Fox, 2005).

2. See also Novotny Lawrence, *Blaxploitation Films of the 1970s: Blackness and Genre* (New York: Routledge, 2008); Donald Bogle, *Toms, Coons, Mulattoes, Mammies, and Bucks: An Interpretative History* (New York: Continuum, 1994); Randall Clark, *At a Theater or Drive-In Near You: The History, Culture, and Politics of the American Exploitation Film* (New York: Garland, 1995).

3. Stephane Dunn, *"Baad Bitches" and Sassy Supermamas: Black Power Action Films* (Urbana: University of Illinois Press, 2008), 111.

4. Lorna Jowett, *Sex and the Slayer: A Gender Studies Primer for the Buffy Fan* (Middletown, CT: Wesleyan University Press, 2005), 43.

5. Gwendolyn D. Pough, *Check It While I Wreck It: Black Womanhood, Hip-Hop Culture, and the Public Sphere* (Boston: Northeastern University Press, 2004), 18.

6. Jeffrey A. Brown, *Dangerous Curves: Action Heroines, Gender, Fetishism, and Popular Culture* (Jackson: University Press of Mississippi, 2011), 191.

7. Yvonne Sims, *Women of Blaxploitation: How the Black Action Film Heroine Changed American Popular Culture* (Jefferson, NC: McFarland, 2006), 75.

8. *Coffy*, directed by Jack Hill (1973; Santa Monica, CA: MGM Home Video, 2001), DVD.

9. Dunn, *"Baad Bitches" and Sassy Supermamas: Black Power Action Films*, 127.

10. "Dead Things," *Buffy the Vampire Slayer*, 6.13, DVD, written by Steven S. DeKnight, directed James A. Contner (2002: Twentieth Century Fox, 2005).

11. Gwyn Symonds, "Solving Problems with Sharp Objects": Female Empowerment, Sex and Violence in *Buffy the Vampire Slayer*," *Slayage: The Journal of the Whedon Studies Association* 11–12, 3.3–4 (2004): n.pg., http://slayageonline.com/PDF/symonds.pdf.

12. Dunn, *"Baad Bitches" and Sassy Supermamas: Black Power Action Films*, 110.

13. Jennifer Crusie, "Dating Death," *Seven Seasons of Buffy: Science Fiction and Fantasy Writers Discuss Their Favorite Television Show*, ed. Glenn Yeffeth (Dallas: BenBella Books, 2003), 85–96.

14. *Coffy*.

15. Hilary Neroni, *The Violent Woman: Femininity, Narrative, and Violence in Contemporary American Cinema* (Albany: State University of New York Press, 2005), 29.

16. *Cleopatra Jones*.

17. Dunn, *"Baad Bitches" and Sassy Supermamas: Black Power Action Films*, 88–9.

18. *Ibid.*

19. Sims, *Women of Blaxploitation: How the Black Action Film Heroine Changed American Popular Culture*, 91.

20. *Serenity*, directed by Joss Whedon (2005; Los Angeles, CA: Universal Studios, 2007), DVD.

21. Toni Morrison, *Playing in the Dark: Whiteness and the Literary Imagination* (New York: Random House, 1992), 9–10.

22. Ewan Kirkland, "The Caucasian Persuasion of *Buffy the Vampire Slayer*," *Slayage: The Journal of the Whedon Studies Association*, 17, 5.1 (2005). http://slayage online.com/PDF/kirkland.pdf.

23. Cynthia Fuchs, "Did Anyone Ever Explain to You What 'Secret Identity' Means?": Race and Displacement in *Buffy* and *Dark Angel*," *Undead TV: Essays on Buffy the Vampire Slayer*, ed. Elana Levine and Lisa Parks (Durham, NC: Duke University Press, 2007), 96–115.

24. Sims, *Women of Blaxploitation: How the Black Action Film Heroine Changed American Popular Culture*, 192.

25. Kirkland, "The Caucasian Persuasion of *Buffy the Vampire Slayer*."

26. "What's My Line (Part 2)," *Buffy the Vampire Slayer,* 2.10, DVD, written by Marti Noxon, directed by David Semel (1997: Twentieth Century Fox, 2005).

27. Vivien Burr and Christine Jarvis, "Friends Are the Family We Choose for Ourselves": Young People and Families in *Buffy the Vampire Slayer*" (presentation, The Slayage Conference on *Buffy the Vampire Slayer*, Nashville, TN, May 28–30, 2004).

28. M. Belinda Tucker and Angela D. James, "New Families, New Functions: Postmodern African American Families in Context," *African American Family Life: Ecological and Cultural Diversity*, ed. Vonnie C. McLoyd, Nancy E. Hill, and Kenneth A. Dodge (New York: Guilford Press, 2005), 86–108.

29. "Lies My Parents Told Me," *Buffy the Vampire Slayer,* 7.17, DVD, written by David Fury and Drew Goddard, directed David Fury (2003: Twentieth Century Fox, 2005).

30. Editors' note: McGee's argument here could be extended to assert that, since a young Robin's presence here distracts Spike from biting Nikki, community saves her in this instance. This interpretation adds an element of irony to McGee's reading, since Nikki rejects the very presence of community that helped avert her death only moments before.

31. Bette J. Dickerson, "Introduction," *African American Single Mothers: Understanding Their Lives and Their Families*, ed. Bette J. Dickerson (Thousand Oaks, CA: Sage, 1995), ix.

32. "Conversations with Dead People," *Buffy the Vampire Slayer,* 7.7, DVD, written by Jane Espenson and Drew Goddard, directed Nick Marck (2002: Twentieth Century Fox, 2005).

33. Dunn, *"Baad Bitches" and Sassy Supermamas: Black Power Action Films*, 5.

34. *Serenity*, DVD, Joss Whedon (2005, Universal City, CA: Universal Studios, 2007).

35. Sims, *Women of Blaxploitation: How the Black Action Film Heroine Changed American Popular Culture*, 188.

36. Cristina Lucia Stasia, "'Wham! Bam! Thank You Ma'am!': The New Public/Private Female Action Hero," *Third Wave Feminism: A Critical Exploration*, ed. Stacy Gillis, Gillian Howie and Rebecca Munford (New York: Palgrave Macmillan, 2004), 175–184.

Someone's Asian in *Dr. Horrible*

Humor, Reflexivity and the Absolution of Whiteness

HÉLÈNE FROHARD-DOURLENT

American popular culture has historically had a very tense and complex relationship with racialized representations, especially in television and film.[1] The dominance of the ideology of whiteness in North American culture means that people of color continue to be underrepresented in popular culture, and that the representations that are available often still draw on stereotypes and racist assumptions about non-white people.[2] Both issues have been raised in relationship to Joss Whedon and his works.[3] More recently, scholars have also pointed out that even so-called positive portrayals of racial and ethnic minorities can have complex ramifications for racial politics. Even the inclusion of racial diversity can contribute to maintaining white hegemony by feeding into a colorblind discourse of progress that views racism as a thing of the past, thus denying the persistence of racism and its significance in shaping people's material conditions and life chances.[4] It is important to note here that the understanding of racism that frames this essay is racism as a systemic phenomenon that does not necessitate intentionality; one can say or do something that sustains or bolsters racism at the interpersonal, institutional and/or systemic level without identifying one's beliefs or actions as racist. Contrary to conventional understandings of the word,[5] then, racism is not primarily about holding (and acting upon) conscious racist beliefs. Rather, with "patterns of discrimination that are institutionalized as 'normal' throughout an entire culture.... It's not one person discriminating at this point, but a whole population operating in a social structure that actually makes it *difficult* for a person *not* to discriminate."[6] As a close reading of the song "Nobody's Asian in the Movies" will demonstrate, even when artists attempt to publically address issues of racialized inequalities in the media, their narratives are mediated by dominant cultural frames that leave little room to talk about systemic racism and white privilege as roots of the problems of racialized representations that persist in American popular culture.

"Nobody's Asian in the Movies" is a song featured on *Commentary! The Musical*, a bonus musical commentary track featured on the *Dr. Horrible's Sing-Along Blog* DVD. *Dr. Horrible* is a three-part web series developed during the Writers Guild of America strike of 2008, written by Joss Whedon, his two brothers Jed and Zack, and his sister-in-law (Jed's wife) Maurissa Tancharoen.[7] Like most products of popular culture, *Dr. Horrible* reflects the larger inequalities of the society in which it was created: the cast of the series is overwhelmingly white (only one minor part is played by a person of color, Tancharoen, who is Asian American) and race is never discussed overtly, with the notable exception of "Nobody's Asian in the Movies," a song that explicitly addresses issues of racism and racialization in the entertainment industry. *Commentary! The Musical*, which was written by all four writers and features both writers and actors singing songs about the process of making *Dr. Horrible*, is written in a decidedly self-mocking tone that opens up a fascinating self-reflexive discursive space; it is an opportunity for the writers to poke gentle fun at themselves, their actors, and the entertainment industry. Yet under the light and silly overtone, the musical commentary also allows the writers to express cynicism and ambivalence towards numerous aspects of the entertainment industry. This tension between a light, joking tone and underlying genuine frustration is at the heart of "Nobody's Asian in the Movies."[8] Co-written by Jed Whedon and Maurissa Tancharoen, and performed by Tancharoen, the song provides a (humorous) commentary on the conspicuous absence of Asian characters in American popular culture, and the struggle of inhabiting a marginalized identity. As such, it is a window into the way that issues of racialized representations can be explored by both artists of color who are directly affected by racism in the media, and also by the very makers of popular culture who are sometimes challenged for not paying enough attention to the political and social implications of the media representations that they help create.

This essay uses the method of close reading to examine the structure and salient themes of the song and answer the following questions.[9] First, how is the issue of racialized inequality framed by the song, and how does this framing function to highlight a particular understanding of racism? Next, how is whiteness implicated in the song's critique of the entertainment industry? And finally, how does the humorous tone of the song both enable and constrain a discussion about the reality and effects of racism? These questions underline the contradictions that exist in the song as a product of dominant framings of racism, and present a challenge to them. By analyzing how modern understandings of racism and racialized inequality are articulated in this song, this paper highlights the ways in which "Nobody's Asian in the Movies," while expressing surface dissatisfaction with the racialized status quo, ultimately fails to address the issue of white privilege and disallows a deeper critical reflection on the workings of systemic racism that maintain that very status quo.

Tancharoen's Story and the Personalization of Racism

The song opens with a (presumably fictional) story of the racism experienced by Tancharoen on the set of *Dr. Horrible* as she is turned down for the part of the female lead, Penny. Lines 1 and 2 ("I wrote all Penny's lines and her song, you know/I even sang her part up on the demo") explicitly note Tancharoen's involvement in the creative process, indicating that the decision not to cast her as Penny was not due to her lack of creative involvement but rather, as lines 3 and 4 establish, the product of overt racism: "When it's time to cast the show / Did they want somebody yellow—hell no."[10] In these lines, the intensifier "hell" adds force to the derogatory expression "somebody yellow," and frames the casting of an Asian lead as an impossibility so self-evident that any suggestion otherwise would be forcefully resisted. The third stanza confirms the harshness of the racism encountered by Tancharoen by contrasting the intensity of her plea to be cast as Penny in line 10 ("I begged and I pleaded please don't pass me by") with the indifference with which the producers respond to her request in line 11–12 ("hey give us a hand / Go stand in the back with that fat guy").[11] The unwillingness of the nameless executives[12] to hire Tancharoen in anything but a minor part situates *Dr. Horrible* within its cultural context, one where white people are seen as more desirable and "safer" choices than people of color, particularly for lead parts.[13] In this sense, the song starts out on a powerful note: in a society where the continued relevance of racism is often denied,[14] the first three stanzas encompassing Tancharoen's story are an unambiguous indictment of current practices in the entertainment industry. They suggest that the invisibility of Asian people in the media is not incidental, but rather the product of specific practices and assumptions on the part of those involved in the entertainment industry. The use of the first person in these stanzas is also a daring linguistic choice, as it functions to implicate the *Dr. Horrible* production team in these problematic practices. This brings racism closer to home by suggesting that this type of racist encounter happens to people we know, and within products of popular culture to which we are connected as consumers.

Yet a number of tensions exist within the three stanzas of Tancharoen's personal narrative. First, the racist "they" of lines 4 ("Did they want somebody yellow") and 11–12 ("They say, hey give us a hand") remains unnamed.[15] No particular individual is actually implicated in the racist practices described in Tancharoen's story, and overt racism remains something that unnamed people practice, not friends or acquaintances. By framing the moment of casting as the site of racist assumptions, the story also shifts the blame from the industry as a whole to a particular set of individuals—those involved in casting decisions, which obscures the complicity of others in the industry, and suggests that the issue of racialized inequality in popular culture is primarily a problem of individuals making prejudiced decisions. More broadly, the fact that Tancharoen's story highlights blatant racism perpetuated by individuals erases the fact that this is not the most pervasive way in which racism persists and functions in our society. In other words, while overt discrimination may play a part in keeping actors of color away from parts, it is by no means the only or even primary mechanism by which racialized inequalities are reproduced in the realm of popular culture. Rather, the problem is perpetuated by a range of racialized belief systems and mechanisms of systemic racism that have little to do with racist individuals making prejudiced decisions. Instead, racialized dynamics in popular culture are perpetuated through a multiplicity of mechanisms that do not stem from individual prejudice but rather from a culture of whiteness, such as: "open" casting calls that are most likely to go to white actors; assumptions about what bodies viewers find attractive and relatable; unconscious racialized schemas that lead decision-makers to cast actors of color in certain parts more readily than in others; and scripts that largely focus on the lives and problems of white people, amongst others.[16] In short, while these first stanzas of the song strongly condemn racism, they also condemn the form of racism that is easiest to recognize and condemn. Though these lines gesture towards racism as an industry problem that shapes how casting decisions are made, the focus on blatant racism obscures the more subtle, ingrained, and systemic mechanisms of racism that make racialized inequalities far more complicated to address than simply to expose individuals who express and enact racist prejudices.

Furthermore, the fact that Tancharoen's story is fictional—the listener is not meant to believe that this actually happened to Tancharoen on the set of *Dr. Horrible*—creates a contradictory effect that partly buffers the accusation of racism. As I have argued, the first-person perspective personalizes the experience of racism in a powerful way. However, the fictional nature of the perspective simultaneously creates distance from the moment of racism, as it allows the songwriters to talk about racist practices without having to incriminate anyone. We are expected to believe that the racists in the story are fictional, that Tancharoen did not experience such blatant racism at the hand of her own family. In other words, the fictional *Dr. Horrible* set of the song could be any set in Hollywood, but it also means that it is no set in particular. The non-specificity created by the fictionalized setting allows (white) listeners to assume that Tancharoen's story is nothing but exaggerated fiction created for the sake of an argument, and that such blatant racism just does not happen anymore.

Finally, the last two lines of the third stanza, which mark the end of Tancharoen's personal narrative, provide yet another moment of tension in the song. In these lines, Tancharoen expresses gratitude for the fact that the part that she obtained does not embody an offensive stereotype (being a Vietcong). These two lines shift our attention to the content of the role rather than its (in)significance; whereas the beginning of the song focused on Tancharoen's dismissal from a lead part, now the focus is on the fact that Tancharoen's minor part "at least" was not based on an offensive stereotype.[17] This shift glosses over the contempt and indifference that "they" have shown for Tancharoen's desire to be cast in a substantial part by offhandedly offering her to "go stand in the back."[18] By closing the stanza on an image of Tancharoen being grateful that her part did not draw on offensive racialized stereotyping, the song downplays the original discrepancy between the hope for a leading role and the actual part Tancharoen is offered. Additionally, the decision to emphasize that Tancharoen's part is not racialized because it "isn't Vietcong, it's comic relief" minimizes the implication of *Dr. Horrible* in the reproduction of racialized inequalities (unlike the rest of Tancharoen's story) by drawing attention to the positive aspect of Tancharoen's casting.[19] Together, both discursive choices leave little room for anger or resentment on Tancharoen's part, echoing the prelude to the song where Tancharoen states tiredly, "it's OK, I didn't want the part of Penny anyway..." (despite the fact that the song suggests that she did).[20] This is important because people of color who express anger at racism, whether their own experience of it or its institutional and cultural mechanisms, are often met with the assertion that they're being "too angry" and the suspicion that they are "playing the race card" and that what they experienced was not "really" racism.[21] While the song does not explicitly play into this narrative, the absence of overt anger or frustration on the part of Tancharoen—and the choice to highlight the "better" part of the casting decision at the end—contributes to erasing the possibility of anger as an appropriate response for encountering racism, and continues to make that reaction an unexpected response that draws criticism from people, particularly white people.

A Ninja, a Physician or a Goofy Mathematician: Broader Racialized Inequalities in the Media

As the song continues, the focus shifts to become less specifically about the production of *Dr. Horrible*, and more about larger patterns of racialized inequalities in the media. The fourth and sixth stanza, for example, underline the fact that Asian American actors are limited to a very restricted list of parts that fit cultural ideas about Asian people, such as the fact that they are supposedly good at martial arts ("ninja"), tech-savvy ("computer technician"), nerdy ("goofy mathematician"), wise ("wise old healer"), and successful in business, if not particularly fluent in English ("thank you prrease" and "we'll be loving you long time").[22] It is worth noting here that some of these stereotypes would be considered "positive" stereotypes, in the sense that they tend to associate Asian people with traits that are valued in American society. While this may make them seem harmless, they are also the traits that contribute to the Asian glass ceiling effect by reifying ideas about Asian Americans as smart but lacking people skills, thus making them unfit for leadership positions.[23] The focus on Asian Americans as a "model minority"[24] (an image sustained by stereotypes about Asians excelling at math and science-related endeavours) also erases the differences that exist within different groups of Asian Americans, and makes it more difficult for Asian people to talk about the racism they encounter by minimizing those experiences. The misguided thinking becomes that Asian Americans are so successful that racism cannot possibly have an impact on their material conditions and life chances.[25]

Using the format of a laundry list of stereotypes to illustrate how Asian Americans are restricted to a pre-existing set of roles also raises some issues. By simply enumerating stereotypes, the list does little to challenge them but rather bolsters their relevance in our cultural imaginary. The presumption that it is obvious that these stereotypes are problematic and/or untrue (and that listeners necessarily share that perspective) assumes that these stereotypes have little actual purchase on our culture, which is not the case. As the "positive stereotype" narrative suggests, many people continue to believe that some stereotypes are valid and harmless, either because they are "based in truth" or because they do not perpetuate an inherently negative image of the marginalized group in question. This dynamic is somewhat disrupted at the very end of the song, when Tancharoen states that her father is a "nerdy, funny scientist."[26] Her reliance on a stereotype is immediately revealed as intentional when Jed Whedon questions her answer with "isn't your dad a transpo guy?" and Tancharoen responds dismissively, "like an Asian could do that."[27] Unlike the laundry list from the song, this exchange highlights the fact that stereotypes limit how we think of people of color, the contradiction that this creates with the real lives of Asian Americans, and finally the tensions that these stereotypes create for people of color who struggle to define themselves within a dominant framework that pre-determines what they should, or should not, excel at. By ending on the uncertainty of the answer, this exchange makes visible the tension between the reality of the lives of Asian Americans, which may or may not conform to stereotypes, and the frustration of being expected to fit stereotypical expectations, reflected in the limited range of parts that Asian American actors are offered in the entertainment industry.

The Persistent Invisibility of Whiteness

By focusing on how the entertainment industry deals with people of color, and Asian Americans in particular, the song leaves aside the second part of the equation: the way that white privilege and whiteness function to create a world where Penny could not be imagined as Asian American. Whiteness is not completely absent from the song, but it is made invisible through two mechanisms. First, it is actively erased through the use of the anonymous "they" as well as "we."[28] Second, it is implicitly present in contrast to the racialized identities that are discussed. For example, the first stanza of the song does not explicitly indicate who is the best choice for the role of Penny if someone Asian is an inconceivable choice; but the fact that listeners would know that white actress Felicia Day was chosen to play Penny establishes an implicit hierarchy between "somebody yellow" and somebody white, moving beyond the fictional into a casting choice that was actually made.[29] As the existing literature suggests, this type of racialized privileging of whites in casting choices runs rampant in the entertainment industry in general, in part due to the assumption that whiteness is universal.[30]

The erasure of whiteness is perhaps most obvious in the fifth stanza, which uses the recurring question "Who do they want before they want an Asian?" to underline that Asian American actors are perceived as so undesirable that they are at the bottom of the racialized hierarchy.[31] In one sense, this stanza gestures towards larger patterns of racialized discrimination in the media by showing that Asian Americans are not the only racial or ethnic minority affected: the laundry list of racial and ethnic identities in this stanza suggests that almost any racial/ethnic minority group is concerned by the issue of lack of representation. The use of the determiner "a" or "an" underlines the pervasiveness of the problem of minimal representation by making it clear that whoever "they" want, "they" only want one person, no more, to embody racial diversity.[32] Two other features of the stanza reinforce this sense that the entertainment industry cares little about featuring accurate and respectful representations of racial minorities. First, throughout the stanza, the terms used to refer to different ethnic and racial minorities are either slightly inexact or potentially contentious: Mexican is used for Latinos, black for African Americans,[33] Persian for Iranians and Middle Eastern people more broadly, and American Indian for Native Americans.[34] This imprecise labeling suggests that who "they" want has little to do with how people of these racialized categories identify, and more to do with how racial minorities are perceived by the entertainment industry, as a handful of homogenous groups that are mostly distinguishable from one another through skin tones.[35] A sense of interchangeability is emphasized by the line "an American Indian played by a Mexican," which suggests that non-white people all look alike and thus can easily stand in for one another, an assumption that is particularly relevant for the representation of Asian Americans.[36] One reading of this stanza is thus a critique of how popular culture features racial diversity, when it features it at all.

Yet this critique is fairly implicit in this stanza. Explicitly, the passage frames the problem of Asian invisibility as an issue of Asians being devalued within the racialized hierarchy of minority groups: Asians are picked last, a sense that is amplified by the mention of racial and ethnic minorities who do not make up as significant a portion of American society. Rather than framing the issue as one of white hypervisibility, the stanza focuses on the struggle of one racial minority to gain visibility over others. In the midst of this interracial competition, there is no space made available for interracial solidarity, including activist organizing that could challenge the system of racism that creates this competition and the dearth of acting opportunities for people of color. The real winner of the race, whiteness, remains unnamed as the stanza glosses over who "they" truly want, more than any of the ethnic and racial minority groups mentioned: white actors.[37] In other words, the system of white privilege that sets up a situation where the choice has to be between an Asian actor and a Mexican actor—where hiring both is unimaginable—is never named or discussed overtly.

In one sense, the invisibility of whiteness is precisely how racialized inequalities are maintained in our society, including within the entertainment industry, so that the song could be read as a commentary on this invisibility; the song does not talk about whiteness because whiteness is not talked about. However, the problem with this interpretation is that the failure to explicitly address the role that whiteness plays in maintaining systemic racism and inequality contributes to perpetuating a dialogue about race that leaves whiteness unexamined. As a result, the few indirect mentions of whiteness do not allow for much unpacking of white privilege and how it functions, and the failure to name white privilege constrains the possibilities for the song to start a conversation about systemic racism. Also limiting the discussion of white privilege, systemic racism, and their dismantling, is the fact that the song is marked by a sense of resignation. Not only does Tancharoen express defeated acceptance of the situation twice, first as she introduces the song ("it's OK, I didn't want the part of Penny anyway") and when she is cast in her minor role as a groupie ("at least it isn't Vietcong"), but the song ultimately frames as somewhat positive the stereotypical parts given to Asian

Americans, because movies "couldn't be made" without Asian Americans being willing to play these parts.[38] Given that the song is void of suggestions for change or insurrection against the prevailing regime of whiteness, no alternative to complicity with systemic racism is made available to the listener, and we are left in the same state of complacency with which we came into the song.

"We need them to play the parts we're not willing to": The Complicated Effects of Humor

So far, I have attempted to illustrate the complexity of the ways that "Nobody's Asian in the Movies" frames the problem of racialized inequality in the media by discussing the contradictions and silences in the song. I now turn my attention to the way that humour functions in the song to make the message about racialized inequality potentially more palatable to its audience, while simultaneously undermining its impact.

First, I would like to discuss the moment where Jed Whedon (a white male) interjects into the song, "But Maurissa, movies couldn't even be made without Asians. We need them to play the parts we're not willing to."[39] The joke contained in these two lines overtly plays on a racist statement: the idea that immigrants (always imagined as people of color) are valuable to the economy because someone is needed to take on the lowest, most strenuous forms of physical labor. As such, the joke can be read as an example of hipster (or ironic) racism, wherein someone makes a racist statement but couches it as a joke, as s.e. smith explains:

> [This type of humour] supposed to be hip and funny because of course "no one really thinks that way." Only, they do, that's the thing, and that's where hipster-ism falls short; it relies on an assumption which simply isn't true, which is that racism, sexism, ableism, and other -isms don't really exist anymore.[40]

Ironic racism is crucial to the way that racism continues to circulate in North American society, as it allows racist ideas and stereotypes to be perpetuated under the guise of humor. It is important to note that Jed Whedon's line functions slightly differently from traditional forms of ironic racism because it imitates, rather than directly reiterates, a racist statement (no one actually argues this about the entertainment industry). This slight disjunction creates self-awareness and explicitly marks the racist humor as preposterous. Yet by portraying racist views as backwards and ludicrous, the joke shares with traditional forms of ironic racism an attitude of dismissal towards the very real presence and force of racism by making it out to be a set of laughable beliefs that only a few isolated individuals could be stupid and prejudiced enough to believe in. This framing of racism closes off opportunities to discuss not only the assumptions contained in these kinds of racist statements when they are said seriously, but more importantly the more complex ways in which racism circulates in American society, through daily assumptions, interactions, and mechanisms that most people do not question.[41]

More broadly, the song raises the question of how the use of humour affects the message on racialized inequality that the song is trying to convey. Tancharoen's defeated tone in the prelude to the song is not humorous, yet the melody and tone of the song remains light-hearted throughout the song. This is a sharp contrast with "Strike!," the other song on the musical commentary soundtrack that deals with a social issue (labor rights), whose lyrics and melody both reflect intense frustration and resentment.[42] It might be that the choice of a humorous tone for "Nobody's Asian in the Movies" stems from an awareness that issues of race and racialized discrimination are a touchy subject in the American context, and that such discussion is often met with resistance; as I have noted before, this is especially true if the conversation is perceived to have a confrontational tone.[43] Broaching the topic of systemic discrimination in the entertainment industry in a serious tone is likely to trigger such resistance; in this context, humor can be seen as a way to start a conversation about racialized inequality without the audience automatically shutting down.

This reading of the humorous tone (as an attempt to defuse knee-jerk hostility to a conversation about racism) is also legitimized by the song's sense of self-awareness and its overt commitment to bringing attention to the problem of racialized casting practices, however limited this lens may be. Additionally, the explicit callousness with which the anonymous racist "they" treat Tancharoen and the lyrics' insistence on the dearth of non-stereotypical parts for Asian American actors leave little doubt that real frustration is being expressed through the song. Yet the light tone of the song simultaneously hinders deeper engagement with questions of racism and racialized inequality by discouraging the expression of legitimate anger. "The humour reminds us not to get too bent out of shape over it," remarks a fan in an online discussion on "Nobody's Asian in the Movies."[44] This response concisely summarizes the limitation of using humor to start a conversation about race: when the only way that we can talk about racist practices and racialized inequality is by downplaying their impact through humor, we reinforce the sense that race cannot—and should not—be talked about seriously. By suggesting that to get "too bent out of shape" over this issue is illegitimate and unjustified, humor (sometimes unintentionally) dismisses the very real impact and effect that racism and racialized inequality can play in the lives of people of color, in the entertainment industry and beyond. In other words, humor in the song works to deflect the very topic to which the song is attempting to bring attention. Ultimately, by downplaying frustration through laughter, humor's potential for resistance against the dominant paradigm is undermined.

By openly addressing the way that people of color, especially Asian Americans, are made both invisible and hypervisible (in stereotypical parts) in the media, "Nobody's Asian in the Movies" begins to illuminate the complex ways in which Asian Americans continue to be disadvantaged in the American entertainment industry. The fact that the song directly implicates *Dr. Horrible* as part of a system that discriminates against actors of color makes the song a particularly powerful critique of an ongoing problem in the entertainment industry. By making visible and denouncing racist practices, Maurissa Tancharoen and Jed Whedon use their privileged position as industry insiders and writers with a guaranteed audience (*Dr. Horrible* fans, and more broadly, Joss Whedon fans) to try to bring attention to the issue and change to the industry. Yet there is an inherent contradiction here between the willingness of Tancharoen and Whedon to point to, and chastise, Hollywood and themselves for contributing to the problematic racialized dynamics of American popular culture and society, and the fact that *Dr. Horrible* itself does little to destabilize these dynamics, and that the song undermines the very possibilities for change that it contains.

In particular, the choice of humor as a medium to facilitate discussion of racism also works to minimize the impact of systemic racism; coupled with the fact that whiteness remains unmarked, humour in the song absolves (white) listeners by allowing them to distance themselves from the issue and their involvement in systemic racism. The message is that racialized inequality and discrimination may exist out there, but other people are to blame: executives, casting directors, producers, and more broadly people who enact racist beliefs. These decisions are unfortunate but do not affect you or what you enjoy watching, because you did not make these decisions and thus you cannot possibly be implicated in the reproduction of racialized inequality. In other words, making the discussion of racism non-threatening also makes acknowledging racism optional.

The very title of the song, "Nobody's Asian in the Movies," functions as a form of hipster anti-racism[45] that allows liberal-minded white people to acknowledge the existence of racism without having to make changes to their own thinking. This title speaks to a crowd that may be willing to acknowledge the racialized landscape of our society—here, the entertainment industry and more broadly the media—but is not prepared to consider what needs to be done to change the situation, let alone to think about how their own practices and beliefs may be implicated in the reproduction of racialized inequality. In other words, the liberal-minded audience gets to feel good about themselves for being able to recognize that there is a problem, while having to change absolutely nothing about their own practices. There are obvious limitations to this type of superficial commitment to anti-racism, most importantly the fact that it does not create an impetus to generate and implement concrete anti-racist liberatory strategies. A critical reading of this song thus requires that we go beyond the question of why there are no Asians in the movies. It is no longer enough to lament stereotypical representations of people of color and the limited opportunities that actors of color often face. We need to ask deeper, harder questions about the role that we, as listeners, viewers, and consumers, play in contributing to a culture where whiteness is allowed to remain the dominant norm, especially if we are white ourselves. Only then will it become possible for change to happen, and for new, different stories to be told and to reach us, including stories that cast somebody yellow in the show without erasing their racialized identity and experiences—hell yes.

NOTES

1. A large number of scholars have written on the racist history of television and cinema's portrayals of people of color, and the complex way in which the politics of representation have shifted in recent decades away from blatantly racist depictions towards more subtle representations that nevertheless continue to perpetuate problematic ideas about people of color. For some examples of books that investigate this history and its implications, see Daniel Bernardi, *Classic Hollywood, Classic Whiteness* (Minneapolis: University of Minnesota Press, 2001); Ward Churchill, *Fantasies of the Master Race: Literature, Cinema, and the Colonization of American Indians* (San Francisco: City Lights, 1998); Darrell Y. Hamamoto, *Monitored Peril: Asian Americans and the Politics of TV Representation* (Minneapolis: University of Minnesota Press, 1994); Stephanie Greco Larson, *Media and Minorities: The Politics of Race in News and Entertainment* (Lanham, MD: Rowman & Littlefield, 2006); David J. Leonard, *Screens Fade to Black: Contemporary African American Cinema* (Westport, CT: Greenwood, 2006); Fred J. MacDonald, *Blacks and White TV: African Americans in Television Since 1948* [Second edition] (Florence, KY: Wadsworth Publishing, 1992); Beretta Smith-Shomade, *Shaded Lives: African American Women and Television* (Toronto: Rutgers University Press, 2002).

2. For some example of stereotypes and images that continue to shape representations of people of color, see Patricia Hill Collins, *Black Sexual Politics: African Americans, Gender and the New Racism* (New York: Routledge, 2004), 119–180; Bradley B. Greenberg, Dana Mastro and Jeffrey Brand, "Minorities and the Mass Media: Television Into the 21st Century," in *Media Effects: Advances in Theory and Research* [Second edition], ed. J. Bryant & D. Zillmann (Mahwah: Lawrence Erlbaum Associates, 2002), 333–352; Entman, R. & Rojecki, A. (2001). *The Black Image in the White Mind: Media and Race in America* (Chicago: University of Chicago Press, 2009). Casting data by the Screen Actors Guild (SAG) shows that non-white actors continue to be underrepresented in film and television, particularly in lead roles: SAG, "Latest casting data follows historical trends and continues to exclude people with disabilities [Press release]," SAGAFTRA website, October 23, 2009, http://www.sagaftra.org/press-releases/october-23-2009/latest-casting-data-follows-historical-trends-and-continues-exclude-p. See also data gathered by Russell K. Robinson on casting breakdowns: Russell K. Robinson, "Casting and Caste-Ing: Reconciling Artis-

tic Freedom and Antidiscrimination Norms." *California Law Review*, 95 (2007), 11–12.

3. By works, I am referring to the shows over which Whedon has had primary creative control: these include *Buffy, Angel, Firefly* and *Dollhouse*, as well as *Dr. Horrible*. These are the works with which his name is mostly readily associated, and the ones with which he has been most heavily involved. For specific critiques of the role of race in Whedon's works, see: Rebecca M. Brown, "Orientalism in *Firefly* and *Serenity*," *Slayage*, 7 (2008); Agnes B. Curry, "We don't say 'Indian': On the Paradoxical Construction of the Reavers" (paper presented at The Slayage Conference on the Whedonverses, Barnesville, Georgia, May 25–28, 2006); Lynne Edwards, "Slaying in Black and White: Kendra as Tragic Mulatta in *Buffy*," in *Fighting the Forces: What's at Stake in Buffy the Vampire Slayer*, eds. Rhonda Wilcox and David Lavery (Lanham, MD: Rowman & Littlefield, 2004); Candra K. Gill, "Cuz the Black Chick Always Gets It First: Dynamics of Race in *Buffy the Vampire Slayer*," in *Girls Who Bite Back: Witches, Mutants, Slayers and Freaks*, ed. Emily Pohl-Weary (Toronto: Sumach Press, 2004); Michaela D. E. Meyer, "From Rogue in the 'Hood to Suave in a Suit: Black Masculinity and the Transformation of Charles Gunn," in *Reading* Angel: *the TV Spin-Off with a Soul*, ed. Stacey Abbott (New York: I. B. Tauris, 2005); Kent Ono, "To Be a Vampire on *Buffy the Vampire Slayer*: Race and ('Other') Socially Marginalizing Positions on Horror TV," in *Fantasy Girls: Gender and the New Universe of Science Fiction and Fantasy Television*, ed. Elyce R. Helford (Lanham, MD: Rowman & Littlefield, 2000)

4. Leonard, *Screens Fade to Black: Contemporary African American Cinema*, 10; Herman Gray, *Cultural Moves: African Americans and the Politics of Representation* (Berkeley: University of California Press, 2005). For broader analyses of the salience and effects of colorblind discourse(s) in modern American society, see: Eduardo Bonilla-Silva, *Racism Without Racists: Color-Blind Racism and Racial Inequality in Contemporary America* [Third edition] (Lanham, MD: Rowman & Littlefield, 2010), particularly pages 29–30; Tim Wise, *Coloblind: The Rise of Post-Racial Politics and the Retreat From Racial Equity* (San Francisco: City Lights, 2010), 132–9.

5. Jennifer L. Eichstedt, "Problematic White Identities and a Search for Racial Justice." *Sociological Forum*, 16 (2001), 458.

6. hepshiba. "Why There's No Such Thing as 'Reverse Racism,'" *Daily Kos*, July 15, 2010, http://www.dailykos.com/story/2010/07/15/884649/-Why-there-s-no-such-thing-as-Reverse-Racism.

7. Jed Whedon and Maurissa Tancharoen, "Nobody's Asian in the Movies," *Commentary! The Musical*, DVD (2008: Mutant Enemy/New Video Group, Inc., 2009).

8. "Nobody's Asian in the Movies," *Commentary! The Musical*.

9. For more information on the practice of close reading please see: Barry S. Brummett, *Techniques of Close Reading* (Thounsand Oaks, CA: Sage, 2009).

10. "Nobody's Asian in the Movies," *Commentary! The Musical*.

11. *Ibid.*

12. Given that the decision maker remains unnamed in the song, I am using the term "executive" as a catch-all for the range of people who are involved in making casting decision on film and television productions, including studio executives, producers, directors, and casting directors. As Russell K. Robinson notes, the title of "casting director" misleads, as casting directors often have little power over final casting decisions; thus we should be careful not to read casting decisions as individual decisions but rather as decisions that occur within a complex system of decision-

making where systemic racism and its assumptions have multiple points of entry. Russell K. Robinson, "Casting and Caste-Ing: Reconciling Artistic Freedom and Antidiscrimination Norms," 6–7.

13. See Dana Calvo, "Applying the First Light Coat," *L.A. Times*, November 20, 1999, http://articles.latimes.com/1999/nov/20/entertainment/ca-35478 and Janine Jackson, "Anything but Racism: Media Make Excuses for 'Whitewashed' TV Lineup," *Fairness & Accuracy in Reporting*, January/February 2000, http://www.fair.org/index.php?page=1019; Russell K. Robinson also cites industry insiders speaking about this phenomenon: Robinson, "Casting and Caste-Ing: Reconciling Artistic Freedom and Antidiscrimination Norms," 8 and note 27.

14. For some examples of the discursive strategies used by white people to deny racism and/or refuse race-conscious approaches, see: Bonilla-Silva, *Racism Without Racists: Color-Blind Racism and the Persistence of Racial Inequality in the United States*; van Dijk, Teun A. "Discourse and the Denial of Racism," *Discourse & Society*, 3 (1992); R. P. Solomon, John P. Portelli, Beverly-Jean Daniel, and Arlene Campbell. "The Discourse of Denial: How White Teacher Candidates Construct Race, Racism and 'White Privilege,'" *Race Ethnicity and Education*, 8 (2005).

15. "Nobody's Asian in the Movies," *Commentary! The Musical*.

16. Robinson, "Casting and Caste-Ing: Reconciling Artistic Freedom and Anti-discrimination Norms," 8–12.

17. "Nobody's Asian in the Movies," *Commentary! The Musical*.

18. *Ibid.*

19. *Ibid.*

20. *Ibid.*

21. For a discussion of the contradictions contained in accusations that people of color are using the "race card," see Bonilla-Silva, *Racism Without Racists: Color-Blind Racism and Racial Inequality in Contemporary America*, 29–30; Tim Wise, *Speaking Treason Fluently: Anti-Racist Reflections from an Angry White Male* (Berkeley: Soft Skull Press, 2008), 32–36. On anger, and the way it is used to dismiss people of color and their experiences (particularly of racism), see Elyse R. Helford, "'My Emotions Give Me Power': The Containment of Girls' Anger in *Buffy*," in in *Fighting the Forces: What's At Stake in Buffy the Vampire Slayer*, eds. Rhonda Wilcox and David Lavery (Lanham, MD: Rowman & Littlefield, 2004), 21; karnythia, "Vikkiage: The White Privilege of White Anti-Racists," Esoterica, 19 May 2011, http://karnythia.tumblr.com/post/5641576585/vikkiage-the-white-privilege-of-white-anti-racists; D. Soyini Madison, "Crazy Patriotism and Angry (Post)Black Women," *Communication and Critical/Cultural Studies, 6*, 323 (2009).

22. "Nobody's Asian in the Movies," *Commentary! The Musical*.

23. Deborah Woo, "The Glass Ceiling and Asian Americans" [Paper 129], *Federal Publications*, http://digitalcommons.ilr.cornell.edu/key_workplace/129.

24. Charles Taylor and Barbara Stern, "Asian-Americans: Television Advertising and the 'Model Minority' Stereotype," *Journal of Advertising, 25* (1997).

25. For discussions of the model minority stereotype and its impact, see: Robert S. Chang, "Toward an Asian American Legal Scholarship: Critical Race Theory, Post-Structuralism, and Narrative Space," *California Law Review, 81*(1993); Linda Holtzman, *Media Messages: What Film, Television, and Popular Music Teach Us About Race, Class, Gender, and Sexual Orientation* (Armonk: M.E. Sharpe, 2000), 223; Stacey Lee, *Unraveling the "Model Minority" Stereotype: Listening to Asian American Youth* (New York: Teachers College Press, 2009); Teresa Mok, "Getting the Message: Media Images and Stereotypes and Their Effect on Asian Americans," *Cultural Diversity and Mental*

Health, 4(1998); Karen Pyke and Tran Dang, "'FOB' and 'Whitewashed': Identity and Internalized Racism Among Second Generation Asian Americans," *Qualitative Sociology,* 26 (2003).

26. "Nobody's Asian in the Movies," *Commentary! The Musical.*

27. *Ibid.*

28. *Ibid.*

29. *Ibid.*

30. See Calvo, "Applying the First Light Coat"; Robinson, "Casting and Caste-Ing: Reconciling Artistic Freedom and Antidiscrimination Norms," 8–9.

31. *Ibid.*

32. *Ibid.*

33. The term "black" is not inexact in itself, and is frequently used by black scholars. It is the use of "black" as a noun rather than an adjective that marks its use as incorrect in the song.

34. "Nobody's Asian in the Movies," *Commentary! The Musical.*

35. *Ibid.*

36. Holtzman, *Media Messages,* 209; Valerie Soe, *All Orientals Look the Same* [Documentary] (Center for Asian American Media, 1986); Robert Lee, *Orientatals: Asian Americans in Popular Culture* (Philadelphia: Temple University Press, 1999), 5.

37. "Nobody's Asian in the Movies," *Commentary! The Musical.*

38. *Ibid.*

39. *Ibid.*

40. s.e. smith, "Glee: The Halfway Point: The Introduction,"*Feminist with Disabilities,* 18 December, 2009, http://disabledfeminists.com/2009/12/18/glee-the-halfway-point-the-introduction/; see also Thea Lim, "The Delusion of Hatred Immunity," *Racialicious,* 23 July, 2008, http://www.racialicious.com/2008/07/23/the-delusion-of-hatred-immunity/

41. For more discussion of how racism operates in daily society, please see Eduardo Bonilla-Silva, *Racism Without Racists: Color-Blind Racism and the Persistence of Racial Inequality in America* (Lanham, MD: Rowman & Littlefield, 2009).

42. Joss Whedon, "Strike!" *Commentary! The Musical,* DVD (2008: Mutant Enemy/New Video Group, Inc., 2009).

43. The expectation that people of color should be able to speak calmly and politely about racism and their experience of oppression is a key mechanism through which white privilege reasserts itself, as it serves to dismiss the concerns of people of color as illegitimate if any anger is expressed. See Naamen Gobert Tilahun, "The Privilege of Politeness," *The Angry Black Woman,* 12 February, 2008, http://theangry-blackwoman.com/2008/02/12/the-privilege-of-politeness/.

44. This comment was made in a thread related to *Commentary! The Musical* on Whedonesque, a community weblog for the discussion of Joss Whedon and his work: http://whedonesque.com/comments/18554#277492.

45. Janani Balasubramanian, "A Guide to Hipster Anti-Racism," *Racialicious tumblr,* 30 May, 2012, http://racialicious.tumblr.com/post/24068580736/aguidetohipsterantiracism. She describes hipster anti-racism as momentary engagements with anti-racism that do not reflect a concrete shift in consciousness or actions, but do bolster one's credentials as respectable in progressive circles.

About the Contributors

Daoine S. **Bachran** is a Ph.D. candidate and Mellon fellow at the University of New Mexico. Her research is the American Gothic, 20th and 21st century written and visual texts, and technology's engagement with race and class. Her dissertation, "From Recovery to Discovery: Ethnic Science Fiction and (Re)Creating the Future," reveals racism in science and explores science fiction written by people of color.

Lynne **Edwards** is a professor of media and communication studies at Ursinus College. She is the author of "Slaying in Black and White: Kendra as Tragic Mulatta in *Buffy the Vampire Slayer*" in *Fighting the Forces* (2002) and co-editor of the anthology *Buffy Goes Dark* (2008). She has also published "Black Like Me: Value Commitment and Television Viewing Preferences of U.S. Black Teenage Girls" in *Black Marks* (2001).

Hélène **Frohard-Dourlent** is a Ph.D. candidate in sociology at the University of British Columbia in Vancouver. Her dissertation focuses on the experiences of educators who work with trans and gender-nonconforming students. Her book chapter on Buffy's relationship with Satsu won the Whedon Studies Association's Mr. Pointy Award for Best Paper in 2010. Her writing has also appeared in such journals as *The Journal of LGBT Youth* and *The Canadian Journal of Higher Education*, among others.

Candra K. **Gill** has presented at PCA/ACA, Slayage, WisCon, and the Nancy Drew and Girl Sleuths conferences. She serves on the editorial board of *Watcher Junior: The Undergraduate Journal of Whedon Studies* and is a co-founder and on the steering committee of the Carl Brandon Society. A former teacher and student affairs professional, she works as a user experience designer.

Joel **Hawkes** is a lecturer in English literature at the University of Victoria, British Columbia. His work is particularly interested in the practices and performances that create the physical and literary spaces we inhabit. His love of gothic and science fiction literature, television and film has led to publications addressing the works of Joss Whedon, including papers in the collections *Joss Whedon's* Dollhouse: *Confounding Purpose, Confusing Identity* (2014), *The Comics of Joss Whedon* (2015), and *After the Avengers* (2015).

Mary Ellen **Iatropoulos** is director of education at Spark Media Project, a non-profit, where she develops and oversees interdisciplinary curricula and assessment, alongside teaching courses in media/digital literacies and multimedia production. She is also an award-winning independent scholar of literature, media, and popular culture. At the 2012 Slayage conference, her paper won the Mr. Pointy Award for Best Paper, and she also won the Northeastern MLA Women/Gender Studies Best Paper prize for her 2014 presentation.

Mayan **Jarnagin** is a high school teacher, British-American Romanticist, medievalist and pop-culturalist. He teaches his students about the perennial objectification of the other by analyzing portrayals of race, creed, sex and class in video games, comic books, cinema, and popular television shows (not to mention canonical literature). A fifteen-year veteran of the armed services, he has a fascination with the portrayal of the military in popular media.

Katia **McClain** teaches at UC Santa Barbara. Her interests include: Eastern European linguistics, literature, folklore, marginalized populations, media representation, science fiction, gender and queer studies. She frequently appears on *Third World News Review*, a local television/radio program and reports on representations of Eastern Europe in popular media. Her essay "Angel vs. the Grand Inquisitor: Joss Whedon Re-imagines Dostoevsky" appeared in *The Literary Angel* (2010).

Masani **McGee** is a Ph.D. candidate at the University of Rochester in Rochester, New York. Her interests pertain specifically to masculinity in genre film and popular culture. Her work has appeared previously in a special issue of *Slayage: The Journal of Whedon Studies*, in addition to a forthcoming edited collection tentatively titled *Assemble! The Making and Re-Making of the Marvel Cinematic Universe*.

Rachel **McMurray** is a writer, editor, and test developer who received an M.A. in English literature from the University of Kansas. Her work has been featured in *The Rumpus*, a pop culture website with essays, reviews, comics, interviews, poetry and more.

Brandeise **Monk-Payton** is a Ph.D. candidate in the Department of Modern Culture and Media at Brown University and a Ford Foundation Dissertation Fellow. She received an M.A. in media, culture, and communication from New York University. Her research focuses on the history and theory of black cultural production and media representation. Her work has been published in *The Black Scholar*, *Reconstruction*, and the edited anthology *From Madea to Media Mogul*.

Samira **Nadkarni**'s publications trace her interest in postmodern poetry and performance, Whedon studies, hermeneutics, ethics, neo/colonialism, fan studies, and digital texts. She serves on the editorial board of *Watcher Junior: The Undergraduate Journal of Whedon Studies*, and is a guest contributor to the *i love e-poetry project*. Her creative writing has been published in *New Writing Dundee*, *Grund Lit*, and *Causeway Magazine*.

Rejena **Saulsberry** is an assistant professor of criminal justice in the Social and Behavioral Sciences Department at the University of Arkansas at Monticello. She graduated from the UALR William H. Bowen School of Law with Honors and was named the William H. Bowen 2007 Outstanding Woman Graduate.

Brent M. **Smith-Casanueva** is a Ph.D. student in cultural studies and a Graduate Council Fellow at Stony Brook University. His dissertation focuses on the dialectic of enlightenment in science fiction television and televisual technology. His work has appeared in *Rupkatha Journal* and *CLCWeb: Comparative Literature and Culture*.

Nelly **Strehlau** is a Ph.D. candidate and lecturer in the Department of English at Nicolaus Copernicus University in Toruń, Poland. Her primary research interests include American and British culture, feminism and postfeminism, gender studies and media studies. She co-edited the volume *Re-Imagining the First World War* (2015). She has presented and published on intersections of gender, class, ethnicity and (post)feminism in television.

Rhonda V. **Wilcox** is a professor of English at Gordon State College and past president of the Whedon Studies Association. She is editor of *Studies in Popular Culture* and coeditor of *Slayage: The Journal of the Whedon Studies Association*. She is the author of *Why* Buffy *Matters* (2005); coeditor, with David Lavery, of *Fighting the Forces* (2002); with Tanya R. Cochran, of *Investigating* Firefly *and* Serenity; and, with Sue Turnbull, of *Investigating* Veronica Mars (2011).

Lowery A. **Woodall** III is an assistant professor of communication and theatre at Millersville University in Pennsylvania. He is the faculty advisor to the campus radio station, WIXQ 91.7-FM. He received a Ph.D. from the University of Southern Mississippi and has written extensively on representations of otherness in popular culture through mass media texts. His most recent works focus on how this intersection is manifested through comic books, popular television and professional wrestling.

Combined Bibliography

Acton, Thomas, and Gary Mundy, eds. *Romani Culture and Gypsy Identity*. Hatfield, England: University of Hertfordshire Press, 1997.

Adams, Michael. "Beyond Slayer Slang: Pragmatics, Discourse, and Style in *Buffy the Vampire Slayer*." *Slayage: The Journal of the Whedon Studies Association* 20. 2006.

Agnew, Robert. "A Revised Strain Theory of Delinquency." *Social Forces*. 1 vol. 64 151–167. 1985.

Agnew, Robert, and Helene Raskin White. "An Empirical Test of General Strain Theory." *Criminology* 30: 475–499. 1992.

Alderman, Naomi, and Annette Seidel-Arpaci. "Imaginary Para-Sites of the Soul: Vampires and Representation of 'Blackness' and 'Jewishness' in the *Buffy/Angel*-verse." *Slayage: The Journal of the Whedon Studies Association* 3(2). 2003.

Alessio, Dominic. "'Things Are Different Now?': A Post-Colonial Analysis of *Buffy the Vampire Slayer*." *European Legacy* 6.6. 2001. 731–40.

Alexander, Bobby. "Ritual and Current Studies of Ritual: Overview." In *Anthropology of Religion: A Handbook*. ed. Stephen D. Glazier. Westport, CT: Greenwood Press, 1997. 139–60.

Alexander, Michelle. *The New Jim Crow: Mass Incarceration in the Age of Colorblindness*. New York: The New Press, 2012. Kindle Reader e-book.

Alim, Samy H. *Articulate While Black: Barack Obama, Language and Race in the U.S.* New York: Oxford University Press, 2012.

Allen, Randall. "Arizona's 2010 Immigration Law: Theoretical, Political, and Constitutional Issues." *Journal of Global Intelligence & Policy*. 3(3). 2010.

Anderson, Lisa. *Mammies No More: The Changing Image of Black Women on Stage and Screen*. Lanham, MD: Rowman & Littlefield, 1997.

Bachman, Richard. *Thinner*. New York: Penguin, 1985.

Bakker, Peter, Milena Hübschmannová, Valdemar Kalinin, Donald Kenrick, Hristo Kyuchukov, Yaron Matras, and Giulio Soravia. *What Is the Romani Language*. Hatfield, England: University of Hertfordshire Press, 2000.

Baldwin, James. "Autobiographical Notes." In *Notes of a Native Son*. Boston: Beacon Press, 1984. 3–9.

Barthes, Roland. "Myth Today." In *A Barthes Reader*, edited by Sonia Sontag, 93–149. New York: Hill and Wang, 1982.

Battis, Jes. *Blood Relations: Chosen Families in* Buffy the Vampire Slayer *and* Angel. Jefferson, NC: McFarland, 2005.

Beety, Valena Elizabeth. "What the Brain Saw: The Case of Trayvon Martin and the

"Need for Eye-Witness Identification Reform." *Denver University Law Review.* 90 (2). 2012. 331–346.

Bentham, Jeremy. *An Introduction to the Principles of Morals and Legislation.* Oxford: Clarendon Press, 1907.

Berman, Sanford. *Prejudices and Antipathies: A Tract on the LC Subject Heads Concerning People.* Metuchen, NJ: The Scarecrow Press, 1971.

Bernstein, Abbie. "Who's the Joss? *The Official* Buffy the Vampire Slayer *&* Angel *Yearbook.*" London: Titan Publishing, 2006. 14–21.

Bianculli, David. "*Fresh Air* Interview with Joss Whedon." In *Joss Whedon: Conversations,* eds. David Lavery and Cynthia Burkhead. Jackson: University Press of Mississippi, 2011. 4.

Bing, Janet, and Dana Heller. "How Many Lesbians Does It Take to Screw in a Light Bulb?" *Humor, 16*(2). 2003. 157–182.

Bogle, Donald. *Toms, Coons, Mulattoes, Mammies and Bucks: An Interpretive History of Blacks in American Films.* 3rd ed. New York: Continuum Publishing Company, 1996.

Bonilla-Silva, Eduardo. *Racism Without Racists: Color-blind Racism and Racial Inequality in Contemporary America.* 3rd ed. Lanham, MD: Rowman & Littlefield, 2010.

_____. "The Strange Enigma of Race in Contemporary America." In *Racism Without Racists: Color-Blind Racism and Racial Inequality in Contemporary America,* 1–24. 3rd ed. Lanham, MD: Rowman & Littlefield, 2010.

Bowser, Eileen. *Biograph Bulletins 1908–1912.* New York: Octagon Books, 1973.

Boyd, Todd. *African Americans and Popular Culture: Theater, Film, and Television.* Santa Barbara: ABC-CLIO, 2008.

Breaking "Gypsy" Stereotypes. N.D. *Voice of Roma.* http://www.voiceofroma.com/culture/gyp_vs_rom.shtml.

Bridger, David. *The New Jewish Encyclopedia.* New York: Behrman House, 1976.

Broidy, Lisa. "A Test of General Strain Theory." *Criminology* 39(1). 9–36. 2001.

Brown, Jeffrey. *Dangerous Curves: Action Heroines, Gender, Fetishism, and Popular Culture.* Jackson: University Press of Mississippi, 2011.

Brown, Rebecca. "Orientalism in *Firefly* and *Serenity.*" *Slayage, 7*(1). 2008.

Brown, Simone, and Ben Carrington. "The Obamas and the New Politics of Race." *Qualitative Sociology.* 35:2. (2013). 113–121.

Brownstein, Ronald. "Americans Are Once Again Divided by Race." *National Journal.* 2013. http://www.nationaljournal.com/columns/political-connections/americans-are-once-again-divided-by-race-20130725.

Brunsdon, Charlotte. "The Feminist in the Kitchen: Martha, Martha and Nigella." In *Feminism in Popular Culture,* eds. Joanne Hollows and Rachel Moseley, 41–56. New York: Berg, 2006.

Burks, Ruth E. "Intimations of Invisibility: Black Women and Contemporary Hollywood Cinema." In *Mediated Messages and African-American Culture,* edited by Venise T. Berry and Carmen L. Manning-Miller, 24–51. London: Sage, 1996.

Byrne, Bridget. "Post-Race? Nation, Inheritance and the Contradictory Performativity of Race in Barack Obama's 'A More Perfect Union' Speech." *thirdspace: a journal of feminist theory & culture.* 10(1). 2011. 1–18.

Cadenas, Kerensa. "Interview with Kai Cole—Producer of *Much Ado About Nothing.*" *Women and Hollywood.* 2013. www.blogs.indiewire.com/womenandhollywood.

Calabresi, Massimo. "The Next Verdict from the Zimmerman Trial." *Time* magazine, July 14, 2013.

Cameron, Marc. "The Importance of Being the Zeppo: Xander, Gender Identity and Hybridity in *Buffy the Vampire Slayer.*" *Slayage: the Online International Journal of Whedon Studies,* 6(3). (2007).

Caminero-Santangelo, Marta. *The Madwoman Can't Speak, Or, Why Insanity Is Not Subversive.* Ithaca: Cornell University Press, 1998.

Campbell, Joseph. *The Hero with a Thousand Faces.* Bollingen Series XVII: Princeton University Press, 1949.

Capehart, Jonathan. "Race and the George Zimmerman Trial." *The Washington Post.* 2013. www.washingtonpost.com.

Čapek, Karel. *R.U.R.* London: Oxford University Press, 1928.

Chang, Robert S. "Toward an Asian American Legal Scholarship: Critical Race Theory, Post-Structuralism, and Narrative Space." *California Law Review,* 81(5): 1243–1322. 1993.

Chimezie, Amuzie. *Black Culture, Theory and Practice.* Shaker Heights: The Keeble Press, 1984.

Chin, Vivian. "Buffy? She's Like Me, She's Not Like Me—She's Rad." In *Athena's Daughters: Television's New Women Warriors,* eds. Frances Early and Kathleen Kennedy, 92–102. Syracuse: Syracuse University Press, 2003.

Chun, Wendy Hui Kyong. "Introduction: Race and/as Technology; Or, How to Do Things to Race." *Camera Obscura.* 24, no. 1. 2009. 7–34.

Churchill, Ward. *Fantasies of the Master Race: Literature, Cinema, and the Colonization of American Indians.* San Francisco: City Lights, 1998.

Clark, Colin. "Severity Has Often Enraged but Never Subdued a Gipsy: The History and Making of European Romani Stereotypes." *The Role of the Romanies: Images and Counter-Images of "Gypsies"/Romanies in European Cultures.* Eds. Nicholas Saul and Susan Tebbutt. Liverpool: Liverpool University Press, 2004. 226–246.

Clemons, Leigh. "Real Vampires Don't Wear Shorts: The Aesthetics of Fashion in *Buffy the Vampire Slayer.*" *Slayage: The Journal of the Whedon Studies Association.* 22. 2006.

Coates, Richard. "Boyz of New Black City." *Time* 137, no. 24. June 17, 1991. 64.

Cohen, Albert. "The Sociology of the Deviant Act: Anomie Theory and Beyond." *American Sociological Review.* 30(1). 5–14. 1965.

Collins, Patricia H. *Black Feminist Thought: Knowledge, Consciousness and the Politics of Empowerment.* New York: Routledge, 1991.

_____. *Black Sexual Politics: African-Americans, Gender and the New Racism.* New York: Routledge, 2004.

_____. "A Telling Difference: Dominance, Strength, and Black Masculinities." *Progressive Black Masculinities.* Ed. Athena D. Mutua New York: Routledge, 2006. 75.

Condon, Bill. *Chicago,* Dir. Rob Marshall Miramax Home Entertainment, 2002.

Connelly, Tom, and Shelley S. Rees. "Alienation and the Dialectics of History in Joss Whedon's *Dollhouse.*" *Slayage: The Online International Journal of Buffy Studies.* 2010.

Coover, Gail E. "Television and Social Identity: Race Representation as White Accommodation." *Journal of Broadcasting & Electronic Media.* v.45 13. 2001.

Cross, William E., Jr. *Shades of Black: Diversity in African American Identity.* Philadelphia: Temple University Press, 1991.

Curry, Agnes. "We Don't Say Indian: On the Paradoxical Construction of the Reavers." Unpublished paper presented at The Slayage Conference on the Whedonverses. Gordon College, Barnesville, GA. 2006.

Dean, Paul. "Gypsies Are Banding Together to Fight Age-Old Stereotypes." *Los Angeles Times.* October 5, 1986.

Delgado, Richard, and Jean Stefancic. *Critical Race Theory: An Introduction.* New York: NYU Press, 2001.

Dicker, Rory Cooke, and Alison Piepmeier. "Introduction." In *Catching a Wave: Reclaiming Feminism for the 21st Century,* eds. Rory Cooke Dicker and Alison Piepmeir, 3–28. Boston: Northeastern University Press, 2003.

Dickerson, Debra J. *The End of Blackness: Returning the Souls of Black Folk to Their Rightful Owners.* New York: Anchor Books, 2005.

Doane, Mary Ann. "Information, Crisis, Catastrophe." In *Logics of Television: Essays in Cultural Criticism,* edited by Patricia Mellencamp, 222–239. Bloomington: Indiana University Press, 1990.

Dobreva, Nikolina Ivantcheva. "The Curse of the Traveling Dancer: Romani Representation From the 19th Century European Literature to Hollywood Film and Beyond." Ph.D. thesis. University of Massachusetts Amherst. 2009.

Dunn, Stephane. *"Baad Bitches" and Sassy Supermamas: Black Power Action Films.* Chicago: University of Illinois Press, 2008.

Durand, Kevin K. "Cannon Fodder: Assembling the Text." In *Buffy Meets the Academy: Essays on the Episodes and Scripts as Texts,* ed. Kevin K. Durand, 9–16. Jefferson, NC: McFarland, 2009.

Durkheim, Emile. "On Anomie." In *Criminological Theory: Foundations and Perceptions,* edited by Stephen Shafer, Richard D. Knudten. New York: Lexington Books, 1972.

Eade, John, and Michael J. Sallnow. "Introduction." In *Contesting the Sacred: The Anthropology of Christian Pilgrimage.* Eds. John Eade and Michael J. Sallnow, Urbana: University of Illinois Press, 2000.

Edgerton, Gary R. "Introduction: Television as Historian: A Different Kind of History Altogether." In *Television Histories: Shaping Collective Memory in the Media Age,* eds. Gary R. Edgerton and Peter C. Rollins, 1–18. Lexington: The University Press of Kentucky, 2001.

Edwards, Lynne. "Slaying in Black and White: Kendra as Tragic Mulatta." In *Buffy. Fighting the Forces: What's at Stake in Buffy the Vampire Slayer,* eds. Rhonda Wilcox and David Lavery, 85–97. Lanham, MD: Rowman & Littlefield, 2004.

Eliade, Mircea. *The Sacred and the Profane: The Nature of Religion.* Translated by Willard R. Trask. London: Harcourt Brace, 1987.

Emmons-Featherston, Sally. "Is That Stereotype Dead? Working With and Against 'Western' Stereotypes in *Buffy.*" In *The Truth of Buffy: Essays on Fiction Illuminating Reality.* Eds. Emily Dial-Driver, Sally Emmons-Fetherston, Jim Ford and Carolyn Anne Taylor. Jefferson, NC: McFarland, 2008. 55–66.

Entman, Robert. "Modern Racism and the Images of Blacks in Local Television News." *Critical Studies in Mass Communication.* 7(4). 1990. 332–345.

Entman, Robert, and Andrew Rojecki. *The Black Image in the White Mind: Media and Race in America.* Chicago: University of Chicago Press, 2001.

Espenson, Jane. "Introduction." *Slayer Slang: A* Buffy the Vampire Slayer *Lexicon.* Ed. Michael Adams. Oxford and New York: Oxford University Press, 2003.

_____. "Playing Hard to 'Get': How to Write Cult TV." In *The Cult TV Book,* edited by Stacey Abbott, 45–53. London: I.B. Tauris, 2010.

_____. "Writing the Vampire Slayer." In *Reading the Vampire Slayer: The New, Updated Unofficial Guide to* Buffy *and* Angel, ed. Roz Kaveney. 100–117. London: Tauris Parke, 2004.

Esposito, Jennifer, J. "What Does Race Have to Do with *Ugly Betty*?: An Analysis of Privilege and Postracial (?) Representation on a Television Sitcom. *Television New Media.* 10, 2012. 521–535.

Estes, Steve. *I Am a Man!: Race, Manhood, and the Civil Rights Movement.* Chapel Hill: University of North Carolina Press, 2005.

Fabian, Jordan. "Zimmerman Acquittal: We Don't Live in a Post-Racial America." *ABC News.* July 14, 2013.

Farrán, Ofelia. "'Cuanto Más Escribo, Más Me Queda Por Decir': Memory, Trauma, and Writing in the Work of Jorge Semprun." *MLN* 116.2. 2001. 266–94.

Ferguson, Christopher J. "Positive Female Role-Models Eliminate Negative Effects of Sexually Violent Media." *Journal of Communication.* 2012. 1–12.

Fisher, Emily L., Grace Deason, Eugene Borgida, and Clifton M. Oyamot. "A Model of Authoritarianism, Social Norms, and Personal Values: Implications for Arizona Law Enforcement and Immigration Policy." *Analyses of Social Issues & Public Policy.* 11(1). 2011. 285–299.

Foucault, Michel. "Film and Popular Memory." *Edinburgh Magazine.* 1977. 2.

Fraser, Angus. *The Gypsies.* Cambridge and Oxford: Blackwell, 1992.

Fritts, David. "Buffy's Seven Season Initiation." In *Buffy Meets the Academy: Essays on the Episodes and Scripts as Text*, ed. Kevin K. Durand, 32–44. Jefferson, NC: McFarland, 2009.

_____. "Warrior Heroes: *Buffy the Vampire Slayer* and *Beowulf.*" *Slayage: The Online International Journal of* Buffy *Studies.* Issue 17. 2005.

Fuchs, Cynthia. "'Did Anyone Ever Explain to You What "Secret Identity" Means?' Race and Displacement in *Buffy* and *Dark Angel.*" In *Undead TV: Essays on Buffy the Vampire Slayer.* Eds. Elana Levine and Lisa Parks. Durham: Duke University Press, 2007. 96–115.

Fuller, Linda. *The Cosby Show: Audiences, Impact and Implications* Westport, CT: Greenwood Press, 1992.

Gallardo, Ximena C., and Jason C. Smith. *Alien Woman: The Making of Lt. Ellen Ripley.* New York: Continuum, 2004.

_____. "From 'Figurative Males' to Action Heroines: Further Thoughts on Active Women in the Cinema." *Screen* 40.1. 38–50. 1999.

George, David. "On Origins: Behind the Rituals." *Performance Research: A Journal of Performing Arts.* 3 (3). 1–14. 1998.

Giddens, Anthony. *The Consequences of Modernity.* Cambridge: Polity Press, 1990. 102.

Giddens, Anthony, and Christopher Pierson. *Conversations with Anthony Giddens. Making Sense of Modernity.* Cambridge: Polity Press, 1998. 94.

Gill, Candra K. "'Cuz the Black Chick Always Gets It First": Dynamics of Race in *Buffy the Vampire Slayer.*" In *Girls Who Bite Back: Witches, Mutants, Slayers and Freaks.* Ed. Emily Pohl-Weary. Toronto: Sumach Press, 2004. 39–55.

Girard, René. *Violence and the Sacred.* Translated by Patrick Gregory. Baltimore: Johns Hopkins University Press, 1979.

Glajar, Valentina, and Domnica Radulescu, eds. *"Gypsies" in European Literature and Culture.* New York: Palgrave, 2008.

Gocić, Goran. *Notes from the Underground: The Cinema of Emir Kusturica.* London: Wallflower Press, 2001. 93.

Golden, Christopher, Stephen R. Bissette, and Thomas E. Sniegoski. Buffy *the Vampire Slayer: The Monster Book.* New York: Pocket Books, 2000.

Golden, Christopher, and Nancy Holder. *Buffy the Vampire Slayer—The Watcher's Guide.* New York: Simon & Schuster, 1998.

Golden, Christopher, Eric Powell, Drew Geraci, Keith Barnett and Guy Major. *Spike and Dru: All's Fair*. Milwaukie, OR: Dark Horse Comics, 7 December 2000.

Gray, Herman. *Watching Race: Television and the Struggle for "Blackness."* Minneapolis: University of Minnesota Press, 1995.

Greenberg, Bradley, Dana Mastro, and Jeffery Brand. "Minorities and the Mass Media: Television into the 21st Century." In *Media Effects: Advances in Theory and Research*. Eds. Jennings Bryant and Dolt Zillmann. 2nd edition. Mahwah, NJ: Lawrence Erlbaum Associates, 2002. 333–352.

Greene, Eric. "The Good Book." In *Serenity Found: More Unauthorized Essays on Joss Whedon's* Firefly *Universe*. Ed. Jane Epenson. Dallas: BenBella Books, 2007.

Hall, Stuart. "Cultural Identity and Cinematic Representation." *Framework*. 36. 68–81. 1989.

_____, ed. *Representation: Cultural Representations and Signifying Practices*. London: Sage Publications, 1997.

_____. "What Is This 'black' in Black Popular Culture?" *Social Justice*. 20 (1/2). 1993. 104–14.

Hancock, Ian. "The 'Gypsy' Stereotype and the Sexualization of Romani Women." *"Gypsies" in European Literature and Culture*. Eds. Valentina Glajar and Domnica Radulescu. New York: Palgrave MacMillan, 2008. 181–191.

_____. *A Handbook of Vlax Romani*. Columbus, OH: Slavica, 1995.

_____. "The Origin and Function of the Gypsy Image in Children's Literature." *The Lion and the Unicorn*. 11 (1). 47–59. 1987.

_____. *The Pariah Syndrome: An Account of Gypsy Slavery and Persecution*. Ann Arbor, MI: Karoma Publishers, 1987.

_____. *We Are the Romani People*. Hertfordshire: University of Hertfordshire Press, 2002.

Hardt, Michael, and Antoni Negri. *Empire*. Cambridge: Harvard University Press, 2000.

Harvey, David. *A Brief History of Neoliberalism*. Oxford: Oxford University Press, 2005.

Havens, Candace. *Joss Whedon: The Genius Behind Buffy*. Dallas: BenBella Books, 2003.

Hawk, Julie L. "Hacking the Read-Only File: Collaborative Narrative as Ontological Construction in *Dollhouse*." *Slayage: The Online International Journal of Buffy Studies*. 2010.

Hayles, Katherine N. *How We Became Posthuman: Virtual Bodies in Cybernetics, Literature, and Informatics*. Chicago: University of Chicago Press, 1999.

Heinecken, Dawn. *The Warrior Women of Television: A Feminist Cultural Analysis of the New Female Body in Popular Media*. New York: Peter Lang Publishing, 2003.

Helford, Elyce, R. 2002. "My Emotions Give Me Power": The Containment of Girls' Anger in *Buffy*." In *Fighting the Forces: What's at Stake in* Buffy the Vampire Slayer. Eds. Rhonda V. Wilcox and David Lavery. Lanham, MD: Rowman and Littlefield. 2002. 18–34.

Hiatt, Robert M. "Revised LS Subject Headings." *Cataloging Service Bulletin* 93 (2001). 50–56.

Hill, Matthew B. "'I Am a Leaf on the Wind': Cultural Trauma and Mobility in Joss Whedon's *Firefly*." *Extrapolation*. 50 (3). 2009. 484–511.

Hoagland, Ericka, and Reema Sarwal. "Introduction to *Science Fiction*." In *Imperialism and the Third World: Essays on Postcolonial Literature and Film*, eds. Ericka Hoagland and Reema Sarwal. Jefferson, NC: McFarland, 2010.

Holder, Nancy. *Buffy the Vampire Slayer: The Watcher's Guide.* Vol. 2. New York: Pocket Books, 2000.

hooks, bell. *Ain't I a Woman: Black Women and Feminism.* Boston: South End Press, 1984.

_____. *Black Looks: Race and Representation.* Boston: South End Press, 1992.

_____. *Feminism Is for Everybody: Passionate Politics.* Cambridge: South End Press, 2000.

_____. *Feminist Theory: From Margin to Center.* Boston: South End Press, 1984.

_____. *Killing Rage: Ending Racism.* New York: Henry Holt, 1995.

_____. *Outlaw Culture: Resisting Representations.* New York: Routledge, 1994.

_____. *Reel to Real.* New York: Routledge, 2009.

_____. *Talking Back: Thinking Feminist, Thinking Black.* Boston: South End Press, 1989.

Hoskin, Anthony. "Explaining the Link Between Race and Violence with General Strain Theory." *Journal of Ethnicity in Criminal Justice.* 9 (1). 2011. 56–73.

Hughey, Matthew. "Show Me Your Papers! Obama's Birth and the Whiteness of Belonging." *Qualitative Sociology.* 35(2). 2012. 163–181.

Hung, Eric. "The Meaning of 'World Music' in *Firefly.*" In *Buffy, Ballads, and Bad Guys Who Sing: Music in the Worlds of Joss Whedon,* Ed. Kendra Preston Leonard. Lanham, MD: The Scarecrow Press, 2011. 255–273.

Hunt, Darnell M. *Channeling Blackness: Studies on Television and Race in America.* Oxford: Oxford University Press, 2004.

_____. "Making Sense of Blackness on Television." *Channeling Blackness: Studies on Television and Race in America,* Ed. Darnell M. Hunt. Oxford: Oxford University Press, 2004.

Hurwitz, Jon, and Mark Peffley. "Public Perceptions of Race and Crime: The Role of Racial Stereotypes." *American Journal of Political Science,* 41(2). 1997. 375–401.

Iordanova, Dina. "Mimicry and Plagiarism: Reconciling Actual and Metaphoric Gypsies." *Third Text.* 22 (3). 2008.

Isaksson, Malin. "Buffy/Faith Adult Femslash: Queer Porn with a Plot." *Slayage: The Journal of the Whedon Studies Association.* 7.4. 2009.

Jameson, Fredric. "Cognitive Mapping." In *Marxism and the Interpretation of Culture,* eds. Cary Nelson and Lawrence Grossberg, 347–360. Urbana and Chicago: University of Illinois Press, 1998.

Jameson, Fredric. "Fear and Loathing in Globalization." In *What Democracy Looks Like: A New Critical Realism for a Post-Seattle World,* eds. Amy Schrager Lang and Cecila Tichi, 123–130. New Brunswick, NJ: Rutgers University Press, 2006.

Jeffries, Michael P. *Paint the White House Black: Barack Obama and the Meaning of Race in America.* Palo Alto, CA: Stanford University Press, 2013.

Jenkins, Alice, and Susan Stuart. "Extending Your Mind: Non-Standard Perlocutionary Acts in 'Hush.'" *Slayage: The Journal of the Whedon Studies Association.* 3.1. 2003.

Jewell, Sue K. *From Mammy to Miss America and Beyond: Cultural Images and the Shaping of US Social Policy.* New York: Routledge, 1993.

Johnson, Allan G. *Privilege, Power, and Difference.* 2nd ed. New York: McGraw-Hill, 2006.

Jowett, Lorna. *Sex and the Slayer: A Gender Studies Primer for the Buffy Fan.* Middletown, CT: Wesleyan University Press, 2005.

Kaplan, Brett Ashley. "'The Bitter Residue of Death': Jorge Semprun and the Aesthetics of Holocaust Memory." *Comparative Literature.* 55 (4). 320–337. 2003.

Karras, Irene. "The Third Wave's Final Girl: *Buffy the Vampire Slayer.*" *thirdspace: a journal of feminist theory & culture.* 1 (2). 2002.

Kaufman, M. Joanne, and J. Ceaser Rebellon, Sherod Thaxton, and Robert Agnew. "A General Strain Theory of Racial Differences in Criminal Offending." *The Australian and New Zealand Journal of Criminology.* 41 (3). 421–439. 2008.

Kauffman, Stanley. *American Film Criticism: From the Beginnings to Citizen Cane.* New York: Livright, 1972. 7–8.

Kaveney, Roz. *Reading the Vampire Slayer: An Unofficial Critical Companion to Buffy and Angel.* London: I.B. Tauris, 2001.

Kenrick, Donald. *Historical Dictionary of the Gypsies (Romanies).* 2d ed. Lanham, MD: The Scarecrow Press, 2007.

Kenrick, Donald, and Grattan Puxon. *Gypsies Under the Swastika.* Hatfield, England: University of Herfordshire Press, 1995.

Kirkland, Ewan. "The Caucasian Persuasion of *Buffy the Vampire Slayer.*" *Slayage: The Online International Journal of Buffy Studies,* 5(1). 2005.

Kleinen, John. "Framing 'the Other.' A Critical Review of Vietnam War Movies and Their Representation of Asians and Vietnamese." *Asia Europe Journal,* 1(3). 433–451. 2003.

Klímova-Alexander, Ilona. *The Romani Voice in World Politics: The United Nations and Non-State Actors.* Hants, England: Ashgate, 2005.

Knight, Gladys L. *Female Action Heroes: A Guide to Women in Comics, Video Games, Film, and Television.* Santa Barbara, CA: ABC-Clio, 2010.

Kochhar, Rakesh, Richard Fry, and Paul Taylor. "Wealth Gaps Rise to Record Highs Between Whites, Blacks and Hispanics." *Pew Research Center.* July 26 2011.

Kociemba, David. "Understanding the Espensode." In *Buffy Goes Dark: Essays on the Final Two Seasons of* Buffy the Vampire Slayer *on Television.* Eds. Lynne Y. Edwards, Elizabeth L. Rambo, and James B. South, 23–29. Jefferson, NC: McFarland, 2009.

Koontz, K. Dale. "Czech Mate: Whedon, Čapek, and the Foundations of *Dollhouse.*" *Slayage* 8 (2&3).

_____. *Faith and Choice in the Works of Joss Whedon* Jefferson, NC: McFarland, 2008.

Köpping, Klaus-Peter, Bernard Leistle, and Michael Rudolph. "Introduction." In *Ritual and Identity: Performative Practices as Effective Transformations of Social Reality,* eds. Klaus-Peter Köpping, Bernard Leistle, and Michael Rudolph. Berlin: Lit Verlag, 2006.

Langer, Lawrence. *The Holocaust and the Literary Imagination.* New Haven: Yale University Press, 1975.

Lantz, Victoria P. "Numero Cinco, Border Narratives, and Mexican Cultural Performance in *Angel.*" In *The Literary* Angel: *Essays on Influences and Traditions Reflected in the Joss Whedon Series,* eds. AmiJo Comeford and Tamy Burnett, 98–111. Jefferson, NC: McFarland, 2010.

Larson, Stephanie Greco. *Media and Minorities: The Politics of Race in News and Entertainment.* Lanham, MD: Rowman & Littlefield, 2006.

Lavender, Isaiah III. *Race in American Science Fiction.* Bloomington: Indiana University Press, 2011.

Lavery, David A. *Joss Whedon: A Creative Portrait.* London: I.B. Tauris, 2013.

_____. "I wrote my thesis on you: *Buffy* studies as an academic cult." *Slayage Online Journal,* 13/14 (4.1–2). 2004.

Lee, Ronald. "Roma in Europe: 'Gypsy' Myth and Romani Reality—New Evidence For Romani History." In *"Gypsies" in European Literature and Culture*, eds. Valentina Glajar and Domnica Radulescu, 1–28. New York: Palgrave, 2008.

Leggatt, Judith. "Critiquing Economic and Environmental Colonization: Globalization and Science Fiction in *The Moons of Palmares*." In *Science Fiction, Imperialism and the Third World: Essays on Postcolonial Literature and Film*, eds. Ericka Hoagland and Reema Sarwal, 127–140. Jefferson, NC: McFarland, 2010.

Lenin, Ronit. *Israel and the Daughters of the Holocaust: Reoccupying the Territories of Silence*. New York: Berghahn Books, 2000.

Lerner, Neil. "Music, Race, and Paradoxes of Representation: Jubal Early's Musical Motif of Barbarism in 'Objects in Space.'" In *Investigating* Firefly *and* Serenity: *Science Fiction on the Frontier*, eds. Rhonda Wilcox and Tanya R. Cochran, 183–190. London: I.B. Tauris, 2008.

Levi, Primo. *The Drowned and the Saved*. Trans. Raymond Rosenthal. New York: Vintage Books, 1989.

Levitt, Steven. "The Changing Relationship Between Income and Crime Victimization." *Economic Policy Review*. 5. 87–98. 1999.

Lichter, Robert, and Daniel Amundson. "Distorted Reality: Hispanic Characters in TV Entertainment." In *Latin Looks: Images of Latinas and Latinos in the U.S. Media*, eds. Clara E. Rodríguez, 85–103. Boulder: Westview Press, 1997.

Lim, Thea. "Joss Whedon and the Blurry Line Between Homage and Appropriation." *Racialicious*. February 16, 2009.

Little, Tracy. "High School Is Hell: Metaphor Made Literal in *Buffy the Vampire Slayer*." In *Buffy the Vampire Slayer and Philosophy: Fear and Trembling in Sunnydale*, ed. James South, 282–293. Chicago: Open Court, 2003.

Logan, Michael. "Sarah Smiles." *TV Guide*. 1998. 19–29.

Looby, Christopher. "'As Thoroughly Black as the Most Faithful Philanthropist Could Desire': Erotics of Race in Higginson's *Army Life in a Black Regiment*." In *Race and the Subject of Masculinities*, eds. Harry Stecopoulos and Michael Uebel. Durham: Duke University Press, 1997.

Lorraine, Ali, Jeff Giles, and Marc Peyser. "Newsmakers." *Newsweek*. 14 January 2002.

Lowe, Edward T., and Perley Poore Sheehan. *The Hunchback of Notre Dame*. DVD. Dir. Wallace Worsley. Hollywood, CA: Image Entertainment, 1923.

Lyotard, Jean-Francois. *Heidegger and "the jews."* Translated by Andreas Michael and Mark Roberts. Minneapolis: University of Minnesota Press, 1990.

MacDonald, Fred J. *Blacks and White TV: African Americans in Television Since 1948* [Second edition]. Florence, KY: Wadsworth Publishing, 1992.

Magana, Lisa, and Erik Lee. *Latino Politics and Arizona's Immigration Law SB 1070*. New York: Springer, 2013.

Makward, Christiane. "To Be or Not to Be ... A Feminist Speaker." In *The Future of Difference*, eds. Hester Eisenstein and Alice Jardine. 95–105. New Brunswick, NJ: Rutgers University Press, 1985.

Malahy, Lori Wu, Mara Sedlins, Jason Plaks, and Yuichi Shonda. "Black and White, or Shades of Gray? Racial Labeling of Barack Obama Predicts Implicit Race Perception." *Analysis of Social Issues & Public Policy*. 10(1). 207–222. 2010.

Mandala, Susan. "Representing the Future: Chinese and Codeswitching in *Firefly*." In *Investigating* Firefly *and* Serenity: *Science Fiction on the Frontier*. Eds. Rhonda V. Wilcox and Tanya R. Cochran. London: I.B. Tauris, 2008.

Masson, Cynthea. "'Evil's Spreading, Sir—And It's Not Just Over There!': Nazism in *Buffy* and *Angel*." In *Monsters in the Mirror: Representations of Nazism in Post-*

War Popular Culture, eds. Sara Buttsworth and Maartje Abbenhuis, 179–199. Oxford: Praeger, 2010.

_____. "'Is That Just a Comforting Way of Not Answering the Question?': Willow, Questions, and Affective Response in *Buffy the Vampire Slayer*." *Slayage: The Journal of the Whedon Studies Association* 5 (4). 2006.

Masson, Cynthea, and Marni Stanley. "Queer Eye of That Vampire Guy: Spike and the Aesthetics of Camp." *Slayage: The Journal of the Whedon Studies Association* 6 (2). 2006.

Matras, Yaron. *Romani: A Linguistic Introduction*. Cambridge: Cambridge University Press, 2002.

_____. "What the Hell?: *Angel*'s 'The Girl in Question.'" Presented at *SC3: the Slayage Conference on the Whedonverses*. Henderson State College, Arkadelphia, Arkansas, 2008.

Matthews, Jodie. "Back Where They Belong: Gypsies, Kidnapping and Assimilation in Victorian Children's Literature." *Romani Studies*. 20 (2). 137–159. 2010.

Matua, D. Athena. "Theorizing Progressive Black Masculinities." In *Progressive Black Masculinities*, ed. Athena D. Mutua, 21–22. New York: Routledge, 2006.

McKee, Alan. "'Superboong! ...': The Ambivalence of Comedy and Differing Histories of Race." *Media and Cultural Studies*. 10(2). 44–59. 1996.

McIntosh, Peggy. "White Privilege: Unpacking the Invisible Knapsack." In *Understanding Prejudice and Discrimination*, ed. Scott Plous, 191–196. New York: McGraw-Hill, 2003.

McRobbie, Angela. "Young Women and Consumer Culture: An Intervention." *Cultural Studies*. 22. 531–550, 2008.

Merimee, Prosper, and Charlie Chaplin. *A Burlesque on Carmen*, directed by Charlie Chaplin in *Chaplin's Essanay Comedies*, Vol. 03 (1915; Image Entertainment, 1999).

Merton, K. Robert. "Social Structure and Anomie." *American Sociological Review*. 3 (5). 672–682. 1938.

Meyer, Michaela D. E. "From Rogue in the 'Hood to Suave in a Suit: Black Masculinity and the Transformation of Charles Gunn." In *Reading Angel: The TV Spin-off with a Soul*, ed. Stacy Abbott, 180–183. London: I.B. Tauris, 2005. 176–188.

Middents, Jeffery R. "A Sweet Vamp: Critiquing the Treatment of Race in *Buffy* and the American Musical Once More (with Feeling)." In *Buffy, Ballads, and Bad Guys Who Sing: Music in the Worlds of Joss Whedon*, ed. Kendra Preston Leonard, 119–132. Lanham, MD: The Scarecrow Press, 2011.

Mignolo, Walter. "The Geopolitics of Knowledge and the Colonial Difference." In *Coloniality at Large: Latin America and the Postcolonial Debate*, ed. Mabel Moraña, Enrique Dussel, and Carlos A. Jáuregui, 229–231. Durham, NC: Duke University Press, 2008.

_____. *The Idea of Latin America*. Malden, MA: Blackwell, 2005.

Mitchell, W.J.T. "Imperial Landscape." In *Landscape and Power*, edited by W.J.T. Mitchell. 5–34. Chicago: University of Chicago Press, 2002.

Mohanty, Chandra Talpade. *Feminism Without Borders: Decolonizing Theory, Practicing Solidarity*. Durham: Duke University Press, 2004.

Mok, Teresa. "Getting the Message: Media Images and Stereotypes and Their Effect on Asian Americans." *Cultural Diversity and Mental Health*. 4(3). 185–202. 1998.

Money, Mary Alice. "The Undemonization of Supporting Characters in *Buffy*." In *Fighting the Forces: What's at Stake in Buffy the Vampire Slayer*, eds. Rhonda V. Wilcox and David Lavery, 98–107. Lanham, MD: Rowman and Littlefield, 2002.

Morinis, Alan. "Introduction." In *Sacred Journeys: The Anthropology of Pilgrimage*, ed. Alan Morinis. Westport, CT: Greenwood Press, 1992.

Morris, Nicola. *The Golem in Jewish American Literature: Risks and Responsibilities in the Fiction of Thane Rosenbaum, Nomi Eve and Steve Stern.* New York: Peter Lang, 2007.

Muntersbjorn, Madeline. "Disgust, Difference, and Displacement in the *Dollhouse*." *Slayage* 8(2&3). 2010.

Murphy, Tab, Irene Mecchi, Bob Tzudiker, Noni White, and Jonathan Roberts. *The Hunchback of Notre Dame.* DVD. Dir. Gary Trousdale and Kirk Wise. Hollywood, CA: Walt Disney Studios Home Entertainment, 1996.

Murray, Mark. "America's Race Relations Take Hit After Zimmerman Verdict, NBC News/WSJ Poll Finds." www.msnbc.com. 2013.

Nama, Adilifu. *Black Space: Imagining Race in Science Fiction Film.* Austin: University of Texas Press, 2008.

Neroni, Hilary. *The Violent Woman: Femininity, Narrative, and Violence in Contemporary American Cinema.* Albany: State University of New York Press, 2005.

Newman, Alex. "The Exploitation of Trayvon Martin's Death." *New American.* 28(9). 20–26. 2012.

Nietzsche, Friedrich. *Thus Spoke Zarathustra: A Book for All and None.* London, 1986.

Noxon, Marti. "'Surprise' Shooting Script, November, 17, 1997." In Buffy the Vampire Slayer: *The Script Book: Season Two, Volume Three.* New York: Simon Pulse, 2001.

Nussbaum, Emily. "Must-See Metaphysics." *New York Times.* 9 September 2011. In *Joss Whedon: Conversations*, eds. David Lavery and Cynthia Burkhead, 64–70. Jackson: University Press of Mississippi, 2011.

O Yanko le Redjosko (Ian Hancock). *American Romani Cultural Vocabulary*, online resource. University of Texas at Austin: Romani Archive and Documentation Center. 2007.

Ono, Kent A. "Domesticating Terrorism: A Neocolonial Economy of Difference." In *Enterprise Zones: Critical Positions on Star Trek*, eds. Taylor Harrison, Sarah Projansky, Kent A. Ono, and Elyce Rae Helford, 157–186. Boulder, CO: Westview Press, 1996.

_____. "To Be a Vampire on *Buffy the Vampire Slayer*: Race and ('Other') Socially Marginalizing Positions on Horror TV." In *Fantasy Girls: Gender and the New Universe of Science Fiction and Fantasy Television*, ed. Elyce Rae Helford, 163–186. Lanham, MD: Rowman & Littlefield, 2000.

Oreck, Alden. *The Golem.* The Jewish Virtual Library. N.D.

Overbey, Karen Eileen, and Lahney Preston-Matto. "Staking in Tongues: Speech Act As Weapon in *Buffy*." In *Fighting the Forces: What's at Stake in Buffy the Vampire Slayer*, eds. Rhonda Wilcox and David Lavery, 73–84. Lanham, MD: Rowman & Littlefield, 2002.

Owen, Susan A. "*Buffy the Vampire Slayer*: Vampires, Postmodernity, and Postfeminism." *Journal of Popular Film and Television.* 27(2). 24–25. 1999.

Park, Ji Hoon, Nadine Gabbadon, and Ariel Chernin. "Naturalizing Racial Differences Through Comedy: Asian, Black, and White Views on Racial Stereotypes in Rush Hour 2." *Journal of Communication.* 56(1). 157–177. 2006.

Pateman, Matthew. *The Aesthetics of Culture in* Buffy the Vampire Slayer. Jefferson, NC: McFarland, 2006.

_____. "You Say Tomato: Englishness in *Buffy the Vampire Slayer*." *Cercles: Revue Pluridisciplinaire du Monde Anglophone.* 8. 103–113. 2003.

Pedwell, Carolyn. "The Limits of Cross-Cultural Analogy: Muslim Veiling and 'Western' Fashion and Beauty Practices." In *New Femininities: Postfeminism, Neoliberalism and Subjectivity*, eds. Rosalind Gill and Christina Scharff, 192–197. Houndmills, Basingstoke, Hampshire: Palgrave Macmillan, 2011.

Pender, Patricia. "Kicking Ass Is Comfort Food: Buffy as Third Wave Feminist Icon." In *Third Wave Feminism: A Critical Exploration*, eds. Stacy Gillis, Gillian Howie, and Rebecca Munford, 164–174. New York: Palgrave Macmillan, 2004.

Perdigao, Lisa K. "'This One's Broken': Rebuilding Whedonbots and Reprogramming the Whedonverse." *Slayage: The Online International Journal of Buffy Studies.* 2010.

Pickering, Michael. "Race, Gender and Broadcast Comedy: The Case of the Black Kentucky Minstrels." *European Journal of Communication.* 9(3). 311–333. 1994.

Playdon, Zoe-Jane. "'The Outsiders' Society': Religious Imagery in *Buffy the Vampire Slayer*." *Slayage: The Journal of the Whedon Studies Association.* 2(1). 2002.

Potts, Donna L. "Convents, Claddagh Rings, and Even The Book of Kells: Representing the Irish in *Buffy the Vampire Slayer*." *Studies in Media & Information Literacy Education.* 3(2). 1–9. 2003.

Prata Miller, J. "'The I in team': Buffy and Feminist Ethics." In *Buffy the Vampire Slayer and Philosophy: Fear and Trembling in Sunnydale*. Popular Culture and Philosophy, ed. James South, 35–48. Peru, IL: Open Court, 2003.

Pye, Douglas. "Movies and Tone." In *Movies and Tone; Reading Rohmer; Voices in Film*, eds. John Gibbs and Douglas Pye, 1–80. Close-Up Series 02. London: Wallflower, 2007.

Pyke, Karen, and Tran Dang. "'FOB' and 'Whitewashed': Identity and Internalized Racism Among Second Generation Asian Americans." *Qualitative Sociology.* 26(2). 147–172. 2003.

Quijano, Aníbal. "Coloniality of Power, Eurocentrism, and Social Classification." In *Coloniality at Large: Latin America and the Postcolonial Debate,* eds. Mabel Moraña, Enrique Dussel, and Carlos A. Jáuregui, 181–220. Durham, NC: Duke University Press, 2008.

Rabb, J. Douglas, and J. Michael Richardson. "Reavers and Redskins: Creating the Frontier Savage." *Investigating Firefly and Serenity: Science Fiction on the Frontier*, eds. Rhonda V. Wilcox and Tanya R. Cochran, 127–138. New York: I.B. Tauris, 2008.

Ramasubramanian, Srividya. "Pride, Prejudice, and Policy Preferences: Exploring the Relationships Between TV Stereotypes, Racial Attitudes, and Support for Affirmative Action." Paper presentation, Annual Meeting of the International Communication Association, 2009.

Ramírez Berg, Charles. "Stereotyping in Films in General and of the Hispanic in Particular." In *Latin Looks: Images of Latinas and Latinos in the U.S. Media*, ed. Clara E. Rodríguez, 85–103. Boulder, CO: Westview Press, 1997.

Randall, Kay. "What's in a Name? Professor Takes on Roles of Romani Activist and Spokesperson to Improve Plight of His Ethnic Group." University of Texas at Austin, 2003. https://web.archive.org/web/20050205135317/http://www.utexas.edu/features/archive/2003/romani.html.

Rich, A. John. *Wrong Place, Wrong Time: Trauma and Violence in the Lives of Young, Black Men*. Baltimore: The John Hopkins University Press, 2009.

Richardson, J. Michael, and J. Douglas Rabb. *The Existential Joss Whedon: Evil and Human Freedom in Buffy the Vampire Slayer, Angel, Firefly and Serenity*. Jefferson, NC: McFarland, 2007.

Rieder, John. *Colonialism and the Emergence of Science Fiction*. Middleton, CT: Wesleyan University Press, 2008.

_____. "Spectacle, Technology and Colonialism in SF Cinema: The Case of Wim Wenders' *Until the End of the World*." In *Red Planets: Marxism and Science Fiction*, eds. Mark Bould and China Miéville, 83–99. Middletown, CT: Wesleyan University Press, 2009.

Riordan, E. "Commodified Agents and Empowered Girls: Consuming and Producing Feminism." *Journal of Communication Inquiry. 25* (3). 280–297. 2001.

Román, Ediberto. "Who Exactly Is Living La Vida Loca? The Legal and Political Consequences of Latino-Latina Ethnic and Racial Stereotypes in Film and Other Media." *The Journal of Gender, Race, and Justice.* 4(1). 37–68. 2000.

Rosenhaft, Eve. "Blacks and Gypsies in Nazi Germany: The Limits of the 'Racial State.'" *History Workshop Journal.* 72. 161–170. 2011.

Rosman, Katherine. "Before He Was President, Mistaken for a Waiter: A 2003 Encounter with Obama." *Wall Street Journal Online.* 7 Nov 2011.

Rowley, Michelle V. "'It Could Have Been Me': Really? Early Morning Mediations on Trayvon Martin's Death." *Feminist Studies.* 38(2). 519–529. 2012.

Ryan, William. *Blaming the Victim*. 2nd ed. New York: Random House, 1976.

Said, Edward. *Culture and Imperialism*. New York: Alfred A. Knopf, 1993.

_____. *Orientalism,* New York: Random House, 1979.

St. Louis, Renee, and Miriam Riggs. "'And Yet': The Limits of *Buffy* Feminism." *Slayage: The Journal of the Whedon Studies Association.* 8.1 (2010).

Saul, Nicholas, and Susan Tebbutt. *The Role of the Romanies*. Liverpool: Liverpool University Press, 2004.

Scott, Monique. *Rethinking Evolution in the Museum. Envisioning African Origins*. New York: Routledge, 2007.

Screen Actors Guild (SAG). "Latest Casting Data Follows Historical Trends and Continues to Exclude People with Disabilities." Press release, 2009. http://www.sag.org/press-releases/october-23-2009/latest-casting-data-follows-historical-trends-and-continues-exclude-p.

Seidman, Steven. "From Polluted Homosexual to the Normal Gay: Changing Patterns of Sexual Regulation in America." In *Thinking Straight: The Power, Promise and Paradox of Heterosexuality*, ed. Chrys Ingraham, 39–62. New York: Routledge, 2004.

Seiter, Ellen. "Stereotypes and the Media: A Re-Evaluation." *Journal of Communication, 36*(2): 14–26. 1986.

Semprun, Jorge. *Le Grand Voyage*. Paris: Gallimard, 1963.

Sen, Rinku. "Building a New Racial Justice Movement." *Colorlines.com.* 2013.

Shim, Doobo. "From Yellow Peril Through Model Minority to Renewed Yellow Peril." *Journal of Communication Inquiry, 22*(4), 385–409. 1998.

Shohat, Ella, and Robert Stam. *Unthinking Eurocentrism: Multiculturalism and the Media*. London: Routledge, 1994.

Simon, Scott. *The Films of D.W. Griffith*. Cambridge: Cambridge University Press, 1993.

Simpson, Scott, and Jessica Sheffield. "Neocolonialism, Technology, and Myth in the *Stargate* Universe." In *Siths, Slayers, Stargates, and Cyborgs: Modern Mythology in the New Millenium*, eds. David Whitt and John Perlich, 73–98. New York: Peter Lang, 2008. 73–98.

Sims, Yvonne. *Women of Blaxploitation: How the Black Action Film Heroine Changed American Popular Culture*. Jefferson, NC: McFarland, 2006.

Smith, William Robertson. *Lectures on the Religion of the Semites: The Fundamental Institutions*. London: A. & C. Black, 1927.

Smith-Shomade, Beretta. *Shaded Lives: African-American Women and Television*. Toronto: Rutgers University Press, 2002.

Sonneman, Toby F. "Dark Mysterious Wanderers: The Migrating Metaphor of the Gypsy." *Journal of Popular Culture*. 32 (4). 1999.

Spicer, Arwen. "'It's Bloody Brilliant!' The Undermining of Metanarrative Feminism in the Season Seven Arc Narrative of *Buffy*." *Slayage: The Journal of the Whedon Studies Association*. 4.3. 2004.

Spivak, Gayatri Cakravorty. "Can the Subaltern Speak?" In *Marxism and the Interpretation of Culture*, eds. Cary Nelson and Lawrence Grossberg, 66–111. Urbana: University of Illinois, 1988.

Stafford, Niki. *Bite Me!: An Unofficial Guide to the World of Buffy the Vampire Slayer: The Chosen Edition*. Toronto: ECW Press, 2007.

Steele, Claude. "A Threat in the Air: How Stereotypes Shape Intellectual Identity and Performance." *American Psychologist*, 52(6): 613–629. 1997.

Steele, Shelby. *A Dream Deferred: The Second Betrayal of Black Freedom in America*. New York: Harper Perennial, 1998.

Stern, Marlow. "Joss Whedon's Passion Project." *The Daily Beast*. June 5 2013.

Stevenson, Stevenson. *Televised Morality: The Case of* Buffy the Vampire Slayer. Dallas: Hamilton, 2003.

Stradling, Linda. *Production Management for TV and Film: The Professional's Guide*. New York: Bloomsbury Methuen Drama, 2010.

Sugrue, Thomas J. *Not Even Past: Barack Obama and the Burden of Race*. Princeton, NJ: Princeton University Press, 2010.

Sutherland, Anne. *Gypsies: The Hidden Americans*. Prospect Heights, IL: Waveland Press, 1986.

Tasker, Yvonne. *Spectacular Bodies. Gender, Genre and the Action Cinema*. London: Routledge, 1993.

Taylor, Charles, and Barbara Stern. "Asian-Americans: Television Advertising and the 'Model Minority' Stereotype." *Journal of Advertising*, 25(2). 47–61. 1997.

Tegel, Susan. 2003. "Leni Riefenstahl's 'Gypsy Question.'" *Historical Journal of Film, Radio and Television*. 23(1). 3–10.

Tesler, Michael, and David O. Sears. *Obama's Race: The 2008 Election and the Dream of a Post-Racial America*. Chicago: University of Chicago Press, 2010.

Tichenor, Daniel J., and Alexandra Filindra. "Raising Arizona v. United States: Historical Patterns of American Immigration Federalism." *Lewis & Clark Law Review*. 16. No 4 (2012), 1215–1247.

Torevell, David. *Losing the Sacred: Ritual, Modernity and Liturgical Reform*. Edinburgh: T & T Clark, 2000.

Trepagnier, Barbara. *Silent Racism: How Well Meaning White People Perpetuate the Racial Divide*. Boulder, CO: Paradigm Publishers, 2010.

Trumpener, Kate. "The Time of the Gypsies: A 'People Without History' in the Narratives of the West." In *Identities*, eds. Kwame Anthony Appiah and Henry Louis Gates, Jr. Chicago: The University of Chicago Press, 1995. 338–379.

Turner, Victor. *Dramas, Fields and Metaphors: Symbolic Action in Human Society*. Ithaca: Cornell University Press, 1974.

_____. *From Ritual to Theatre: The Human Seriousness of Play*. New York: PAJ Publications, 1982.

U.S. Commission on Civil Rights. 2013. Web. www.usccr.gov.

Upstone, Sara. "'LA's Got It All': Hybridity and Otherness in *Angel's* Postmodern City." In *Reading Angel: the TV Spin-off with a Soul*, ed. Stacey Abbott, 101–113. New York: I.B. Tauris, 2005.

Vande Berg, Leah R. "Liminality: Worf as Metonymic Signifier of Racial, Cultural, and National Differences." In *Enterprise Zones: Critical Positions on Star Trek*, ed. Taylor Harrison, 51–68. Boulder, CO: Westview Press, 1996.

Van Dijk, Teun A. *Discourse and Power*. New York: Palgrave Macmillan, 2008.

Van Gennep, Arnold. *The Rites of Passage*, translated by Monika B. Vizedon and Gabriel L. Caffee. London: Routledge & Kegan Paul, 1960.

Vaught, Sabrina E. *Racism, Public Schooling, and the Entrenchment of White Supremacy: A Critical Race Ethnography*. Albany: State University of New York Press, 2011.

Vint, Sherryl. "Killing Us Softly? A Feminist Search for the 'Real' Buffy." *Slayage: The Journal of the Whedon Studies Association*. 2.1. 2002.

Walters, Suzanna D. *All the Rage: The Story of Gay Visibility in America*. Chicago: University of Chicago Press, 2001.

Weaver, Simon. "The 'Other' Laughs Back: Humour and Resistance in Anti-Racist Comedy." *Sociology*, 44.1 (2010), 31–48.

Weber, Kathryn. "Exploding Sexual Binaries in *Buffy* and *Angel*." In *Sexual Rhetoric in the Works of Joss Whedon*, ed. Erin B. Waggoner, 248–261. Jefferson, NC: McFarland, 2010.

Webster, Noah. *An American Dictionary of the English Language*. New York: Converse, 1828.

Wegner, Phillip E. "Soldierboys for Peace: Cognitive Mapping, Space, and Science Fiction as World Bank Literature." *World Bank Literature*, ed. Amitava Kumar, 280 296. Minneapolis: University of Minnesota Press, 2003.

West, Cornell. *Race Matters*. New York: Vintage Books, 1994.

Weyrauch, Walter. *Gypsy Law: Romani Legal Traditions and Culture*. Berkeley: University of California Press, 2002.

Whedon, Joss. "An Evening with Joss Whedon." Lecture, *Film Society at Lincoln Center*. 2013.

_____. "High Stakes Poker." Interview with *Entertainment Weekly*. October 1, 1999. 20–49.

_____. "Joss Whedon's Selection of His Favorite *Buffy* Episodes." *The Chosen Collection* DVD Boxed Set Episode Guide. Twentieth Century Fox Home Entertainment. 1–4, 2005.

_____. "*Much Ado About Nothing* Screening and Q & A." *Brooklyn Academy of Music (BAM)*. May 31, 2013.

_____. "A Personal Message from Joss Whedon." April 23, 2013. Retrieved from http://www.digitalbits.com/mytwocentsa72.html.

_____. Reddit.com Ask Me Anything. Web. April 2012.

_____. "10 Questions for Joss Whedon." *New York Times*. 2003. Web. http://www.nytimes.com/2003/05/16/readersopinions/16WHED.html.

_____, and Jane Espenson, Marti Noxon, Eliza Dushku. Season 3 Overview. *Buffy the Vampire Slayer The Complete Third Season DVD Special Features*. DVD. Hollywood, CA: Twentieth Century Fox, 2001.

Wilcox, Rhonda V. "The Darkness of Passion: Visuals and Voiceovers, Sound and Shadow." *Spotlight: Joss Whedon*, ed. Robert Moore. *PopMatters*. Web.

_____. "Dating Data Miscegenation in *Star Trek: The Next Generation*." In *Enterprise Zones: Critical Positions on Star Trek*, eds. Taylor Harrison, Sarah Projansky,

Kent A. Ono, and Elyce Rae Helford, 69–92. Boulder, CO: Westview Press, 1996.

_____. "Echoes of Complicity: Reflexivity and Identity in Joss Whedon's *Dollhouse*." *Slayage: The Online International Journal of Buffy Studies*. 2010.

_____. "Much Ado About Whedon." Keynote speech, Joss in June: A Conference on the Works of Joss Whedon. 29 June 2013.

_____. "Show Me Your World: Exiting the Text and the Globalization of *Buffy*." In *Why Buffy Matters: the Art of Buffy the Vampire Slayer*. 90–107. London: I.B. Tauris, 2005.

_____. "Unreal TV." In *Thinking Outside the Box: A Contemporary Television Genre Reader*, edited by Brian G. Rose and Gary R. Edgerton, 201–225. Lexington: The University Press of Kentucky, 2005.

_____. *Why* Buffy *Matters: The Art of* Buffy *the Vampire Slayer*. London: I.B. Tauris, 2005.

Wilson, Melanie. "She Believes in Me: Angel, Spike, and Redemption." In *Buffy Meets the Academy*, ed. Kevin K. Durand, 137–49. Jefferson, NC: McFarland, 2009.

Wise, Tim. *Between Barack and a Hard Place: Racism and White Denial in the Age of Obama*. San Francisco: City Lights Publishers, 2009.

Woo, Deborah. "The Glass Ceiling and Asian Americans" [Paper 129]. *Federal Publications*, 1994. http://digitalcommons.ilr.cornell.edu/key_workplace/129.

Worden, Daniel. "Neo-Liberalism and the Western: HBO's *Deadwood* as National Allegory." *Canadian Review of American Studies*. 39 no. 2 (2009), 221–24.

Yancy, George, and Janine Jones. *Pursuing Trayvon Martin: Historical Contexts and Contemporary Manifestations of Racial Dynamics*. Lanham, MD: Lexington Books, 2012.

Yen, Hope. "New College Graduates Facing Bleak Employment Landscape." *Community College Week*. 24 (20). May 14 2012.

Zanger, Anat. "Desire Ltd: Romanies, Women, and Other Smugglers in *Carmen*." *Framework*. 44 (2). 2003. 81–93.

Zettl, Herbert. *Television Production Handbook*. Independence, KY: Cengage Learning, 2011.

Zhang, Angela. "*Buffy* and *Dollhouse*: Visions of Female Empowerment and Disempowerment." *Popmatters.com*, 7 April 2011.

Index